MYSTERIUM PASCHALE

MYSTERIUM PASCHALE

The Mystery of Easter

Hans Urs von Balthasar

Translated with an Introduction
by
Aidan Nichols, O.P.

IGNATIUS PRESS   SAN FRANCISCO

Contents

Preface   vii
Introduction   1

Chapter 1   Incarnation and Passion   11
(1) The Incarnation as Ordered to the Passion   12
(2) Endorsement in Scripture   14
(3) Confirmation in Tradition   20
(4) The Kenosis and the New Image of God   23
(5) Literature   36

Chapter 2   The Death of God as Wellspring of
Salvation, Revelation and Theology   49
(1) The Hiatus   49
(2) The 'Word of the Cross' and its Logic   52
(3) The Cross and Philosophy   56
(4) The Bridge over the Hiatus   66
(5) Experiential Approach to the Hiatus   71

Chapter 3   Going to the Cross: Good Friday   89
(1) Jesus' Life as Directed to the Cross   89
(2) The Eucharist   95
(3) The Mount of Olives   100
(4) Surrender   107
(5) Trial and Condemnation   112
(6) The Crucifixion   119
(7) Cross and Church   129
(8) Cross and Trinity   136

Chapter 4   Going to the Dead: Holy Saturday   148
(1) Preliminaries on Method   148
(2) The New Testament   152

Contents

(3) Solidarity in Death   160
(4) The Being Dead of the Son of God   168

Chapter 5   Going to the Father: Easter   189
(1) The Fundamental Theological Affirmation   190
(2) The Exegetical Situation   225
(3) The Imagistic Development of the Theological
     Aspects   246
Index   291
Bibliography   281

Preface to the Second Edition

This book appeared for the first time as a constituent chapter of a large-scale dogmatics. Since in that context the doctrine of God as one and triune was treated elsewhere, there was no need to examine in any more fundamental a way the delicate problem (so warmly discussed nowadays) of the Kenosis of the Son of God in his Incarnation and, above all, in his Passion. Here, by contrast, it seems incumbent on me to say a word – no doubt, too condensed – by way of addressing the root of this mystery. I hope that it will be clear enough, at any rate, to remove certain misunderstandings of the grosser sort.

For a number of years, indeed, the idea of a suffering God has become virtually omnipresent. Kitamori put it into official circulation. American 'Process Theology' nourished it. Then there were the polemics against the divine 'impassibility' (so strongly affirmed by the Church Fathers), and against God's 'immutability' (denied, or so it seemed, by numerous Old Testament passages), as well as the Hegelianising theology of Jürgen Moltmann in his *Theology of Hope, The Crucified God,* and *The Trinity and the Kingdom of God.* All that appeared to suggest to Christians that the older dogmatics had blundered on an essential point of its interpretation of biblical revelation.

Doubtless the Kenosis of the Son will always remain a mystery no less unsoundable than that of the Trinity of hypostases in the single God. And yet, by placing the emphasis, in the doctrine of the Kenosis, so exclusively on the human nature assumed by the Son, or on his act of assuming that nature – the divine nature remaining inaccessible to all becoming or change, and even to any real relationship with the world – one was running the risk of under-estimating the weight of the assertions made in Scripture, and of succumbing at once to both Nestorianism and Monophysitism. Only the 'Jesus of history' would do the suffering, or perhaps the 'lower faculties' in Christ's being, whereas the 'fine point' of his soul remained, even in the moment of the abandonment, united to the Father in a beatific vision which could never be interrupted.

It seems to me that the only way which might avoid the two opposed and incompatible extremes is that which relates the event of the Kenosis of the Son of God to what one can, by analogy, designate as the eternal 'event' of the divine processions. It is from that supra-temporal yet ever actual event that, as Christians, we must approach the mystery of the divine 'essence'. That essence is forever 'given' in the self-gift of the Father, 'rendered' in the thanksgiving of the Son, and 'represented' in its character as absolute love by the Holy Spirit.

According to the great Scholastics, the inner-divine processions are the condition of possibility for a creation. The divine 'ideas' for a possible world derive from that everlasting circulation of life, founded as it is on the total and unconditional gift of each hypostasis to the others. *De necessitate si est productio dissimilis praeintelligitur productio similis* (Saint Bonaventure). *Ex processione personarum divinarum distinctarum causatur omnis creaturarum processio et multiplicatio* (Saint Thomas).

We shall never know how to express the abyss-like depths of the Father's self-giving, that Father who, in an eternal 'super-Kenosis', makes himself 'destitute' of all that he is and can be so as to bring forth a consubstantial divinity, the Son. Everything that can be thought and imagined where God is concerned is, in advance, included and transcended in this self-destitution which constitutes the person of the Father, and, at the same time, those of the Son and the Spirit. God as the 'gulf' (Eckhart: *Un-Grund*) of absolute Love contains in advance, eternally, all the modalities of love, of compassion, and even of a 'separation' motivated by love and founded on the infinite distinction between the hypostases – modalities which may manifest themselves in the course of a history of salvation involving sinful humankind.

God, then, has no need to 'change' when he makes a reality of the wonders of his charity, wonders which include the Incarnation and, more particularly, the Passion of Christ, and, before him, the dramatic history of God with Israel and, no doubt, with humanity as a whole. All the contingent 'abasements' of God in the economy of salvation are forever included and outstripped in the eternal event of Love. And so what, in the temporal economy, appears as the (most real) suffering of the Cross is only the manifestation of the (Trinitarian) Eucharist of the Son: he will be forever the slain Lamb, on the throne of the Father's glory, and his Eucharist – the Body shared out, the Blood poured forth – will never be abolished, since the Eucharist it is which must gather all creation into his body. What the Father has given, he will never take back.

Hans Urs von Balthasar

Abbreviations

AJSL	*American Journal of Semitic Languages and Literatures* (Chicago 1895–1941)
Anal. Greg.	*Analecta Gregoriana* (Rome 1930ff)
BZ	*Biblische Zeitschrift* (Paderborn 1903ff)
BZNW	*Beihefte zur Zeitschrift für die Neutestamentliche Wissenschaft* (Berlin 1923ff)
CSEL	*Corpus Scriptorum Ecclesiasticorum Latinorum* (Vienna 1866ff)
DACL	*Dictionnaire d'archéologie chrétienne et liturgie* (Paris 1903–1953)
DBS	*Dictionnaire de la Bible. Supplément* (Paris 1928ff)
DLZ	*Deutsche Literaturzeitung* (Berlin 1880ff)
D–S	*Enchiridion symbolorum. Ed. H. Denzinger/A. Schönmetzer* (Freiburg^{33} 1965)
DSAM	*Dictonnaire de spiritualité, ascétique et mystique* (Paris 1932ff)
EO	*Echos d'Orient* (Bucharest 1897–1943)
ET	*Expository Times* (Edinburgh 1889ff)
EvTh	*Evangelische Theologie* (Munich 1934ff)
GCS	*Die griechischen christlichen Schriftsteller der ersten drei Jahrhunderte* (Berlin 1897ff)
GuL	*Glaube und Lehre* (Witten 1953ff)
Greg.	*Gregorianum* (Rome 1920ff)
JBL	*Journal of Biblical Literature* (Philadelphia 1889ff)
JLW	*Jahrbuch für Liturgiewissenschaft* (Münster 1921–1941)

JThS	*Journal of Theological Studies* (Oxford 1899–1949; 1950ff)
KuD	*Kerygma und Dogma* (Göttingen 1955ff)
LThK	*Lexikon für Theologie und Kirche* (Freiburg ²1957–1968)
MthZ	*Münchener theologische Zeitschrift* (Munich 1950ff)
NRT	*Nouvelle Revue Théologique* (Louvain 1869ff)
NT	*Novum Testamentum* (Leiden 1956ff)
NTS	*New Testament Studies* (Cambridge 1854ff)
OrChrP	*Orientalia Christiana periodica* (Rome 1935ff)
PG	*Patrologia Graeca* (Paris 1857–1866; 1928–1936)
PL	*Patrologia Latina* (Paris 1841–1849; 1850–1855; 1862–1864; 1958–1970)
RAM	*Revue d'ascétique et de mystique* (Toulouse 1920ff)
RB	*Revue Biblique* (Paris 1892ff)
RGG	*Die Religion in Geschichte und Gegenwart* (Tübingen ³1956–1965)
RHE	*Revue d'histoire ecclésiastique* (Louvain 1900ff)
RQ	*Römische Quartalschrift für christliche Altertumskunde* (Freiburg 1887ff)
RSPhTh	*Revue des sciences philosophiques et théologiques* (Paris 1907ff)
RSR	*Recherches de science religieuse* (Paris 1910ff)
RThAM	*Recherches de théologie ancienne et médiévale* (Louvain 1929ff)
Rev.Apol.	*Revue apologétique* (Paris 1921ff)
THQ	*Theologische Quartalschrift* (Tübingen 1818ff)
ThLZ	*Theologische Literaturzeitung* (Leipzig 1876ff)
ThW	*Theologisches Wörterbuch zum Neuen Testament* (Stuttgart 1933ff)
ThZ	*Theologische Zeitschrift* (Basle 1945ff)
TU	*Texte und Untersuchungen zur Geschichte der altchristlichen Literatur* (Berlin 1882ff)
VD	*Verbum Domini* (Rome 1921ff)
VF	*Verkündigung und Forschung. Theologischer Jahresbericht* (Munich 1940ff)

VS	*La Vie Spirituelle* (Paris 1946ff)
ZAM	*Zeitschrift für Aszese und Mystik* (Innsbruck 1925–1944)
ZKS	*Zeitschrift für Kirchengeschichte* (Stuttgart 1877ff)
ZKTh	*Zeitschrift für katholische Theologie* (Vienna 1876ff)
ZKG	*Zeitschrift für Kirchengeschichte* (Stuttgart 1877)
ZNW	*Zeitschrift für die neutestamentliche Wissenschaft* (Berlin 1900ff)
ZSTh	*Zeitschrift für systematische Theologie* (Berlin 1923ff)

Introduction

Balthasar, his Christology, and the Mystery of Easter

Aidan Nichols OP

Balthasar was born in Lucerne in 1905.[1] It is probably
significant that he was born in that particular Swiss city,
whose name is virtually synonymous with Catholicism in
Swiss history. The centre of resistance to the Reformation in
the sixteenth century, in the nineteenth it led the Catholic
cantons in what was virtually a civil war of religion, the War
of the *Sonderbund* (which they lost). Even today it is very
much a city of churches, of religious frescoes, of bells.
Balthasar is a very self-consciously *Catholic* author. He was
educated by both Benedictines and Jesuits, and then in 1923
began a university education divided between four
Universities: Munich, Vienna, Berlin – where he heard
Romano Guardini, for whom a Chair of Catholic Philosophy
had been created in the heartland of Prussian Protestantism[2]
– and finally Zürich.

In 1929 he presented his doctoral thesis, which had as a
subject the idea of the end of the world in modern German
literature, from Lessing to Ernst Bloch. Judging by his
citations, Balthasar continued to regard playwrights, poets and
novelists as theological sources as important as the Fathers of
the Schoolmen.[3] He was prodigiously well-read in the literature
of half a dozen languages and has been called the most
cultivated man of his age.[4] In the year he got his doctorate,

he entered the Society of Jesus. His studies with the German Jesuits he described later as a time spent languishing in a desert, even though one of his teachers was the outstanding Neo-Scholastic Erich Przywara, to whom he remained devoted.[5] From the Ignatian *Exercises* he took the personal ideal of uncompromising faithfulness to Christ the Word in the midst of a secular world.[6] His real theological awakening, however, only happened when he was sent to the French Jesuit study house at Lyons, where he found awaiting him Henri de Lubac and Jean Daniélou, both later to be cardinals of the Roman church. These were the men most closely associated with the 'Nouvelle Théologie', later to be excoriated by Pope Pius XII for its patristic absorption.[7] Pius XII saw in the return to the Fathers two undesirable hidden motives. These were, firstly, the search for a lost common ground with Orthodoxy and the Reformation, and secondly, the desire for a relatively undeveloped theology which could then be presented in a myriad new masks to modern man.[8] The orientation to the Fathers, especially the Greek Fathers, which de Lubac in particular gave Balthasar did not, in fact, diminish his respect for historic Scholasticism at the level of philosophical theology.[9] His own metaphysics consist of a repristinated Scholasticism, but he combined this with an enthusiasm for the more speculative of the Fathers, admired for the depths of their theological thought as well as for their ability to re-express an inherited faith in ways their contemporaries found immediately attractive and compelling.[10]

Balthasar did not stay with the Jesuits. In 1940 they had sent him to Basle as a chaplain to the University. From across the Swiss border, Balthasar could observe the unfolding of the Third Reich, whose ideology he believed to be a distorted form of Christian apocalyptic and the fulfilment of his own youthful ideas about the rôle of the eschatology theme in the German imagination. While in Basle Balthasar also observed Adrienne von Speyr, a convert to Catholicism and a visionary who was to write an ecstatic commentary on the Fourth Gospel, and some briefer commentaries on other New Testament books, as well as theological essays of a more sober kind.[11] In 1947, the *motu proprio Provida Mater Ecclesia* created the possibility of 'secular institutes' within the Roman Catholic Church, and, believing that these *Weltgemeinschaften* of laity in vows represented the Ignatian vision in the modern world, Balthasar proposed to his superiors that he and Adrienne von Speyr together might found such an institute within the Society of Jesus. When they declined, he left the Society and in 1950 became a diocesan priest under the bishop of Chur, in eastern Switzerland. Soon Balthasar had published so much that he was able to survive on his earnings alone, and moved to Einsiedeln, not far from Lucerne, where, in the shadow of the venerable Benedictine abbey, he built up his publishing house, the *Johannes Verlag*, named after Adrienne von Speyr's preferred evangelist. She died in 1967, but he continued to regard her as *the* great inspiration of his life, humanly speaking.

In 1969 Balthasar was appointed by Pope Paul VI to the International Theological Commission, and, after that date, he was drawn increasingly into the service of the Church's teaching office. In 1984, Pope John Paul II symbolized his high regard for Balthasar by awarding him the Paul VI prize for his services to theology. These included not only the unbroken stream of his own writing, but his founding, in 1972, of the international Catholic review *Communio* – a critical sifting, in the light of theological tradition, of the abundant but often confusing wares made available by post-conciliar Catholicism. Balthasar died in Basle on 26 June 1988, three days before his investiture as a cardinal of the Roman church. His remains are buried in the family grave, under the cloister of Lucerne cathedral.

Balthasar's writings are formidable in number and length. Any one area of his publications would constitute a decent life's work for a lesser man. In patristics he wrote accounts of Origen, Gregory of Nyssa and Maximus the Confessor.[12] In literature, he produced a major study of Bernanos[13] as well as translations of Claudel, Péguy and Calderón. In philosophy he turned his thesis into three massive tomes under the title *Apokalypse der deutchen Seele,*[14] from Lessing through Nietzsche to the rise of Hitler. Although a major idea of this work is the notion that the figure of Christ remained a dominant motif in German Romanticism, more significant for Balthasar's later Christology is his essay *Wahrheit: Die Wahrheit der Welt*,[15] in which he argues that the great forgotten theme of metaphysics is the theme of *beauty*.

Balthasar presents the beautiful as the 'forgotten transcendental', *pulchrum*, an aspect of everything and anything as important as *verum*, 'the true', and *bonum*, 'the good'. The beautiful is the radiance which something gives off simply because it is something, because it exists. A sequel to this work, intended to show the theological application of its leading idea, was not written until forty years later but Balthasar had given clear hints as to what it would contain. What corresponds theologically to beauty is God's *glory*. The radiance that shows itself through the communicative forms of finite being is what arouses our sense of transcendence, and so ultimately founds our theology. Thus Balthasar hit upon his key theological concept, as vital to him as *ens a se* to Thomists or 'radical infinity' to Scotists. In significant form and its attractive power, the Infinite discloses itself in finite expression, and this is supremely true in the biblical revelation. Thus Balthasar set out on his great trilogy: a theological aesthetics,[16] concerned with the perception of God's self-manifestation; a theological dramatics,[17] concerned with the content of this perception, namely God's action towards man; and a theological logic[18] dealing with the method, at once divine and human, whereby this action is expressed.

Balthasar insisted, however, that the manner in which theology is to be written is Christological from start to finish. He defined theology as a mediation between faith and revelation in which the Infinite, when fully expressed in the finite, i.e. made accessible as man, can only be apprehended by a convergent movement from the side of the finite, i.e. adoring, obedient faith in the God-man. Only thus can theology be Ignatian and produce 'holy worldliness', in Christian practice, testimony and self-abandonment.[19] Balthasar aimed at nothing less that a Christocentric revolution in Catholic theology. It is absolutely certain that the inspiration for this derives, ironically for such an ultra-Catholic author, from the Protestantism of Karl Barth.

In the 1940s Balthasar was not the only person interested in theology in the University of Basle. Balthasar's book on Barth,[20] regarded by some Barthians as the best book on Barth ever written,[21] while expressing reserves on Barth's account of nature, predestination and the concept of the Church, puts Barth's Christocentricity at the top of the list of the things Catholic theology can learn from the *Church Dogmatics*.[22] Not repudiating the teaching of the First Vatican Council on the possibility of a natural knowledge of God, Balthasar set out nevertheless to realize in Catholicism the kind of Christocentric revolution Barth had wrought in Protestantism: to make Christ, in Pascal's words, 'the centre, towards which all things tend'.[23] Balthasar's acerbity towards the Catholic theological scene under Paul VI derived from the sense that this overdue revolution was being resisted from several quarters: from those who used philosophical or scientific concepts in a way that could not but dilute Christocentrism, building on German Idealism (Karl Rahner), evolutionism (Teilhard de Chardin) or Marxism (liberation theology), and from those who frittered away Christian energies on aspects of Church structure or tactics of pastoral practice, the characteristic post-conciliar obsessions.[24]

In his person, life, death and resurrection, Jesus Christ is the 'form of God'. As presented in the New Testament writings, the words, actions and sufferings of Jesus form an aesthetic unity, held together by the 'style' of unconditional love. Love is always beautiful, because it expresses the self-diffusiveness of being, and so is touched by being's radiance, the *pulchrum*. But the unconditional, gracious, sacrificial love of Jesus Christ expresses not just the mystery of being – finite being – but the mystery of the *Source* of being, the transcendent communion of love which we call the Trinity.[25] Thus through the *Gestalt Christi*, the love which God *is* shines through to the world. This is Balthasar's basic intuition.

The word 'intuition' is, perhaps, a fair one. Balthasar is not a New Testament scholar, not even a (largely) self-taught one like Schillebeeckx. Nor does he make, by Schillebeeckx's exigent standards, a very serious attempt to incorporate modern exegetical studies into his Christology. His somewhat negative attitude towards much – but, as *Mysterium Paschale* shows, by no means all – of current New Testament study follows from his belief that the identification of ever more sub-structures, redactional frameworks, 'traditions', *perikopai*, binary correspondences, and other methodological items in the paraphernalia of gospel criticism, tears into fragments what is an obvious unity. The New Testament is a unity because the men who wrote it had all been bowled over by the same thing, the glory of God in the face of Christ. Thus Balthasar can say, provocatively, that New Testament science is not a science at all compared with the traditional exegesis which preceded it. To be a science you must have a method adequate to your object. Only the contemplative reading of the New Testament is adequate to the glory of God in Jesus Christ.[26]

The importance of the concept of contemplation for Balthasar's approach to Christ can be seen by comparing his view of perceiving God in Christ with the notion of looking at a painting and seeing what the artist has been doing in it.[27] In Christian faith, the captivating force (the 'subjective evidence') of the artwork which is Christ takes hold of our imaginative powers; we enter into the 'painterly world' which this discloses and, entranced by what we see, come to contemplate the glory of sovereign love of God in Christ (the 'objective evidence') as manifested in the concrete events of his life, death and resurrection.[28] So entering his glory, we become absorbed by it, but this very absorption sends us out into the world in sacrificial love like that of Jesus.

This is the foundation of Balthasar's Christology, but its *content* is a series of meditations on the mysteries of the life of Jesus. His Christology is highly concrete and has been compared, suggestively, to the iconography of Andrei Rublev and Georges Rouault.[29] Balthasar is not especially concerned with the ontological make-up of Christ, with the hypostatic union and its implications, except insofar as these are directly involved in an account of the mysteries of the life.[30] In each major moment ('mystery') of the life, we see some aspect of the total *Gestalt Christi*, and through this the *Gestalt Gottes* itself. Although Balthasar stresses the narrative unity of these episodes, which is founded on the *obedience* that takes the divine Son from incarnation to passion, an obedience which translates his inner-Trinitarian being as the Logos, filial responsiveness to the Father,[31] his principal interest – nowhere more eloquently expressed than in the present work – is located very firmly in an unusual place. This place is the mystery of Christ's Descent into Hell, which Balthasar explicitly calls the centre of all Christology.[32] Because the Descent is the final point reached by the Kenosis, and the Kenosis is the supreme expression of the inner-Trinitarian love, the Christ of Holy Saturday is the consummate icon of what God is like.[33] While not relegating the Crucifixion to a mere prelude – far from it! – Balthasar sees the One who was raised at Easter as not primarily the Crucified, but rather the One who for us went down into Hell. The 'active' Passion of Good Friday is not, at any rate, complete without the 'passive' Passion of Holy Saturday which was its sequel.

Balthasar's account of the Descent is indebted to the visionary experiences of Adrienne von Speyr, and is a world away from the concept of a triumphant preaching to the just which nearly all traditional accounts of the going down to Hell come under.[34] Balthasar stresses Christ's solidarity with the dead, his passivity, his finding himself in a situation of total self-estrangement and alienation from the Father. For Balthasar, the Descent 'solves' the problem of theodicy, by showing us the conditions on which God accepted our foreknown abuse of freedom: namely, his own plan to take to himself our self-damnation in Hell. It also demonstrates the costliness of our redemption: the divine Son underwent the experience of Godlessness. Finally, it shows that the God revealed by the Redeemer is a Trinity. Only if the Spirit, as *vinculum amoris* between the Father and the Son, can re-relate Father and Son in their estrangement in the Descent, can the unity of the Revealed and Revealer be maintained. In this final humiliation of the *forma servi*, the glorious *forma Dei* shines forth via its lowest pitch of self-giving love.

Mysterium Paschale could not, however, be an account of

the *paschal* mystery, the mystery of Easter, unless it moved on, following the fate of the Crucified himself, to the Father's acceptance of his sacrifice, which we call the Resurrection. Whilst not over-playing the rôle of the empty tomb – which is, after all, a *sign*, with the limitations which that word implies, Balthasar insists, in a fashion highly pertinent to a recurrent debate in England, as well as in Continental Europe, that the Father in raising the Son does not go back on the Incarnation: that is, he raises the Son into *visibility*, rather than returns him to the pre-incarnate condition of the invisible Word. The Resurrection appearances are not visionary experiences but personal encounters, even though the Resurrection itself cannot be adequately thought by means of any concept, any comparison.

Finally, in his account of the 'typical' significance of such diverse Resurrection witnesses as Peter, John and the women, Balthasar offers a profound interpretation of the make-up of the Church, which issued from the paschal mystery of Christ. In his portrayal of the inter-relation of the masculine and feminine elements in the community of the Crucified and Risen One – the Church of office and the Church of love, Balthasar confirms the words spoken in his funeral oration by Cardinal Joseph Ratzinger:

> Balthasar had a great respect for the primacy of Peter, and the hierarchical structure of the Church. But he also knew that the Church is not only that, nor is that what is deepest in the Church.[35]

What *is* deepest in the Church, as the concluding section of *Mysterium Paschale* shows, is the spouse-like responsiveness of receptivity and obedience to the Jesus Christ who, as the Church's Head, 'ever plunges anew into his own being those whom he sends out as his disciples'.

References

[1] Balthasar's own estimate of his life and work is in *Rechenschaft* (Einsiedeln 1965).

The most thorough study of his theology to date is A. Moda, *Hans Urs von Balthasar* (Bari 1976); for his Christology see also G. Marchesi, *La Cristologia di Hans Urs von Balthasar* (Rome 1977).

[2] See H. U. von Balthasar, *Romano Guardini. Reform aus dem Ursprung* (Munich 1970): the title is significant.

[3] See especially, *Herrlichkeit. Ein theologische Ästhetik* (Einsiedeln 1961–1969), III/1. Et: *The Glory of God* (Edinburgh and San Francisco 1983–).

[4] By H. de Lubac in 'Un testimonio di Cristo. Hans Urs von Balthasar', *Humanitas* 20 (1965) p. 853.

[5] H. U. von Balthasar 'Die Metaphysik Erich Pyrzwara', *Schweizer Rundschau 33* (1933), pp. 488–499. Przywara convinced him of the importance of the analogy of being in theology.

[6] Balthasar has compared the 'evangelicalism' of the *Exercises* to that not only of Barth but of Luther. See *Rechenschaft*, op. cit., pp. 7–8.

[7] See R. Aubert's summary of the *Nouvelle Théologie* in *Bilan de la théologie du vingtième siècle* (Paris 1971), I. pp. 457–460.

[8] Pius XII, *Humani Generis* 14–17.

[9] Stressed by B. Mondin, 'Hans Urs von Balthasar e l'estetica teologica' in *I grandi teologi del secolo ventesimo* I (Turin 1969), pp. 268–9.

[10] De Lubac spoke of Balthasar enjoying 'una specie di connaturalità' with the Fathers; but he has never suffered from that tiresome suspension of all criticism of patristic theology which is sometimes found, not least in England. In *Liturgie Cosmique: Maxime le Confesseur* (Paris 1947) he points out that the Fathers stand at the beginning (only) of Christian thought, pp. 7–8.

[11] H. U. von Balthasar, *Erster Blick auf Adrienne von Speyr* (Einsiedeln 1967), with full bibliography.

[12] *Parole et mystère chez Origène* (Paris 1957); *Présence et pensée. Essai sur la philosophie religieuse de Grégoire de Nysse* (Paris 1942); *Kosmische Liturgie. Höhe und Krise des griechischen Weltbilds bei Maximus Confessor* (Freiburg 1941).

[13] *Bernanos* (Cologne 1954).

[14] *Apokalypse der deutschen Seele* (Salzburg 1937–9).

[15] *Wahrheit. Wahrheit der Welt* (Einsiedeln 1947).

[16] Thus *Herrlichkeit*, op. cit.

[17] *Theodramatik* (Einsiedeln 1973–6).

[18] The *Theologik* took up the earlier *Wahrheit. Wahrheit der Welt*, op. cit., re-published as *Theologik* I, and united it to a new work, *Wahrheit Gottes. Theologik II*. Both appeared at Einsiedeln in 1985. Also relevant to this project is his *Das Ganze im Fragment* (Einsiedeln 1963).

[19] 'Der Ort der Theologie', *Verbum Caro* (Einsiedeln 1960).

[20] *Karl Barth. Darstellung und Deutung seiner Theologie* (Cologne 1951).

[21] By Professor T. F. Torrance, to the present author in a private conversation.

[22] op. cit. pp. 335–372.

[23] *Pensées* 449 in the Lafuma numbering.

[24] See Schleifung der Bastionen (Einsiedeln 1952); *Wer ist ein Christ?* (Einsiedeln 1965); *Cordula oder der Ernstfall* (Einsiedeln 1966). The notion that, because Christian existence has its own form, which is founded on the prior *form* of Christ, Christian

proclamation does not (strictly speaking) need philosophical or social scientific mediations, is the clearest link between Balthasar and Pope John Paul II. See, for instance, the papal address to the South American bishops at Puebla.

[25] *Herrlichkeit* I pp. 123–658.

[26] *Einfaltungen. Auf Wegen christlicher Einigung* (Munich 1969).

[27] Cf. A. Nichols OP, *The Art of God Incarnate* (London 1980), pp. 105–152.

[28] For an excellent analysis of Balthasar's twofold Christological 'evidence', see A. Moda, op. cit., pp. 305–410.

[29] By H. Vorgrimler, in *Bilan de la Théologie du vingtième siècle*, op. cit., pp. 686ff.

[30] We can say that, had Balthasar been St Thomas, he would have begun the *Tertia pars* of the *Summa* at Question 36: *de manifestatione Christi nati*.

[31] 'Mysterium Paschale', in *Mysterium Salutis* III/2 (Einsiedeln 1962), pp. 133–158.

[32] *Glaubhaft ist nur Liebe* (Einsiedeln 1963), p. 57.

[33] 'Mysterium Paschale', art. cit., pp. 227–255. Balthasar speaks of a 'contemplative Holy Saturday' as the centre of theology, in contra-distinction to G. W. F. Hegel's 'speculative Good Friday'.

[34] See J. Chaine, 'La Descente du Christ aux enfers', *Dictionnaire de la Bible, Supplément* II.

[35] Translated from the French, alone accessible to me, of Cardinal Joseph Ratzinger, 'Oraison funèbre de Hans-Urs von Balthasar', *Communio* XIV, 2 (March–April 1989), p. 8.

The translator is grateful to the editor of *New Blackfriars* for permission to re-publish, in modified form, some material originally found in that journal (66.781–2 [1985]) as 'Balthasar and his Christology'.

I

Incarnation and Passion

Our task now is to consider that problem, and that teaching, which so often are passed over in silence, but which – for that very reason – I want to study with all the more eagerness. That precious and glorious divine Blood poured out for us: for what reason and to what end has such a price been paid?[1]

Here we have the question of the meaning of the Passion. Once the Incarnation has taken place, is not the Passion something that might be dispensed with? Should we not, at any rate, agree with the Scotists when they describe the Passion as an accidental addition in terms of the principal aim of the Incarnation, the glorification of the Father by the Son who unites all things in himself?[2] Were we to take the contrary position, and regard the Passion as the centre of everything, with the Incarnation simply a means to that end, should we not then make God's self-glorification in this world dependent on human sin, and reduce God himself to an instrument for promoting the purposes of the creation? In what follows, we shall leave to one side all attempts to patch up a superficial harmony between these two points of view. At the same time, we shall show that to focus the Incarnation on the Passion enables both theories to reach a point where the mind is flooded by the same perfect thought: in serving, in washing the feet of his creatures, God reveals himself even in that which is most intimately divine in him, and manifests his supreme glory.

In this Introduction, so as to gain an overview of the central place of the *Triduum Mortis* for all theology: we shall first survey the entire economy of salvation in a fashion as yet abstract in character. After this, we shall investigate the resources of Scripture and Tradition. Finally, we shall close by considering the problem of the Kenosis, wherein the Incarnation takes on the quality of the Passion from the very start.

(1) The Incarnation as ordered to the Passion

(a) The image of man which revelation sets before us differs radically from the idea of the *animal rationale, mortale* which empirical enquiry suggests. In point of fact,[3] man is 'destined' and chosen 'before the foundation of the world' to be 'blessed . . . with every spiritual blessing', so that he might stand 'holy and blameless' before his Creator 'in the Beloved', that is, in the Son and 'through his blood' (Ephesians 1, 3–4). In this way, the entire order of sin and redemption appears inclusively integrated. This first idea of what man is already bears the determining mark of the Trinitarian economy. No doubt, to the eyes of God, 'man' is not that 'first man, Adam (who) become a living being' without some finalising reference to the Second Adam, who was 'life-giving Spirit' (I Corinthians 15, 45). For death, entering the world 'through sin' (Romans 5, 12), tears apart the being of man as God envisaged it. Neither philosophy nor religion can restore to the status of a rounded, meaningful whole this fragment of earthly life, slipping away as it is toward death.[4] Nor, besides, can they contrive in the realm beyond death some complementary piece – be it the 'immortality of the soul', the 'transmigration of souls', or whatever – which, once added, makes the broken self entire. The shattered image can only be restored by God, by the Second Adam who is 'from heaven'. And the mid-point of this restorative action is necessarily the place of the original rupture: death, Hades, lostness far from God. This is a locus of enquiry which lies outwith current anthropology, or on its margins. The philosophical adage by which we are informed that living means learning how to die fails to apprehend it.

(b) Starting from the theme of man's mortality, the most one could hope to do by way of illuminating this question is to invoke the notion that the person who lives towards the 'act of death' is always free to seal his existence as a whole with this or that total meaning. For this view, so long as one lives, such a total meaning remains in suspense. Now this does not mean that, in the recapitulating act of death, a human being is personally capable of giving his existence that transcendent meaning which God has foreseen for it. What it tells us is, rather, that the meaning of earthly life remains undecided and obscured, as long as life lasts. Only in death, through the divine judgment, does a man receive his definitive orientation. This is why Christ's redemption of mankind had its decisive completion not, strictly speaking, with the Incarnation or in the continuity of his mortal life, but in the hiatus of death.

(c) Looking at this from the divine perspective, if God wished to 'experience' (*zein peira*, cf. Hebrews, 2, 18; 4, 15)[5] the human condition 'from within', [6] so as to re-direct it from inside it, and thus save it, he would have to place the decisive stress on that point where sinful, mortal man finds himself 'at his wit's end'. And this must be where man has lost himself in death without, for all that, finding God. This is the place where he has fallen into an abyss of grief, indigence, darkness, into the 'pit'[7] from which he cannot escape by his own powers. God has perforce to place the emphasis on this experience of being 'at one's wit's end', in order to bind together the fractured extremities of the idea of man. And this is what we actually find in the identity that holds good between the Crucified and the Risen One.

(d) If God himself has lived out this ultimate experience of this world, a world which, through human freedom, has the possibility of withdrawing obedience from God and so of losing him, then he will no longer be a God who judges his creatures from above and from outside. Thanks to his intimate experience of the world, as the Incarnate One who knows experientially every dimension of the world's being down to the abyss of Hell, God now becomes the measure of man. The Father, as Creator, grants to the Son as Redeemer 'all judgment' (John 5, 22; cf. Enoch 51), which henceforth will mean:

> Behold, he is coming with the clouds, and every eye will see him, every one who pierced him, and all the tribes of the earth will wail on account of him ... (he who is) the Alpha and the Omega ... who (as the Pierced One) is, and was and is to come (Apocalypse 1, 7–8; John 19, 37; Zechariah 12, 10–14).

The Cross (Matthew 24, 30) or, better, the Crucified, is, therefore, the term to which all human existence, whether personal or social, tends. It is a term which is final judgment and redemption 'as through fire' (I Corinthians 3, 15). We must show how, in all this, the fundamental prophetic charge of the Old Testament is brought to its fulfilment. But above all, if we can speak in one breath of these four points, we should say that, in this happening, not only is the world enabled by God to reach its goal (compare the term 'soteriology'), but God himself, in the moment of the world's very perdition, attains his own most authentic revelation (compare 'theology') and glorification (compare 'doxology').

(2) Endorsement in Scripture

It is clear from the internal structure of the gospels, as from their place in the context of the preaching of the primitive Church, that those gospels are indeed, as M. Kähler wrote, 'passion stories preceded by a developed introduction'. The apostles, in their first homilies, spoke, fundamentally, only of the death and resurrection of Christ – a procedure which finds justification in a saying of the Lord himself:

> Thus it is written, that the Christ should suffer and on

the third day rise from the dead, and that repentance
and forgiveness of sins should be preached in his name
to all nations, beginning from Jerusalem. You are
witnesses of these things (Luke 24, 46–8).

The disciples bore their witness by reporting what they had
experienced and by making themselves answerable for it. Paul
will take further just this very line. The evangelists will
confirm it by their way of presenting their own materials.
But as the text here cited shows, all draw in the first place on
the evidential value of the Old Testament.

(a) 'Christ died for our sins *in accordance with the Scriptures,*
. . . he was buried, . . . he was raised on the third day *in
accordance with the Scriptures*' (1 Corinthians 15, 3; cf. Acts 26,
22ff): Paul cites this affirmation as a matter of 'tradition'.
Similarly according to First Peter 1, 11, the prophets at large
were concerned to seek out beforehand, 'the sufferings of
Christ and the subsequent glory' in 'the Spirit of Christ'. In
his speech at Pentecost (Acts 2, 25ff, 34ff), Peter brings
forward scriptural proofs for the death and resurrection, while
his discourse in the Temple (Acts 3, 18, 22ff) speaks of God
as fulfilling what he had declared in advance 'by the mouth
of all the prophets': namely, the sufferings of the Messiah and
his resurrection. That perspective of 'fulfilment' is certainly
necessary if the whole 'typical' existence of Israel is to be seen
converging on the *Triduum Mortis*. And yet that convergence,
though it cannot be inferred from particular texts such as
Isaiah 53, Hosea 6, 2, Jonah 2, 1 or Psalms 16 and 110, is
nonetheless rigorously demonstrable. It follows from the
whole meaning of that direction in which the nation was led
towards its transcendent goal; from the theology of sacrifice
(Romans 4, 25; the Letter to the Hebrews), and, above all,
from the theology of the Mediator who steps in between
God and man – that person who, from the Moses of the
book of Deuteronomy (1, 37; 3, 26; 4, 21), via Hosea,
Jeremiah and Ezekiel, right up to the 'Servant of the Lord',
takes on increasingly the features of a go-between joining
God and the people, heaven and earth, since, weighed down

by the world's sin as he is, he has the power to set the Covenant to rights. Admittedly, were the point of convergence not given by God in the New Testament it could not be construed on the basis of the Old Testament alone. But the very infinity of his transcendence, and the human impossibility of unifying the symbols and theological ideas in which that transcendence finds expression, form together a negative proof of the correctness of the positive assertions of the New Testament.[8]

(b) It is recognised that for Paul the proclamation of the Gospel coincides with that of the Cross of Jesus Christ – a Cross which, through his resurrection, is known to be salvation (cf. I Corinthians 1, 17).[9] At Corinth, Paul wishes to know nothing other than the Cross of Christ (I Corinthians 1, 23; 2, 2). To the Galatians, he will boast of nothing save the Cross (Galatians 6, 14). That Cross is the mid-point of saving history, all the promises are realised in it, every aspect of the Law, with its quality as curse, is dashed to pieces on the Cross. The Cross is the centre of the world's history, for it transcends the categories of 'elect' and 'non-elect' by reconciling all human beings in the crucified body which hangs there (Ephesians 2, 14ff). It is the mid-point, too, of all creation and predestination, inasmuch as we were predestined, in Christ's blood, to be the children of God 'before the foundation of the world' (Ephesians 1, 4ff). Paul himself simply intends to carry out the ministry of preaching, by way of service to the reconciliation of the world to God in the Cross of Jesus (II Corinthians 5, 18). What he takes it upon himself to announce thereby is not just one historical fact among others, but that complete upheaval, that re-creation of all things, which the Cross and Resurrection brought about. 'The old has passed away, behold, the new has come!' (II Corinthians 5, 17). Here, then, is the innermost truth of history. This truth appears to the Jews to be a stumbling-block, to the pagans as folly, since it seems to speak of the 'weakness and foolishness of God'. Yet it so speaks in such a way that it is endowed with an unconditional power to test, to judge, to discriminate and to separate. In the Cross,

then, is manifested the entire 'power of God' (I Corinthians
1, 18, 24). This power is so great that, paradoxically, it can,
in the very act of falling whereby Israel stumbles over the
stumbling-stone (Romans 9, 30ff), catch and save her (Romans
11, 26). Christian existence is a 'reflection' of the form of
Christ: as one has died for all so, at the deepest level, all have
died (II Corinthians 5, 14). Faith must ratify this truth
(Romans 6, 33ff); life must manifest it (II Corinthians 4, 10).
And if this death happened out of love 'for me' (Galatians 2,
20), then my response must be a 'faith' which consists in total
self-gift to this divine destiny. In this way, scandal and
persecution become titles of glory for the Christian (Galatians
5, 11; 6, 12–14).

(c) The Synoptics recount the pre-history of the Passion only
in the two-fold light of the Cross and Resurrection. The
Cross is there.

> no isolated happening ... but *the* event towards which
> the history of his life is oriented and through which its
> other episodes receive their meaning.[10]

The constant penetration of Jesus' life-story by the light of
the Resurrection only lengthens the shadow of the Cross. In
no way does the effect of that light suggest Docetism. The
life of Jesus stand under the *dei* or 'must' of 'suffering much'
(Mark 8, 31 and parallels; luke 17, 25; 22, 37; 24, 7, 26, 44). It
is to this end that his attitude of serving tends. Though he has
the right to reign, his service extends to the giving over of
his soul as a ransom for the many (Mark 10, 45). The same
meaning attaches to the temptation of Jesus, which cannot be
reduced to the temptations in the wilderness (Luke 4, 13).
The Writer to the Hebrews, indeed, sees Jesus' tempting as
connected with all the suffering of his life, with the 'groaning'
of Jesus at the race among whom he must live (Mark 8, 12),
and which seems to him 'insupportable ' (Mark 9, 19). As
soon as a sufficient number of signs of his divine mission are
forthcoming, he poses the decisive question of his identity;
immediately after this episode, a rhythm, made up of

predictions of suffering ahead, enters in to give pattern to the interval before his Passion (Mark 8, 31ff; 9, 30ff; 10, 32ff). To the first of these passion predictions, the disciples respond by asking 'what the rising of the dead meant' (9, 10); on the second occasion, they do not understand, and fear to ask him questions (9, 32); and the third time, as Jesus walks before them with 'his face set' towards Jerusalem (Luke 9, 51), the disciples were 'amazed, and those who followed . . . afraid' (Mark 10, 32). When he talks about discipleship, he speaks of the Cross as the fundamental form and synthesis of self-renunciation (Mark 8, 34ff). It consists in 'drinking the cup' that he must drink, and 'being baptised' with the baptism with which he must be baptised (10, 38). He himself longs for this ending (Luke 12, 50), just as he longs for the supper where he will be able at last to distribute his immolated flesh and poured out blood (Luke 22, 15). Despite the divine 'must' which determines his journey, all of this takes place in perfect freedom, in a sovereign disposition of self. He knows what he is doing when he provokes his opponents (who soon enough seek to 'destroy him', Mark 3, 6), by violating the customs of the Sabbath, by distinguishing between what in the Law is original, and what has been super-added, and lastly by raising himself above the authority of the Law itself whose sole authentic interpreter he is (Matthew 5, 21ff). His authority is power over the entire realm of what opposes God: he is 'the stronger' (Mark 3, 27). Numerous miracles give evidence of this *exousia*, but he reckons with their cost by paying in his own strength, as in the Pauline formula 'When I am weak, then I am strong' (II Corinthians 12, 10). And just as in Luke there is mention of the Passion during the incident of the Transfiguration (Luke 9, 31), so in Mark, immediately after the Transfiguration story, we hear of the Precursor John (compare Elijah) that they (Herod, or Jezabel) treated him as they would. So will it be with the Son of Mark (Mark 9, 12ff): in just the same way his life is oriented towards martyrdom.

The Gospel of John is also dominated by this 'must' (3, 14; 20, 9; cf. 12, 34), which at the same time is sovereign freedom (John 10, 18; 14, 31b; 18, 11). But here the journey and the goal (the latter being passage to the Father in the unity of death and resurrection) are so integrated that Jesus' Passion (18, 4–8) can be interpreted as the personal consecration of Jesus for the men whom God has given him (17, 19), and as a proof of supreme love for his friends (15, 10). This love asks as its return not only the same 'laying down our lives for the brethren' (I John 3, 16), but also the joyous self-abandonment whereby the beloved Lord was drawn into that death which brought him back to the Father (John 14, 28). And yet the shadow cast by the Cross is so heavy to bear that Jesus, while on his way, 'weeps' and is 'deeply moved' (11, 33ff), wishes to flee from this 'hour' and yet remains faithful (12, 27–28). 'Becoming flesh', since it involves 'not being received' (1, 14, 11), is for that reason a crushing of the self (6, 54, 56). It is dying into the earth, disappearing (12, 24), yet being 'lifted up' in death-and-resurrection like the serpent in which all poison at once gathered and met its antidote (3, 14). For this is the One who, light of heart, was sacrificed for the multitude – and for more, indeed, than his murderers thought (11, 50ff) – as the bread of life which vanishes in the mouth of the traitor (13, 26), and the light which shines in the darkness that does not comprehend it and therefore cannot extinguish it (1, 5). If he who is subsistent Judgment itself does not judge of himself (12, 47; 3, 17), nevertheless, by his existence as love he necessarily causes an inexorable division, a crisis. Is it to be adherence or refual (3, 19ff)? This choice is the more profound in its implications according to the level of depth at which the word of love is disclosed. To gratuitious love there corresponds gratuitous hate (15, 22ff). Christians have to stand under the same law of opposites (15, 18ff, 16, 1–4). A direct line joins the Prologue to the Footwashing – that gesture which sums up the distinctively Johannine unity of intransigence and tenderness, of total abasement and a purification that exalts. And the same trajectory links that gesture to the great prayer of farewell which, for the 'hour' of the Cross, hands over all things to the Father, as also to the scene by the Lake of Tiberias where the Church of office is placed beneath the law of the greater love and so is commissioned to follow, in discipleship, the way of the Cross.

The New Testament is wholly oriented towards the Cross
and Resurrection, just as it proceeds from them also. In this
perspective, the Old Testament can be considered a first
approach to the *Triduum*, itself at once the mid-point and the
end of the ways of God.

(3) Confirmation in Tradition

There can surely be no theological assertion in which East
and West are so united as the statement that the Incarnation
happened for the sake of man's redemption on the Cross.
Not only has the East – to confine ourselves for the moment
to that – shown at all times a deep devotion to the Cross.[11]
More than that: it has never failed to expound its own theory
namely, that the assuming of an individual taken from
humanity as a whole (understood as a kind of *universale
concretum*) affects and sanctifies the latter in its totality, except
in relation with the entire economy of the divine redemptive
work. To 'take on manhood' means in fact to assume its
concrete destiny with all that entails – suffering, death, hell –
in solidarity with every human being. Let us listen to the
words of the Fathers themselves.
Tertullian writes, 'Christus mori missus nasci quoque
necessario habuit ut mori posset'.[12]
Athanasius has this to say:

> The Logos, who in himself could not die, accepted a body
> capable of death, so as to sacrifice it as his own for all.[13]

And again:

> The passionless Logos bore a body in himself . . . so as
> to take upon himself what is ours and offer it in sacrifice
> . . . so that the whole man might obtain salvation.[14]

Gregory of Nyssa remarks:

> If one examines this mystery, one will prefer to say, not

that his death was a consequence of his birth, but that the birth was undertaken so that he could die.[15]

In the tradition of Irenaeus, Hippolytus insists that Christ had to take on the same matter as that from which we are made, else he would have been unable to ask of us things he had not accomplished himself.

> To be considered as like ourselves, he took upon him pain; he wanted to hunger, thirst, sleep; not to refuse suffering; to be obedient unto death; to rise again in a visible manner. In all this, he offered his humanity as the first-fruits.[16]

For Gregory Nazianzen, the Incarnation is the taking on of humanity's curse: only because Christ took on all those human factors affected by death – body, soul, spirit – could he, as the leaven in the lump, hallow all men.[17] Chrysostom speaks in no different tones.[18] For Cyril of Alexandria, Christ was made 'a curse' for us, since he accepted embodiment for the sake of saving humankind.[19] At the moment of creation, God foresaw salvation through Christ.[20] From the Greeks, the idea passes, with renewed vigour, into Latin theology. Thus Leo the Great declares, 'In nostra descendit, ut non solum substantiam, sed etiam conditionem naturae peccatricis assumeret'.[21] 'Nec alia fuit Dei Filio causa nascendi quam ut cruci possit affigi.'[22] Hilary considers that, 'In (all) the rest, the set of the Father's will already shows itself: the virgin, the birth, a body; and after that, a Cross, death, the underworld – our salvation'.[23] Ambrose teaches the same.[24] For Maximus Confessor, the succession of Incarnation, Cross, Resurrection means the inauguration, for believer and theological thinker alike, of an ever deeper understanding of the world's making:

> The mystery of the Incarnation of the Word contains, as in a synthesis, the interpretation of all the enigmas and figures of Scripture, as well as the meaning of all material and spiritual creatures. But whoever knows the mystery of the Cross and the burial, that person knows

the real reasons, *logoi*, for all these realities. Whoever, lastly, penetrates the hidden power of the Resurrection, discovers the final end for which God created everything from the beginning.[25]

Nicholas Cabasilas gives the soteriological explanation of this progressive discovery:

As men were triply sundered from God – by their nature, by their sins, and by their death – the Saviour so worked that they might meet him unhindered and come to be with him directly. This he did by removing successively all obstacles: the first, in that he shared in human nature; the second, in undergoing the death of the Cross; and finally, the third wall of division when he rose from the dead and banished wholly from our nature the tyranny of death.[26]

These texts show, in the first place, that the Incarnation is ordered to the Cross as to its goal. They make a clean sweep of that widely disseminated myth of theological textbooks, according to which, for Greek theology, over against Latin, 'redemption' was basically achieved with the Incarnation itself in relation to which the Cross was only a sort of epiphenomenon. And with that, these citations also give the lie to the modern myth (which would like to find support in the one just mentioned) that Christianity is above all an 'incarnationalism': a taking root in the (profane) world, and not a dying to the world.[27]

   Secondly, and more profoundly, the texts offered here also demonstrate that he who says Incarnation, also says Cross. And this is so for two reasons. The Son of God took human nature in its fallen condition, and with it, therefore, the worm in its entrails – mortality, fallenness, self-estrangement, death – which sin introduced into the world. So Augustine tells us, 'Ex quo esse incipit in hoc corpore, in morte est. An potius et in vita et in morte simul est'.[28] And for this reason Bernard can venture the statement, 'Fortasse crux ipsa nos sumus, cui Christus memoratur infixus . . . "Infixus sum in limo profundi"

(Psalm 28, 3): quoniam de limo plasmati sumus. Sed tunc quidem limus paradisi fuimus, nunc vero limus profundi – the mud and muck of the pit'.[29] The second reason to be mentioned has to do not with the man assumed, but with the Logos assuming: to become man is for him, in a most hidden yet very real sense, already humiliation – yes, indeed, as many would say, a deeper humiliation than the going to the Cross itself. And herewith a new question in 'passiology' is opened up – not now the (horizontal) relationship between the Crib and the Cross, but the vertical one between heaven and the Crib. This is the question of the Kenosis.

(4) The Kenosis and the New Image of God.

The doctrine of the Kenosis[30] is so difficult from the viewpoints of exegesis,[31] the history of tradition[32] and of dogma[33] that here we can only touch upon it, and deal with it just so far as it is unavoidable for our theme. Here is the principal affirmation of the very ancient, pre-Pauline hymn, which Paul rounded off in Philippians 2.

> Christ Jesus . . . though he was in the form of God, did not count equality with God a thing to be grasped, but emptied himself, taking the form of a servant, being born in the likeness of men. And being found in human form he humbled himself and became obedient unto death.

Paul adds here, 'even death on a cross'. Then the hymn resumes:

> Therefore God has highly exalted him and bestowed on him the name which is above every name, that at the name of Jesus every knee should bow, in heaven and on earth and under the earth, and every tongue confess that Jesus Christ is Lord, to the glory of God the Father.

It may be taken as read that the subject who thus 'empties'

himself by taking the form of a servant is not the already incarnate Christ but he who abides beyond this world, being in the form of God. Moreover, it is also an assured conclusion that in this primary Kenosis the second is already contained: As man, not only does he tend to the same condition (*homoiōma* and *schēma* mean approximately the same as *morphē* here) as other human beings. He goes yet further, in obedience, by stopping lower still, down to the death of the Cross. If the fundamental assertion is thus made of the Logos prior to the creation of the world, then *harpagmos* or 'prize' here refers to the 'form of God', the divine condition. In other words, it indicates not something which is to be conquered by force, or unjustly, but rather 'something precious, to be preserved at all cost, though legitimately possessed. And this can be nothing other than the '(form of) glory' ascribed in the last verse of the hymn to the Father, and, in the Kenosis, let go of. No doubt E. Käsemann[34] is correct in not wishing to overload the text by introducing here the dogmatic teaching on the two natures. It is better to interpret it instead in terms of 'the succession of different phases in the continuity of a single drama of salvation', and so to speak, with P. Henry, of 'conditions' rather than natures, in which the subject exists. And yet the question remains: if one wishes to understand the (perhaps, to begin with 'mythical') schema presented here in a Christian fashion, and if, for this reason, one is compelled to interpret it in the framework of Christology and so eventually of Trinitarian theology, then one must allow an 'event' into the God who is beyond the world and beyond change. This event, described in the words 'emptying' and 'humiliation' consists in abandoning equality with God, *isa Theōi*, in what touches the precious possession of 'glory'.

The real problem was concealed so long as, with the Arians, people denied the equality of essence of the Son with the Father (it little matters in this connexion whether the *harpagmos* was interpreted as a *res rapienda* or a *res rapta*), or when, with the Gnostics, they ascribed to the Logos only an apparent body (which excluded a Kenosis) or when again, with Nestorius, they placed their emphasis on the 'promotion' of a man to the dignity of being the God-Man. In all these cases, only the second part of the hymn was taken seriously. Against this tripartite heretical front, orthodoxy had the advantage in the fray that it took the text *à la lettre*, the intrinsic difficulty of its particular interpretation notwithstanding. It was necessary to steer a narrow course. On the one hand, God's changelessness must not be defended in such a manner that in the pre-mundane Logos nothing real took place. On the other hand, this real event could not be allowed to degenerate into theopaschism.[35]

The first fundamental notion which suggested itself to the orthodox, and was used by Athanasius against Arius and Apollinarius, by Cyril against Nestorius and by Leo against Eutyches had it that the divine decision to let the Logos become man meant for the Word a genuine humiliation and lowering, the more so when the historic condition in which sinful humanity found itself was taken into consideration. Athanasius describes the basic movement of the event of Jesus Christ as descent, not ascent. He cites Philippians 2, and goes on:

> What could be clearer or more probative than these words? He did not pass from a more wretched state to a better one, but, being God, took the form of a slave and, by that act of assuming, was not lifted up but cast himself down.

It was, rather, the human being who needed to rise, 'because of the lowliness of the flesh, and of death'. The Logos, who needed no exaltation, took this form and 'suffered death in the flesh on our account as man, in order that he might offer himself for us in death to the Father', and raise us up with him to those heights which from all eternity were his.[36] Here lies Cyril's chief strength in his struggle against a Nestorian Christology which we today might describe as a 'dynamic and transcendental anthropology'. Cyril does not start out from the 'open' structure of man's transcendence', but from God's self-abnegation, and the Love that stoops down.[37] For God, the Incarnation is no 'increase', but only

emptying.[38] No doubt, to Cyril's mind it changes nothing in
the divine form (and so in the glory) of the eternal Logos.
Yet in the perspective of pre-existence it is a fully voluntary
action whereby the Logos accepts the limits (the word *metron*
recurs frequently), and the *adoxia*,[39] 'ingloriousness', of
human nature -which means to say an 'emptying out of
fulness' and a 'lowering of what was exalted'.[40] Leo the
Great shows the same concern to relate the undiminishedness
and impassibility of the Godhead with the promotion of
man through the humiliating assumption (*divinitatem usque ad
humana submisit*) of the *conditio naturae peccatricis*.[41] And in
the same tradition, which is what we wish to underline here,
Hilary says of the Incarnation (and not expressly of the Cross):
'His humiliation is our nobility; his weakness is our honour'.[42]
Hilary speaks too of the 'abasement of his uncircumscribable
power, right down to the docile assumption of a body'.[43] In
the same line of reflection, Louis of Granada will declare
that, for God, the Incarnation is more humiliating than the
Cross.[44] It was with a stooping down, remarks Augustine,
that the Incarnation began.[45]

But is this assertion something which in itself can be
combined with an affirmation of the unchangeability of God
– and so of the continuing glory of the Son with God the
Father?

If we look back from the mature Christology of Ephesus
and Chalcedon to the hymn of Philippians 2, and do so with
the intention of not exaggerating its capacity for 'dogmatic'
assertiveness, we can hardly help registering a 'plus factor' in
its archaic language – stammering out the mystery as this
does – to which the established formulae of the
unchangeability of God do not really do justice. One senses
here a further residue of meaning, with which the German,
English and Russian kenoticists of the nineteenth and
twentieth centuries sought to come to terms.

There were, however, the almost super-human efforts of
Hilary to explicitate without reducing the mystery of the
Kenosis. While his attempts were not wholly satisfactory,
they set us, perhaps, on the right path. For Hilary, the whole
affair proceeds in the sovereign freedom (and so in the power

and majesty) of the God who has the power to 'empty himself, in obedience, for the (eventual) taking of the form of a servant, and from out of the divine form itself'.[46] And so God, whilst abiding in himself (for everything happens in his sovereign power) can yet leave himself (in his form of glory). Were the two forms (*morphai*) simply compatible (as the three great teachers just mentioned thought), then nothing would really have happened in God himself. The Subject, doubtless, remains the same – 'non alius est in forma servi quam in forma Dei est' – but a change in the condition of the Subject is unavoidable:

> cum accipere formam servi nisi per evacuationem suam
> (!) non potuerit qui manebat (*hyparchōn!*) in Dei forma,
> non conveniente sibi formae utriusque concursu.[47]

A bifurcation takes place, which will only be brought to an end when the form of the servant is raised up into the form of the glory of the Kyrios.[48] Between the two lies the *vacuitatis dispensatio*,[49] which does not change the Son of God (*non demutatus*), but signifies, within his innermost being, an act of self-concealing (*intra se latens*), of 'self-emptying at the inmost centre of his powers' (*intra suam ipse vacuefactus potestatem*)[50] – without, then, the loss of that power in its freedom and divinity (*cum virtutis potestas etiam in evacuandi se potestate permaneat*).[51]

To these affirmations there is lacking just one dimension: the Trinitarian dimension, that is, the dimension of the Persons in their processions, relations and missions. At the New Testament level, this dimension is glimpsed in the hymn of Philippians 2, even though there it does not yet possess for its own self-expression any other conceptual materials than those already used by the Old Testament in its notion of God. The stress, therefore, falls on the affirmation that, though being in the form of God (in dogmatic terms: participating in divinity *homoousiōs*), he did not believe it necessary to hold on to that condition as to some possession, precious, inalienable, all his own. If this will to 'hold on' might be described as a fundamental characteristic of the God

of the Old Testament, who shares with no other his honour
and glory, and indeed *cannot* share them with any other, since
he would fall into self-contradiction should he offer them
round, this property does not henceforth pertain to 'Jesus
Christ' – considered as a premundane and thus divine Subject.
He can, so to say, let himself renounce his glory. He is so
divinely free that he can bind himself to the obedience of a
slave. In this reciprocal detachment of two images of God,
the self-emptying Son stands opposed, for a moment, to God
the Father who is still (Philippians 2) in some way depicted in
the colours of the Old Testament palette. But theological
reflection at once evens out this difference: it is in fact the
Father himself who 'does not believe it necessary to hold on
to this Son', but 'delivers him over' (*tradere: John 19, 11;
Romans 4, 25; 8, 32; dare*: John 3, 16; 6, 32, etc.), as indeed the
Spirit is continuously described as the 'Gift' of them both.

The question of some kind of 'mythical' premundane
temptation of the Son (as primordial Man) does not, then,
arise. It is not a matter of an incapacity to master the highest
degree of glory without undergoing Incarnation. There is,
therefore, no parallel with Adam who, anticipating the
reward of the divine command to obey, 'grasped'[52] the apple
for himself. What is at stake, at least in a perspective of
depth, is an altogether decisive turn-about in the way of
seeing God. God is not, in the first place, 'absolute power',
but 'absolute love', and his sovereignty manifests itself not in
holding on to what is its own but in its abandonment – all
this in such a way that this sovereignty displays itself in
transcending the opposition, known to us from the world,
between power and impotence. The exteriorisation of God
(in the Incarnation) has its ontic condition of possibility in
the eternal exteriorisation of God – that is, in his tripersonal
self-gift. With that departure point, the created person, too,
should no longer be described chiefly as subsisting in itself,
but more profoundly (supposing that person to be actually
created in God's image and likeness) as a 'returning (*reflexio
completa*) from exteriority to oneself' and an 'emergence from
oneself as an interiority that gives itself in self-expression'.
The concepts of 'poverty' and 'riches' become dialectical.

This does not mean, however, that God's essence becomes itself (univocally) 'kenotic', such that a single concept could include both the divine foundation of the possibility of Kenosis, and the Kenosis itself. It is from here that many of the mistakes of the more modern kenoticists take their rise. What it *does* mean − as Hilary in his way tried to show − is that the divine 'power' is so ordered that it can make room for a possible self-exteriorisation, like that found in the Incarnation and the Cross, and can maintain this exteriorisation even to the utmost point. As between the form of God and the form of a servant there reigns, in the identity of the Person involved, an analogy of natures − according to the principle *maior dissimilitudo in tanta similitudine* (DS 806).

Here for the first time a way is cleared to the speculative penetration of two propositions which Scripture and the patristic tradition articulate, certainly, but whose understanding was, to speak, closed off by the taking up of anti-heretical positions, whether in defence of the unchangedness of the form of God, and so of the Son's glory even during his Kenosis, or of the unchangeability of God in general. The first of these two propositions is the Johannine affirmation that, in the uttermost form of a slave, on the Cross, the Son's glory breaks through, inasmuch as it is then that he goes to the (divine) extreme in his loving, and in the revelation of that love. The second proposition affirms that in the Incarnation the triune God has not simply helped the world, but has disclosed himself in what is most deeply his own. Truth to say, this latter claim does not appear in its fulness in the Trinitarian doctrine of the Fathers and of Augustine but only in that of Richard of Saint-Victor.

It is in this perspective that many of the assertions of the Fathers become fully luminous for the first time. Take, for example, Origen's declaration

One must dare to say that the goodness of Christ appears greater, more divine, and truly in the image of the Father, when he humbles himself in obedience unto death − the death of the Cross − than had he clung onto his equality with the Father as an inalienable gift, and had refused to become a slave for the world's salvation.[53]

Or again that of John Chrysostom:

No event is so sublime as this: the blood of God has been poured out for us. It is more than our adoption as children, more than anything other thing, that God did not spare his only Son ... That is by far the greatest thing.[54]

Cyril can even speak of a *felix culpa* not for us, but for the Son of God, since the Fall gave him the opportunity to attain in his abasement a new glory.[55] Taking his stand on such texts, Lossky interprets the Kenosis as a revelation of the entire Trinity.[56] This permits one to grasp how, on occasion, the thought arises, tentatively and obscurely, that when the Creator first made man the ideal Image he had in mind was the Incarnate Son as our Redeemer.[57]

If one takes seriously what has just been said, then the event of the Incarnation of the second divine Person does not leave the inter-relationship of those Persons unaffected. Human thought and human language break down in the presence of this mystery: namely, that the eternal relations of Father and Son are focussed, during the 'time' of Christ's earthly wanderings, and in a sense which must be taken with full seriousness, in the relations between the man Jesus and his heavenly Father, and that the Holy Spirit lives as their go-between who, inasmuch as he proceeds from the Son, must also be affected by the Son's humanity. This is the question which the modern kenoticists in their own way tried to tackle: beginning with the Lutherans Chemnitz (1522–1586) and Brentz (1499–1570), both of whom admitted a *communicatio idiomatum* between the divine and human natures of Christ. They understood this to mean that the humanity must share in the omnipotence and omnipresence of the divinity. For Chemnitz this participation was only potential where continuous possession was concerned but actual in terms of use, *chrēsis*, if and when the will of Christ allowed it (which meant the Eucharist). For Brentz, the condition of *exinanitio* is always co-extensive with that of exaltation, and yet this omnipresence, of which Christ enjoys the constant disposition, remains, in the perspective of the Economy, something frequently hidden (*krypsis*). The school of Giessen followed Chemnitz, that of Tübingen Brentz. The latter was the more serious in its implementation of the Lutheran *communicatio idiomatum*, whereas the school of Giessen was reproached with falling into the *extra calvinisticum*. According to the latter, the Logos, *extra carnem*, did not abandon his governance of the world during Jesus' earthly sojourn and death, but rather carried out the Incarnation and the death as, so to say, one occupation alongside others. This must also have been the belief of Augustine[58] and Thomas Aquinas[59] to judge from the character of their premisses. The problematic of both Lutheran schools does not, however, disengage what is central in the problem of the Kenosis. For they consider above all the immanence of the finite in the infinite, even if they do regard the latter as significantly affected by the former. Moreover, they lack the categories of divine personality which we have drawn out. They somehow contrive to consider the divine attributes in an Old Testament fashion and situate the Incarnation within that framework.

The kenoticists of nineteenth century Germany[60] wrote under the influence of Hegel for whom the absolute Subject, to become concrete and 'for-himself', renders himself finite in nature and world history. These theologians take up, therefore, the opposite standpoint: to their mind, the subject of the Kenosis is not he who became man, but he who becomes man. What is at stake is a 'self-limitation of the Godhead', as Thomasius puts it. According to this writer, the Son renounces those divine properties which are 'relative' to the world – such as omnipotence, omnipresence, ubiquity and so forth – so as to keep those properties – such as truth, holiness, love – which are immanent in God himself. Since this self-limitation of the Godhead takes place in absolute freedom, being the work of love, it does not suppress God's divinity. Frank spoke more radically of a selfdepotentialisation of the consciousness of the eternal Son in a finite self-consciousness which, however, still allows the incarnate Son awareness of his own identity as Son of God. The being of man as the image of God becomes the receptacle for a divine content gathered and funnelled into its limited space. Gess goes further still: the Logos made man renounced even the immanent divine properties and his own eternal self-consciousness. In this system, the Logos ends up by losing himself in the process of world history, and the Trinity is only constituted by means of the economy. Doubtless Thomasius' position was still close enough to the intuitions of Hilary, yet with his distinction between immanent and transcendent properties – a distinction itself wholly unworkable – he was not really able to go beyond the horizon of the Old Testament.

If German kenoticism was manifestly provoked by speculative Idealism, what A. M. Ramsey called the 'kenotic flood' in Anglican theology between 1890 and 1910 was no doubt also aroused in an indirect manner, thanks to the influence of T. H. Green, by Hegel, and the idea of a cosmic evolution reaching its summit in Christ. Essentially, though, it was an independent attempt to reconcile patristic Christology with that earthly realism about the man Jesus of Nazerath which research into the gospels had highlighted. The group's weakness lay in the fact that, while speculative Idealism had identified the problem of the person with the problem of consciousness, they stressed the empirical aspect of Jesus' self-awareness which, as something human and historical, was necessarily also limited. For Charles Gore, moreover, the creation, and still more the Incarnation, is a 'self-limitation of God' – yet precisely in this lies God's self-revelation. For sheer 'physical power ... makes itself felt only in self-assertion and pressure; it is the higher power of love which is shown in self-effacement'. Frank Weston follows Gore[61] here in his *The One Christ* (1907). He criticises the weak points in Gore's account, and seeks to reconcile the traditional ontic categories with their counterparts in the Idealist philosophy of self-consciousness. This Weston does in as much as while, assuredly, accepting the existence in Christ of two natures, each with its faculties of knowledge and will, he posits one sole self-consciousness in him, since, when these divine and human faculties are actively engaged, each set co-determines the other. There is neither action nor suffering of the Son made man in which the divine nature does not participate. Similarly, there is no relationship of the eternal Son to the Father, and to the world, that is not conditioned by the self-limitation of the man Jesus. From the standpoint of the single consciousness, he is on earth a limited man under obedience, while in heaven he is the ruler of the world. However, these speculations lead nowhere: their only result is to bring to our attention in striking fashion how deep the mystery of the Kenosis lies. Just as the ancient ontic theology was impotent to render credible the idea that the Incarnation was a 'complementary factor' added to the immutable divine nature (for the Kenosis is not a *harpagmos*, a gain), so too the theology of consciousness – whether in speculative or empirical guise – did not succeed in finding a 'third' position from which the interplay of the divine and human consciousness might be surveyed. The *paradox* must be allowed to stand: in the undiminished humanity of Jesus, the whole power and glory of God are made present to us.

P. Althaus was right when he wrote:

> Christology must be thought out from the vantage-point of the Cross. In the total powerlessness, the death anguish, of the Crucified – from which one cannot keep unscathed the 'divine nature' – the full undiminished divinity of God is at work. What Paul heard as a word of the Lord for his own life – 'My powers is made perfect in weakness' (II Corinthians 12, 9), we recognise through faith in Jesus Christ as a law of the divine life itself. With this recognition, it is true, the old conception of God's immutability breaks into pieces. Christology must take seriously the fact that, in the Son, God himself really entered into suffering, and in that very entrance is and remains entirely God.[62]

Accordingly, one can only agree with those Fathers who not

only identified the Kenosis – as God's self-limitation and self-renunciation – with the divine *freedom*, over against every way of thinking that would posit here a process of a natural (Gnostic) or logical (Hegelian) character, but went on to see in the powerlessness of the Incarnate and Crucified One the shining forth of God's *omnipotence*. One could speak here of a 'concentration' of the Son, realised in freedom[63], so that the 'mustard seed', which was the smallest of all seeds, might, thanks to the power within it, grow to a height that out-tops all the rest.[64] This is why Hilary, when writing of the sufferings of the Cross, can underline, almost to the point of Docetism, that divine freedom on which the form of a slave depends.[65] Lastly, Gregory of Nyssa can say:

> The fact that the all-powerful nature was capable of stooping down to the lowliness of the human condition is a greater proof of power than are the miracles, imposing and supernatural though these be ... The humiliation of God shows the super-abundance of his power, which is in no way fettered in the midst of conditions contrary to its nature ... The greatness is glimpsed in the lowliness and its exaltation is not thereby reduced.[66]

There is a theological truth which mediates between the two irreconcilable extremes: those of, on the one hand, a 'divine immutability' for which the Incarnation appears only as an external 'addition', and, on the other a 'divine mutability' of such a sort that, for the duration of the Incarnation, the divine self-consciousness of the Son is 'alienated' in a human awareness.[67] The truth which intervenes between them concerns the 'Lamb slain before the foundation of the world' (Apocalypse 13, 8; cf. 5, 6, 9, 12). Here, clearly enough, two lines meet. The 'slaying' is in no sense conceived in a Gnostic manner, as a heavenly sacrifice independent of that of Golgotha. It designates, rather, the eternal aspect of the historic and bloody sacrifice of the Cross (Apocalypse 5, 12) – as indeed Paul everywhere presupposes. Nevertheless what is indicated here is an enduring supratemporal condition of the

'Lamb' – not only, as the 'French School' would have it, the continuing 'sacrificial state' of the Risen One, but also a condition of the Son's existence co-extensive with all creation and thus affecting, in some manner, his divine being. Recent Russian theology,[68] though not immune from temptations of a Gnostic or Hegelian sort,[69] was right to give this aspect a central place. It should be possible[70] to divest Bulgakov's fundamental conviction of its sophiological presuppositions while preserving – and unfolding in its many facets – that basic idea of his which we agreed just now to give a central place high on our list of priorities. The ultimate presupposition of the Kenosis is the 'selflessness' of the Persons (when considered as pure relationships) in the inner-Trinitarian life of love. There is, next, a fundamental Kenosis given with the creation as such, since God from all eternity takes on responsibility for its flourishing (not least in regard to human freedom), and in his providence, foreseeing sin, includes the Cross (as foundation of the creation) in his 'account'. 'The Cross of Christ is inscribed in the creation of the world since its basis was laid.'[71] Finally, in the actual world, marked as it is by sin, 'his redemptive Passion begins with his Incarnation itself'.[72] And since the will to undertake the redemptive Kenosis is itself indivisibly trinitarian.' God the Father and the Holy Spirit are for Bulgakov involved in the Kenosis in the most serious sense: the Father as he who sends and abandons,[73] the Spirit as he who unites only through separation and absence.[74] All this is true of the 'economic Trinity' who, according to Bulgakov, must be distinguished from the 'immanent' Trinity. But one sees how, through adoption of a perspective borrowed from the philosophies of Schelling and Hegel, the economic Trinity is 'from time immemorial assumed' in the immanent Trinity, in such a way, however, that the process of establishing and experiencing the world remains for God a perfectly free decision.

The outstanding Congregationalist theologian P. T. Forsyth in his own way placed the heavenly sacrifice of the Lamb at the nodal point where God and the world are joined in mutual relation. Designedly, Forsyth call this the 'crucial act' wherein creation and redemption intersect and unite.

Christ's sacrifice began before he came into the world, and his Cross was that of a lamb slain before the world's foundation. There was a Calvary above which was the mother of it all. His obedience, however impressive, does not take divine magnitude if it first rose upon earth, nor has it the due compelling power upon ours. His obedience as man was but the detail of the supreme obedience which made him man.[75]

In *Christus Veritas* (1924), the Anglican William Temple will interpret this to mean that the Cross is 'the unveiling of a mystery of the divine life itself'[76] – not in the sense that God becomes the immediate subject of our suffering, but rather that, for the Creator and Redeemer, nothing of what happens in the creation for which he has 'paid' and taken responsibility is alien or external. Had not Origen already tried to go beyond the dogma of the pure *apatheia* of God when, in the presence of the Son suffering on the Cross, he believed he had to say, 'Perhaps the Father too is not without *pathos*'?[77] And what does the 'sublime altare tuum' of the Roman Canon mean if not the everlasting aspect of the sacrifice of Golgotha, which is likewise represented in the Lamb slain before time began, seated eternally with the Father on that throne from which issue the 'flashes of lightning, and voices and peals of thunder' (Apocalypse 4, 5) of God's glory?[78]

(5) Literature

In what follows, we will have to do with a 'theology of the Passion, of the Descent into Hell, and of the Resurrection'. By way of opposition, then, to the customary School theology which takes as its themes such abstract notions as 'redemption', 'justification' and so forth, this theology takes as its chief object the personal *concretissimum* of the God-man who suffers 'for me', 'for us', descends into Hell and rises again. It is beyond doubt that the abstract manner of approaching things came into prominence through the heresiological struggles of the first centuries (from Irenaeus, via Athanasius, Cyril and the Cappadocians to Damascene and Scholasticism), even if the ultimate objective of those controversies about ideas always remained the concrete person of Christ in his (primary) function as Redeemer and (secondarily) as Revealer. But alongside this conciliar and Scholastic dogmatics it was necessary – if the personal element was to receive its theological primacy – for there always to be a counter-movement, setting out from the implicit theology of the great saints and their encounter with Christ and seeking to resolve itself, more or less felicitously and with varying degrees of success, into an explicit theology of the Passion. Neither the Middle Ages nor the modern period ever succeeded in bringing about the complete fusion of 'scientific' theology with what was called, in a slightly pejorative phrase, 'affective' theology. Today the latter is still less appreciated: even an 'existential' type of reflection takes as the limits of its vision not, in the first place, Christ himself but the subject whom he is to redeem.

One must, however, take notice of the fact that the starting-point and model of all theology, namely Holy Scripture, provides us with a shining example of the perfect identity between concrete and abstract (or, better, universal) ways of looking. That is true of its treatment of the decisive prophetic situations of the Old Testament (salvation and judgment, the role of the Mediator, and so forth) as of all the facets of New Testament 'Passiology'. For Paul, the whole understanding of faith, justification and sanctification is rooted in the 'Son of God, who loved me and gave himself for me' (Galatians 2, 20), and thus delivered to us the living Trinitarian proof of the Father's gracious love (Romans 8, 32), the outpoured love of the Spirit (Romans 5, 5). For the entire Christology of John, person and function are essentially one, while God's love renders itself concrete with an almost terrifying exclusivity in the person and work of Christ (I John 4, 2, 9–10). The same is true of the Synoptics: all of Christ's 'titles' show him to be the unique personal individual in whom God manifests himself as Redeemer of the world. The same unity is present, and with a strongly affective accentuation in Ignatius of Antioch. Enveloped in a Hellenistic idiom, yet clearly recognisable, we also find it in Clement of Rome.

With the Apologists on the one hand, and Irenaeus and Tertullian on the other there arises an abstract discourse, at once 'diplomatic' and 'polemical', which will be sustained in theological and conciliar documents throughout the patristic period. A new voice, personal, affective, is heard with Origen: his commentary on the Song of Songs will influence Bede and Bernard directly, Francis and the Rhenish mystics indirectly.[79]

But above all the source, ever flowing, ever fresh, of the theology of the Passion lies in the great holy figures of Church history. Their charism consisted in the ability to re-immerse themselves, beyond everything that convention might dictate, in a 'contemporaneity' with the Gospel so as to bequeath the legacy of their intimate experience to their spiritual children. Mentioning names will suffice. Anthony of Egyot's much famed demonic temptations are no doubt primarily experiences of the Passion;[80] the Rules of saint Basil, and their introductions, breathe the spirit of the Cross.[81] As for the relevant aspects of Eastern spiritual theology, from Evagrius and Nilus to Maximus and Symeon, there will be an opportunity to treat of this later,[82] in connexion with the theme of divine abandonment. Augustine's conversion unfolded in two stages: first, to the only good God (of Plotinus), and then to the weak, crucified God (*Confessions* VII. 18), for it is only in the Crucified One that God becomes concrete (X. 43), and all the splendour of the redeemed world arises from out of the 'root planted in thirsty ground' of the suffering God.[83] The early Middle Ages draws its 'affective theology' from here, though the stream of Augustinian influence is crossed by that of an apophatic theology, coming in continuous waves, from its source in the Pseudo-Denys. This latter is certainly not a theology of the Passion in the proper sense of that phrase. Only rarely do the two streams mingle in harmony:[84] that is not the case even in Bonaventure. Benedict's restrained theology of the Passion appears indirectly in his 'The Grades of Humility', and shows itself in new guise in Anselm's astonishing prayers on the

Passion, and in the mysticism of Gertrude of Helfta. Bernard's powerful impulse did not come to full term within his own school, and even less so in that of St-Victor: it was criss-crossed by Neoplatonic schemes of mystical ascent (Augustinian or Dionysian in colour). The experience of the *Poverello*, Francis of Assisi, on Mount Alverna – the highpoint of his meditation on the Cross – is deflected by his pupils in one of two directions: by Bonaventure into another 'ascension' scheme, and by the Spiritual Franciscans into a Joachimism for which, despite all its affective piety, the Passion is fundamentally rendered otiose by the coming of the age of the Spirit. And so the great work of Ubertino di Casale, *Arbor vitae crucifixae Jesu*, formally dependent on Bonaventure as this is,[85] does not contain what its title promises.[86] The finest fruit on the Franciscan tree might well be that of Elizabeth of Hungary, though Jacopone da Todi should also be mentioned in this connexion. The classic period in the theology of the Passion extends from 1300 to 1700. Whereas Suso's loyalties were divided (concern with sharing the Passion, but also devotion to 'Wisdom'), Tauler became the father of a theology of the Cross which (through Surius) spread out in a broad fan, exercising a determining influence on all the European countries as well as the great Orders (Dominicans, Jesuits, Carmelites, and so on). Among women, Passion mysticism frequently took on a splendid expression.[87] A new impulse derives from the meditation on the Passion found in Ignatius of Loyola – by no means independent, this, of the concrete contemplation of the late Middle Ages. Yet in Loyola's mysticism of the 'call' of Jesus from the Cross and of 'conversation with the Crucified' (*Exercises* 97f., 165f., 53f., 61), he inaugurates a theology which is novel in its style of personal dialogue. By the side of Ignatius, whose own theology of the Cross was not made explicit, there stands the Augustinian Luther, who, from his early Catholic period (the Cross, and the humiliation of God) right down to his last years did not cease to build up his theology from the elements provided by the Passion event. Despite the major impulses given by the saints the official theology did not succeed in constructing a genuine theology of the *Triduum Mortis* to complement the abstract soteriology. By and large, that was because, on the one hand, the implicit theology of the saints was at times narrowed down to a specialised 'affective' or 'spiritual' theology, while on the other hand it was taken captive by anthropocentric schemata of ascent and purificiation, still dominant in the doctor of the Church John of the Cross himself.

If we leave aside the multiplicity of more popular devotions which took the Passion as their focus: devotion to the Way of the Cross,[88] to the Heart of Jesus, essentially a meditation on the Passion, and one which has brought into being a whole christocentric theology of its own,[89] the countless great Passion plays, sometimes lasting for days on end and containing a rich theological content,[90] the literary flood leaves only a few theological high-water marks behind it. Jacob Gretzer's standard work, *De Cruce Christi*, comprising a first volume in four books (1588) and a second, with Greek texts and supplement (1600) is of little interest to us here, since on the one hand, it confines itself to the historical materiality of the Cross, its veneration and appearance in art, and on the other hand (in book four) remains on the level of the 'spiritual Cross' of the Christian man: a true theology of the Cross is, therefore, lacking here. By contrast, two pre-eminent works must be mentioned. At the end of the Renaissance, Jean de la Ceppède writes his *Théorèmes sur le Mystère Sacré de Notre Rédemption*:[91] three books each with a hundred sonnets on the Passion, and a fourth with the fifty sonnets on the Descent into Hell, followed by three further books with one hundred and sixty five sonnets on the Resurrection, the Ascension and the Outpouring of the Spirit. The entire work is of a high literary order, and is supplied with copious commentaries from the Church Fathers and the Scholastics. Its inspiration is Ignatian. At the opening of the Baroque age, the Oratorian J. J. Duguet composed a *Traité de la Croix de Notre Seigneur Jésus-Christ* in fourteen volumes, and in addition, in two volumes, *Le Tombeau de Jésus-Christ* (1733f).[92] These theological meditations, coloured by Jansenism though they are, both draw into their compass the whole gamut of patristic speculation. A high-point of rigorist theology of the Passion whose editor, Père F. Florand, O.P., has shown to belong to a whole current of tradition, is Louis Chardon's *La Croix de Jésus* (Paris 1647),[93] to which we shall return. After the Enlightenment, no work of similiar intensity was published.[94]

These works have been mentioned here because, at the very least, they represent attempts to harmonise a personal and concrete devotion to the Passion with the patristic vision of the whole economy of salvation – the Cross as the acme of the entire redeeming and revealing work of the triune God. The equilibrium in question is a *perpetuum mobile*: not even the historic Liturgy has achieved it in a permanent fashion.[95] The concretising of particular mysteries in the form of feasts (as memorials of particular situations in the saving drama) always carries the danger of losing sight of the unfolding of the drama as a whole, and so of its specific dramatic structure. On the other hand, such concretising (as in, for example, Paul) is in no way identical with a return to the *Christos kata sarka*.[96] What is necessary today, after long experience of the history of theology, is an effort at an authentic *theological* deepening of the particular mysteries of salvation in their incarnationally concrete character – without surrendering thereby to an untheological historicising interest, and, above all, without losing to view the Trinitarian background and so the functional aspect of the work of Jesus, which means no less than the relations within the Trinity that define his Person.

References

[1] Gregory Nazianzen, *Oratio* 45 (PG 36, 653A).

[2] For the precise delimitation of the question between Thomists and Scotists, cf. A. Spindeler, *Cur Verbum Caro Factum?* (Paderborn 1938), pp. 13–38. We shall not, it follows, speak, with Suarez, of a 'twofold principal motive of the Incarnation': bibliography in *Summa Theologiae* (Madrid 1953, Biblioteca de Autores Cristianos), pp. 14–24.

[3] H. de Lubac, *Le Mystère du Surnaturel* (Paris 1965); idem., *Etudes historiques* (Paris 1946). In Athanasius (*De Incarnatione* 3, PG 25, 101BC) the vocation of the 'first Adam born from the earth' to share in the second Adam and in eternal salvation

in God is described in a naïve and grandiose way: since God saw that humankind was 'incapable, according to the law of its own nature, of subsisting for ever, he gave it something more ... by giving them a share in the pwer of his own Word'. More penetrating is the most polished of the early apologists, Athenagoras, whose 'On the Resurrection of the Dead' (after 177) is 'by far the best ... of what the ancients have written about the Resurrection' (Otto, ed., *Corpus Apologetorum* VII, 1857, pp. 187–291; = Altaner-Stuiber 74). Though an Athenian philosopher, he completely abandons the idea that man is fundamentally an immortal soul (fallen into the flesh from which he must be delivered). On the contrary, man is inseparably body and soul: destined, through the Creator's goodness, to know God's being and will. From the eternity of the perceived object (perceived already on earth), namely, the wisdom and glory of God, there follows the eternity of the subjective act of knowledge and love. But the subject is precisely that human being who is inseparably body and soul. Therefore, right from the moment of man's creation, God wills his Resurrection. The selfsame truth can either be shown apologetically (God has the wisdom, the power and the will to render man imperishable), or dogmatically – from God as primordial cause, who has created man for himself and so has lifted him above the beasts that perish, and from the two-fold nature of man, who always posits all his acts (whether of enjoyment or renunciation, good or evil) as a total subject composed of body and soul, or finally, from the world-guiding providence which must allow an appropriate judgment to be made on the body-soul existence of the human being destined for eternity, a judgment which itself can only be just if it grants the body its part. One should not criticise this remarkable Christian anthropology for allegedly deducing the Resurrection as a postulate of nature, since, for Athenagoras, everything rests on a first grace of the Creator God: the distinction between 'natural' and 'supernatural' does not enter his field of vision. One might at most approach it with playing down a 'certain disaccord' (*tis anōmalia*, n. 16), in regarding death as the 'brother of sleep', rather than as the destructive consequence of sin. This is also why it fails to express the archetypal place occupied by Christ's death and Resurrection in the re-unification of 'man identical with himself' (n. 25). But what is important for our purposes here is uniquely the idea of the inseparability between the human being, made up of body and soul, and his eternal, death-surviving, determination.

4 See on this particular point: H. U. von Balthasar, *Das Ganze im Fragment. Aspekte der Geschichtstheologie* (Einsiedeln 1963), II: 'Die Vollendbarkeit des Menschen', pp. 61–123.

5 J. Coste, 'Notion grecque et notion biblique de la "Souffrance éducative"', RSR 43 (1955), pp. 481–523.

6 Athanasius, *De Incarnatione* 44 (PG 25, 173C–176A)

7 C. Barth, *Die Errettung vom Tode in den individuellen Klage- und Dankliedern des Alten Testaments* (Zollikon 1947), pp. 52ff; 82.

8 See on this our volume 'Alter Bund' in *Herrlichkeit* II/2, 1 (Einsiedeln 1967).

9 A. Oepke, *Die Missionspredigt des Apostels Paulus* (Gütersloh 1920); U. Wilckens, *Weisheit and Torheit* (Tübingen 1959).

10 P. Tillich, *Systematische Theologie* II (Stuttgart 1958), p. 171.

11 P. Bernardakis, 'Le culte de la Croix chez les Grecs', EO 5 (1905), pp. 193–202;

257–264; A. Rücker, 'Die *adoratio crucis* am Karfreitag in den orientalischen Riten', in *Miscellanea Liturgica Mohlberg* I (Rome 1948), pp. 379–406; S. Salaville, 'Le coup de la lance et la plaie du côté dans la liturgie orientale', *L'Unité de l'Eglise* 8 (1920), pp. 77–86; J. Vogt, 'Berichte über Kreuzerscheinungen im 4. Jahrhundert', in *Pankrateia. Mélanges Henri Grégoire* I, = *Annales de l'Institut de Philologie et d'Histoire Orientales et Slaves* 9 (1949), pp. 593–606.

[12] *De Carne Christi* 6 (PL 2, 764A).

[13] *De Incarnatione* 20 (PG 25, 152B); A. Spindler, *Cur Verbum Caro Factum?* (Paderborn 1938) sums up Athanasius' thought in this way: 'We are to recover grace after sin not only from without but from within; we are to receive divinisation in relation to the body', p. 53; redemption is not 'a simple effacing of sin, . . . (It) is realised in a superabundant fulness of life, . . . by the Incarnation of God, and through this incarnate God's blood and sacrifice', p. 55.

[14] *Epistola ad Epictetum* 6–7 (PG 26, 1061A).

[15] *Oratio Catechetica* 32 (PG 45, 80A); the Incarnation without the Redemption would have been superfluous: *Antirrhetikos* 51 (PG 45, 1245B).

[16] *Adversus Haereses* X. 33 (PG 16/3, 3452C). On Irenaeus, cf. ibid., V. 14, 1 (also: III. 16, 9; IV. 5, 4; V. 1, 1; 17, 1). If Irenaeus speaks of 'recapitulation' in such a fashion that it denotes above all the Incarnation, that is, particular actions in the life of Jesus which appear to bring about the return of Adam's race to unity with God, nevertheless, at all the decisive points, the new Adam's obedience is contrasted with the disobedience of the old: the 're' signifies conversion and so liberation, effected by the God-Man, in regard to the 'powers', namely death and the Devil.

[17] *Oratio Theologica* 4, 21 (PG 36, 13B).

[18] *In Epistolam ad Hebraeos* 5, 11 (PG 63, 46); *In Epistolam ad Ephesianos* 1 (PG 62, 14).

[19] *Thesaurus*, XV (PG 75, 265).

[20] Ibid., PG. 75, 282A.

[21] *Sermo* 71, 2 (PL 54, 387).

[22] *Sermo* 48, 1, (PL 54, 298). Cf. Tomus I (54, 763); *Sermo* 46, 1 (54, 292); *Sermo* 59, 8 (54, 342) etc.

[23] *De Trinitate* II. 23 (PL 10, 66A).

[24] *De Incarnatione Domini* 54 (PL 16, 831).

[25] *Capita Theologica et Oecumenica* I, 66 (PG 90, 1108B).

[26] *De Vita in Christo* III (PG 150, 572CD).

[27] Cf. the diagnoses and warnings given in H. de Lubac, *Paradoxes* (expanded edition, Paris 1959). pp. 41ff; 'Arian Christianity is perfectly incarnate: there one is Christian by birth from the flesh'; 'What a fine plan for incarnate Christianity Satan presented to Jesus in the desert! Jesus preferred a crucified Christianity'; 'The mystery of Christ is also our own. What was achieved in the Head must be achieved in the members. Incarnation, death and ressurection: that is to say, en-rooting, detachment and transfiguration. There is no Christian spirituality which does not comprise this threefold rhythm': 'Christ did not come to carry out the work of incarnation: the Word became incarnate so as to carry out the work of redemption'. 'To humanise before Christianising? If the enterprise

succeeds, Christianity will come too late, its place will be filled. And do they think that Christianity has no humanising value?'.

[28] *De Civitate Dei* 13, 10 (PL 41, 383); cf. *Confessiones* I. 6; C. Hartmann, 'Der Tod in seiner Beziehung zum menschlichen Dasein bei Augustinus', *Catholica* 1 (1932), pp. 159–190.

[29] *In Vigiliam Nativitatis Sermo* 4 (PL 183, 103B). For the whole, see the subtle study by J. P. Jossua, *Le Salut. Incarnation ou mystère pascal chez les Pères de l'Eglise de S. Irénée à S. Léon le Grand* (Paris 1968), where the thesis, sustained earlier by, above all, P. Malevez, which ascribes to the Greek fathers an 'incarnationalism' is transcended in the direction of a common understanding, at once Eastern and Western, of the Redemption (with the Cross as centre).

[30] Earlier general accounts: O. Bensow, *Die Lehre von der Kenose* (Leipzig 1903); H. Schumacher, *Christus in seiner Präexistenz und Kenose* (2 volumes, Rome 1914 and 1921); P. Henry, 'Kénose', DBS V (1957), pp. 7–61 (with a comprehensive bibliography, alphabetical order: Käsemann's analysis, however, is omitted).

[31] Some recent studies of a fundamental kind: E. Käsemann, 'Kritische Analyse von Phil. 2, 5–11), ZThK 47 (1950), pp. 313–360 cited from idem., *Exegetische Versuche und Besinnungen* I (Göttingen 1965⁴), pp. 51–95; A. Feuillet, *L'Homme-Dieu considéré dans sa condition terrestre de serviteur et rédempteur* (=Vivre et Penser 2, Paris 1942); J. Dupont, 'Jésus-Christ dans son abaissement', RSR 37 (1950), pp. 500–514; L. Cerfaux, 'L'hymne au Christ-Serviteur de Dieu', in *Recueil Lucien Cerfaux* (Paris 1954), pp. 425–437; O. Michel, 'Zur Exegese von Phil. 2, 5–11' in *Theologie als Glaubenswagnis. Festschrift für K. Heim* (Hamburg 1954), pp. 79–95; L. Krinetzki, 'Der Einfluss von Is. 52, 13–53, 12 par. auf Phil. 2, 6–11', ThQ 139 (1959), pp. 157–193; 291–388.

[32] J. Gewiss, 'Zum altkirchlichen Verständnis der Kenosisstelle', ThQ 128 (1948), pp. 463–487; exhaustive discussion of all the patristic texts in P. Henry, art. cit., pp. 56–136.

[33] On the dogmatics, and especially the dogmatic errors, of the modern period (the kenoticists of the sixteenth to seventeen centuries, and of the nineteenth century), see M. Waldhauser, *Die Kenose und die moderne protestantische Theologie* (Mainz 1912); P. Henry, art. cit., pp. 136–158 deals with Bulgakov in detail; for the Anglicans, see A. M. Ramsey, *From Gore to Temple* (London 1960).

[34] Op. cit., p. 80.

[35] In what follows, we leave the exegetical question to one side.

[36] *Adversus Arium* I, 40–41 (PG 26, 93CD; 96CD).

[37] 'The Incarnation is in itself an abasement. Cyril says that so often that we cannot doubt it', Spindeler, op. cit. p. 110: he sees therein the principal argument against Nestorius, pp. 112–113.

[38] *Apologia pro 12 Capitis*, anathema 10 (PG 76, 366); *Epistola 55 in Sanctum Symbolum* (PG 77, 304).

[39] *Dialogus de Trinitate* 5 (PG 75, 933B).

[40] *Ad Reginas* 2, 19 (PG 76, 1360B).

[41] Leo, *Sermo* 3, 2 (PL 54, 145); *Sermo* 71, 2 (PL 54, 387): on the Reincarnation as *inclinatio majestatis* and so *humilitas*, *Sermo* 26, 1 *In Nativitatem* 6 (PL 54, 212–213).

[42] Hilary, *De Trinitate* II. 25 (PL 10, 67A).

43 Ibid., XI. (PL 10, 432A).

44 Louis of Granada, *Oeuvres complètes* (Paris 1868), XIII. 217.

45 *In Joannem Tractatus* 104, 3 (PL 35, 1903).

46 *De Trinitate* VIII. 45 (PL 10, 270).

47 Ibid., IX. 14 (PL 10, 292B).

48 Ibid., IX. 39 (PL 10, 312A).

49 Ibid., 41 (PL 10, 314B).

50 Ibid., XI. 48 (PL 10, 432A).

51 Ibid., XII. 6 (PL 10, 437B).

52 On such, and other, presumed sources for the hymn, see P. Henry, art. cit., pp. 38–56; according to this author, and to Krietzki, the Servant Songs may have influenced the hymn, though this is not certain.

53 *In Joannem* I. 32 (Preuschen IV. 41).

54 *In Ephesianos* I (PG 62. 14).

55 *De Trinitate* 5 (PG 75, 968).

56 *Théologie mystique de l'Eglise d'Orient* (Paris 1944), p. 140: 'This renunciation of his own will is not moreover a voluntary decision, it is not a particular act, but it is, so to say, the very being of the three divine Persons, who have only one single will, belonging to their common nature . . . The Kenosis . . . (and) the work of the incarnate Son are the work of the most holy Trinity as a whole, from which one cannot separate Christ'.

57 Tertullian, *Adversus Praxean* 12 (PL 2, 167); Pseudo-Gregory of Nyssa, *De Eo Quid Sit ad Imaginem* (PG 44, 1328); Anastasius of Sinai, *In Hexaemeronem*, Liber 6 (PG 89, 930): 'Since God, the Trinitarian Creator, says 'Let us make man to our image', that image is already by anticipation the incarnate Son, and in this word is found equally as well the Son's consent to the Incarnation'; ibid. (935B): 'Christ is thus the only one by whom the task conferred on man in Paradise – to govern all creation – was carried out'.

58 Augustine's position may be characterised in the following single saying: 'Sic se exinanivit formam servi accipiens, non formam Dei amittens; forma servi *accessit*, non forma Dei discessit', *Sermo* 183, 4, 5 (PL 38, 990). But this simple 'addition' to the already present divine contradicts the meaning of the 'to empty oneself' in Philippians 2 and the 'to become poor' in II Corinthians 8, 9, as well as the affirmations cited from the Greek fathers to the effect that the Logos acquired nothing new by the Incarnation but lowered himself to the condition of a slave.

59 For Thomas Aquinas, cf. *Summa Theologiae* III. q, 14, a. 1, ad ii; a. 2 c.; q. 15. a. 5, ad iii, where the question is treated of the limits to the blessedness in Christ's soul: This happens *dispensative*, so restrained by the incarnate Word himself that blessedness no longer passes from the *mens* to the *vires sensibiles*. With a similar freedom of will Christ makes himself submit to the limits of the human, and thereby to what is natural and involuntary. But the subject of these limiting acts is the Son made man himself. The sense of these affirmations is that 'Christ's ontology' must be defined in a functional and soteriological manner.

60 Above all: G. Thomasius, *Christi Person und Werk* (Erlangen 1853–61; 1886–88², para. 40ff; K. T. A. Liebner, *Christliche Dogmatik aus dem christologischen Prinzip* (Göttingen 1849, more strongly Hegelian): F. H. R. Frank, *System der christlichen*

Wahrheit (Erlangen 1878–80; 1885–6², para. 34); W. F. Gess, *Christi Person und Werk* (Basle 1887). For other writers, see O. Bensow, op. cit., pp. 61ff; 91ff. With their approach is associated the Congregationalist A. M. Fairbairn, *Christ in Modern Theology* (London 1893).

61 Bampton Lectures (London 1891), p. 160.

62 P. Althaus, 'Kenosis', RGG III. 1245ff.

63 P. Nautin (ed.), *Homélies pascales* I, 165: *sunathroisas kai sunagagōn tosoutos ēlthen hosos ethelēsen.*

64 Gregory of Elvira, *Tractatus* 7 (PL Supplement I, 464).

65 *De Trinitate* X. 10 (PL 10, 350AB); cf. S. Thomas, *Summa Theologiae* IIIa., q. 15, a. 5, ad i.

66 *Oratio Catechetica* 24 (PG 45, 64CD).

67 On this see D. M. Baillie, *God was in Christ: an Essay on Incarnation and Atonement* (London) who asks correctly of the modern kenoticists why the Kenosis, for them, is simply a temporary affair, and does not last for as long as Christ remains man, and thus into eternity? The same objection was already made by Weston against Gore.

68 Cf. N. Gorodetsky, *The Humiliated Christ in Modern Russian Thought* (London 1938): on, primarily, Soloviev, Tareev, Bulgakov.

69 Very clear in Bulgakov when he makes Sophia, as both uncreated and created reality, a 'condition of possibility' for the union of the two natures in Christ, and thus, so to speak, a suprachristological scheme for christology: see *Du Verbe incarné: Agnus Dei* (Paris 1943) pp. 113f; 121ff. The notion that the historic Cross is only the phenomenal translation of a metaphysical Golgotha is Gnostic (ibid., pp. 238ff).

70 Cf. P. Henry's final criticism of Bulgakov, art. cit., pp. 154ff.

71 Bulgakov, op. cit., p. 281.

72 Ibid.

73 Ibid., pp. 289; 305ff.

74 Ibid., p. 306.

75 *The Person and Place of Christ* (London 1909), p. 271; cf. the fundamental article by K. Rosenthal, 'Die Bedeutung des Kreuzesgeschehens für Lehre and Bekenntnis nach Peter Taylor Forsyth', KuD 7 (1961), pp. 237–259.

76 Op. cit., p. 262. On the relations between Eucharist and Passion, see below, chapter II.

77 *In Matthaeum* 17, 17 (Klostermann X. 637).

78 A contribution to a trinitarian foundation for the Kenosis is also found in Marius Victorinus who calls even the first origination of the Logos a *recessio* and, thereby, a *passio* though, admittedly, he draws in here the Plotinian *hulē noētē: Adversus Arium* IV. 31 (PL 8, 1135D). Yet this foundation permits him to avoid a Kenosis in the modern sense: 'Intellegamus autem ipsum se exinanisse, non in eo esse quod potentiam suam alibi demiserit aut se privaverit, sed ad sordida quaeque se humiliaverit, ad postrema officia descendens', *In Philippenses* II (PL 8, 1208). Cf. P. Henry, art. cit., pp. 114–117.

79 F. Bertrand, *Mystique de Jésus chez Origène* (Paris 1951). Already in G. Bardy, *La Vie spirituelle d'après les Pères des trois premiers siècles* (Paris 1935), pp. 214ff; H. de Lubac, *Histoire et Esprit. L'intelligence de l'Ecriture d'après Origène* (Paris 1950).

80 Cf. in the *Vita Antonii* of Saint Athanasius: chs. 75, 78, 79 (PG 26, 948–953).

81 PG 31, 619ff.

82 See below, ch. II.

83 *Sermo* 44, 1–2 (PL 38, 259ff): 'Ascendit ... sicut radix in terra sitienti. Crevit illud granum sinapis. Unde haec tanta pulchritudo? De nescio qua radice surrexit ... Quaeramus radicem. Consputus est, humiliatus est, flagellatus est, cruficixus est, vulneratus est, contemptus est ...'.

84 The most astonishing example, no doubt, of an authentic fusion is once again the founder of an Order: Paul of the Cross, founder of the Passionists. Cf. S. Breton, *La Mystique de la Passion. S. Paul de la Croix* (Paris 1962).

85 F. Callaey, *Etude sur Ubertin de Casale* (Louvain 1911), pp. 73ff.

86 Reprinted Turin 1961, with introduction and bibliography by C. T. Davis.

87 Above all: Mechtild of Magdeburg, Gertrude of Helfta, Angela di Foligno, Margaret Ebner (edited by J. Prestel, Weimar, 1939) and Catherine of Siena. Later, this mystical tendency was renewed by Marie de l'Incarnation (*Oeuvres complètes*, 4 vols., Paris 1929).

88 K. A. Kneller, *Geschichte der Kreuzwegandacht von den Anfängen bis zur völligen Ausbildung* (Freiburg 1908). In relation to this, the festal calender of the Liturgy should also be considered: the *Triduum Mortis*, the Finding of the Holy Cross (cf. here J. Staubinger, *Die Kreuzauffindungslegende*, Paderborn 1913), the Exaltation of the Holy Cross, the feast of the Precious Blood, the feasts of the Seven Dolours of the Blessed Virgin Mary etc., around which a theology all their own has developed. Taking as one's starting point just the *Triduum Mortis*, one can develop a theology of the entire paschal mystery, (thus: L. Bouyer, *Le Mystère pascal*, Paris 1957[5]), yet in this case Holy Saturday will necessarily receive less than its due attention.

89 For devotion to the Heart of Jesus, the opening of that heart on the Cross has a central importance: cf. Richstätter, *Die Herz-Jesu-Verehrung im deutschen Mittelalter* (Munich 1924[2]); A. Bea, H. Rahner, H. Rondet, F. Schwendimann, *Cor Jesu* (2 vols., Rome 1956[2]); J. Heer, *Der Durchbohrte* (Rome 1966).

90 Like the 'Christus patiens' attributed to Gregory of Nazianzus (XI–XII Centuries, PG 38, 133–338), or the highly representative play *Le Mystère de la Passion* by Arnoul Gréban: 30, 574 verses, written before 1452, and contextualising the Passion by, on the one side, the history of creation and salvation, and, on the other, an eschatological conclusion (Paris 1878, edited by G. Paris and G. Raynaud). For bibliography on Passion plays: see LThK IX (1964), pp. 374ff.

91 Reprinted, with an introduction by J. Rousset, (Geneva 1966).

92 On this work, see A. Guny, 'Duguet', DSAM III (1957), cols. 1759–1569, especially 1766.

93 Reprinted Paris 1937. On this, see H. Bremond, *Histoire du sentiment religieux en France*, 8: 'La métaphysique des saints', II (Paris 1930), pp. 19–77; Y. Congar, 'La Croix de Jésus du P. Chardon', VS Supplément 51 (1937), pp. 42–57; re-printed in idem., *Les voies du Dieu vivant* (Paris 1962), pp. 129–141.

94 For the whole, see B. de S. Pablo, *La espiritualided de la Pasión* (Madrid 1961); DS III (1957), cols. 767ff.

95 O. Casel, 'Art und Sinn der ältesten Osterfeier', JLW 14 (1934), pp. 58ff; 69ff.

For the Middle Ages, consult above all: H. de Lubac, *Corpus Mysticum* (Paris 1949²); A. Franz, *Messe im deutschen Mittelalter* (Freiburg 1902).

[96] Too unilateral here is F. X. Arnold, 'Das gott-menschliche Prinzip der Seellsorge und die Gestaltung der christlichen Frömmigkeit', *Chalkedon* III, pp. 287–340.

2

The Death of God as Wellspring of Salvation, Revelation and Theology

(1) The Hiatus

If without the Son no one can see the Father (John 1, 18), nor anyone come to the Father (John 14, 6), and if, without him, the Father is revealed to nobody (Matthew 11, 27), then when the Son, the Word of the Father is dead, then no one can see God, hear of him or attain him. And this day exists, when the Son is dead, and the Father, accordingly, inaccessible. Indeed, it is for the sake of this day that the Son became man – as Tradition has shown us. One can, no doubt, say: he came to bear our sins on the Cross, to take up the account-sheet of our debt, and to triumph thereby over principalities and powers (Colossians 2, 14f): but this 'triumph' is realised in the cry of God-forsakenness in the darkness (Mark 15. 33–37), in 'drinking the cup' and 'being baptised with the baptism' (Mark 10, 38) which lead down to death and hell. Then the silence closed around, as the sealed tomb will close likewise. At the end of the Passion, when the Word of God is dead, the Church has no words left to say. While the grain of corn is dying, there is nothing to harvest. This state of being dead is not, for the Word made man, one situation among others in the life of Jesus – as if the life thus briefly interrupted were simply to resume on Easter Day (though certain sayings of Jesus, aimed at consoling his

disciples about the 'little while', may sound like that).
Between the death of a human being, which is by definition
the end from which he cannot return, and what we term
'resurrection' there is no common measure. In the first place,
we must take with full gravity this affirmation: in the same
way that a man who undergoes death and burial is mute, no
longer communicating or transmitting anything, so it is with
this man Jesus, who was the Speech, the Communication and
the Mediation of God. He dies, and what it was about his life
that made it revelation breaks off. Nor is this rupture simply
the quasi-natural one of the dying man of the Old Testament,
who descends into the grave, returning to the dust from
which he was made. This is the plunging down of the
'Accursed One' (Galatians 3, 13) far from God, of the One
who is 'sin' (II Corinthians 5, 21) personified, who, falling
where he is 'thrown' (Apocalypse 20, 14), 'consumes' his
own substance (Apocalypse 19, 3; 'Thou hast made the city a
heap, the fortified city a ruin' Isaiah 25, 2):

> Terror, and the pit, and the snare
>   are upon you, O inhabitant of the earth!
> He who flees at the sound of the terror
>   shall fall into the pit;
> and he who climbs out of the pit
>   shall be caught in the snare.
>   (Isaiah 24, 17f, = Isaiah 48, 43f)

This is the essence of the second death: that which is cursed
by God in his definitive judgment (John 12, 31) sinks down
to the place where it belongs. In this final state, there is no
time.

The danger is very real that we, as spectators of a drama
beyond our powers of comprehension, will simply wait until
the scene changes. For in this non-time, there appears to be
no possibility of following him who has become non-Word.
In Hymn 35 Romanos *ho Melōdos* sang of Mary at the foot
of the Cross, and, in the dialogue between Mother and Son,
he has the Son explain to his Mother how, like a doctor, he
must strip off his clothes, so as to reach that place where the

mortally ill are lying, and there heal them. The Mother pleads
to be taken with him. He warns her: the whole creation will
be shaken, earth and sea will flee away; the mountains will
tremble; the tombs will be emptied . . . Then the dialogue is
broken off, and the poet directs his prayer to the Son as 'the
owner of agony'.[1] We are not told whether it is possible to
follow the Son through the chaos of a world that is falling
apart, or whether all that remains is the anguished following
gaze of Mary as her Son disappears into the inaccessible
darkness where no one can reach him.[2] The apostles wait in
the emptiness. Or at least in the non-comprehension that
there is a Resurrection and what it can be (John 20, 9; Luke
24, 21). The Magdalen can only seek the One she loves –
naturally, as a dead man – at the hollow tomb, weeping
from vacant eyes, groping after him with empty hands (John
20, 11 and 15). Filmed over with an infinite weariness unto
death, no stirring of a living, hoping faith is to be found.

The poet makes Christ say:

> I descended as low as being casts its shadows, I looked
> into the abyss, and cried, 'Father, where are you?'. But I
> heard only the everlasting ungovernable storm . . . And
> when I looked from the unmeasurable world to the eye
> of God, it was an empty socket, without foundation,
> that stared back at men. And eternity rested on the
> choas, gnawing at it, ruminating.[3]

This 'vision' has frequently been regarded as the departure-
point of modern 'Death-of-God' theology. More important
for our purposes is the point that the emptiness and
abandonment which it expresses are more profound than
what an ordinary human death can bring about in the world.
In other words: the real object of a theology of Holy Saturday
does not consist in the completed state which follows on the
last act in the self-surrender of the incarnate Son to his Father
– something which the structure of every human death, more
or less ratified by the individual person, would entail. Rather
does that object consist in something unique, expressed in the
'realisation' of all Godlessness, of all the sins of the world,

now experienced as agony and a sinking down into the 'second death' or 'second chaos', outside of the world ordained from the beginning by God. And so it is really God who assumes what is radically contrary to the divine, what is eternally reprobated by God, in the form of the supreme obedience of the Son towards the Father, and, thereby, in Luther's words, *sub contrario* discloses himself in the very act of his self-concealment. It is precisely the unsurpassable radicalness of this concealment which turns our gaze to it, and makes the eyes of faith take notice. It now becomes extraordinarily difficult to keep together in our sights the 'absolute paradox' which lies in the hiatus, and the continuity of the Risen One with the One who died, having previously lived. And yet this is asked of us, and it presses the paradox further still. If we rest content with the simple *sub contrario*, then we shall be forced to take the path that travels from Luther to Hegel. A purely dialectical Christology becomes transformed into a sheerly 'philosophical' dialectic, into a 'worldly' discourse. On the other hand, the tracklessness (*aporia*) which confronts us like a yawning abyss in that hiatus of the death of man and of God must at all costs be preserved from the attempt to render it innocuous through an intellectually comprehensible 'analogy' between the before and the after, the mortal Jesus and the risen Kyrios, earth and heaven. The 'stumbling block of the Cross' must not be 'removed' (Galatians 5, 11); the 'Cross of Christ' must not be 'emptied of its power' (I Corinthians 1, 17).

(2) The 'Word of the Cross' and its Logic

In an article with this title,[4] E. Stauffer has worked out the right approach to this problem. He sets out from II Corinthians 8, 9: Jesus Christ

> though he was rich, yet for your sake he became poor,
> so that by his poverty you might become rich.

Stauffer shows that this double affirmation, which moves in

two contrary directions, is a central topic of Pauline preaching
(cf. Galatians 4, 5; 3, 13ff; II Corinthians 5, 21; Romans 8,
3ff; Galatians 2, 19; Romans 7, 4): In each case it is a question
of expressing the *skandalon*, but with its consequences and
efficacy for us and for the world. By means of this efficacy,
the unique historical fact which is, beyond all conditional
clauses, what we are speaking about and that which can never
be left out of consideration, shows itself as a 'principle'
conjointly affecting the being (and concrete existence) of
every created thing. 'One has died for all; therefore all have
died' (II Corinthians 5, 14). The universality of the second
affirmation cannot be detached from the singularity of the
first.

But this 'being dead with him' does not at all imply a
'being drawn with him into the abyss', since: he died for all,
that those who live might live no longer for themselves but
for him who for their sake died and was raised (ibid., v. 15).
The descent of One alone into the abyss became the ascent of
all from the same depths, and the condition of possibility for
this dialectical change-about lies on the one hand in the 'for
all' of the descent (and so not just in the 'dying', but in
becoming a holocaust as the scapegoat outside the camp of
God, Hebrews 13, 11ff), and on the other in the prototypical
Resurrection with which this passage deals. Without that
Resurrection Christ would sink into the abyss, but 'all' would
not be raised. He must be, then, the 'first-fruits of those who
have fallen asleep' (I Corinthians 15, 20), the 'first-born from
the dead' (Colossians 1, 18).

But if it is true that in Luther's *sub contrario* the 'absolute
paradox' (of Kierkegaard) comes to expression, there can be,
nonetheless, no resting with this static form of expression.
The paradoxical formulation has, rather, an inner dynamism
which manifests itself in purposiveness (became poor, *so that*
you might become rich). This finality kindles a light in the
darkness of rational incomprehensibility. This light is the light
of love, and it is by love's logic that Paul draws the conclusion
(*krinantas*) we have been discussing. (According to II
Corinthians 5, 14, 'the love of Christ' presses and constrains
him to this conclusion and to accepting the conclusions for

his own existence which follows from it.) It is in the measure that Jesus' death is a function of absolute love – 'he died *for* all' – that this death has, first and foremost, the validity and the efficacious power of a principle. There is, of course, no question here of a 'formal logic'; what is involved is a logic whose content is the uniqueness and personality of the eternal Logos become man, a logic created by him and identical with him. And this unique efficaciousness belongs with the 'scandal' and must not be 'watered down' or 'emptied out'. Of any other logic than this, the New Testament knows nothing.

E. Stauffer can, therefore, describe the Pauline *topos* here studied as a 'breakthrough formula'. He considers it to be a 'further development of an original kind', going beyond the mythical schema of descent and ascent inasmuch as

> The paradoxical fractured quality of the affirmation is overcome by the dialectical counter-movement of the purpose clause with the result that paradox and reason, *skandalon* and *sophia*, death and life, reciprocally condition each other, so that here all understanding of God, the world, and history . . . either stands or falls.[5]

There is possible neither a theology which fails to take its intrinsic character and structure from the 'Word of the Cross', nor one which would stop short at the great struggle (or 'offence') as between God and man, both in being and in thought. (At any rate, such a dialectical theology would not be Pauline.)

This is also true of the provocative dialectical formulae of I Corinthians 1, 17 and following, whose polemically anti-Gnostic character U. Wilckens has demonstrated.[6] The 'wisdom' of the Corinthians saw to it that the believer was thoroughly well established on the further side of the Cross, by claiming that the Christ (Sophia), who descended unrecognised by the angels and the 'archontes' of the world, had been crucified in error by those powers – Paul himself takes up this ideology in a reflective piece of polemic in I Corinthians 2, 8 – whereas the entire force of his self-disclosure lay in his exaltation and Resurrection. Over against this position, Paul wants above all to abide by the paradox of the Cross. God's power shows itself in his weakness; in his folly he demonstrates his superiority *vis-à-vis* the wisdom of men. Thus it is that, in the presence of those people who have left the Cross behind them, Paul wishes to 'know nothing ... except Jesus Christ and him crucified'. In him salvation has its centre. But this polemical abridgement carries nevertheless the dynamism of breakthrough. If God's weakness is stronger than man, God's folly wiser than man, then, we may say:

> these surprising comparatives would be absurd paradoxes if they were not intended to point up something in the event of the Crucifixion ... which is really strong and really wise ... That, evidently, is ... the event of the Resurrection which took place at God's hands ... but is here registered in such a way that it cannot be separated from the affirmation of Christ's Crucifixion, with which it is, in its inmost reality, most closely united.[7]

This explains why Paul speaks quite consciously of the 'crucified *Christ*' (I Corinthians 1, 23; 2, 2).

> That person is a pneumatic who has the Spirit of the crucified Christ ... the whole pathos of the self-expression of the gnostic must therefore be claimed here for the proclamation of a crucified Christ, into whose service it is now pressed[8]

– and even to the point of ambiguity where the polemical turns of phrase are not subsequently balanced by other formulations of doctrine.

One should not draw from this fact – the claim that the power of Christ's resurrection is manifested precisely in the communion of believers, and especially of the apostle, in his death – the conclusion that the dialectic of death and life is a closed dialectic, which turns in upon itself. On the contrary, this community of destiny, in its paradoxical character, demonstrates the outright – and in no sense merely dialectical – superiority of the power of the Resurrection and indeed of God's very Glory, and abolishes the equal balance between the 'daily dying of the old man' and the 'daily renewal of the new' by virtue of an 'eternal weight of glory beyond all comparison' (II Corinthians 4, 16ff).

If theology is to be Christian, then it can only be a theology which understands in dynamic fashion the unsurpassable scandal of the Cross. Certainly, such a theology will understand the Cross as a 'crisis', but it will see the crisis in question as a turning-point between the old aeon and the new, in the tension between the 'world's situation' and the 'world's goal'. What ensures the connexion between these two is no immanent evolution, but that inconceivable moment between Holy Saturday and Easter. That can also be seen clearly enough from the side of anthropology, since 'evolution', no matter how one understands it, will never re-unite the two extremities of interiorly ruptured man but at best must consider sick and broken human individuals as constituting the *dépassé* pre-history of a humanity progressing towards health. Jesus, however, did not come to encourage those who were well, but to cure those who were sick (Mark 2, 17 and parallels). And in any case authentic theology, faced with the 'death of God' in the *Triduum Mortis* is so thoroughly absorbed in its supreme object that it has no time to lose itself in idle questions.[9]

(3) The Cross and Philosophy

What we have just said shows how difficult it is to draw the line between a genuinely theological statement about the *Tridum Mortis* and its (frequently unnoticed) transformation into a universal and generally knowable philosophical truth detachable from faith. The difficulty intensifies if we re-introduce the problem, described earlier, of that Kenosis whose subject is the pre-mundane Logos – and therefore God himself – in relation to the 'eternal sacrifice of the Lamb'.

Even when one excludes those kinds of philosophy which have self-evidently made their exit from the space of Christian theology, there remains an ample supply of ambiguous thought-forms, or of thought-forms which, according to context and emphasis, may be conceived either as theological or as philosophical affirmations.

a. The first example is already disconcerting. Those theologies of the Cross found in the apocryphal Acts of the Apostles occupy an inter-mediary position, difficult to determine precisely, between a non-Christian philosophical Gnosis and a Christianity on which Gnostic or Neo-Platonic themes have been, in a purely external manner, draped. For Valentinus (here presented in simplified fashion), the true Cross is identical with the Logos (Christ) who leaves the heavenly *plērōma* in order to save Sophia (Achamoth) who has fallen from that plenitude and allowed matter to come forth from her. The 'heavenly Cross' has two fundamental functions (*duo energeias*): that of fortifying (what would otherwise disintegrate) – which renders the Cross *horos*, 'limit', and that of dividing from or separating off (what is chaotic and material).[10] The revelations of the *Acts of John* (97ff) must be interpreted in this context: while Jesus, surrounded by the crowd, suffers or appears to suffer on the Cross of wood, John receives from the heavenly Christ enlightenment about the true Cross, the 'unshakeable Cross of light', also called by men Logos, Reason, Bread, Resurrection, Truth, Faith, and so forth. This Cross is the 'limitation of all things', the 'harmony of wisdom', and signifies a purely gnostic 'passion'.

> Thou hearest that I suffered, yet did I not suffer; that I suffered not, yet did I suffer . . . Perceive thou therefore in me the . . . slaying . . . of the . . . Word (Logos), the piercing of the Word, the blood of the Word, the wound of the Word, the hanging up of the Word, the suffering of the Word, the nailing . . . of the Word, the death of the Word.

But all that took place on Calvary was 'contrived . . . symbolically and by a dispensation toward men . . .'[11]

And yet whilst the Valentinian conception (even in its presuppositions) constitutes a philosophical deformation of Christian themes, Plato's *Timaeus* (36b) provided a representation of the Demiurge cutting up the world-soul in a cruciform way, in the form of a X (*chi*). On this foundation, erudite Platonism (as in Albinus) develops further speculative gambits, which make up, it seems, the background to the theology of the Cross in the *Acts of Andrew*. Here too the Cross is 'planted in the world to establish the things that are unstable'.

> The one part of thee stretcheth up toward heaven that thou mayest signify the heavenly Word . . ., the head of all things . . .

The arms, to left and to right, put to flight the enemy forces of chaos and re-gather the cosmos, while the lower part of the Cross, grounded in the depths, unites what is lowest to what is most high. The Cross, then, has cosmic dimensions. It is praised for having 'bound down the mobility of the world' ('The Martyrdom', I. 4).[12] Linked to these speculations is the homily *On the Pasch* of the Pseudo-Hippolytus, a text whose orthodoxy is not in doubt, and which ascribes to the Cross a pan-cosmic significance, expressed in images which throw back the mind not only to Plato but also to Buddhism.[13]

> This tree is for me a planting of eternal salvation; I find my nourishment from it . . . By its roots I am rooted, by its branches I am spread out . . . This tree of heavenly dimensions rises up from the earth to heaven. It is fixed, as an everlasting growth, in the midst of heaven and of earth. It is the sustenance of all things, the prop of the universe, the support of the whole inhabited earth and the axis of the world. It holds together the variety of human nature, fixed as it is by the invisible pegs of the Spirit so that, divinely adjusted, it may never more be

detached from God. By its pinnacle touching the summit of the heavens, by its foot stabilising the earth, and by its immense arms restraining on all sides the manifold spirits of the air between heaven and earth, it exists whole and entire in everything, everywhere.[14]

Here the theological theme of the Cross has, without losing its historical reality, replaced a philosophical theme or even absorbed that theme within itself.

It is harder to situate the theology of the *Acts of Peter* (of Vercelli),[15] where Peter (37–39) insists on being crucified upside down, and himself discloses the 'mystery of the Cross ... hidden (in his) soul'. Here the re-establishment in uprightness of the first (archetypal) man who, in the beginning, fell from heaven comes about through his inversion, which restores him to his rightful dimensions, though this idea should not be regarded as an encroachment on the significance of the Cross. Here, encratite and docetic themes serve simply as trimmings for a theology whose intentions are Christian: in 'popular peity', 'many elements which theologians have been pleased carefully to separate become neighbours again'.[16] H. Schlier has shown that there are reflections of the Gnostic idea of the heavenly Man and the heavenly Cross even in Ignatius, who is aware of the fact, yet clearly calls back his readers to the genuine Cross of Christ and his genuine suffering.[17]

If we take a retrospective glance at what has been said above about the Kenosis and the Lamb slain in heaven (namely, Christ as archetype of man), we should realise that those representations which see in the Cross of Christ a principle that founds, and hold together, the cosmos do not necessarily abandon the terrain of Christian theology. This is just what Augustine says in the *De Civitate Dei* X. 20 in describing the meaning (the fulfilment) of the world as the attachment of humankind as a whole to the eternal sacrifice of adoration offered by Christ to the Father.

(b) That domain is, however, abandoned wherever the Cross becomes a general symbolic idea, analogically expressed in

the most diverse religions and world-views, and, among
others, in Christianity. We may take as an example (and
without even mentioning the Rosicrucians and Freemasons)
R. Guénon, *Le symbolisme de la Croix*.[18] In that work, to be
sure, an historically real element is part and parcel of the
reality of the symbol, yet:

> If Christ died on the Cross, it was, we can say, because
> of the symbolic value that the Cross possesses in itself
> and which it has always been accorded by all the
> traditions.[19]

The chief meaning of the Cross (its foundational meaning) is
its 'metaphysical' meaning: the rest being 'so many contingent
applications'.[20] Logically, then, a metaphysic of being was
developed, identical with a metaphysic of the primordial
cosmic Man. The point where all the dimensions of the world
intersect is also the point of indifference between all
contraries, and so the point of redemption – and so forth. In
all that Christian theology is uninterested. What that theology
must do is to discern whether the kind of universality which
confronts it belongs to the unique historical fact of the
Crucifixion and Resurrection of Christ, or to a general idea.
In the latter case, emphasis may fall either on the symbolic,
imagistic form, or on upon the concept, conceived as a law
of history or of existence, but in any of these versions the
Cross of Christ is regarded as a particular instance of
something, if perhaps a remarkable one. That is theologically
unacceptable. One can see, however, that this 'special case'
might be nudged into becoming a 'supreme case' and from
there attain the status of an all-determining idea. And so a
scrupulous investigation is required, in order to fix the limits
of what can count as theology. When C. R. Raven, in his
1951–1952 Gifford Lectures, *Mind, Life and Spirit* wants to see
creation and redemption as a unity in which nature and
supernature are indistinguishable, and where a general law of
'die and become', of resurrection out of death, holds good,
he acknowledges the Cross and Resurrection of Christ as the
high-point of and the key to this total law of the world.

Something similar can be accepted in the case of Teilhard de Chardin, in conformity to the rhythm of his thinking as a whole: the gradual elevation of a structure through evolution, in the course of which this structure becomes, by way of a 'death', sublimated or re-engendered as a higher, and completely renewed form. And this law of 'inversion', 'conversion' or 'ex-centering', this 'phase of rupture' through which must pass both the monad and the universe[21] in obedience to a law understood throughout as a law of the world, but also as a law of mounting personalisation, finds in the Cross of Christ its 'certainly supernatural, but, in relation to the fulfilment of humanity, physically assigned, term'.[22] Teilhard is conscious that the balance which he sees between law of the world and law of Christ is very hard to find, and that in all his formulae a tension remains between his unconditional faith in the Cross and his attempt to see the Cross and the world's development as a unity. He may stand here as representative for those countless others who have attempted such a synthesis.[23]

(c) A third approach consists in a radical denial of all such continuity and a letting-be of the Cross as sheer paradox. Luther pressed this to an extreme in certain of his formulations in which he gave to the paradox of the Cross an expression at once formal and static. Linked as it is to the uniqueness of Christ, this paradox, for Luther, because it is completely without analogy and yet imposes itself with a claim to absolute validity, tends of its own volition to become a key for the unlocking of every door, a 'dialectical method'. And so E. Seeberg can sum up his analysis of Lutheran theology in these terms:

> It is, then, in Christ that Luther discovers the fundamental law which holds good in life: he is simultaneously cursed and blessed (*simul maledictus et benedictus*), simultaneously living and dead (*simul vivus et mortuus*), simultaneously grieving and joyful (*simul dolens et gaudens*). In him is prefigured the great 'simultaneously' which constitutes the fundamental idea

of the doctrine of justification – simultaneously just, and a sinner (*simul justus et peccator*) – which so easily and so quickly is distorted into a 'one after the other' ... In Christ, we see the way in which God acts at large, namely, in opposition to reason, evidence and so on.[24]

But once in Christ the law of universal Providence has been read off, one may then ask whether the same law is not discernable in exactly the same way in Socrates or in the 'crucified just man' of Plato. The danger lies close at hand that we may:

> also dogmatise the paradox of God's acting *sub contrario* and make of it an inviolable schematisation for the understanding of history.[25]

– which is what happened to Hegel in between the *Early Writings* and the *Logik* of his Jena years. At a level incomparably higher than that of Valentinian Gnosis, we see repeated here the same process of turning the mystery of the Cross into a piece of philosophy, and in both cases the God-man (the primordial Man), by his self-revelation, coincides in the last analysis with the self-understanding of man himself. Doubtless Hegel was entirely in earnest about his 'speculative Good Friday' and his 'God himself is dead' ('the feeling on which the religion of modernity rests') – intellectual places, these, where the ideas of absolute freedom, and hence of absolute suffering, arise –[26] but just so does this new Good Friday replace that which 'formerly was historic'.[27] Even if, in the *Phenomenology of the Spirit*, room is set aside for the historic form, it remains cut off from the 'dogmatics' of the Christian religion, which is not believed but simply known about. And furthermore, it should be observed that Luther's static dialectic between Law and Gospel (Old Testament and New), continues in a sense the ancient static dialectic of Gnosis, and of Marcion, while Hegel's early writings take us back, via Luther, to this primordially gnostic Anti-Judaism: the Cross, in the final analysis, is the 'tearing apart' of Judaism – that Judaism which becomes, with the New Testament, itself a tearing force. It is no longer, then, the Cross of Jesus but a 'dialectical situation' (with Marcion, located between the true God and the world-ruler) in which one can only suffer.

(d) In his remarkable study *La Passion du Christ et les philosophes*,[28] Stanislas Breton has traced the path which leads from Hegel, through Feuerbach, to Alain, and on whose length a new theme appears in the turning of the Cross into philosophy. If freedom is something absolute, then, so Hegel already maintained, there is in God absolute suffering. But, so adds Feuerbach, should one not make subject and predicate here change places? 'Suffering for others is divine': but the subject of this 'divinity' is man himself. In Christianity, God indeed had to become man, so as to suffer.[29]

> Where the personal God is the object of a genuine heartfelt distress, he must himself suffer distress. Only in his suffering is the certitude of his reality to be found, in that suffering alone does the essential impact and force of the Incarnation consist. Only in the blood of Christ is the thirst for a personal, that is, a human, participating, feeling God, slaked.[30]

Behind Feuerbach's formulations there lies a subtle notion which had already found practical expression in Greek tragedy. Suffering man stands higher than the god who cannot suffer. In the work of Alain, this occupies a central place.[31] Right at the start, the sign of the Cross is there:

> It is the all-naked sign, where will breaks forth; it is the sign that announces nothing other than itself; and so it recalls man to man. All the great ideas finish there, and the image of the crucified just man adds nothing to them: the sign speaks more clearly. In solitude: better; clumsily fashioned: better.[32]

That sounds like Guénon, but its intention goes farther. It refers to what is most interior in man, termed by Alain 'spirit'. To spirit must be sacrificed everything that is worldly, carnal power, to that spirit which itself is pure impotence.

> The Cross is the 'No' that is opposed to power, and it is a revolution in the concept of God himself.

People say that God is almightiness, but almightiness cannot be loved, and so the mighty one is poorer than all. 'Only weakness is loved.' Again, in the Old Testament, existence is seen as characterised by contradiction. Over against the God of power is set the 'scandalously executed man'.[33]

> In the Bible there is no grace. Spirit is an absolute tyrant. Such is its manner of existing. Spirit, in its decrees, is worse than anything.

When that statement is de-mythologised, it reads

> The first school for the understanding is necessity.

That was the training offered by the Old Testament.[34] In the New Testament, on the other hand, this necessity discloses itself as the freedom to suffer. The Christian is a free-thinker: spirit imposes itself on him as the freedom to be impotent, and to suffer absolutely. Take the Christmas picture:

> Look now at the child. This weakness is God. This weakness that has need of everyone is God. This being, which, without our care for it, would cease to exist, is God ... The child does not pay, it asks, and it asks again. It is the spirit's severe rule that spirit does not pay, and that no one can serve two masters ... I could show, following Descartes, that there is no truth, not even any verified truth, or useful truth, that is not the daughter of an unverified truth, a useless truth, a truth without any power at all. Whereas industrial truth is a thankless child, leaving one punished a hundred times over as her reward ... Perhaps the spirit will one day renounce every type of power, and that will be the climax of its reign. Now, Calvary announces that

consummation, in so eloquent and violent a fashion that
I can add no further comment.[35]

Many other names might be mentioned of those who have
sought to interpret the Cross anthropologically or
ontologically, in a pre-Christian way (as Simone Weil in her
Intuitions préchrétiennes of 1951) or in a pan-tragic way (the
tendency of Reinhold Schneider). Then the crucified Christ
becomes a symbol, denser perhaps than the rest of reality put
together, but a symbol all the same. And he is thereby sub-
ordinated to what is universal, whether the latter engulf him
as law or as the absolute freedom of man. Here theology is
transcended, and is replaced by anthropology.

In all these forms of philosophical outmanoeuvring of
theology, the frontier line is often difficult to make out. It
can happen that one experiences the Cross of Christ as 'the
world's Cross' (Franz von Baader),[36] as bearing down, in
anonymous fashion, upon existence, without one's changing
places thereby with the true Cross-bearer. Pascal, Hamann,
Kierkegaard, Dostoievskii, experienced profane existence as
determined by the Cross of Christ, even if this existence
from its side, also determines that Cross. Nevertheless, in
each instance, a choice (known only to God) is made in the
depths of the soul. Is man placed under a law of absolute love
which 'goes right to the end', or does he ultimately claim
rights over the law in his own interest?

Philosophy can speak of the Cross in many tongues; when it is
not the 'Word of the Cross' (1 Corinthians 1, 18), issuing from
faith in Jesus Christ, it knows either too much or too little. Too
much: because it makes bold with words and concepts at a point
where the Word of God is silent, suffers and dies, in order to
reveal what no philosophy can know, except through faith,
namely, God's ever greater Trinitarian love; and in order, also,
to vanquish what no philosophy can make an end of, human
dying so that the human totality may be restored in God. Too
little, because philosophy does not measure that abyss into which
the Word sinks down, and, having no inkling of it, closes the
hiatus, or deliberately festoons the appalling thing with
garlands:

> The Cross is thick bestrewn with roses: who has joined roses to the Cross?[37]

in place of Jerome's 'naked, to follow the Naked One'. Either philosophy misconceives man, failing, in Gnostic or Platonic guise, to take with full seriousness his earthly existence, settling him elsewhere, in heaven, in the pure realm of spirit, or sacrificing his unique personality to nature or evolution. Or, alternatively, philosophy forms man so exactly in God's image and likeness that God descends to man's image and likeness, since man in his suffering and overcoming of suffering shows himself God's superior. Here God only fulfils himself and manages to satisfy his own desires by divesting himself of his essence and becoming man, in order, as man, 'divinely' to suffer and to die. If philosophy is not willing to content itself with, either, speaking abstractly of being, or with thinking concretely of the earthly and worldly (and no further), then it must at once empty itself in order to 'know nothing ... except Jesus Christ and him crucified' (I Corinthians 2, 2). Then it may, starting out from this source, go on to 'impart a secret and hidden wisdom of God, which God decreed before the ages for our glorification' (ibid., 2, 7). This proclamation, however, rises up over a deeper silence and a darker abyss than pure philosophy can know.[38]

(4) The Bridge over the Hiatus

Christian preaching is proclamation of the Risen Crucified One. It can, therefore, only be the continuation, carried out by commission, of his *self*-proclamation – since only he can bridge over the hiatus. He sinks into the hiatus, so that it may suffer shipwreck in him. He must make himself know as '*the* Life', as '*the* Resurrection' (John 11, 25), insofar as *He* alone can constitute the identity of what which for God alone (who dies not) and for man alone (who does not rise again) would be sheer contradiction. It is not some 'generally usable category' of dying and rising gods which provides a 'pre-understanding' of this event (the disciples expressly deny having had anything of the kind):[39] for here it is a man, and no mythic figure, who is dead. Nor again, was the proper pre-understanding to be taken over from the category (allegedly available in Late Judaism) of resuscitated men,[40] for such a conception was, at best, of the eschatological order (and so formed part of the general resurrection) whereas for the disciples time continues.[41] With that, there explodes in the faces of the witnesses the elemental problem of theological time, a problem they are utterly unable to resolve while remaining on their own level. Where do they stand in this event? With the Risen One beyond ('at the end of') time, or still in time's midst? What does it mean that Christianity is 'last-time-ly', eschatological? How is it possible that the end of time, now attested as present, should be for the witnesses themselves (after the Ascension) and for the Church and the world something in the future? That indeed earthly time *is* blown apart shows itself in the fact that the Risen One

> died, and behold I am alive for evermore, and I have the keys of Death and Hades
> (Apocalypse 1, 18)

He is not then someone who 'returns' into time, and might die again.

> For we know that Christ being raised from the dead will never die again; death no longer has cominion over him. The death he died he died to sin once for all (*ephapax*), but the life he lives he lives to God
> (Romans 6, 9–10; cf. I Peter 3, 18; Hebrews 9, 26)

– a life, then, lived beyond the hiatus and so also in death in an unconditional self-identity ('the same yesterday and today and for ever', Hebrews 13, 8) to be expressed in the Resurrection appearances by the signs of 'my hands and my feet' (Luke 24, 29) and by letting the hand of Thomas be placed in the wounds of his side (John 20, 27). Not unscarred, as the beast of the Apocalypse is unscarred (Apocalypse 13, 3, 14) does he carry the 'mortal wound': he has, rather, taken up the hiatus into his own continuity. Now in what way may such an event be 'thought', for at any rate in some approximate way it must be thought if it is to be announced? The content of preaching must be the closing of the hiatus itself, the salvific healing by God of man who, in the death of sin, lay irremediably torn open and apart. That content must be the event itself, and not merely some of its symptoms (like the 'empty tomb') or even simply the 'appearances' which could have been, perhaps, hallucinations (Luke 24, 11) and might leave behind 'doubts' (Luke 24, 38; Matthew 28, 17; John 20, 27). Here we can only offer some indications:

(a). If we suppose that the lost ending of *Mark*, which some claim was replaced by 16, 9–20, never actually existed, then the original data will constitute: the story of the empty tomb, which the women, 'amazed' (v. 5) discover before them; the announcement by the 'young man' that Jesus has 'risen', and – if with W. Marxsen we strike out verse 7 as a redactional addition – the flight of the women full of 'trembling and astonishment' which prevents them from communicating their news. Mark (according to Marxsen) would have added the reference to a future seeing in Galilee: and in that way, the Church, emigrating as it was to Galilee (perhaps to Pella) would move towards the event of Resurrection and Parousia ('as he told you'), considered as one and the same reality. This reminder of Jesus' promise that he would appear again leaves intact, even if one retain verse 7, the identity of the Resurrection and the Parousia. The vision of the Risen One thus remains for preaching something in the future, and with a marked eschatological slant. What does become visible is, first of all, the empty tomb (16, 4) filled as it is with heavenly radiance (16, 5). John strongly emphasises the simultaneity of the emptiness, the absence and the heavenly light ('two angels in white, sitting where the body of Jesus had lain, one at the head, and one at the feet'. 20, 12): from out of the emptiness of the death of God streams forth glory (*doxa*) and sounds the resurrection word. For the genuine Mark, the Church, in going towards Galilee, would thus be journeying towards the eschatological event of the Resurrection, just as, for John, the

Magdalen perceives the Lord in the *event* of his Resurrection, coming out of Sheol and going to the Father ('I have not yet ascended') and is invited to let the event take its course ('do not hold me', 20, 17). This first aspect allows the message of the closing of the abyss to emerge from the (already transfigured) abyss itself, and in the strongest possible way accentuates the authentically eschatological character of the 'other shore'.

(b) The second bridge to be mentioned is thrown across thanks to the *word* of Jesus which announced in explicit terms the death and resurrection and fulfilled them in a self-evident way. In his word, he is the identity of promise and fulfilment. Considered in the perspective of the disciples, he is the bridge created between their total non-understanding previously and their lucid comprehension subsequently. *Luke* exploits this moment in the fullest way. The two angels at the tomb already turn the argument to their service:

> Remember how he told you, while he was still in Galilee, that the Son of man must (*dei*) be delivered into the hands of sinful men, and be crucified, and on the third day rise. (24, 6–7)

And in fact Luke has not only the three Passion predictions found in Mark, but six or seven. Next, he lets Jesus himself explain the decisive *dei* to the disciples on the road to Emmaus (24, 26), and again in due form before the assembled disciples (24, 56) where he shows not only his own identity in word, but that of the entire Word of God ('the law of Moses, and the prophets and the psalms', 24, 44) with himself as the Risen One: all this on one single Easter Day. The spiritual experience of the *attunement*, its absolute coherence right across the hiatus – and this last cannot be left out of count in that harmony – turns out to be the solid foundation of an intelligible proclamation, sustained, simply, by the sensuous signs (the empty tomb and the appearances). This proclamation is made by Jesus Christ, the God who, in history, has lived, died and is risen, declaring himself in his living and harmonious Word.

(c) In his Farewell Discourses, *John* goes one step further, since he allows Jesus himself, in these discourses, to throw a bridge across the hiatus, by way of anticipation, and in virtue of the almightiness of his love. Just as he offers a meticulous account of the (sacrament of the) Eucharist in addressing himself to the disciples and the Father, so John shows Jesus taking thought for his disciples against the moment of his leave-taking. He is on the verge of setting foot on the 'way' to the Father (13, 36; 14, 4, 12; 16, 5, 28; 17, 11, 13), a way which they 'know' (14, 4), and on which they cannot now follow him (13, 33), although they will later (13, 36). The opening abyss, in whose depths they will seek him in vain (13, 33), that interval for whose duration they will 'weep and lament' (16, 20), and 'see (him) no more' (16, 16), he calls 'a little while' (seven times in 16, 16–19; cf. 13, 33). As in Mark, this is the interval which precedes both the Resurrection and the Parousia. The abyss may perhaps be transformed by his love and his promises into sheer 'joy' (this joy seems to be demanded, 14, 28); truly 'sorrowful' (16, 6) will they be only in denying him (13, 38), and 'leaving (him) alone' (16, 32). But, over against the cry of abandonment in Mark and Matthew, the Johannine Jesus, even in his abandonment, is 'not alone': 'for the Father is with me' (ibid.). The hiatus of the 'little while' acquires a multifold meaning: to blaze a trail, so as to prepare for them a dwelling-place (14, 3), a 'room' in the Father's house (14, 2); to disappear, so that the Spirit can come who will explain the interrupted Word of Jesus (16, 12) in its fullness (16, 13–15); so that, together with the Father, he may live interiorly in those who believe and love and disclose himself (14, 21), and that, finally, the mediation between the world and the Father may bring into immediate relationship those who are its recipients (first 14, 13ff, then 16, 26ff). For the time of the hiatus he puts aside (like a swimmer stripping off) everything which is his own, leaving it partly with them, partly with the Father. To them he leaves behind his peace (14, 27), his word (15, 7), that is: his love unto death, in which they ought, and are able, to abide (15, 12ff), his joy (15, 11), but also his existence in the midst of the world's unfounded hatred (15, 18–25), an existence which, certainly, also includes a community of destiny expressed by the persecution of Christians (16, 2). He leaves with the Father the most precious thing he has on earth: the disciples, who have believed his word (17, 6–8), and who, while he is no longer in the world, themselves remain in the world (17, 11). At his plea, the Father must take over the work which, during the 'little while', he cannot carry further: to 'guard' them and 'keep' them (17, 12, 15), and, so as to confer on his prayer infallible fulfilment, he 'consecrates' himself for them, down into the hiatus (17, 19). And more, in this he takes them with him by anticipation on to the other side (to 'be with me where I am', 17, 24), so that between his coming to fetch them home to their eternal dwelling (14, 3) and his return to them with the Father (14, 23), no distance intervenes. Here too the Easter event is eschatological, making present the last times. Correspondingly, the future tense of Jesus' promise no longer to speak with the disciples in the parabolic mode drawn from everything that is transient, is responded to by them, as representatives of the post-Easter Church, with a present tense (of an eschatological kind, 16, 29–30).

In this threefold manner, the Church has a divinely given possibility to proclaim at one and the same time both the hiatus (and so the dissolution of continuity) and its bridging over by Jesus (and so the unique re-establishment of continuity in his person). And yet, at the point which we have reached so far, this paradox retains a wholly formal character: so far as its content is concerned, nothing has yet been said about the hiatus in which 'God is dead'.

(5) Experiential Approach to the Hiatus

In the Gospel of Mark we have, where the words from the Cross are concerned, only the cry of abandonment and the call at the moment of death, to which must be added the artfully constructed[43] scene of the agony on the Mount of Olives in which Jesus falls into a fear (*ekthambeisthai*), into the anguish of aloneness (*a-dēmonein*, anguish in separation from

the 'people'), into a grief that overwhelms from all sides
(*peri-lupos*), so great that it leads him in advance, in the midst
of life, 'right into the death' which it represents by
anticipation. It is *hē hōra*, the hour (Mark 14, 34ff).
Abandonment by the disciples who fail him and sleep on,
continuance of relationship with the Father only now by way
of the chalice which he would, if possible, have removed
from him, yet 'not what I will, but what thou wilt': this 'not
. . . but' is the entire remaining relationship with God, and
on the Cross it will, finally, be experienced only as the
Father's abandonment. In the 'great cry' in the 'darkness', he
sinks into the realm of the dead, from out of which no word
of his any longer makes itself heard. The aloneness, or rather
the quite decisive uniqueness of that suffering seems to cut
off all access to its own inwardness: at the most a silent
'assisting', from a distance, is all that is possible (Mark 15,
40). For the rest, what we have described for us are the
worldly aspects of the process, aspects which afford barely a
glimpse of the inner drama. And yet, for Christian faith, in
this inner space all the world's salvation lies enclosed. Is there
no kind of access to it?

If there *are* ways of approach, they must be found within
the space of the Old Testament, and of the Church. They
must correspond, therefore, to a twofold demand: they must
be a genuine approach (by the grace of God), but they must
also safeguard that distance which protects the uniqueness of
the Passion of the Redeemer from invasion.

(a) From the side of the Old Testament

That the Passion of Christ was not only predicted in the Old
Testament, but was in many ways pre-experienced, emerges
clearly enough for anyone familiar, if only in quite external
fashion, with the relations between the Passion and the Old
Testament themes of the 'delivering up of the just man',[44]
the 'suffering of the innocent', [45] martyrdom for the faith,[46]
especially in the latter's atoning and meritorious character,[47]
and, above all, the themes found in the Servant Songs with
their powerful influence on the New Testament.[48] But we

will not here follow these lines, on whose course the literary influence of the Old Testament on the story of the Passion is chiefly sought. For more than pointers and images – and we shall not lose these to view – the Old Testament cannot offer, if it is true that the decisive breakthrough by way of the 'wrath of God' into the uttermost abyss came about only on the Cross.[49]

We shall begin appropriately from the detailed word-portraits of terror found in Leviticus 26, 14–39 and Deuteronomy 28, 15–68. Delivered up to enemies, trembling with anguish, under 'heavens like iron', the reprobated people falls far from God, an object of derision for all the world, those of whom it is said, 'The Lord will take delight in bringing ruin upon you and destroying you'; he will send them down to Egypt, the land of perdition and curse ... With this one should compare the later symbolic description of Egyptian darkness in the book of Wisdom: that darkness is made up essentially of inner anxiety (in the face of nothing, of phantoms! Wisom 17, 3; cf. Leviticus 26, 36), 'shut up in a prison not made of iron', 'with one chain of darkness ... bound', in the midst of the anxiety which 'beset them from the recesses of powerful Hades'.[50] This is, in essence, isolation, the loss of communication, the withdrawal of all reality, where light is found only in an obscure counter-light, which itself is full of 'terror' (17, 6).

Two points must now be made by way of essential supplement: first, the genuineness of the people's abandonment by God at the moment when the presence of God leaves the Temple and the holy city (Ezekiel 10, 18ff; 11, 22ff), driven away as it is by the cult of idols (Ezekiel 8, 6). And second, the genuineness of the divine abandonment of individuals, who either represent the people (Jeremiah) or fall alone (Job). The divine abandonment of the people is authentic and unique because Israel alone has known a true and unique presence of God in her very midst.[51] In exile from the Holy Land and in the ruins of the holy temple, she learns by experience what it means to say that God has turned away and become 'an enemy' (Lamentations 2, 5), and can be spoken of only as one who is absent, 'Hast thou utterly rejected us? Art thou exceedingly angry with us?' (5, 22). The abandonment of individuals stretches from the mediatorial figure of Moses in Deuteronomy through Jeremiah, the psalms of lament (Psalm 22, 1: 'My God, my God, why hast thou forsaken me?) and Ezekiel to Job and the Second Isaiah. Job experiences the absolute disproportion between guilt and punishment, as also the excessive demands put upon him in his suffering and, in that way, the complete darkening over of the image of a righteous and good God. That is why there is left to him in his suffering only a purely exterior dialogue with a (self-contradictory) God. Interiorly, the dialogue is broken off, and a third, reconciliatory court of appeal is not to be found.

> If I speak, my pain is not assuaged,
> and if I forbear, how much of it leaves me? (Job 16, 6).

He is truly abandoned by God, 'hedged in' (3, 23), 'besieged' (19, 12); pitted against such a super-power, he has lost in advance and can only complain that God wishes to 'despise the word of (his) hands' and to 'destroy' it (10, 3 and 8). He is 'given up' (16, 1). The thought of God makes him paralytic with fear:

> I am terrified at his presence;
>   when I consider, I am in dread of
>   him;
> . . . Darkness draws me in,
>   night veils me with its presence (23, 15 and 17)

In whatever way Job's insoluble problematic may finally be resolved (and that it cannot be before Christ), one thing only is important: that Israel underwent such experiences, and expressed them in a representative work of literature which, like all the rest, is a fore-shadowing of Christ.

The Servant of the Lord' speaks more discreetly, more mysteriously, of 'divine abandonment' (strangely radicalised[52] by the Septuagint: 53, 6cd, 12c, 12f), of his disfigurement by the sins with which he is burdened, of the contempt he is made to share, of his dumbness. It is an 'unheard of' event, which 'has never been told before'. 'It was the will of the Lord to bruise him, to put him to grief' (53, 10). Yet, in contrast to Job, he was not rebellious' (50, 5), he who 'poured out his soul to death, and was numbered with the transgressors' (53, 12).

The images of these two last figures at least go beyond the fall gamut of representations of the 'realm of the dead' with its absence of hope. To be sure, in Sheol communication with God is at an end, since it presupposes a living subject (Psalm 6, 6; 30, 10; 88, 11–13; 115, 17; Isaiah 38, 18; Sirach 17, 27). But in the book of Lamentations, in Job and in the Servant Songs Israel experiences something much more terrible: active aversion on God's part, the overcharge of God's will, the weight of the world's sin in its *more* than deathly frightfulness. Deeper than Sheol is the experience of the 'lowest pit' (Psalm 55, 24; 140, 11),[53] the 'place of perdition' (*abbadon*: Psalm 88, 12; Job 26, 6; 28, 22; Proverbs 15, 11; Apocalypse 9, 11), of imprisonment and immuring (Psalm 142, 8; 88, 9; Lamentations 3, 7; Job 19, 8 etc.), of the fire of everlasting wrath threatened in the prophecies of Jeremiah ('with none to quench it', 21, 12). The images and representations could be multiplied. What is important is that, flowing as they do from the idea of covenant with God, they make us feel the loss of covenantal grace, the sin of infidelity, the act of divine reprobation as something more vital and heavy with consequence than a mere sinking into the realm of death, and that, therefore, at the end of the Old Testament period the notion arises[54] of 'Gehenna' as a place of eternal punishment (Isaiah 66, 22ff, but see already Jeremiah 7, 30ff, and 18, 6ff), and that for living sinners (Ethiopian Enoch 90, 26ff; 54, 1ff; etc.). This notion the New Testament will take over as to its essential substance (not in its mythic and imagistic representations) and in its implication of a waiting for a definitive redemption promised by God.

(b) From the side of the New Testament

The Spirit who 'takes what is mine' so as to lead Christians into all truth (John 16, 14 and 13), and who is also Lord of the freely distributed charisms (I Corinthians 12, 11), also initiates Christians throughout the centuries, by his teaching at large as well as through special charisms, into the inexpressible depths of the Cross and the Descent into Hell. This takes place inasmuch as there are fulfilled the Lord's promises that believers will be hated and persecuted, made into witnesses by blood, imprisoned (Acts 5, 18 etc.), beaten (5, 40), stoned (II Corinthians 11, 25), crucified (John 21, 19), cursed, calumnied and treated as the refuse of the world (I Corinthians 4, 12ff), but also inasmuch as Christians freely take upon themselves 'many a sleepless night, in hunger and thirst, often without food, in cold and exposure' (II Corinthians 11, 27), and do not reject the opprobrium of the Cross in any of its forms (Hebrews 11, 26, 35ff; 12, 1ff; 13, 13).

But there is, to be sure, a series of intermediary stages between the universal being crucified, dying and rising again with Christ in baptism and Christian living (Romans 6, 3–6; Colossians 3, 3) and the especial being 'co-crucified' of a Paul (Galatians 2, 19; 6, 14), his 'bearing on his body the marks of Jesus' (Galatians 6, 17), his 'carrying in the body the death of Jesus' (II Corinthians 4, 10), even if we cannot determine with exactness the content of this charism.

An uninterrupted charismatic re-interpretation of the Cross (and this is our sole topic here, presented by calling to mind some exemplary cases) runs through the centuries of the Church's life. It constitutes the New Testament reflection of the Old Testament experience of God-abandonment and of what the doctor of the Church John of the Cross experienced and described as the 'dark night'. That experience has frequently been considered, both before John and after him, as an experience of damnation, of Hell. It may be useful to recall by way of preamble that, for one entire Christian line of tradition, 'Hell' has been conceived primarily as an inner condition (and not as a 'place' or an 'exterior ordeal'). Beginning with Augustine,[55] this tendency continues via, for example, Honorius of Autun[56] and Dietrich of Freiberg,[57] not to speak of Scotus Eriugena or Nicholas of Cusa. To this there corresponds the notion that, in Hell, a particular experience of time reigns, that of a *tempus informe*: a bringing to a standstill of the runaway course of time (and so a paradoxical pendant to the structure of eternity in the sense of the life everlasting).[58] As we move towards the modern period, 'Hell' will be regarded increasingly as the condition of the self-enclosed 'I', the 'I' unliberated by God, to the point of becoming a constitutive dimension, no less, of present existence.[59]

But it is not that sort of Hell which we shall be looking at here. Our topic is, rather, those charismatic experiences of night and abandonment already met with in the Greek monks and spiritual fathers, and continuing, at any rate in the West, until the modern epoch. It will be necessary to draw attention to the fact that, in the East, experiences of the Cross are closely connected with the idea of struggle against the demons (the entry-permit of the soul striving for God into the realm of the divinely cursèd impure spirit), whereas in the West, such experiences (up to and including the Cross) are conjoined with, on the one hand, the Neo-Platonic and Areopagitic comprehension of the 'radiant darkness' of the unknown God, and, on the other hand, with the idea of the soul's purification through the 'tests' of God-abandonment.[60] Origen is aware of the duty of a vicarious struggle with the demons. He interprets in a spiritual fashion the journeyings through the Wilderness and the storm by night on the Lake, as well as the forsaking of the soul, the bride, by the bridegroom in the Song of Songs.[61] In Gregory of Nyssa and the (semi-) Messalians who lie behind the Homilies of 'Macarius', there is a marked experience of inner spiritual separation from God.[62] The anti-Messalian Diadochus of Photike knows from experience the same 'testings', *peirasmoi*, and gives them classic description.[63] Even Evagrius is clear on the point:[64] every exertion towards God seems vain; *akēdia* (which, for the Greeks, is not just the soul's tedium, but the feeling of futility, despair, God-abandonment) makes the soul undergo the experience of Hell.[65] In Isaac of Nineveh, it is a matter not only of a spiritual hell' (*noētē geennē*), and of a 'taste of Hell', *geusis tēs geennēs*, but also of the timelessness of this experience

Such a man no longer believes that a change might intervene and that he could re-find peace ... Hope in God and the consolation of faith have quite disappeared from his soul, which latter is completely filled with doubt and anguish.[66]

Maximus the Confessor, taking up the ideas of Diadochus and Evagrius, lists four kinds of God-abandonment: first, that found in Christ, in the context of the economy of salvation; where 'by apparent abandonment the abandoned had to be saved'; secondly, abandonment imposed as a test; thirdly, that which is sent for the purposes of purification; fourthly, the kind of abandonment with constitutes a punishment, on the grounds of a turning away from God, as with the Jews. All four types serve the work of salvation.[67]

In the West, the experiences of abandonment recounted by Bernard (in his commentary on the Song of Songs) long remained overlaid by Augustinianism and the Areopagitic system, but proceeded to create for themselves an expression of their own in: Angela of Foligno,[68] Mechthild of Magdeburg,[69] Suso[70] and Tauler,[71] Margaret Ebner,[72] Catherine of Siena,[73] Hilton,[74] Marie des Vallées,[75] Magdalana dei Pazzi,[76] Rosa of Lima[77] and many others. At Manresa, Ignatius experienced something similar;[78] the young Francis de Sales believed himself damned and handed in to God a written declaration that he wished to serve him even in Hell.[79] Nor can Luther go unmentioned in this context.[80] Surin depicted the mystical night as a Hell with all of Hell's pains.[81] The great Theresa can on occasion allude to these torments of Hell.[82] John of the Cross describes them in detail.[83] The little Thérèse speaks of a sub-terranean journey which she undertakes without knowing where she is going or how long she will have to endure there.[84] It is not possible here to investigate either the authenticity or the particular character, or again the special theological significance of all these experiences. But frequently enough they are the response made to the generous offer of souls to be damned in the place of others.[85] This makes the New Testament experiences a mirror of those of the Old: only the person who has truly 'possessed' God in the Covenant, knows what it means to be truly abandoned by him. But all the experiences of night in both Old and New Testaments are at best approaches, distant allusions to the inaccessible mystery of the Cross – so unique is the Son of God, so unique is his abandonment by the Father.

(6) Cross and Theology

In the presence of the hiatus, the 'logic' of theology can in no way rest on the (unbroken) continuity of human and scientific) 'logic', but only on that theo-'logic' established by God himself in the hiatus of the 'death of God'. For even the affirmation, 'The Logos of God is dead' has for its grammatical subject the divine Logos and so – if it is really the Logos *of God* – for its ontic subject also. But the Logos of God is eternal life. He alone can take responsibility for the affirmation that he, as eternal life, is simultaneously dead – and dead with the death of those who are accursed. The believing theologian (and there is no other kind) ventures his logic only on the basis of what the Logos takes responsibility for affirming of himself (the *Theos legōn* in the moment of his self-interpretation becomes the *Theos legomenos* and, thereby, he who can be re-spoken by men). But the death, and the dying away into silence, of the Logos so become the centre of what he has to say of himself that we have to understand precisely his non-speaking as his final revelation, his utmost word: and this because, in the humility of his obedient self-lowering to the death of the Cross he is identical with the exalted Lord. What founds the continuity is the absolute love of God of man, manifesting itself actively on both sides of the hiatus (and so in the hiatus itself), and his triune Love in its own intrinsic reality as the condition of possibility for such a love for man.

This is why we may leave to Karl Barth the closing word on the doctrine of the Kenosis and its theological consequences. Barth wished to speak not of 'two successive conditions, *status*, of Jesus Christ' but of 'two sides or

directions or forms of what *happened* in Jesus Christ for the
reconciliation of man with God'. By the terms 'abasement'
and 'exaltation' is described simply the two-fold *action* of
Jesus Christ, the materials of his *work*:

> his single work which must not be parcelled out into
> different stages or times in his existence, but which, in
> this two-fold form, fills and constitutes, rather, his *entire*
> existence. Ask yourself if this does not correspond better
> to the New Testament witness about Jesus Christ.
> Where and when is he not both the humiliated One
> and the Exalted One: already exalted even in his
> humiliation, and still the Humiliated One even in his
> exaltation? For example, in Paul: the Crucified who is
> *not yet* the Risen One, or the Risen One who is not
> *precisely* the Crucified?

From this perspective, a Christology such as that of Chalcedon
can doubtless be considered as 'objectively true and necessary'
– not, however, in abstraction from the living action of God
in this event of Christ, but in constant recollection of the
way in which

> what Jesus Christ is as true God and true man and what
> *happens* in his humiliation and his exaltation, as a divine
> reconciling work, do to throw light upon each other.

It is, moreover, in this perspective that the doctrine of the
Kenosis is definitely illuminated (in that same meaning, which
we have tried to give it in the above). In his self-emptying,
God does not divest himself of his Godhead, but rather does
he give it precise confirmation in that he:

> submits himself to the chains and wretchedness of the
> human creature; that he, the Lord, becomes a servant,
> and to that measure, and in exactly this, distinguished
> thereby from the false gods, *lowers* himself; and that
> man in Jesus Christ, man without, similarly, loss or
> mutilation of his humanity, is, in the power of his

divinity, and so in the power of, and thanks to, the humiliation of God ... man ... not divinised but rather ... divinely exalted. Thus we get: the abasement of *God* and the exaltation of *man*, and indeed the abasement of God is his supreme honour, since it confirms and demonstrates nothing other than his divine being – and the exaltation of man, as a work of God's grace, consists in nothing other than the restoration of his true humanity.

Everything depends on the fact that this God who thus acts:

confirms and discloses himself as he who is in a concrete way *divinely* free, that is, as he who in his freedom confirms and discloses *in love*.[86]

It is only in the revelation which God makes of himself on the basis of his Word that we learn to understand and to say after him that the God–Man can surrender himself to God-abandonment, without resigning his own reality as God, because, as God, he is as interior to the world he has made as he is superior to it.

He makes his own the being of the man who is opposed to him; but he does not collaborate in his opposition.

By becoming man, he enters into what is alien to him and there remains at the same time true to himself.

In him, there is no paradox, no antinomy, no division

because, by acting as he did, he:

proves to us precisely that he is *capable* of this, that to do such a thing lies absolutely in his *nature*. He thus manifests himself as more sovereign, greater, richer than we would have thought before.[87]

Everything turns on his inner-trinitarian Love which alone explains that an act of obedience is not necessarily foreign to God himself.[88]

The inner-divine relationship between the one who governs and commands in the heights and the one who obeys in humility is identified, in the work of the world's reconciliation with God, with the relationship, so different of its nature, between God and one of his creatures, a man.[89]

Once we realised that even the most extreme Kenosis, inasmuch as it is a possibility in the eternal love of God, is englobed in that love which takes responsibility for it, then the opposition between a *theologia crucis* and a *theologia gloriae* is fundamentally overcome – even though those two may not dissolve the one into the other.

A *theologia gloriae*, celebrating what Jesus Christ in his Resurrection, received for us, and what he is for us as the Risen One, would have no meaning unless it also contained in itself the *theologia crucis*: the praise of what he has done for us in his death and of what he is for us as the crucified. But no more would an abstract *theologia crucis* have meaning. One cannot celebrate in proper fashion the passion and death of Jesus Christ, if this praise does not already contain in itself the *theologia gloriae*: the praise of him who, in his Resurrection, receives our justice and our life, the One who rose for us from among the dead.[90]

In these words, there is once again confirmed what, in the foregoing, we said about the dynamic character of the Pauline 'breakthrough formulae' for the Cross, while the limits of the Lutheran *sub contrario* are also shown up for what they are.

To affirm this is not to collapse theology into a non-dialectical, or even a dialectical, philosopy which has 'understood' the Cross. For who would want to understand the love of God in its folly and weakness? Or who (even if, in the presence of this divine self-revelation, one may speak of 'gnosis' and 'sophia') would wish to lay claim to any other course of action than hanging on the lips of God, whose word remains inseparably connected with his historic Cross and Resurrection, and keeping silence, before the 'love ... which surpasses knowledge' (Ephesians 3, 19), at that moment when the word of God falls silent in the hiatus, since there it takes away from every human logic the concept and the breath?

References

[1] Romanos ho Melodos, *Hymnes* IV, 13–17 (Paris 1967), pp. 179–187.

[2] A. von Speyr, *Kreuz und Hölle* (privately printed, 1966), pp. 49, 80. 120ff, 134ff, 144, 147ff, 316–324. Christ's descent into Hell could not be contained in Mary's 'Yes': p. 141.

[3] J. Paul, 'Siebenkäs', *Werke* II (Munich 1959), p. 269.

[4] 'Vom *logos tou staurou* und seiner Logik', *Theologische Studien und Kritiken* 103 (1931), pp. 179–188.

[5] Ibid., p. 186.

[6] U. Wilckens, *Weisheit und Torheit. Eine exegetische-religionsgeschichtliche Untersuchung zu I Kor. 1 and 2* (Tübingen 1959); idem., 'Kreuz und Weisheit', KuD 3 (1957), pp. 77–108.

[7] Ibid., p. 87.

[8] Ibid., p. 92.

[9] One can only regret that scholastic theology has so little understood the full significance of Holy Saturday, and that it let itself be absorbed by the futile question as to if and how Christ, during the time of his death, remained a man and the God-Man: a vigorously contested question in the twelfth century. Texts in Robert of Melun, *Quaestiones de Divina Pagina 59* (ed. Martin), p. 30, n. Also: S. Landgraf, 'Das Problem "utrum Christus fuerit homo in triduo mortis" in der Frühscholastik', in *Mélanges A. Pelzer* (Louvain 1947), pp. 109–158; and F. Pelster, 'Der Oxforder Theologe Richardus Rufus, O. F. M., über die Frage: "Utrum Christus in triduo mortis fuerit homo"', RThAM 16 (1949), pp. 259–280.

[10] Irenaeus, *Adversus Haereses*, I. 2, 2; I. 3, 5 (PG 7. 453B–456A; 475A).

[11] K. Schäferdiek, 'Joannesakten', in W. Schneemelcher, *Neutestamentliche Apokryphen* II (Berlin 1964), pp. 157–159, and the remarks on p. 143. The English translation given here is from M. R. James, *The Apocryphal New Testament* (Oxford 1924; 1969), pp. 254–256.

[12] M. Hornschuh, 'Andreasakten', in W. Schneemelcher, op. cit. II. pp. 292–3. English translation from M. R. James, op. cit., pp. 359–360. Cf. W. Bousset, 'Platons Weltseele und das Kreuz Christi', ZNW 14 (1913), pp. 280ff

[13] H. de Lubac, *Aspects du Bouddhisme* (Paris 1950), ch. 2: 'Deux arbres cosmiques', pp. 55–79. For notes on this see ibid., pp. 157–170. Comments are also available

here on the frequently found giant-figure, whether Christ or Buddha, as other texts about the cosmic function of the Cross. See also idem., *Catholicisme* (Paris 1952²), pp. 327ff On the cosmic Cross see further Dom S. Steckx, *Introduction au monde des Symboles* (Paris 1966), pp. 25–49; 365–373.

14 P. Nautin (ed.) 'Une homélie inspirée du traité sur la Pâque d'Hippolyte', in: *Homélies Pascales* I (Paris 1950), pp. 177–179. In the same tradition are: Lactantius, *Divinae Institutae* IV. 26, 36 (CSEL 19, 383); Firmicus Maternus, *De Errore Profanarum Religionum* 27 (CSEL 2, 121); Gregory of Nyssa, *Oratio de Resurrectione* (PG 46, 621–625); idem., *The Great Catechism* 32 (PG 75, 81C); Cyril of Jerusalem, *Catecheses* 13 (PG 33, 805B); Maximus of Turin, *Homilia 50 de Cruce* (PL 57, 341ff). Other texts in H. Rahner, 'Das Mysterium des Kreuzes', in idem., *Griechische Mythen in christlichen Sicht* (Zurich 1945), I: 'Das Kreuz als kosmisches Mysterium', pp. 77–89. We may add a word here on a theme which concerns us only indirectly and which constitutes the object of the important research of E. Dinckler (cf. by this author, *Das Apsismosaik von S. Apollinare in Classe*, Cologne-Opladen 1964, and *Zur Geschichte des Kreuzsymbols*, 1951, reproduced in *Signum Crucis. Aufsätze zum Neuen Testament und zur christlichen Archäologie*, Tübingen 1967). Interpreting the radiant crosses in the apse of St Apollinaris and the *clipeus* of the mausoleum of Galla Placidia, Dinckler relates them to representations of the Transfiguration of Jesus, and the latter to the representation of his eschatological Parousia. These luminous crosses (and other analogues) should not, then, be interpreted in a Gnostic fashion but in an eschatological. They are the sign, blazing forth, judging and redeeming, of the Son of Man returning upon earth (*stauros phōtoeidēs*), the One towards whom the Church is moving. It is clear that the Apocrypha have exercised an influence here (*Apsismosaik*, pp. 80ff) – above all, the Apocalypse of Peter but probably also the Acts of John. That the Jewish sign of 'sealing', the *tau*, and the Platonic *chi* were adopted but re-interpreted by the Christian theology of the Cross is for us less important than the adoption of the sign of the Cross in imperial art (towards the year 400) which led the Cross to become a sign of worldly victory, something which could seriously threaten its character as a scandal.

15 W. Schneemechler, 'Petrusakten' in idem., op. cit., II. pp. 219–220; English translation in M. R. James, op. cit., pp. 334–335.

16 W. Schneemelcher, op. cit., p. 187.

17 H. Schlier, 'Religionsgeschichtliche Untersuchungen zu den Ignatiusbriefen', ZNW 8 (1929), pp. 102–110.

18 Paris 1931.

19 Ibid., p. 13.

20 Ibid., p. 14.

21 *Hymne de l'Univers* (Paris 1961), pp. 30–31.

22 In *Études* 20 (June 1921: reproduced in *La Vision du Passé* Paris 1959, p. 37). Cf. H. de Lubac, *La Pensée religieuse du P. Teilhard de Chardin* (Paris 1962), ch. XVIII: 'Création, Cosmogénèse, Christogénèse', pp. 281 295.

23 Cf. for example, H. Scott Holland, *Logic and Life* (London 1882), where the Cross is presented as principle of the world.

24 *Luthers Theologie* II (Stuttgart 1937), pp. 8ff

[25] E. Benz, *Der gekreuzigte Gerechte bei Plato, im Neuen Testament und in der alten Kirche* (Mainz 1950).

[26] K. Leese, *Die Religion des protestantischen Menschen* (Munich 1948[2]), pp. 248.

[27] 'Glauben und Wissen', *Werke* I (Berlin 1832) p. 157.

[28] Teramo 1954.

[29] *Das Wesen des Christentums* (Leipzig 1841): *Werke* 6, 77. 90ff

[30] Ibid., p. 177.

[31] Alain's most important writings are gathered in *Les Arts et les Dieux* (Paris 1958).

[32] *Système des Beaux-Arts* (Paris 1963), p. 184.

[33] S. Breton, op. cit., p. 39.

[34] Alain, *Les Arts et les Dieux*, op. cit., pp. 1324ff

[35] Ibid., p. 1352.

[36] 'Bemerkungen über einie antireligiöse Philosopheme unser Zeit', *Werke* III (Leipzig 1851), p. 492.

[37] Goethe, 'Die Geheimnisse'.

[38] To the *Theologia crucis* there must correspond a real *Philologia crucis* also. It was, above all, Hamann who tried to understand this, and to bring it about. (Cf. W. Leibrecht, 'Philologia crucis. J. G. Hamanns Gedanker über die Sp-rache Gottes', KuD 1 (1955), pp. 226–242). This language is neither directly symbolic (against R. Unger), nor directly dialectical (against F. Lieb), neither does it wish to identify directly the Word of God with the biblical word (against E. Peterson). 'Every attempt to divide the Word into the form of glory and the form of a slave is for him a day-dream' (Leibrecht, p. 235). It is a matter of such brokenness of utterance that precisely in that fragmentation there appears, through the Spirit, wholeness and the state of salvation.

[39] Luke 24, 11, 22, 38 and 41; John 20, 9, 14 and 27.

[40] Cf. Mark 9, 10ff; 6, 12–16. The grotesque anecdotes about resuscitation by rabbis (Strack-Billerbeck I, 557, 560) come from a notably later epoch. Nothing else is alleged about Matthew 14, 2. For other parallels, see P. Seidensticker, *Zeitgenössische Texte zur Osterbotschaft der Evangelien* (Stuttgart 1967); H. Braun, 'Der Sinn der neutestamentlichen Christologie', ZThK 54 (1957), pp. 341–377.

[41] Even if, according to Mark 1, 14 (and contrary to John 3, 24) Jesus only began to preach after the arrest of the Baptist, the popular opinion reproduced in Mark 6, 14, for which Jesus would be John *redivivus* could only mean a kind of transmission to Jesus (now at least thirty years old) of the prophetic powers of the one who had been 'yielded up': cf. II Kings 2, 9ff or, more primitively still, a kind of 'transmigration of the soul'. Herod himself adopts this opinion (mark 6, 16) by reason of his bad conscience. The representation of a return by the (not deceased!) Elijah, applied to Jesus (Mark 6, 15) or to John (Mark 9. 13) is purely eschatological (Malachi 3, 23).

[42] W. Marxsen, *Der Evangelist Markus* (Göttingen 1959[2]), p. 54.

[43] E. Lohmeyer, *Das Evangelium des Markus* (Göttingen 1953[12]), p. 313: 'An achieved totality of unique and enduring validity'. That does not disallow the possibility that different traditions may be united, just as different theological themes may com-penetrate each other while remaining in mutual tension.

[44] W. Popkes, *Christus traditus. Eine Untersuchung zum Begriff der Dahingabe im Neuen Testament* (Zürich 1967), with bibliography.

[45] J. J. Stamm, *Das Leiden des Unschuldigen in Babylon und Israel* (Zürich 1946), with bibliography.

[46] H. W. Surkau, *Martyrien in judischer und frühchristlicher Zeit* (Göttingen 1938); N. Brox, *Zeuge und Märtyrer* (Munich 1961): for the Old Testament, pp. 132, 173.

[47] W. Wichmann, *Die Leidenstheologie. Eine Form der Leidensdeutung im Spätjudentum* (Stuttgart 1930).

[48] H. Hegermann, *Jesaia 53 in Hexapla, Targum und Peschitta* (Gütersloh 1954); H. W. Wolff, *Jesaia 53 im Urchristentum* (Berlin 1952[3]). See also on this E. Käsemann, VF (1950), pp. 200ff

[49] Cf. S. Augustine, *Contra Adversarios Legis et Prophetarum* I. 16, 32 (PL 42, 620): 'Quod enim diluvium comparari aeternis ignibus potest?', etc.

[50] For a theological analysis, see H. U. von Balthasar *Der Christ und die Angst* (Einsiedeln 1953[2]), pp. 16–33.

[51] This is why the Sumerian and Akkadian lamentations deploring a destroyed sanctuary may perhaps be literary models for Israel's lamentation songs, but in no way theological parallels to them. Cf. our study 'Alter Bund', in *Herrlichkeit* III/2. 1, p 258, note 1.

[52] W. Popkes, op. cit., pp. 30ff

[53] 3 Here as cursing formula on the evil, who either ought to be expelled or were (Kore!).

[54] The later speculative relationship between Sheol and Gehenna need not concern us: see J. Nelis, 'Gehenna' in *Bibel-Lexikon* (Einsiedeln 1968[2]), p. 530.

[55] *De Genesi ad Litteram* VIII. 5, 9ff (PL 34, 376–377); XII. 32, 61ff (PL 34, 480–481), perhaps in furtherance of Wisdom 17 mentioned above.

[56] *De Animae Exilio et Patria* 14 (PL 172, 1246D).

[57] Texts in E. Krebs, *Meister Dietrich* (Theodoricus Teutonicus de Vriberg). *Sein Leben, seine Werke, seine Wissenschaft* (Münster 1906), pp. 105, 108, n. 1.

[58] Augustine, *De Civitate Dei* XX. 21, 4; 21, 1–4; 22, 30 (PL 41, 693, 709–714, 801); cf. Alexander of Hales, *Summa* I, 69–70.

[59] In the *Theologia Deutsch*, personal will is Hell. The idea is transferred to S. Franck, Cepko, Silesius. See also L. Malevez, *Le Message Chrétien et le Mythe. La théologie de R. Bultmann* (Brussels 1954), p. 158; L. Grünhut, *Eros und Agape* (Leipzig 1931), pp. 31–41.

[60] I. Hausherr, 'Les Orientaux connaissent-ils les 'nuits' de S. Jean de la Croix?', OrChrP 12 (1946), pp. 1–46; M. Lot-Borodine, 'L'aridité dans l'antiquité chrétienne', *Études Carmelitaines* 25 (1937), p. 196.

[61] Texts in H. de Lubac, *Histoire et Esprit*, op. cit., pp. 185ff; I. Hausherr, art. cit., pp. 24–26.

[62] H. Dörries, *Symeon von Mesopotamien* (Leipzig 1941), pp. 15ff; I. Hausherr, art. cit., pp. 20–22.

[63] *Centurie über die geistliche Vollkommenheit* ed. by J. E. Weis-Liebersdorf (Leipzig 1912), ch. 69, p. 87; ch. 27, p. 30; ch. 81, p. 104.

[64] *Centuriae* I. 37 (Frankenberg), p. 81: the most terrible experiences of this kind are, according to Evagrius, reserved for the perfect.

[65] *Praktikos* 19 (PG 40, 1226).

[66] Texts in I. Hausherr, art. cit., pp. 26ff; 31ff.

[67] *Centuriae de Caritate* IV. 96 (PG 90, 1072C. Cf. the mystical descent into Hell in *Ambigua* (PG 91, 1384C).

[68] Angela di Foligno, *Le Livre de l'expérience des vrais fidèles*, ed. M.-F. Ferré (Paris 1927), 96ff; *Letter 3*, pp. 494ff

[69] Mechthild of Magdeburg, *Das fliessende Licht der Gottheit* (Einsiedeln 1955), I.5; III.10 (pp. 60 and 141).

[70] 'Zehn Jahre Gottverlassenheit', in *Biographie* (ed. Bihlmeyer 1907), ch. 23, pp. 66ff

[71] J. Tauler, *Predigten*, ed. by W. Lehmann (Jena 1923²), I. 9 (pp. 42ff); II. 50 (pp. 30–31; 35); 53 (p. 47); 55 (pp. 56ff); 76 (pp. 223ff).

[72] P. Strauch, *Die Offenbarungen der Margaretha Ebner und der Adelheid Langmann, ins Neuhochdeutsche übertragen von Josef Prestel* (Weimar 1939), passim.

[73] Catherine of Siena, *Dialogo della divina Provvidenza*, ed. I. Taurisano (Rome 1947), I. 13; cf. Raymond of Capua, *Vie de Sainte Cathérine de Sienne* (Paris 1859²), I. 11. 2ff (pp. 71ff); III. 2–3 (pp. 287ff).

[74] W. Hilton, *The Scale of Perfection* (London 1927), I.37; II.45.

[75] E. Dermenghen, *La vie admirable et les révélations de Marie des Vallées* (Paris 1926), pp. 36, 38ff

[76] V. Puccini, *Vita della venerabile Madre Suor Maria Maddalena de' Pazzi* (Florence 1611), I. 34–40.

[77] Cf. I. Görres, *Christliche Mystik* II (Regensburg 1840), pp. 286ff: 'She was daily visited by the most frightful nights of the soul which ... for hours so caused her anxiety that she knew not if she were in Hell ... She groaned beneath the dreadful burden of the darkness ... Her will wanted to tend to love, but was paralysed as if solidified in ice. The memory forced itself to evoke at least the images of previous consolations, but in vain ... Terror and anguish took possession of her totally, and her heart, overwhelmed, cried out: My God, my God, why have you forsaken me? But no one replied ... Yet what was worst in her sufferings was that these ills presented themselves as having to last eternally; that no glimpse was given of an end to the distress; and that, since a wall of bronze made all escape impossible, no exit from the labyrinth could be found ...'.

[78] *Autobiography*, 24.

[79] Texte in M. Hamon, *Vie de Saint François de Sales* (new edition, Paris 1922), pp. 56ff

[80] Sed et ego novi hominem qui has poenas saepius passum se asseruit, brevissimo quidem temporis intervallo, sed tantas ac tam infernales, quantas nec lingua dicere nec calamus scribere nec inexpertus credere potest, ita ut, si perficerentur aut ad mediam horam durarent, immo ad horae decimam partem, funditus periret et ossa omnia in cinerem redigerentur, Weimar Ausgabe I, 557, 32.

[81] 'De l'enfer de l'âme', in *Guide Spirituel pour la Perfection* (Paris 1963), pp. 303ff

[82] *Moradas* VI. 1.

[83] For the dark night as infernal torment, see the 'Dark Night' II. 5f; II. 20, 2.

[84] *Manuscrits autobiographiques* (Lisieux 1956); *Selbstbiographische Schriften* (Einsiedeln 1958), p. 219; cf. p.97.

[85] Alvarez de Paz, *Tractatus de Vita Spirituali* I. 4, p. 3, c. 12 (Lyons 1608); J. E.

Nierenberg, *Flammae Amoris Divini* 3 (Madrid 1639); D. Schram, *Théologie mystique* I (Paris 1872), para. 275 (cf. para. 274).

[86] *Kirchliche Dogmatik* IV/1 (Zollikon 1953), pp. 145–147. On the historic doctrine of the Kenosis, ibid, pp. 196–199; 205ff

[87] Ibid. pp. 202–204.

[88] Ibid., p. 211.

[89] Ibid., p. 222.

[90] Ibid., p. 622.

3

Going to the Cross: Good Friday

(1) Jesus' Life as Directed to the Cross

Our introduction has already shown that, according to the witness of both Scripture and Tradition, the whole life of Jesus should be conceived as a going to the Cross. But that still needs to be presented concretely, and from various perspectives. For the question arises: to what extent do the earlier events[1] in Jesus' life announce the Cross, and even, in a determinate sense, belong with it already?

(a) *Existence in Kenosis as obedience to the death of the Cross*

To the hymn of Philippians 2, which speaks of obedience to the Cross as the consequence of the Son's emptying and abasement, there corresponds the Johannine *mandatum a Patre* (10, 18; 12, 49, 50) which Jesus executes: *sic facio*. Since for the eternal Son, who is the subject here, there can be no question of a subsequent confrontation with the Father's command, which he then might decide to obey, Chrysostom,[2] Anselm[3] and Thomas[4] sought to illuminate the perfect unity of the wills of the Father and the Son, and therewith the voluntary (*sponte*) character of all the Son's acting – something which Thomas rates higher than obedience to an order. At the most, one might venture the view that in the unshakeable will to give self, there was something like an 'inspiration', an attraction by the Father, and that in this sense the language of obedience can be justified.[5] P. Galtier asks whether this interpretation does justice to the biblical text.[6] He fills it out by an idea which he claims to find in Ambrose, Augustine and, above all, Irenaeus: the natural solidarity of Jesus with all human beings. But human beings are, thanks to the curse befalling Adam and his posterity, a suffering and mortal race:

> From the very fact of the Incarnation, he (the divine Son) found himself in the presence of a judgment to death which touched him too.[7]

But since he is sinless (and here Galtier has explicit recourse to, once again, saint Anselm), Jesus accepted the dying which he had to undergo physically in his 'existence unto death' not as a personal punishment but by a free and spontaneous intention. As man, he is, before God, a 'servant'; as bearer of a sinful nature he is 'destined to an accursed death'; whereas, as the eternal Son, he remains free in his gift of self (cf. John 10, 18). This reasoning seems to overlook two points. First, Jesus does not only not only accept the (to be sure, accursed) mortal destiny of Adam. He also, quite expressly, carries the sins of the human race and, with those sins, the 'second death' of God-abandonment. Secondly, in the 'condition of a servant' it is not an anonymous destiny that he obeys but the person of the Father.[8] These viewpoints must be integrated in our account, though they should be gone beyond also.

For that we need to return to the mystery of the Kenosis whose first result is the Incarnation, followed by the whole human existence of Jesus. If the person who lowers himself to the condition of a servant is that of the *divine* Son, with his entire servant-existence remaining, therefore, the expression of his divine freedom, in unanimous accord with the Father, then the obedience which determines that whole existence of his is not simply a function of what he has *become* (*en homoiōmati anthrōpōn, schēmati hōs anthrōpos* and thus 'existence unto death'). It is also a function of what, in his self-emptying and self-abasement, he *willed* to become. By letting go of the 'form of God' that was his (and so his divine power of self-disposal) he willed to become the One who, in a remarkable and unique manner, is obedient to the Father – in a manner, namely, where his obedience presents the kenotic translation of the eternal love of the Son for the 'ever-greater' Father. To this extent, that 'inspiration' by the Father which we spoke of above is not simply the inner *élan* of his love, but submission to the rule and leading of the Holy Spirit of mission) who 'impels' him (Luke 4, 1 and 14, etc.). In the time of the Son's abasement, the Spirit (proceeding eternally from Father and from Son) receives a primacy over the Son who obeys him (and by him obeys the Father): this constitutes the expression of the fact that all of his existence is ordered, functionally and kenotically, to the Cross. Even those great affirmations which begin with the word 'I' are not the language of 'self-consciousness' but of mission.

(b) Existence in awareness of the coming hour

And with this recognition we can see that the apparent dialectic between 'being Lord' and 'being a servant' in the words and deeds of Jesus does not have as its primordial condition some retrojection of the post-Easter understanding of Christ onto the time before Easter – in such a way that he appeared to the disciples now as *Kyrios*, now as Servant of Yahweh – an antinomy which could only be reconciled by artifice (as in the 'messianic secret' of Mark). On the contrary, this dialectic is objectively surmounted, already and always, in the existence of Christ. It is so surmounted on the basis of his mission, which called for the coming of Jesus into the world, both with *exousia* and with 'meekness and mildness'. This unity, which is not further divisible in the life of Jesus, and is only in seeming a 'dialectical' one, throws light on everything. In *Mark*, the Baptist on his 'arrest' (1, 14) is displaced by the more mighty person, 'baptising with the Spirit' (1, 8) whom he had foretold. The latter, at once establishing a solidarity with sinners (2, 16), and provoking the 'righteous' as he does so, pardons sins (2, 10), raises himself above the limits of the Law (2, 18–3, 6), and, for this reason, is judged to be out of his mind (3, 21). He makes the hardest demands (3, 31ff), brings all things into the light (4, 21), and distributes blame without pity (7, 18; 8, 17 and 21). Three times he announces 'plainly' (8, 32) his future suffering, and drags his stupefied disciples behind him (10, 32) towards the Passion in which he will 'give his life as a ransom for many' (10, 45).

Without changing the principal contours of the story, *Luke* discloses more deeply the heart of the Son who bows so low in his will to help and save (4, 18ff). The latter will become a sign of contradiction, and a sword will pierce through the heart of his Mother (2, 34ff), something which begins when Mary seeks uncomprehending for the young boy (2, 48). He inhabits the realm of the Evil One's temptations (4, 13; 22, 28), enrages his compatriots (4, 28) and above all his adversaries (6, 11), divides his hearers between those whom he proclaims 'blessed' and those on whom he pronounces woes (6, 20ff), yet he shares in the suffering of the afflicted (7, 14; 10, 33 and 37; 15, 20). In the parables of the Good Samaritan and the Good Shepherd (15, 3ff), he unveils his own heart; in those of the Prodigal Son and the Great Banquet, that of the Father (14, 21); in the word to the good thief and the word of forgiveness he discloses the meaning of his Cross (23, 34 and 43). Even the scene of the Transfiguration has the Passion as its centre (9, 31). Towards it he 'sets his face' (9, 51) as he walks – he had already seen Satan fall from heaven (10, 18). He who is to baptise 'with the Holy Spirit and with fire' (3, 16) presses towards the baptism of the Cross which he must receive and without which he cannot bring fire upon the earth (12, 49ff). Lazarus at the gate must be fed (16, 19ff): it is with an 'earnest desire' that Jesus wants to give himself to his own as their food and drink (22, 15ff), and that as totally as the widow who 'put in all the living that she had' (21, 4).

Matthew has the life of Jesus begin with the flight into Egypt and a great blood-bath of the innocent (2, 13ff): how, then, could Jesus *not* be a marked man? This is why, from the moment of the first miracles, Isaiah 53 is expressly cited: (8, 17). The 'bearing of our griefs' through his miracles cannot be thought through without reference to his substitutionary death. But above all, behind the first programmatic discourse there lies already the whole ethic of the Cross. What is posed as demand is 'guaranteed' beforehand by the Cross: it is a true *logos tou staurou* (5, 20; 39; 44 and 48; 7, 13). The situation is no different in the missionary discourse which, in advance, associates the disciples, and the whole meaning of their existence with the Cross which is his destiny (10, 5–39). The sign of Jonah too is interpreted in terms of the Passion (12, 40).

For *John*, the entire life of the Jesus who 'dwelt among us' is already that which 'enlightens every man . . . in the world' (1, 9), and, thereby, 'shines in the darkness' (1, 5). In it, the return to the Father is initiated (16, 28). Everything that was 'a figure' passes over into 'plainness' (16, 25), in a way which is almost Gnostic and yet is most profoundly anti-Gnostic because throughout what is at stake is 'the flesh' (1, 14), the 'blood and water' gushing forth from the heart (19, 34), the flesh and blood which are 'food indeed . . . and drink indeed' (6, 55), the inseparable 'water and Spirit' (3, 5) and 'Spirit, water and blood' (I John 5, 8). Jesus lives in prior readiness for his 'hour': by its distance he decides what to do and what to leave be (2, 4; 7, 30; 8, 20; 12, 23 and 27; 13, 1; 16, 32; 17, 1). The Cross, which he does not anticipate, and the knowledge of which he leaves to the Father's discretion (Mark 13, 32), is the measure of his existence.

(c) Existence as anticipation of the Passion?

It is tempting to combine the considerations ventured in the two previous sections, so as to arrive at the idea that the whole existence of Jesus was, from the start, interiorly identical with the Cross. The 'French School' indeed, looked away from the succession of events to the innermost and in some sense timeless states, *états*, of the Redeemer, characterised essentially by his will to give himself, to bear the sin of the world, and that on the basis of his Kenosis, his *abaissement*[9] Thomas Leonardi, O.P., drew the final inference in his little book entitled, *Christus crucifixus sive de perpetua cruce Jesu Christi a primo instanti suae conceptionis usque ad extremum vitae.*[10] For the thesis expressed in that title, one can refer not only to Bérulle and Bourgoing but also to Francis de Sales,[11] Bellarmine[12] and perhaps authors as early as Richard of Saint-Victor, Albert, Tauler and Ruysbroeck, Thomas à Kempis, Catherine of Siena and others. The already mentioned Louis Chardon will develop his theology of the Cross in the same sense.[13] Bossuet and Bourdaloue follow him, and more recent authors such as the English Oratorian Faber take further the same teaching.[14] Rejection of this theory must be tempered by care, since it tries to express something of the pervasive mystery of the Kenosis which is the basis of the existence of the God-man. But if at first sight it seems to constitute the very antithesis of a gnostic Docetism, it may also be said to contain, nevertheless, a kind of counter-gnosis. The condition, *état*, of abasement in which the Bringer of salvation finds himself already coincides, for this theory, with the historic event of the Cross, and that calls into question, at another level, the authentic temporality of the 'hour' and so the genuineness of his humanity and incarnation. Moreover, the hymn to the Kenosis in Philippians 2 does not put the accent on the suffering as such but on the obedience, and so on the humble *indiferencia* (Ignatius of Loyola) whereby the servant of God receives everything from the Father, the 'rejoicing in the Holy Spirit' (10, 21) as well as the 'sorrow even unto death' (Mark 14, 24). In the texts, the 'hour, and the power of darkness' (Luke 22, 43) are clearly distinguished from what precedes them. Much more does it belong to perfect obedience that knowledge of the hour does not absorb the awareness of the One who obeys to such a point that other contents, given by God, are narrowed down or even left unreceived altogether.

(d) Existence in sharing

Jesus' life is unthinkable without the dimension of 'being-with' – indeed, without that sharing with those others whom he freely and expressly chose out for that purpose (Mark 3, 13ff), taking them along his special way while communicating to them something of his own 'plenary power' (Mark 1, 17;

3, 14; 6, 7), initiating them into his mysteries (Mark 4, 11) –
above all, those of his Passion (8, 31, etc.). Here lies an
irresoluble paradox: his way of suffering is essentially unique,
on its decisive stretch it is, for the moment, impossible to
follow him (John 13, 33); even those who seek to follow him
and vow to do so (Matthew 26, 33 and parallels; John 11, 16)
'must' be deceived in his regard and betray him. Only after
the hiatus of death, when alone he has accomplished his whole
work, will they be in a position to follow him to the Cross
as his witnesses, through their life and their death (John 21,
19). To make plain this singular 'analogy' between the leader
and the failing disciple one could appeal to the pre-Christian
Jewish theology of martyrdom which might have given the
disciples some sort of 'pre-understanding'. But the texts speak
otherwise. Jesus does not present himself as the supreme
instance of something universally intelligible, under whose
concept the way of the disciples might also be subsumed.
Rather does he call others on a way which is at first without
analogy, a way which can only be elucidated through him,
so that he can make available of himself, that is, on the basis
of his finished work on the Cross, access to his own person.
Only much later, at something of a tangent and in order to
illustrate this singularity, can the Jewish theology of
martyrdom be utilised in a new fashion.[15] In the event of
sharing, the Eucharist signifies at one and the same time a
limit, and the over-passing of that limit. Until this point, the
disciples have 'continued with' him (Luke 22, 28). From now
on, they will be 'scattered' (Matthew 26, 31), and yet, since
they have eaten his flesh and drunk his blood, they are taken
beyond their own limits into him. Or, to put it the other
way round, they become thereby receptacles in which (as in
his members) he can suffer as he will.[16]

(2) The Eucharist

The Eucharist cannot be dealt with here as a subject in its
own right, but it can be considered in its relation to the
Passion. So as to prevent a unitary whole crumbling into

fragments of source analysis, it is worthwhile looking at the different strands of tradition in their theological convergence, in their indispensability for an overall understanding.

(a) A spontaneous gift in view of the Passion

For Jesus, this meal is a long desired culmination whose meaning is only clarified by the additional phrase 'before I suffer' (Luke 22, 15), and the negative formulation of the eschatological perspective: 'I shall not eat . . . I shall not drink' (vv. 16, 18), as by the mention of the traitor whose hand is with that of Jesus on the table (v. 21). This is the 'hour' which has 'come', but in such a way that, at its beginning, Jesus can still dispose of his own affairs, and that in a decisive manner (John 13, 1). It is an hour which cannot be transcended, and to which men must return time and again (as the formulation of the command repeatedly to 'do this' indicates). For beyond it there is nothing, save the bringing to completion of what it freely inaugurates: dying. Yet it is itself eschatological, in that it goes *eis telos*, to the final end of love (John 13, 1). Two traditions describe its content, though they are unable to do without each other: a report about the meal with its self-distribution and its reference to the enactment of a new covenant (expressed through features of Old Testament ritual), and a report about Jesus' last act of service, and the serving mind-set which he established, in a perspective of eschatological fulfilment (Luke 22, 15–20; 27–30; John 13 and the Farewell Discourse). The interior mind-set (symbolised in the Foot-washing) becomes a definitive action in the self-distribution which anticipates and introduces the Passion. John 6 points to the unity of what is otherwise virtually irreconcilable: on the other hand, 'spirit and life', 'faith', 'words of eternal life', 'the flesh is of no avail' (vv. 63–69); and, on the other hand, 'eating' and 'drinking' the flesh and the blood as an indispensable condition for resurrection (vv. 53–59). To suppress this second aspect, as does Bultmann, is hardly feasible in the light of the programmatic *Verbum-Caro* (1, 4), expressed precisely in the tension between these two sets of affirmations. It is neither a matter of pure presence in language,[17] nor of the 'reification' of Christ's bodiliness, but of the indivisible unity of his self-gift 'for the multitude' – and this gift is not just an 'attitude' but an integrally human enactment carried out precisely by virtue of the bodiliness which discloses in a deeper way the identity between the person of Jesus and his soteriological function. In that function, he is at once a disposer (as institutor of the Eucharist, the new covenant in his blood) and the disposed of (in obedience to the hour, when, at the Father's disposition, he will be handed over.)

(b) Bread and wine: meal and sacrifice

The definitive character of the hour in the awareness of the founder would be thoroughly misconceived if one failed to see there the simultaneous fulfilment of the institutions of the Old Testament. That is true, even if the various strands were, at first, only gradually distinguished from each other in any clear way. Thus we have: the culmination of the legal foundation of the covenant in 'my blood of the covenant'[18] (Mark, Matthew, cf. Exodus 24, 8); of the prophetic promise in the 'cup of the new covenant' (Paul, Luke, cf. Jeremiah 31, 31); and of the substitutionary theology of Second Isaiah (influenced by the Jewish theology of martyrdom?) in the self-gift and promise 'for the multitude' (Mark 14, 24, a Semitism equivalent to 'for all', whereby the Old Testament barrier which excluded the pagans from eschatological salvation is broken down).[19] Here too there converge in a final way the ideas of sacrifice and meal, ideas always interlinked (Exodus 24, 8 and 11, etc.), no matter what transformations that link may have undergone (even to the point of introducing the idea of sacrifice into that of meal). And if the formula pronounced over the bread gives prominence to the meal aspect (to some degree over against the Passover, which was understood by Jews as a *sacrificial* meal), the formula pronounced over the wine, with its mention of the outpoured blood and, in that exclusive context, its eschatological perspective, underlines, rather, the aspect of sacrifice. The emphasis on the separation of flesh and blood (doubtless made clear originally by the separation in time of the word over the bread and the word over the wine) sends us back, on the one hand, to the toleration of the use of flesh from the time of Noah (Genesis 8, 21), and, on the other, to the prohibition of the use of blood (Genesis 9, 2ff; Leviticus 7, 27), the rationale for the complete draining off of the blood in a sacrificial animal. (cf. Acts 15, 20 and 29; 21, 25). The blood, the seat of life, belongs to God alone, so much so that the blood of a murdered man can be divinely proffered to the murderer as an element of forensic proof, while the blood of the murderer himself can be reclaimed (either by way of vendetta or, later, through a judicial sacrifice of expiation). But if, in Isaiah 53, instead of an animal led to the abattoir there steps forth a representative man who shed his blood for our transgressions and 'poured out his soul to death' (Isaiah 53, 12c), and if this blood, belonging as it does to God, has such value in God's sight that it 'justifies many', then the idea is already emerging that the 'precious blood' (I Peter 1, 19), reserved for God yet used by him for the good of many, might one day be made over to men as his most precious gift, even though they be the executioners and assassins of his Son. The Capharnaite horror of blood is already interiorly transcended in that Israel lives, and is justified by the death of the Servant of the Lord. In the *Verbum-caro* the final consequence is drawn therefrom for the eucharistic meal. It matters little, then, whether the Last Supper was celebrated, as the Synoptics would have it, in the course of a passover meal, representing the detachment of the one covenant from the other in a tangible way by the juxtaposition of the two rites, or whether, as in John, that detachment took place in the simultaneity of passover and Cross, and so in the replacement of the substitutionary animal sacrifice by the bloodly self-offering of the Servant of the Lord. What is really important is that Christ, at the end of the ages, once for all, by his own blood, has passed both through the heavens to the Father (Hebrews 9, 12) and into those sharing the meal, as the sacrificial victim poured out as a libation. If the theologian contemplates simultaneously the consequences of the *Verbum-Caro* and the implications of the way sacrifice and meal are presented in the Temple liturgy and by the prophets, the convergences between the two rise up to meet the eye in almost a priori fashion. There ceases to be any 'either/or' as between body-and-blood in their literal pertinence, and spirit-and-life as their inner kernel of meaning, since the two pairs coincide perfectly in the Eucharist. The Son thanks the Father (*eucharistein, eulogein*) for having allowed him to be so disposed of that there comes about, at one and the same time, the supreme revelation of the divine love (its glorification) and the salvation of humankind.

(c) Community

Since what is at stake is the welcoming of the *Word* under the form of flesh and blood, the decisive factor on the part of the recipient is faith, that is, the readiness to follow where the Word wills and indicates (John 6, 63ff; whence the 'crisis': I Corinthians 11, 27–29). Thus the dialectic of discipleship described above (III 1d) returns in a sharpened form. To receive into me the One who was sacrificed for me means to grant him space in, and power of disposition over, my whole existence, both spiritual and physical, and thereby to follow him – at a distance, since it is he (in a masculine fashion) who decides, whilst I (in a feminine fashion) let him act, but also in unity, since, through my letting him act, he will decide in me only in accordance with the meaning of his own *disponibilité*. And so the meal becomes the Church's real sharing in Jesus' flesh and blood in their condition of victimhood (I Corinthians 10, 16ff). The Church's sacrifice is, therefore, at once distinct from that of Christ and identical with his, since it consists in a (feminine) consenting to the sacrifice of Christ (and to all the consequences that flow therefrom for the Church).[20] Christ's kenotic condition – as bread to be 'eaten' and wine poured out – appears to confer on the table-guests an active and absorbing rôle; but 'when I am weak, then am I strong' (II Corinthians 12, 10) and 'the weakness of God is stronger than men', precisely in the

Eucharist. There Christ actively incorporates the participants
into his mystical body.

(3) The Mount of Olives

(a) Isolation

The Passion 'properly so called' – here we are disregarding its
continually actualised preparatory stages in the life of Jesus:
temptation, the weeping over murderous Jerusalem as over
the mighty power of death, wrath, weariness, disgust and so
forth – begins, in the earliest narrative, that of Mark, with
Jesus 'fallen to the ground' (Mark 14, 35, a phrase weakened
by Matthew who presents this moment as an act of adoration
by Jesus who prostrates himself, his face touching the earth,
as by Luke who reduces it to the action of kneeling). Jesus
falls down, so as to undergo, dashed to the ground, the
eschatological testing, *peirasmos*. Everything starts from
within: in fear, *ektnambeistai*, and the horror which isolates,
adēmonein, Mark 14, 33. This is isolation vis-à-vis the God
who distances himself, but has not yet disappeared, and on
whom Jesus calls with pleading tenderness, 'dear Father',
Abba. And yet no communication with the Father follows
save that of the Lucan angel who strengthens Jesus in his
suffering, or, in John, the confirmatory voice from heaven
which affirms the glorification of the Father (not of Jesus!)
through the suffering. Isolation, too, from the disciples whom
Jesus takes with him yet also leaves at a distance, according to
a dialectic whose theological meaning is developed in various
ways: first, as the assignation of a place for the exercise of
obedience[21] (you 'here', myself 'there' – Matthew); secondly,
as graduated accompanying – three chosen ones may come
within earshot but no nearer (Mark, Matthew); thirdly, as
union in prayer ('Pray!'), but with this distinction, that Jesus
prays *in* the *peirasmos*, whereas the disciples pray to be
preserved *from* it; fourthly, as the going and coming of Jesus
(three times in Mark and Matthew) which underlines his
distance and his closeness; fifthly, as the incapacity of the

disciples (excused by Luke as 'sadness') to sustain Jesus in his solitary struggle in prayer, which earns for Peter (Mark) and the two others (Matthew) a disappointment-filled reproach. This dialectic of an absent presence of the Church at the side of the suffering Head is irresoluble. The 'ought' (heard by the Church's parenesis an issuing from the mouth of Jesus) stands in contradiction to the impotence disclosed for judgment in the Passion.

(b) The entrance of sin

In place of the 'terror which isolates' of Mark, John speaks of 'being troubled' (11, 33 and 38; 12, 27; 13, 21). What this truly implies can only be grasped when the anxious prayer-agony is placed in the context of enduring the 'hour', and draining the chalice (of eschatological wrath), as described in the Mount of Olives stories (and also John 18, 11), and besides the great soteriological affirmations of Paul (such as II Corinthians 5, 21; Romans 8, 3; Galatians 3, 13ff, and so forth) and of John (12, 31; 16, 11, etc.). Then the 'hour' and the 'chalice' became the entry of the sin of the world into the personal existence, body and soul, of the representative Substitute and Mediator. It does not suffice (precisely because of this confrontation of the narrative with the soteriological reflection) to argue from the unique 'dignity' of the substitutionary person, and his innocence and freedom, in order to make acceptable the reality of his work of atonement (whether ontological or forensic). It is much more important to offer a deepened description of how the hypostatic union constitutes the condition of possibility of a real assumption of universal guilt. In earlier theology, a two-fold obstacle seemed to stand in the way of this: first, the theological hypothesis for which the soul of Christ, even during the Passion, persisted in its (beatific?) vision of the Father, something which appeared to exclude Christ's being the total subject and 'experiencer' of sin, and secondly, a doctrine of predestination which excluded expiatory suffering (at the least, a prayer of intercession on the part of the sufferer) for those certainly condemned by God to damnation. These two barriers, which ancient thought came up against and already, at times, partially broke through, are no longer a serious obstacle for today's thinking.[22]

On the supposition that this two-fold barrier has fallen, let us listen to certain affirmations of the Middle Ages. In the *Sententiae Divinitatis*, the following question is posed: in his anguish on the Mount of Olives, did Christ know the *timor gehennalis?*

> Some say that he knew it in his (ecclesial) members. But we say, to the contrary, in his own person – not for himself, but for his members. Indeed, if he had already experienced a true consternation, and a true grief, and shed real tears on account of the temporal death of Lazarus, with much better reason could he feel anguish and grief in himself because of the eternal damnation which he foresaw would be inflicted on the Jews on his account.[23]

If we replace the affirmation 'would be' here by a conditional 'could be' we shall come close to Paul: in his Passion, Christ surmounted even the guilt (and therewith the merited punishment) of his murderers (Romans 5, 16).

Robert Pullus also poses the question of the *timor gehennalis* in Christ. The Psalms testify to it, yet Christ's foreknowledge of his glorification argues against it.

> How, then, did the anguish dominate? Did he, for example, experience the anguish which is ours when we face some prospect that we know by reason will not eventualise? At night, we fear to encounter a dead man, but we know that that will not happen. Or again, when we find ourselves on an exposed height, a feeling of vertigo takes us over completely, so that we are anxious lest we fall over a precipice, even though our reason tells us that we are quite safe, and our anxiety is baseless. Now if it is superstitious in such a state of anxiety to pray that what we fear may not happen, while we know, however, that it will not happen, how could the

prayer of Christ be rational (admitting that the feeling of being damned did seize him) if it was a persistent request to escape damnation but if too Christ remained, despite that, convinced that he was saved?[24]

The solution provided for this so curiously posed problem is this: Christ was not certain of his salvation by any other means than his prayer of supplication. The fear of falling into Hell is, doubtless, the 'beginning of wisdom', yet Christ could experience that fear not in himself but only in his (mystical) members.

The commentary on some difficult christological affirmations of Hilary by the Master of the Sentences (III. distinctio 16) gave rise to numerous speculations as to the manner in which the uniqueness of Christ's sufferings was conditioned by the uniqueness of the hypostatic union. Along with Odo Rigaldus, the *Summa* of Alexander of Hales sets up a contrast:

> In ourselves (as sinners) the possibility (of suffering) is bound up with the necessity of suffering and the will not to suffer which, however, cannot stop suffering from taking place . . . In the Lord, the possibility (which was no merely remote, *indisposita*, one, as in Adam) is not bound up with the necessity of suffering, as in us, but with an inclination to suffer and a will which would have had the power to prevent suffering.[25]

That indicates (however haltingly) something quite special about the constitution of the God-man, owing to the voluntary character of his Kenosis, which conditions and structures his human nature, and allows it to house a quite different measure of suffering than that of the sinner whose suffering is constrained.

Bonaventure brings a more penetrating light. Having showed that the 'beatific vision of God' does not prevent the most spiritual parts of the soul of Christ from involvement in suffering, since the 'entire sinful soul must be healed',[26] he introduces a distinction between passion and compassion

whereby the latter can only be understood aright when it is
seen as a genuine 'co-suffering'. And so his thesis is:

> In what concerns the pain of suffering, *passio*, Christ
> suffered more intensely in his sensibility; in what
> concerns the pain of co-suffering, *compassio*, he suffered
> more intensely in his spiritual nature. But the pain of
> co-suffering was greater than the pain of suffering.

The distinction, taken over from Bernard and Hugh, was put
to use in two contrary ways: the physical pain inflicted on
Christ drew his soul into co-suffering, while the psychic pain
occasioned by our sins took along the body with it, and so
Christ wept over us. This spiritual suffering was the more
intense, because its ultimate cause was so much deeper –
offence against God and our separation from God, and also
because Christ's excess of love made him the more inclined
to suffer. The stronger love is, the more painful are the
wounds of co-suffering.

> And so his co-suffering goes beyond all other co-
> suffering, just as his suffering goes beyond all other
> (bodily) suffering, for the excess of his love transcends
> that of his suffering, compared with that of other people,
> even though in both respects he far went beyond
> them.[27]

These different attempts at a solution can be understood as
convergent, and thus as pointing to the fact that, on the
Mount of Olives, Christ's anguish was a co-suffering with
sinners, of such a kind that the real loss of God which
threatened them (the *poena damni*) was assumed by the
incarnate Love of God in the form of a *timor gehennalis*. Since
the sin of the world is 'laid' upon him, Jesus no longer
distinguishes himself and his fate from those of sinners – the
less so, according to Bonaventure, the more the love is – and
thus in that way he experiences the anxiety and horror which
they by rights should have known for themselves. The
possibility of such a real assumption of the sinful being of all

sinners may be rendered intelligible from three points of view:

(1) from the determination of the entire human consciousness of Jesus by the Logos and his eternal attitude of love towards the Father.

(2) through the absolute readiness, inherent in this determination, of Christ's human nature to be disposed of as a space for sheer (co-) suffering – a readiness to serve which expresses the Kenosis of the Logos in absolute obedience.

(3) through the real communication (solidarity) of the humanity assumed with the reality of humankind as a whole and its eschatological fate. (The rôle of judgment in all of this will be spoken of later.)

(c) Reduction to obedience

The prayer-agony on the Mount of Olives has as its unique object a saying 'Yes' to the will of the Father. The latter is content and form, excluding every other perspective. Here assuredly, there comes to its fulfilment the wider programme of living which Jesus had formulated in John's reporting (4, 34; 5, 19; 6, 38; 8, 55; 12, 49) and which received its final illustration in the gesture of the Footwashing, that pure piece of slave's service (13, 13ff). The sayings about service in the Synoptics have the same sense (Mark 10, 42ff, and parallels), Mark associating this service, in the end, with Jesus' words about giving his life as a ransom. The interpretation of his life in terms of the theology of the Servant of the Lord, found in the early apostolic preaching, confirms this manner of looking at things; the hymn found in Philippians 2, 5 and the Letter to the Hebrews extend this obedience (regarded as a summary of the life of Jesus) to the realm of pre-existence: his inclination was, in the large, already an act of obedience (Hebrews 10, 5–10). In both cases, however, obedience-existence moves towards a climax: for Philippians 2, 8, death on a cross, that is, the most shameful of deaths, and for Hebrews 5, 7ff the prayer-agony of Gethsemane, where he 'learned obedience'. What it is essential to note is that, at this culminating point, all broadly-based, that is, universally applicable, categories fall away. If the first Passion predictions explicitly mention Resurrection on the third day, and so exaltation after abasement, on the Mount of Olives all such peep-holes into future glorification are walled off. If, on the basis of both the early declarations and later, interpretative textual material, Jesus' destiny can be included within the Old Testament, and Jewish, scheme of the 'suffering righteous man' subsequently exalted and rewarded, on the Mount of Olives, with its narrow ways – 'my will, thy will' – every such schematism dissolves before the unique event, the one thing necessary.[28] No more can the categories of the late Jewish theology of martyrdom light up our problem, for the manifold   motivations   and   blessing-filled   effects   of martyrdom[29] remain as much outside this field of vision as do the specific attitudes, at once ethical and heroic, of the martyrs themselves. All 'meaning' is inexorably reduced to the humble preference for the will of the Father, as loved for its own sake. If the immortality hope of later apocalyptic and sapiential theology dulls provisionally the sting of death, there is no question of this here (cf. Wisdom 2, 24; 3, 2ff).

From the wider context only one element may be adduced in interpreting this 'culminating point': the rationale of the fundamental anxiety involved is, above all, 'shame' or 'infamy'. This already appears in the earliest stratum of the passion predictions (*apodokimasthēnai*: 'to be declared useless', Mark 8, 31; Luke 9, 22; 17, 25). It is developed in Paul (I Corinthians 4, 10ff, etc.), in First Peter 2, 19ff, and, at length, in the Letter to the Hebrews where the author speaks of 'the shame of the Cross' (12, 2) and of 'abuse for the Christ' (11, 26), and where the carrying of the Cross bespeaks essentially 'bearing abuse for him' (13, 13; cf. 10, 33). This is the final consequence of the 'I do not seek my own glory' (John 8, 50). Over against the martyrs' prayer of Daniel 3, 34, that God should not abandon those who suffer 'right to the end', *eis telos*, John sets down in conscious opposition the contrary affirmation – Jesus has continued his own 'right to the end', *eis telos*, 13, 1), namely, without looking to anything beyond the death in abuse that was his.

And yet, in contra-distinction to what happened in the

Temptations, the entire Passion proceeds without reference to the Devil. The whole story of the Passion passes him by, played out, as it is, between the Father and the Son. What matters in it is the bearing away of the sins of the world (John 1, 29). By that event, the enemy power is 'disarmed' (Colossians 2, 15) without the appearance of struggle against it.[30]

(4) Surrender

The principal concept which the term *tradere* (*paradidonai*)[31] represents becomes highly relevant at the close of the scene on the Mount of Olives, when Judas and the band of soldiers come into view.

> It is enough; the hour has come; the Son of man is betrayed into the hands of sinners. Rise, let us be going. See, my betrayer is at hand (Mark 14, 41–2; = Matthew 26, 45b–46).
>
> But this is your hour, and the power of darkness (Luke 22, 53).
>
> This 'handing over' has already been the frequent topic of the Passion predictions (Mark 9. 31 and parallels; 10, 33 and parallels; 10, 45 and parallels), the verb always taking the passive form and having as its subject the 'Son of man'. He is 'delivered up into the hands of men' or 'sinners', or, again, 'pagans'; the expected outcome is the Passion, itself expressed in a variety of formulae. As to the Baptist, he is also described as delivered up (Mark 1, 14, = Matthew 4, 12), doubtless in dependence on the story of the Passion of Jesus, with the additional comment (Mark 9, 13), 'they did to him whatever they pleased'.
>
> This is the continuation of the sacred tradition of the Old Testament where God as active subject delivers Israel from her enemies, from captivity, or from other evils for the sake of his covenant justice, Leviticus 26, 25; Deuteronomy 1, 27). But in the holy war God can

also deliver to his people the enemies of Israel (Numbers 21, 2 and 3 and frequently elsewhere). Compare First Samuel 24, 5a:
Behold, I will give your enemy into your hand, and you shall do to him as it shall seem good to you

This divine acting is in each case an act of judgment, that is, an act of the divine wrath.[32] 'He who is thus handed over is, in the truest sense of the word, abandoned by God.'[33] God ceases to dispose of him, and his enemy does so instead. At a later time, avenging angels can appear as executors (Ethiopian Enoch 63, 1). The apocrypha, the apocalypses and rabbinic literature take over this understanding of the idea unchanged.[34] Paul, at the beginning of the Letter to the Romans, makes a threefold use of it (Romans 1, 24, 26 and 28). The problem of knowing how God 'hands over' even the 'just' and 'innocent' is posed early and with increasing insistence, and finds a varied response. The notions of expiation and merit become central. At the same time, the three texts which speak of the Servant of the Lord as handed over (Isaiah 53, 6c and d, 12c) occupy an isolated position, and remain unused by the tradition up to Jesus and, again, after him, although the Septuagint gives them, *vis-à-vis* the Hebrew Bible, a marked emphasis (the Hebrew says once only that he was delivered, v. 12).

By contrast, from Daniel and Maccabbees onwards, the idea of martyrdom takes a premier place. This is the thought of the voluntary sacrifice of the just man (on behalf of God and the people, with expiating effect), lived out in such a fashion that the divine will to hand over and the human will to be handed over end up by coinciding.[35] The handing over of self is a 'total existential commitment',[36] which does not necessarily entail dying, yet risks dying as a consequence of totally obedient service to God.[38] In later Judaism, where reward and punishment after death were presumed, courage before the prospect of death is no longer the supreme courage, and the wise man, from a kind of observation post, is able to contemplate the lot of the good and the evil here below and there beyond. The wicked condemn the just to 'a shameful death, for, according to what he says, he will be protected', but the just (having been disciplined a little, . . . will receive great good', whereas the impious, who despised the just, will undergo punishment (Wisdom 2–3).

If here the drama of the Passion of Jesus seems to receive in advance a sort of objective frame, it is a frame which, as an 'event of promise', is melted down in the definitive fulfilment. In the passive mood of the 'being delivered into the hands of sinful men', God remains he who acts, and does so with the inexorable, ineluctable character (*dei*) of an act of judgment, even if what is at stake is no longer the wrath of God but 'the definite plan and foreknowledge of God' (Acts 2, 23), and ultimately of his love, since 'he did not spare his own Son but gave him up for us all' (Romans 8, 32). No more does 'condemnation' follow (Romans 8, 3). The later texts of the New Testament complete the picture by expressing ever more clearly the self-gift which Jesus made of himself. The crucial change can be observed when the causal *dia*, found in the pre-Pauline parallel saying, 'he was put to death for, *dia*, our trespasses and raised for, *dia*, our justification' (Romans 4, 25) is replaced by a final *anti*, 'for the sake of', something which occurs for the first time, in the celebrated half-verse,[39] removed from its context, which is Mark 10, 45b: 'to give his life as a ransom for many', or by a final *huper* (I Corinthians 11, 24; Luke 22, 19, a Eucharistic reference; I Peter 2, 21; Romans 8, 3, using *peri*); to 'give himself' appears explicitly in Galatians 2, 20, and in numerous parallels.[40] At the decisive moment, Luke replaces the ultimate *paradōsis* by the Father, namely, the Son's cry of abandonment on the Cross, with the ultimate *paradōsis* by the Son, who gives over his spirit into the hands of his Father (Luke 23, 46, citing Psalm 31, 6; cf. John 19, 30). To this there corresponds the warning in First Peter 2, 23, to bear suffering with patience, since 'Christ trusted to him who judges justly' (in the sense that he 'commended himself').

It conforms to the *Verbum-Caro* of the New Testament,[41] and to the co-humanity which it implies, that besides the Father who hands over, and the Son who is handed over, there appear as a third actor the traitor who is a hander-over also. Judas, one of the Twelve, is 'he who hands over', the *traditor*. On the other hand, by his action, he becomes the representation of unbelieving and faithless Israel, which rejects its Messiah, and is thereby itself delivered up (for a time: Romans 11). The inter-play between the God who hands over and the sinners who, in handing over, betray, has an extremely paradoxical character, although as early as the Old Testament, God has human executors of his justice who are nonetheless not exonerated from the blame of their actions but obliged to take cognisance of the judgment that weighs in turn on them. The inter-play can be interpreted by reflexion as a mystery of God's providence (Acts 2, 23), and in terms of the relative ignorance of the Jews (Acts 3, 17: cf. also the mitigating 'repentance' of Judas in Matthew 27, 3), but it can also be misused in a polemical fashion as the means of identifying a personal or national 'black sheep'.[42] The eschatological situation requires us to see a link between this betrayal and all powers hostile to God (John 13, 27). The stereotypical character[43] of the gospel formulations allows this to take on an adamantine objectivity and in that way pays homage to God. On the one hand, Judas steps forward with Israel, for the time of the world's history, in the visible 'rôle' of reprobation,[44] but, on the other hand, from the perspective of the universalist affirmations of the New Testament, he is the visible agent of all that sinners – Christians, Jews, pagans – do in common (Romans 5, 12ff; I Timothy 2, 6; John 12, 32, etc.).

The handing over of Jesus in the Passion remains a mystery; for this reason, the concurrently operative elements cannot be strait-jacketed into any comprehensible system. And if, in the textual history of the New Testament, there are different levels of interpretation, this differentiation should not be understood unilaterally as the replacement of primitive aspects by others which arise later and come to predominate, but must be taken theologically as the slow integration of such aspects. To be sure, there stands at the outset the inexorable judging activity of God: Jesus, the 'servant of God' (Acts 3, 13 and 26; 4, 27, etc.), the 'just one' (Acts 3, 14) was delivered by God, like the just of the Old Testament, into the hands of sinners − by sinners but also for sinners, since he who was handed over consented so to be, in his absolute obedience (Philippians 2). From this point on there arises the Trinitarian theme which develops in three forms: simultaneously: God the Father hands over his Son ('does not spare his Son'), thanks to his love for us (Romans 8, 32; John 3, 16), but it is also due to Christ's love for us (Romans 8, 35; Galatians 2, 20; Ephesians 5, 1, etc.), in such a way that in Christ's gratuitous self-gift (John 10, 18) the Father's unconditional love becomes plain.[45] Undeniably, paranesis increasingly takes pride of place. Jesus' gift of self becomes the model for our imitation. First, it is Paul who is selected to reproduce in himself Christ's sufferings; afterwards (I Peter 2, 18ff; Hebrews 10, 32ff), it is every individual suffering unjustly, or suffering for faith. The late Jewish theology of martyrdom is introduced laterally into the theology of the Passion and produces a flattening out of a moralising kind which threatens the absolute originality of Christ's Passion. Over against this 'fall' we must hold fast to the original aspect of judgment, the fundamental affirmation involved, in all its inexorable character − whether despite or precisely because of the stepping forth into visibility of the love of God, and despite a certain imitability of this action by grace. Even Christ's self-giving remains obedience (Philippians 2, John 5), and the harshest obedience, bitter obedience, at that (the scene on the Mount of Olives), and the enemy to which Christ is delivered remains the 'power of darkness' (Luke 22, 53).[46] Christ's 'shackling' and 'being led away' by Judas and the troop of soldiers shows that in an image.

The theology of the delivering up can only be maintained in a Trinitarian fashion. That God 'hands over' his Son

> forms part of the most unheard of affirmations of the New Testament. We must understand the expression to 'hand over' in its proper meaning, without diluting it to a mere 'mission' or 'gift'. Here was done what Abraham was spared from doing in Isaac. The Christ was deliberately given over by the Father to a deadly destiny. God rejected him and delivered him to the death-dealing

powers, whether these be called 'man' or 'death' . . .
'God made him to be sin' (II Corinthians 5, 21), the
Christ is the accursed of God . . . Here the *theologia
crucis* comes to expression in a way than which none
more radical can be conceived.[47]

But this aspect is only true to the New Testament if it is
completed by reference to the active gift which Christ made
of himself – a gift which, however, cannot, once again, be
treated as an isolated moment without running the risk of
losing sight of the eschatological horizon, and slipping back
into a theology of martyrdom. Christ must be God if he is so
to place himself at the disposal of the event of love which
flows from the Father and would reconcile the world with
itself that in him the entire darkness of all that is counter to
God can be judged and overcome. In this happening, the
active handing over by men can only play a subordinate role,
and the very contradiction between human treason and the
love of God in giving his Son must be bonded together with
the 'contradiction of the Cross' and there find its resolution.
But for that to happen, the handing over, the arrest, the
placing in chains, and the leading away by myrmidons must
be taken with historical seriousness of an absolute kind.

(5) Trial and Condemnation

Here we are dealing simply with the theological content of
the great trial scenes,[48] a content which presupposes an
original unity of meaning in the reports, despite the diversity
of these scenes and the fact that they result from the synthesis
of various traditions.[49] We must consider: (1) the theology of
Jesus' condemnation by mankind in its entirety; (2) the
attitude of the Church in this event; (3) the attitude of Jesus.

(a) Christians, Jews, pagans as judge and jury

The theme of the 'handing over' (*paradidonai*) must now be
developed in the ampler context of the theological structure

of humankind, which consists of the mass of those who are non-elected (the pagans), the chosen people (the Jews), and the disciples, chosen anew from out of that people (the Christians). The one who 'hands over' in the strict sense is Judas, one of the Twelve (Mark 10, 4, etc.) who delivers Jesus to the Jews; the latter 'deliver' him to Pilate (Mark 15, 1), Pilate then 'sends him away' to Herod who again 'sends him back' (Luke 23, 7 and 11), but finally 'hands him over' to the Jews (Mark 15, 15; Matthew 27, 26; John 9, 16) and 'delivers him up to their will' (Luke 23, 25). The chain of these handings-over is forged theologically. Judas is interiorly attached to the profane ideal of the Messiah shared by the leading Jews; he denies his New Testament faith in favour of an alleged Old Testament alternative. But the Jewish leaders have never understood the theological themes of the 'Messiah' and 'Son of God' (Mark 14, 61) save politically. This is why the political turn which their indictment before Pilate takes (Luke 23, 2: agitation among the people; refusal to pay taxes; desire to rule) does not, as they opine, correspond to a diplomatic disguise for their religious motives, but rather unmasks their convictions for the fundamentally heathen politicking which they are: 'We have no king but Caesar' (John 19, 15). So the question as to whether Jesus was judged by a Jewish tribunal or a Roman one, and whether he was condemned because of his claim to the title of Messiah or as 'King of the Jews' is an insignificant one, as is even, indeed, in the last analysis, the question of whether his Messianic identity was explicitly posed before the Sanhedrin, or whether, alternatively, his claim to be the eschatological Saviour in person implicitly entailed his Messiahship. An express confession of that Messiahship before his judges would, no doubt, at that unique point of intersection render history and Christian faith coincident,[50] but a situation where all this was simply implicit would amount, practically speaking, to the same thing.[51] The three-fold handing-over (by Christians to the Jews; by Jews to the pagans; by pagans to death) was for the early Church so theologically impressive that the Acts of the Apostles gives it a post-fulfilment in Paul (21, 27ff). Moreover, it constitutes the manner in which, prior to all subsequent differentiation, all of humanity's representatives, considered theologically, are integrated from the outset into guilty responsibility for Jesus' death. As Romans 11, 32 puts it:

> For God has consigned all men to disobedience, that he may have mercy on all.

Only afterwards can a certain graduated ascription of responsibility be theologically envisaged, in terms of the descending scale of seriousness of the actions whereby Jesus is betrayed. 'Satan entered' into Judas (John 13, 27); he is 'lost', the 'son of perdition' (John 17, 12), whose frightful end (Matthew 27, 3–10) corresponds to the prophetic word and becomes a ghastly public warning (Acts 1, 18ff).[52] Only when Christendom has acknowledged this shameful stain on its escutcheon can it look around for another scape-goat and come to underline the guilt of the Jews which, in the assertion of the Johannine Jesus, exceeds that of Pilate (John 19, 11). That the story of the Passion was, from the earliest Christian times onwards, contemplated and commented on within the framework of Old Testament events (and thus *theologically*),[53] allows the great period of rejection (described by Jeremiah and Ezekiel) to form the background for the new, and more acute, situation of guilt and reprobation – even though the latter is not to be assessed as absolutely definitive (cf. the themes of ignorance, Luke 23, 24; Acts 3, 17, and the divine faithfulness to the promises Romans 11, 1 and 29). However this be, the fundamental refusal to let oneself be led by God (Isaiah 7, 9b; 28, 16; 30, 15), as in the days of Jeremiah, and the political claim to superior knowledge remain the principal causes of their misjudgment, which comes to its climax in the decisive question and answer, 'Are you the Christ?', 'I am' (Mark 14, 61ff).

Three elements of theological demonstration are adduced, but that in merely illustrative guise. They are: 1. the historically certain 'saying about the temple' (even if Mark 14, 57 is a later insertion), in which Jesus applied to himself the ancient prophecies about the destruction of the Temple

and its eschatological re-building (Jeremiah 26; Ezekiel 40ff);
2. the use of Psalm 110 and Daniel 7, 13 to underline his
dignity as Messiah (Matthew 26, 64; Mark 14, 62, and Luke
drop the apocalyptic text from Daniel, retaining only the
text of the enthronement psalm); 3. lastly – in the move
from the Jewish tribunal to the pagan one – the title of king,
put forward in Pilate's presence (Mark 15, 2), as the
inscription affixed to the Cross proves (Mark 15, 26), and
which in John (where the word 'king' appears twelve times)
is interpreted in function of its theological significance. In this
title, the primitive Old Testament idea of theocracy (Judges
8, 23) is united with the authentic concept of the Israelite
king as God's representative (II Chronicles 9, 8), an idea
further elevated by the prediction of a Davidide king
(II Samuel 7, 16) who will be yet higher than David himself
(Psalm 110, in Matthew 22, 41), and must therefore be a
'king who is not of this world' (John 18, 36ff; 19, 11).

If the three-fold chain of the men who hand over convicts
all human beings in their guiltiness, the same is no less true of
the way in which all the guilty try to offload their
responsibility for the crime. So Judas who, through
'repentance', brings back the money (though indeed it is not
accepted); so the Jews who do not put the blood-money in
the Temple treasury but use it to acquire a burial-ground for
strangers(!); so, in the game of exchanges, Pilate who, more
than any of the others, would have liked to release the
prisoner; so Herod who, disappointed in the entertainment
he had hoped for, sends back the condemned man; so the
leaders of the people who invoke their lack of political
authorisation to judge the issue (John 8, 31), whilst Pilate,
constrained to pronounce judgment by political pressure of
the gravest kind (John 19, 12) declines to accept any moral
responsibility (Matthew 27, 24). No one wishes to be
responsible. That is why they are all guilty.

(b) The attitude of the Church

From the manner in which the Church has imaged herself in
the story of the Passion her realisation that there can be no

immediate 'imitation of Christ' is evident. Peter's betrayal and the flight of the other disciples may well, and to one's heart's content, be placed under a prophetic 'This had to be' (Matthew 26, 31ff) and find themselves predicted by the Lord himself (John 16, 32). But this in no way prevents the disciples from being unmasked thereby in their faithlessness, cowardice, inconstancy, and from being pilloried before the world. Only John situates himself on the further side of this problematic, in that he covers the flight by Jesus' words of farewell (18, 8). Yet he cannot omit the denial of Peter, since he needs it as a theological element in his teaching on Peter's investiture with his office (21, 17, as presupposed in 21, 19). Everything that Peter essays in the context of the Passion is wrongheaded: his request that the Lord should not suffer, which makes him 'Satan, whose thoughts are not those of God but of man' and approximates him to Judas (Matthew 16, 23; cf. Luke 22, 31); his solemn affirmation that he will not betray, even if all the others do so – he will be the principal author of the denial (Matthew 26, 34 and parallels); his assiduity in shielding the Master from attackers – if he draws the profane sword, he will perish by it (John 18, 11; Matthew 26, 52), and Jesus, by curing Malchus, takes up a position against him (Luke 22, 51); his feeling of responsibility, which makes him believe he should observe the proceedings – precisely at this watching-post, he fails lamentably (Mark 14, 66 and parallels). The only way of being there left to him is to stand to one side, and weep bitterly – more over himself than over the Lord. The others fly, head over heels, and the young man of the Gospel of Mark who abandons his only piece of clothing in order to escape (Mark 14, 52) forms the symbolic and paradoxical antitype to Jesus' stripping of his garments – what the latter lets befall by obedience is for the former an involuntary deprivation. But behind the disappearing Church of males, and of office, there appears, 'at a distance' a persevering element: the Church of women who 'followed him and ministered to him': 'several', says Mark, in addition to the three whom he enumerates (15, 41). They will be present at the burial and make up the first Easter witnesses. They stand there 'looking' (*theōrousai*), contemplative, not active or co-suffering or – differently from the mourning women of Jerusalem whom Jesus rebuffs – ascribing to themselves a positive part by their tears. On this occasion, the only active participant is an outsider, on whom the Cross is imposed (Luke 23, 26), along with the two 'malefactors' with whom Jesus crucified forms a new community of the condemned. They it is who enjoy now pre-eminence over against the elect.

In the face of all this, the Johannine account brings a mysterious clarification: the presence of a Church of love at the foot of the Cross (in contradistinction to the absent Church of office), represented above all by the *Mater dolorosa* and the 'disciple whom Jesus loved' to whom he entrusts his mother: a nucleus, here stepping forth into visibility, of the Church which 'stands by' the Cross, and which afterwards (in the question addressed to Peter, Do you love me *more* than these?) is absorbed into the petrine Church, there to 'remain' (21, 22ff), despite everything, as a residue inexplicable by Peter and resistant to its own reduction.

(c) The attitude of Jesus

At the end of the prayer-agony, *disponibilité* in its fulness is re-conquered. 'It is enough' (*apechei*, Mark 14, 41).[54] Now Jesus is free from every bond, whether exterior or interior. At the moment of the first arrest, and the binding (Mark 14, 46; Matthew 26, 50; John 18, 12), the voluntary character of the self-surrender is strongly emphasised: there was no point at which he was not at their disposal (Mark 14, 48ff and parallels, transferred by John to the scene before Annas, no doubt correctly, and over against Luke 22, 52). John extends this majestic liberty almost to the boundary with Docetism (18, 6). Mark and Matthew locate the binding in terms of the authority of Scripture, without being able to indicate any particular text (Mark 14, 49; Matthew 26, 56). But the self-surrender is, on the one hand, obedience to the Father (John 18, 11), and, on the other, a decision in favour of defencelessness – renunciation of the 'twelve legions of

Angels' (Matthew 26, 53),[55] whence his order countermanding the attempt to defend him (Luke 22, 51 and parallels) and the instruction to Judas, 'Do your business', *eph' ho parei* (Matthew 26, 50; cf. John 13, 27); whence also the ever more dogged silence since now every speech would only come up against unbelief ('If I tell you, you will not believe', Luke 22, 67; = John 10, 25), a silence that arouses wonderment and which Mark 15, 45ff registers, incontestably, against the background of Isaiah 53, 7: the lamb that opens not its mouth). Whatever historical form the mockery and sarcastic play with the prisoner may have taken – and probably there were two principal scenes, one after the nocturnal interrogation at the house of Annas (and, less plausibly, after the morning session of the Sanhedrin), the other in the courtyard of the Roman soldiers' barracks – theologically, they are *résumés* of Old Testament antecedents, especially Isaiah 50, 6: 'I hid not my face from shame and spitting'. The game for which the blindfolded prisoner is struck, and must say by whom he is struck, has several layers of significance: for Luke it is a commonplace farce perpetrated by the soldiers; for Mark, the 'Servant of the Lord' shines through; for Matthew, finally, Christ appears as prophet, and as messianic high-priest.[56] He rolls like a ball between the competitors, thrown from one to another, held by none, undesired by all. The passover amnesty opens, on the human level, a lucky possibility: Pilate would like to ally himself with popular opinion against their leaders, but the political prisoner is the preferred candidate, and appeal to the intermediate authority, Herod Antipas, has no better fortune. At whatever point, historically, the Johannine *Ecce homo* scene (which presupposes the flagellation and the crowning with thorns) took place, whether in the middle of the trial or at its end, it constitutes an image which draws together a multiplicity of aspects: the surrendered one is ushered out with a 'Here's the man!' onto the stage of the world, and in the *Ecce homo* we hear an *Ecce Deus* also. Here now is the only valid and obligatory image of what the sin of the world is like for the heart of God, made visible in 'the' man. In the image of the complete Kenosis, there shines 'the light of the

knowledge of the glory of God in the face of Jesus Christ'
(II Corinthians 4, 6).

(6) The Crucifixion

(a) The Cross as judgment

Above all, the Cross is the full achievement of the divine
judgment on 'sin' (II Corinthians 5, 21) summed up, dragged
into the daylight and suffered through in the Son. Moreover,
the sending of the Son in 'sinful flesh' took place only so as
to make it possible to 'condemn (*katakrinein*) sin in the flesh'
(Romans 8, 3).

In John, judgment formulae seem contradictory: on the
one hand, Jesus is the holder of all judgment (5, 22), he
exercises judgment (8, 16 and 26), for which function he has
come (9, 39); but on the other hand, he has come not to
judge, but to save (3, 17; 12, 47). However, he accomplishes
judgment by means of his existence (3, 18), and that,
evidently, is bound up with his elevation on the Cross (12,
31); his advocate, the Spirit, will undertake the defence of his
innocence, at his trial, on the basis of, precisely, the Cross,
and over against the world (16, 7ff). In what follows, we can
respond only partially to the question as to the relation
between Cross and judgment. To respond fully, it would be
necessary to deal with the doctrine of justification (expounded
elsewhere in the series *Mysterium Salutis* of which *Mysterium
Paschale* originally formed part). It would have to be shown
how the just man is condemned with justice, so that the
unjust and the sinner may be with justice justified. Only the
first part of this affirmation, expressive as it is of the central
drama of revelation, will be studied here.

To understand the concluding (Johannine) statements about
judgment, the best route to follow is what which leads from
the Old Testament to Paul, and from Paul to John. In the
Old Testament, God is judge inasmuch as he is guardian of
the Law which he instituted with the Covenant (*mishpat*),
and so on the basis of his covenantal grace and fidelity.

Wherein he shows himself, for what he is: the veracious one, ever the same, to whose Name it belongs to preserve the covenant in its gracious character. And this is supremely true where the deficient partner, man, opposes himself to this grace, setting his own injustice against the justice of God, and so has need of 'correction' in order to return to covenant righteousness (cf. Augustine and Anselm: *rectitudo*). In the Old Testament, the Law which God establishes is the foundation of all confidence, all hope; his justice is simply another, and indispensable, aspect of his mercy, his faithfulness and his patience. That God 'is righteous, he loves righteous deeds' (Psalm 11, 7) is, for the man who knows the true God, a tautology. As the Just One, he is the God of grace, and vice versa. How could he answer man's refusal to dwell in the space of his covenant grace save by his own refusal to see the justice he has founded and guaranteed attacked and contradicted, and how could he not, then, give his refusal an effective form? He will and must 'himself be judge' (Psalm 50, 6). He who by grace has involved himself with man and concluded with him a pact that is – from God's side – indissoluble, must, for the sake of his own faithfulness and veracity, 'become enraged', rather than turn away, in a non–Godlike superior indifference, from the devastation of his work, 'letting the odd be called even'. Rather must he take seriously his covenant partner and by judgment, correction, punishment lead him back to the law which the deviant is incapable of restoring by himself. For what human being can re-establish the right of God that he has destroyed? Can it be done *sola compunctione*? Whoever is minded to support that point of view should take to heart Anselm's answer to Boso's suggestion: 'Nondum considerasti quanti ponderis sit peccatum'.[57] This man is

> before God completely and irretrievably impossible. For unrighteousnessness is horror and loathing before him. It must, simply and straightforwardly, be gone. So majestic is God's righteousness evermore against unrighteousness. Its existence is insupportable in his presence. It is gripped by the life of God, consumed, and annihilated as dry wood by fire.[58]

The perpetrator of injustice *as such* cannot appeal to God without having to expect the repudiation of his sin. And only inasmuch as he *as such* is repudiated can the grace of God turn towards him. But there is only *one* human being there, just as God too is *one*, he who is wrathful *because* he is gracious. How can this necessarily two-faceted event work itself out? Perhaps in the manner portrayed in the Deuetronomic History, with its constant succession of acts of correction and engracement, until finally the excess of sin demands a definitive reprobation, from out of which there survives only the promise (or hope) of final salvation (since God must indeed be faithful to himself, Ezekiel 36, 21ff)? To this *polumerōs kai polutropōs* (Hebrews 1, 1) of the Old Testament the *ephapax* of the New Testament (9, 12) puts an end. For God guarantees henceforth both sides of his covenant, the divine and the human, and as the God-man actualises his entire righteousness, the *dikaiosunē theou*. The injustice is not cleared away by half-measures and compromises, but by drastic measures which make a clean sweep of it, so that all the world's injustice is consumed by the total wrath of God, that the total righteousness of God may be accessible to the sinner. That is the Gospel according to Paul[59] who sees the fulfilment of the directional meaning of the entire Old Testament in the Cross and Resurrection of Christ. No one other than God himself was capable of *this* purification – in no case was man who, in his entirety, is a sinner before God, there being no distinction possible here between a fallible empirical 'I' and an infallible or transcendental counterpart. Only God, taking manhood in Christ, becomes in one single Person both 'subject and object' of judgment and justification, and places himself on the side of men so to defend, on their behalf, the cause of God. The *justitia Dei* acquired for us by Christ on the Cross in the judgment of God is certainly first and foremost a *justitia aliena*, insofar as it is the righteousness of *God*, established by him and of course in the *alienum* of the sinful world. But precisely in this way, that justice becomes our very own, valid for us, and able to be appropriated by us, *propria*, and so for the first time truly the *justitia propria Dei* in us, (since it makes us God's sons and *familiares*). Just as are 'in Him at home',[60] so is he at home in us. All of that presupposes for Paul the judgment of the Cross wherein God, as the man Christ, takes upon himself the totality of 'Adam's' guilt (Romans 5, 15–21) in order that, as the 'bodily' incorporation of sin and enmity (II Corinthians 5, 21; Ephesians 2, 14), he might be 'handed over' (Romans 4, 25) to be 'condemned through God' (Romans 8, 3), and as the Life of God, which died in God-forsakenness and was buried, to be divinely 'raised for our justification' (Romans 4, 25). That is not myth, but the central biblical message and, where Christ's Cross is concerned, it must not be rendered innocuous as though the Crucified, in undisturbed union with God, had prayed the Psalms and died in the peace of God.

It is precisely the John[61] who has been suspected of underlining the divinity of Christ in his Passion to the limit of Gnosticism[62] who presents the judgment character of the Cross with a radical force beyond even that of Paul. Over against W. Thusing, J. Blank has shown that the Son's return to the Father does not, in John, take place in two stages: first, the 'lifting up' on the Cross ('as the serpent was lifted up', 3, 14; cf. 12, 32ff, the 'lifting up' indicating the kind of death involved), and then a subsequent 'glorification' in Resurrection and Ascension, but, on the contrary, the 'lifting up' and the 'glorification' are, for John, a single indivisible happening, so that the Cross, precisely, though together with the Resurrection, forms part of the glorification. That is why

> the event of the death on the Cross is seen from the start otherwise than in its isolated historical and purely earthly facticity

namely, in a way very close to that of Paul, as the objective, eschatological event of judgment, the 'hour' when God 'glorifies' himself (12, 28) or glorifies his 'Name'[63] (in the righteousness of his love), and, to be sure, glorifies himself in his Son who embodies his judgment, making the Son thereby the real manifestation of his glorification. Now in 12, 20–36 the 'hour' is characterised at once as 'glorification' and as 'judgment' – at once objective judgment (*krisis*) and subjective being judged (the experience of judgment, *taraché*). The latter ('Now is my soul troubled', 12, 27) means that

> he who came to conquer death lets himself be seized by the knowledge of the potency, hostility and counter-Godliness of this power whose conquest is at stake.[64]

The expressions 'to be troubled' and 'to be deeply moved' (*enebrimēsato*, 11, 33; cf. Matthew 9, 30; Mark 1, 43) are closely related. Jesus must 'suffer to the end' the counter-godly power, and that 'in the Spirit' – which is 'not a magnitude of the psychological order' but the selfsame reality in which, in 4, 23, 'the Father is worshipped'. By the additional remark that Jesus 'bears testimony', this 'trouble' is

> still more stoutly fortified than the figure of speech in 11, 33 against misinterpretation a simple feeling impulse ... As *taraché* the suffering comes ultimately from the Father and is something accepted.

What we are dealing with here is one of those 'pointed' Johannine expressions, which contain more than the customary use of language allows, and which aim to mark out a unique Christological event in an analogical manner.

> A spiritual motion takes possession of Jesus, having such strength that it would throw other men into utter confusion.[65]

It is the same with the 'cup' which Jesus must drink (John 18, 11 and parallels). It is not a matter of just any suffering, but the Old Testament, and also apocalyptic, cup of the divine anger which the sinner must drain (Isaiah 51, 17 and 22; Jeremiah 25,15; Ezekiel 23, 31ff; Psalm 75, 9, etc.). Again, the same holds true of the 'baptism' with which he must be baptised, which corresponds to the Old Testament sinking beneath the destroying flood (Isaiah 43, 2; Psalm 42, 8; 68, 2ff, etc.). But what unrolls in our context is the *krisis* on the world as a whole (John 12, 31), the wholly objective event of judgment, wherein the sin of the world is, in the fullest way possible, laid bare.

> It is a judgment which unveils, convicts, condemns. It is not only a sentence passed on the state of the world, but a judgment which chastises, which ends, which destroys. Through it, 'this world', the old aion, really ceases to exist, it comes to its end, and – this is the quite decisive point – to Jesus Christ himself.[66]

So too, in Paul, the world-rulers are 'de-potentiated' on the Cross (that is what the 'being cast out' means, John 12, 31; cf. Colossians 1, 20ff; 2, 14; Ephesians 2, 14ff),[67] but not without a prior coming of the 'prince of this world', who advances for the decisive assault against Jesus, but 'finds nothing' in him which would sustain his own claim to lordship (John 14, 30).[68] And so unrighteousness is shattered against the infinite justified righteousness of God and the tormented final humiliation of Jesus becomes his definitive exaltation, his 'enthronement as cosmic Kyrios in the Passion as a whole'. But that means, for John just as for Paul, that 'before any glory . . . there is, definitively, and irreversibly, the Cross', since

> no one can be exalted who has not been crucified. And the glory of Jesus is first understood aright when it is understood as the glory of the Crucified

– manifested in the Resurrection. That also signifies, or so J. Blank concludes in agreement with K. Barth – that in the Cross

> God has made a decision, objectively and independently of any subsequent taking up of a position on the part of man, for the salvation, the rescue, of the world . . . The de-potentialisation of the ruler of this world is the reverse side of the divine decision – a positive decision, ontically real in the Christ event, and not merely a 'judicial' or

'forensic' decision – to save humanity . . . By that is also determined the meaning of Christ's affirmation that, from the exalted Cross, he will 'draw all men' to himself.[69]

(b) The words from the Cross

In the light of their theological interpretation by Paul and John, the Passion accounts as a whole take on their theological visage. Let us take the words from the Cross first. Primacy must go to the cry of abandonment – in Mark the single word from the Cross – and only relativised to the position of the 'fourth word' by an arbitrary decision about ordering in a harmonisation of the gospels. In the theological context, it is, like the Johannine *tarachē*, 'pointed': that word directs us to the unique point which is Jesus, and in no way to the beginning of a psalmic recitation which finishes with the glorification of the suffering individual and insists on being interpreted within its own limits. As we have shown there are, in the Old Testament and in the history of the Church, forms of abandonment deeper than what many of those who placard their veto here – be it theological, historical or[70] exegetical – would wish to tolerate on the Cross. Here truly the axiom that Irenaeus laid down against the Gnostics is valid, that axiom which has it that Christ could not demand of his disciples any suffering that he had not experienced himself as Master. [71] That is why the dreadful testings, *peirasmoi*, in God-abandonment in both Old and New Testaments are not at all, in the first place, tests of a pedagogic kind, or (certainly not!) stages in a Neo–platonic schema of ascent, but must be interpreted, rather, in christological fashion.

Besides this fundamental word, the other words from the Cross could, without any essential narrowing of their bearing, be understood as interpretations of that actual situation of judgment (both objective and subjective) which the events render distinct enough. So the word 'I thirst' in John, which expresses the abandonment in another, no less impressive, way: the source of living water, springing up to eternal life, of which all are invited to drink (4, 10 and 13ff; 7, 37ff) has audibly drained away and itself become thirsty ground. The word must be historically well-founded, since it explains, better than does the cry in Matthew and Mark, the soaking of a sponge with vinegar which follows. The mocking comments about the doctor who helped others but cannot help himself (Matthew 27, 42), who trusted in God and now has to be saved by God if he is the son of God, if truly God loves him, and so forth, point to the same paradox as the cry of thirsting. Similarly, the giving over of the Mother of Jesus to John has an historic probability, since it makes Mary's future living in the house of John intelligible. Yet, while Jesus' loving concern for his Mother occupies the foreground of the picture, its background is a theological meaning: the Son grants the Mother solidarity with the Cross in that he withdraws from her – just as the Father has withdrawn from the Son: *homo purus pro Deo vero*.[72] The Lucan words, whether they be historical or not, interpret the gracious character of the judgment of the Cross: the plea for a pardoning (Luke 23, 34a) is objectively contained in the Passion itself, while the word of grace addressed to the thief understands the crisis of the Cross, first and foremost, by reference to Matthew 25, 31ff, as a separation of the sheep and the goats, yet also, and fundamentally, goes beyond the meaning of this parable in the direction of John: the judgment of the Cross is, as such, a judgment in grace, just as, indeed, in Luke 23, 48, after the death of Jesus, not only does the centurion 'praise God', but 'all the multitudes . . . returned home beating their breasts'. The replacement of Psalm 22, 2 by Psalm 31, 6 (Luke 23, 46a: 'Father, into thy hands I commend my spirit!') interprets the (objective-subjective) abandonment in the sense of John also, since the latter knows, on the one hand, the 'giving over of the Spirit' (19, 30), and, on the other, the completing of the commission ('consummatum est', 19, 30a). The *paratithemai* of Luke thus occupies a half-way position between the simple *exepneusen* of Mark 15, 37, the *aphēken* of Matthew 27, 50 and the very emphatic *paredōken to Pneuma* of John, whose meaning is, without any shadow of doubt, that in the unitary event of *krisis* and glorification which is the Cross, the Spirit becomes 'free' in the moment when Jesus breathes his last (cf. John 7, 39), and thus can be breathed into the Church, undelayed, by the Risen One. (John 20, 22).[73] In Luke himself the Pneuma is stated to be the Spirit of mission while for John the registration (even by Jesus as subject) of the completed nature of the work given him to do (*to ergon teleiōsas*) provisionally in 17, 5) is the solemn confirmation that the *telos* (13, 1), the *eschaton*, has really been reached.

(c) The events of the Crucifixion

Mark, Matthew (especially) and Luke (derivatively) interpret the eschatological dimension in apocalyptic key: first, by the tearing of the temple curtain[74] which only in Mark signifies, in the first instance, the abolition of the ancient Law and cultus, whereas in Matthew its significant background is the destruction of the old aion, for the temple curtain was interwoven with images of the stars, and passed for a reproduction of the cosmos (Philo, Josephus).[75] The cosmic darkening is reported by three Synoptics: it is the way in which they express the objectivity and cosmic significance of the inner 'hour of darkness'. This feature is also incorporated by Matthew into his much wider-ranging apocalyptic tableau for whose design the Cross coincides with the end of the world, with – to be more precise – the 'Day of Yahweh'. The darkness over the whole earth is not primarily, in the light of Amos 8, 9–10, a sympathetic mourning of the cosmos for the death of the Jesus, but a mourning of God himself: 'I will make of this mourning, mourning for an only son' as the echoing word of Zechariah 12, 10 has it. In the other signs too – the quaking of the earth, the splitting open of rocks, the opening of graves, the cosmos is in no way active, but rather is passively shaken to its foundations by the final event. If the happenings concerned are 'familiar eschatological signs'[76] they are not simply set side by side, paratactically, for the earthquake leads to the rock-splitting, the rock-splitting to the grave-opening, and the grave-opening to the emptying of Sheol which, in the presence of this dead man on the Cross, must yield up its prey. The clarification 'after his resurrection' may be a later addition, intended to bring the statement that 'many bodies of the saints who had fallen asleep were raised, and coming out of the tombs ... they went into the holy city and appeared to many' into concord with the non-negotiable affirmation that Jesus is the first-born of those who are raised (I Corinthians 15, 20; Colossians 1, 18). It is a chronological precision, in the midst of eschatology, in the service of theological exactitude. Above all, it offers a superb perspective on the true eschatological event inaugurated by the death of Jesus. Not horizontally, in a worldly future, but in vertical relation to the time of this world, this resurrection leads into the true 'holy city', the 'Jerusalem above' (Galatians 4, 26; Hebrews 12, 22): of this the earthly apparitions are but the parable. Just as the thieves are but parables for the 'co-crucifixion' of Jesus with sinners, so is this legendary scene a symbol for solidarity in the Resurrection.[77] Despite this sudden glimpse of the apocalypse, which allows us to see a supra-temporal identity between the death on the Cross and the last day, the middle of time and its end, Matthew adds on the word of confession of the Roman officer 'and his people', and so a glimpse into the earthly future, inasfar as here we find pagans converting, just as, in a Passion context in John 12, pagans who wished to see Jesus first came into view.

It is to the same context, at once apocalyptic and ecclesiological, that John's testimony about the lance that pierced Jesus' side directs us, since the prophetic word, 'They will look on him whom they have pierced' (Zechariah 12, 10) is cited as appropriately in the genuine historic context of the Passion (John 19, 37) – evidently as an image to be contemplated henceforward – as in the apocalyptic context of the Christ who comes on the clouds for the final judgment (Apocalypse 1, 7). To this image there belong as finally determinative traits: the thrust of the lance, the opening of the heart, and the outflow of blood and water – to which we must return. Depicted with these features, the exalted Pierced One is – even more than the 'Ecce Homo' (19, 5) – the definitive meditation icon, gazed on by John himself and solemnly presented (19, 35), the 'Ecce Deus', the final representation and interpretation of the God whom no one has seen (1, 18). In that image, the theology of the Serpent that was Lifted Up and on whom, for Wisdom 16, 6, our eyes must be set if we are to obtain salvation, also comes to its fulfilment.[78] It is the same image, the icon of the Father, simultaneously transfigured and wondered at, which Thomas is to touch with his hands (20, 26ff), although a believing glance (for John, looking, knowing, believing pass over into each other) would have sufficed. The image is integral, unbroken in the unity of Crucifixion and glorification. That is the import of the circumstantial account showing both the fact and the reason that there was no breaking of the legs but rather the subsequent thrust of the lance instead (19, 31, 34). Certainly, the primary reference is to the true paschal Lamb, whose bones were not to be broken (Exodus 12, 46), and perhaps also to Psalm 34, 20ff, where the Lord keeps all the bones of the just man so that 'not one of them is broken'. According to John (19, 14), Jesus was crucified at the same hour in which, in the Temple, the passover lambs were slaughtered.[79] For the same reason, and a fortiori, Jesus could not be stoned.[80] On the contrary, the rabbinic legislation prescribes, 'Let the heart of the slain lamb be opened, and its blood flow forth'.[81]

(7) Cross and Church

(a) The open heart

That the Cross means solidarity was something that the ancient Church never ceased to see in its very form: spread out in all the world's dimensions, its arms thrown open wide, all-embracing. According to the Didache,[82] the Cross is *sēmeion epektaseōs*, and extension as wide as that only God can achieve:

God has opened wide his arms on the Cross in order to span the limits of the earth's orb wrote Cyril of Jerusalem.[83]

> So God in his suffering spread out his arms and gathered
> in the circle of the earth, so as to announce that, from
> the rising of the sun to its setting, a future people would
> be gathered under his wings[84]

declared Lactantius. O blessed wood, in which God is
extended'.[85] This God can do only as man, who himself is
distinguished from the animals in that 'he stands upright and
can spread out his hands' (Justin).[86] Thus it is that he extends
his arms to the two peoples represented by the thieves and
tears down the separating wall of division (Athanasius).[87]
Even in its outer form the Cross is inclusive.

What shows forth the inner inclusiveness, however, is the
open heart out of which is communicated what is ultimate in
Jesus' substance: blood and water, the sacraments of the
Church.[88] For the Bible, and for the (philosophical)[89] thought
of man as a totality, the heart is the true centre of the spiritual-
physical human being, and, by analogy, the centre of the God
who opens himself to man (I Samuel 13, 14). If in the Old
Testament the heart is still more the seat of spiritual power and
of thought (whilst the entrails, *rachamim*, *splanchna*, are
expressions for the seat of the affections), the two come together
in the New Testament concept of the heart. The turning of 'the
whole heart' towards God is the opening of the whole man to
him (Apocalypse 8, 37; Matthew 22, 37). Thus the hardened
heart (Mark 10, 5, with numerous Old Testament parallels)
must be renewed: from a heart of stone it must become a heart
of flesh (Ezekiel 11, 19, etc.; II Corinthians 3, 3). And if Greek
philosophy, following Homer, saw in the heart the centre of
psychic and spiritual life (for the Stoics, it was the seat of the
hēgēmonikon, the ruling faculty), so New Testament theology
adds to this, on the one hand a factor of incarnation (for the
soul is entirely incarnate in the heart, and the body becomes, in
the heart, the total expressive sphere of the soul), and, on the
other, a factor of personalisation (the Christian man, body and
soul, is, in the call of God, a unique person, and turning to
God, offers with his heart what is thus unique in him).

The account of the lance thrust and the flowing forth of blood and water must be read within the continuity of the Johannine symbolism of water, spirit, blood, to which there belongs the key-word 'thirst'. Earthly water makes one thirsty again, whereas the water of Jesus quenches thirst for evermore (4, 13ff). 'If anyone thirsts, let him come to me and drink, he who believes in me' (John 7, 37ff); thus the thirst of the believer is slaked for ever (6, 35). To this is linked the wondrous promise that, in the one who drinks, water will become a spring leaping up to life eternal (4, 14), a promise accompanied by the scriptural text, 'Out of his heart, *koilia*, shall flow rivers of living water' (7, 38). We have seen above how it is at the moment when he suffers the most absolute thirst that Jesus pours himself forth as the everlasting spring. As for the scriptural citation, it may either be attached, with Audet, to that constantly recurring analogy between water and the word-and-spirit[90] (for the words of Jesus are 'spirit and life'), or, better, with Pythian-Adams,[91] to the source in Ezekiel's renewed Temple (Ezekiel 47; cf. Zechariah 13, 1) to which Jesus has compared, indeed, his body (2, 21). In the context of the Johannine symbolism at large, it can hardly be doubted[92] that John saw in the flowing forth of blood and water the institution of the sacraments of Eucharist and Baptism (cf. Cana: 2, 1ff; the unity of water and spirit: 3, 5; the water, the spirit and the blood: I John 5, 6, with an explicit allusion to 'he who came by water and blood, Jesus Christ'). The opening of the heart is the gift of what is most interior and personal for public use: the open, emptied out space is accessible to all. Moreover, the official proof had to be furnished that the separation of body and blood (a presupposition of the form of the Eucharistic meal) had been carried out right to the end.[93] The (new) Temple, like the newly released drinking water of the source point towards community: the body given over is the site of the new foundation of the Covenant, the new assembly of the congregation. It is at once and the same time space, altar, sacrifice, meal, community and the spirit of them all.

(b) The Church born from the Cross

The birth of the Church on the Cross[94] is a theologoumenon so frequently considered that it can hardly be more than cursorily dealt with here. Two lines of thought meet at this point. For one, the people of the Covenant is wholly re-created out of the single, fully valid representative of that Covenant on earth (to which belongs the beloved patristic image of the birth of the new Eve from the side of the new Adam asleep in death).[95] For the other, the ancient people of God fulfils and transcends its own life in the 'holy remnant', and does so in such a way that in this grace-filled creative transmutation which starts out from the Old Testament, a sort of 'Church-before-the Church' (represented by Mary, John and the believing women) must be pre-supposed. Nothing, indeed, prevents our accepting that pre-Christian faith also lived from the grace of the Cross (Hebrews 11, 26; I Peter 1, 11; John 8, 56 etc.), just as, in particular, Mary must be considered as pre-redeemed (by the sacrifice of Christ). Furthermore, the theology of the Covenant, moving towards its completion as the idea of a bilateral contract between God and man, finds its fulfilment in unison with that of the unilateral promise which preceded that concept of Covenant. Since the God who is in heaven and on earth constitutes the unity of the Covenant ('But God is one', *heis*: Galatians 3, 20), so at the same time are all human beings included in the unity of Christ in this same Covenant ('You are all one, *heis*, in Christ Jesus': Galatians 3, 28), for Christ is man, and man for the sake of all men. From this second encounter, yet another is made possible. The contract, at once unilateral and bilateral, between God and the people in the Old Testament, had always been compared to a marriage Covenant, so pertinent to the holiness of its foundation and the loving faithfulness accordingly demanded. But now that the Word has become flesh and has shown his own loving faithfulness to the very end, the conjugal parable becomes incarnate, and the theology of the Song of Songs is fulfilled therein. It comes to its fulfilment in the bilaterality (something necessarily required, as the second variety of convergence described above indicates) which the Church must in both of its aspects simultaneously be: namely, as the body of Jesus Christ himself (through his Eucharist, I Corinthians 10, 16, as participating in the flesh and blood he bestowed in his dying: I Corinthians 11, 26; John 6) and, precisely in this being body as, in addition, his virginal bride (II Corinthians 11, 2). The possibility of this simultaneity is, however, inscribed in the paradise saga where woman takes her rise from man (Ephesians 5, 30–33) in an indissoluble mutuality: I Corinthians 11, 7;12, so much so that Christ too, from whom the Church originates, was 'born of a woman': (Galatians 4, 4). This implies, in effect, that two affirmations must be made simultaneously: the absolute sovereignty of God, who in Jesus Christ alone set up his new and eternal covenant with humankind; and the obtaining of a consensual 'Yes' of humanity as represented at the Cross – the 'Yes' which Mary had to give, at the moment of the Incarnation (and for all of its implications) *loco totius humanae naturae*,[96] and especially as the nucleus of the new Church.[97] Inasmuch as Christ's vicarious suffering is not exclusive but inclusive,[98] his gesture of comprehension can only be one of letting others suffer with him. From this point on, it becomes clear in a definitive manner that the afore-described approximations to God-abandonment in Old and New Testaments are not to be understood in 'psychological' or 'ethical' terms, but rather, where they are genuine, can only be grasped in christological ones – and must, indeed, be postulated along those lines. Such allowance for co-suffering is especially plain in John, where Jesus deliberately lets the 'one whom he loves' (11, 3) die, and sends no news to the anxious sisters, but leaves them in a forgottenness with the pitch of a dark night, lets this night (brought down on them through him!) submerge himself also (11, 33ff), and thereby gives them a part in his God-abandonment which prefigures that of the Eucharist. This *com-passio* is, therefore, part and parcel of his essential legacy to his Church, and makes it possible for her to survive the hiatus of that day when 'God is dead'.

Here the biblical and theological implications inter-penetrate each other with, at one and the same time, the highest rigour and the most concentrated intensity. Only a very thorough and penetrating thinking through of the synthesis fashioned from out of the 'promises' can keep them all simultaneously within its sights. The synthesis in question cannot be constructed or surveyed by human logic, for it can only be seen against the ultimate horizon of trinitarian faith. Its earthworks are, however, so broadly and lavishly laid out that none of the elements used may be omitted in the integral vision of faith.

Born of the utmost love of God for the world, the Church herself is essentially love. What she is, that she ought to be: her essence is her unique commandment (John 15, 12). It is characteristic here that the love of disciples for Christ (mentioned ten times in John) is rendered by *philein*, and so by a word which stresses, precisely, love between human beings, whereas the love of Christians for each other is always designated by *agapan*, and so by the term applied to divine love.[99] What binds Christians to Christ is the 'friendship' which he has founded and whose proof is that he 'lay down his life for his friends' (John 15, 13, 15). What binds Christians to each other is that they are all brothers under the same Master (Matthew 23, 8), all members of the same superlative Head and, following the law of love laid down by that Head, have to be concerned for one another (Romans 12, 1; I Corinthians 13; Ephesians 4, 11ff; Colossians 3, 13).

(c) Co-crucified

The whole Church, insofar as she is in all seriousness (through the Eucharist) the body of Christ, must be co-crucified with her Head, and that, in the first place, without a retrospect onto the subjective suffering of Christians but rather through the sheer fact of her existence and the logic of her faith. For the content of this faith is that the sinner *as sinner* is hanging on the Cross of Christ – really, and not only in some vague representation – and that, accordingly, Christ dies 'my death of sin' whilst I obtain from beyond myself, in this death, the life of the love of God. Paul, then, expresses the total situation of the Church with great precision when he asserts in Galatians 2, 19–20:

> It is no longer I who live (as an I abiding with itself as home), but Christ who lives in me ... (which means, I am co-crucified with Christ ...). The life I now live in the flesh I live by faith in the Son of God, who loved me and gave himself for me. I do not nullify the grace of God.

That puts into words the essential constitution of the Church's being.[100] To become a Christian means to come to the Cross.[101] When this law (as *forma Christi*: Galatians 4, 19) begins to work itself out in the Christian, then its first necessary consequence is that 'not I suffer, but Christ in me' – the Christ who has created for himself in me an organ for *his* redemption, so that we should not carry *our* suffering, but rather 'the death of Jesus in the body', in order that 'the life of *Jesus* may be manifested in our mortal flesh' (II Corinthians 4, 10ff). Even as his own experienced suffering, this is not the Christian's property, but only a loan, for which, in the ecclesial and feminine word of consent, he is responsible to the true owner.[102] The a priori and objective quality of this being co-crucified in faith is confirmed by the principle, equally presupposed in each and every experience of suffering, and immanent to the sacraments of baptism (Romans 6, 3–11) and of the Eucharist (I Corinthians 11, 26), which gives the whole subjectivity of the Christian its direction. Paul reveals in a paradoxical formulation that for him an objective space has been set aside and left free on the Cross:

> In my flesh I complete (*ant-anapléroō*)[103] what is lacking in Christ's afflictions for the sake of his body the Church (Colossians 1, 24).[104]

One *can* recall here that it would not conform to the authentic human solidarity of Jesus were he to carry through his work of salvation in an exclusive fashion, shutting out all others, or, more exactly, that it would be inhuman not to draw within the exclusivity which befits him as the only Son of God a moment of inclusivity. There *must* therefore, a priori, be a certain taking up of the Old Testament theology of expiatory suffering and of martyrdom into Christology. It is in this sense that we should interpret the logion which grants to the disciples the capacity to drink the cup, and undergo his baptism (Mark 10, 38ff). However, one would do better to let this 'assumption' first disappear into the mystery of Christ so as to understand the making space on the Cross as the sovereignly free grace of the New Testament.

In Christians' co-bearing of the mortal suffering of Christ there is undoubtedly a graduated scale in operation. The promise to Peter that he will be (co-)crucified (John 21, 9), the grace given to John and to Mary that they may stand at the foot of the Cross, the sufferings of Paul – these occupy a place of their own *vis-à-vis* community and Church.[105] In Mary and the women saints at the foot of the Cross, we find a representation of the nuptial character of the new covenant. In Peter and Paul we find the normative representation of the apostolic kerygma, as that which is received 'not as the word of men, but as what it really is, the word of God' (I Thessalonians 2, 13): a preaching, then, with the whole of one's existence, corresponding to the *Verbum-Caro* of the New Testament itself.

(8) Cross and Trinity

Only as the acting of the triune God does the scandal of the Cross become tolerable to the believer, and even become that one unique scandal in which the believer can glory (Galatians 6, 14). The original actor is God the Father

> All this is from God, who through (*dia*) Christ reconciled us to himself and gave us (apostles) the ministry of reconciliation; that is, God was in Christ, reconciling the world to himself.

And the sign that this work of reconciliation succeeded in reaching its goal is the Holy Spirit who brings to those reconciled, 'for whom there is now no condemnation' life and peace' (Romans 8, 1–6); he is the 'Spirit of Christ',

'Christ ... in us' (ibid., 9–10). In this perspective, the Cross of Christ becomes transparent (*dia*); as the medium of reconciliation between the Father and ourselves – we who have become his children through the Spirit who dwells in us (ibid., 11). But the presupposition for this reading of the Cross (the only one possible) is that the entire abyss of man's refusal of God's love has been crossed over: in other words, that God is solidary with us not only in what is symptomatic of sin, the punishment for sin, but also in co-experiencing sin, in the *peirasmos* of the very essence of that negation – though without 'committing' (Hebrews 4, 15) sin himself.

By that are ruled out of court all theories which, missing the point of the actual redemption, start looking at other 'possible' methods for the world's reconciliation: considering whether a simple divine 'decree', or the mere Incarnation, or 'a single drop' of Christ's blood might have sufficed. Over against such free-wheeling speculation in empty space it should not only be remembered that God is in his (ever free!) sovereignty the absolute ground and meaning of his own action, so that only foolishness can cause us to neglect his actual deeds, in favour of scouting round for other possibilities of acting. But, more than this, we must state positively that, to become solidary with the lost is something *greater* than just dying for them in an externally representative manner. It is more than so announcing the Word of God that this proclamation, through the opposition it arouses among sinners, happens to lead to a violent death. It is more than just taking a universally unavoidable mortal fate upon the self, more than simply carrying about consciously, in one's own person, that death which has been a constitutive and immanent aspect of the life of sinners ever since Adam and turning it into a personally responsible act of obedience and self-gift to God, perhaps with such a purity and freedom, denied to all other human beings, who are sinners, that it sets up, in that way, a 'new existential' within the reality of the world.[106] Though all of these have their relative validity, it goes beyond them.

For the redeeming act consists in a wholly unique bearing of the total sin of the world by the Father's wholly unique

Son, whose Godmanhood (which is more than the 'highest case' of a transcendental anthropology) is alone capable of such an office. Who, apart from him would have the 'power to lay down (his) life, and power to take it again' (John 10, 18)? Who would have the power to die 'not for the nation only' (which the martyr in his selflessness could also do) but also to 'gather into one the children of God who are scattered abroad' (John 11, 52), and so to found the true Church of God? Is there any analogy for the 'Second Adam', 'in whom shall all be made alive' (I Corinthians 15, 22), for him who alone 'has ascended into heaven . . ., he who descended from heaven, the Son of man' (John 3, 13)? Is there any transitional stage between the futility of the ancient sacrifices and the sheer power of the equally sheerly unique and unrepeatable sacrifice of Christ? Is there some other point of convergence for all the Old Testament (and if one wishes pagan) sacrifices and liturgies, the religious laws and institutions, prophecies and symbols, sacred and profane offices, all of which remain, in their disparate qualities, separate from each other, and the unique Golgotha, where all of this alike is fulfilled, transcended, abolished, and replaced by that unique action which is *God's*. God as *man*, to be sure, and God *only* as man, in such a way that, as nowhere else, man is valued. Yet not God together with just any man, but God, the absolutely unique, in that absolutely unique man who is unique because he is God, and who, for this reason and no other, can communicate a share in his Cross to his fellow human beings, with whom he is more profoundly solidary than any man can ever be with any other man, and can do that in death itself, where each man is absolutely alone.

If this is so, then this event must tell us not only that sinful man sinks into the nothingness and obscurity of death, but, quite simply, that God hates sin.

> God cannot love moral evil, he can only hate it. Of its very nature, it stands in complete opposition to God's essence. It is the counter-image of his holy love. There is no right love without wrath, for wrath is the reverse side of love. God could not truly love the good unless

he hated evil and shunned it ... Therefore God does not forgive unexpiated sin. A mere amnesty is an ignoring of evil, which takes sin lightly or even recognises in it an existence as of right.[107]

Let us listen to the words of Jesus against the man who leads astray: it would be better for him that a millstone be hung around his neck and he sink into the midst of the sea (Matthew 18, 6). There is the precise articulation of what the wrath of God is as the reverse side of his love (for 'one of these little ones'). It is that wrath which the Son must face in his Passion. The fearful, divinely grounded wrath which blazes up throughout the Old Testament and finally consumes faithless Jerusalem in the fire of the divine glory (Ezekiel 10, 2), Jesus must bring to its eschatological end.

And here we must speak once again of Luther, who, leaving to one side all the indulgent mediations of Scholasticism, was thrown directly into the fire of the absolute wrath and the absolute love, and drew from there his theology of the God who on the Cross is hidden *sub contrario*.[108] We have referred already (II/2) to the limitations of a theology of the Cross, which would set up the 'absolute Paradox' in a static and absolutised fashion. But if Luther, for reasons of controversy, came close to this extreme, it is only a single moment within his theology of the Cross as a whole, one factor found within the mighty movement of the justification idea. More fateful is something different: the interpretation of the Pauline *pro me* (Galatians 2, 20) in an at any rate tendentially anthropocentric sense ('how can *I* find a gracious God?') – which has exerted a baleful influence in Protestant theology down to our the present day. The entire existential seriousness of the *pro me* is only maintained undiminished if the opening up of the Trinitarian love for sinners which there becomes visible is responded to by an integral *pro te*, and if, furthermore, one understand that, in the *pro me* of Christ's self surrender, one is oneself already taken over by that love and yielded up, so that faith is not one's own 'work' but the ratification of what God has done in finished form and, in that, one's transferral to the sphere of the triune Love.[106] The anthropocentric tendency will never be able to keep within view the Trinitarian background of the Cross, since in the last analysis it is concerned with the interpretation of individual 'existence', in a kind of theological transcendentalism, whereas the movement opposed to it is able to make manifest, and to interpret, all that is christological and soteriological by rooting it in the mystery of the Trinity. Only so does the believer match up to the great interpretations of the Cross in Paul and John: the Son's Cross is the revelation of the Father's love (Romans 8, 32; John, 3, 16), and the bloody outpouring of that love comes to its inner fulfilment in the shedding abroad of their common Spirit into the hearts of men (Romans 5, 5).

References

[1] Leo, *Sermo* 60, 3 (PL 54, 344): 'Hoc igitur illud est sacramentum, cui ab initio omnia sunt famulata mysteria'. Even the mysteries of the Old Testament are there enclosed, *Tomus* 1 (PL 54, 775ff).

[2] *Homilia in Joannem* 50 (49), 2 (PG 59, 331): Chrysostom goes almost as far as an inversion of the Johannine formula: 'ekeinō dokei ho egō poiō': 'That which I do, that is what pleases him, what he approves'.

[3] *Cur Deus Homo?* I, 8–10 (Schmitt II, 59ff): the obedience of Jesus is a spontaneous service of the Father, assumed out of love: it is the exercise of his justice, the preaching of his truth, from which results, *as a consequence* the opposition of sinners to him, and his death (I. 9, p. 62, lines 6–8).

[4] *Summa Theologiae* IIa.IIae., q. 104, a 2, ad i; a. 5, ad iii; IIIa., q. 47, a. 2, ad i.

[5] Anselm, op. cit. I. 10 (Schmitt II. 65): 'Quoniam namque voluntate quisque ad id quod indeclinabiliter vult, trahitur (cf. Augustine, *In Johannem Tractatus* 26, 2: PL 35, 1607) vel impellitur, non inconvenienter trahere aut impellere Deus, cum talem dat voluntatem, affirmatur. In quo tractu ... intelligitur ... bonae voluntatis spontanea et amata tenacitas'. As with Chrystostom, it is a matter of an approval by the Father (*approbat*, p. 65, l. 23); cf. Thomas Aquinas, *Summa contra Gentiles* IV. 35, ad 15–16.

[6] P. Galtier, 'Obéissant jusqu'à la mort', RAM 1 (1920), pp. 113–145.

[7] Ibid., p. 131.

[8] With regard to the *hupēkoos* (Philippians 2, 8), E. Käsemann draws attention to the 'remarkable fact' that 'it is not said to whom Christ was obedient', *Exegetische Versuche und Besinnungen* I (Göttingen 1965⁴), p. 77. That may be worthy of remark in the context of critical analysis – the emphasis lies on the humiliation – but for the dogmatic theologian who must come to terms with the *mandatum a Patre* Johannine texts, reference to the Father is 'self-evident', ibid.

9 P. de Bérulle, 'Discours de l'état et des grandeurs de Jésus', *Oeuvres* I (Paris 1644), pp. 261–525.

10 Brussels 1648.

11 *Oeuvres* IX., p. 458.

12 *De Gemitu Columbae* (1617), II. 3, 153.

13 For the whole work, see the introduction by F. Florand, to Chardon, *La Croix de Jésus* (Paris 1937), especially pp. LXXXV–XCVI.

14 In his *Bethlehem* (London 1860).

15 Cf. the thesis, essentially correct, of E. Lohse, *Märtyrer und Gottesknecht* (Göttingen 1963²), pp. 193ff, although his interpretation of Paul needs complementary additions. For Paul, see E. Güttgemanns, *Der leidende Apostel und sein Herr* (Göttingen 1960).

16 This is Chardon's fundamental thesis, developed after his time by J. Nacchiante and, more clearly still, by J.-P. Nazari. According to these theologians, the Eucharist 'est ad illius hypostaticum esse provehi et ad eandem cum illa (Persona) subsistentiam personalem admitti': see Florand, op. cit., p. LXXXXI, n. 1. Christ is the single hypostasis of his mystical body.

17 E. Schweizer, 'Abendmahl', RGG I. 20.

18 J. Jeremias, *Die Abendmahlsworte Jesu* (Göttingen 1966⁴), pp. 186ff.

19 Ibid. pp. 171, 222. On the convergence of the Old Testament sacrificial types, cf. the article by J. Ratzinger, 'Ist die Eucharistie ein Opfer?', *Concilium* III (1967), pp. 299–304.

20 C. Spicq, 'la théologie et la liturgie du précieux Sang', in idem., *Epître aux Hebreux* II (Paris 1953), pp. 271–285. For the theology of the blood, see also: A. M. Stibbs, *The Meaning of the Word 'Blood' in Scripture* (London 1947); L. Morris, 'The biblical use of the term 'blood', JThS N. S. 6 (1955), pp. 77–82; S. Lyonnet, 'Conception paulinienne de la Redemption', *Lumière et Vie* 38 (1958), pp. 45–52; F. Grandchamp, 'La doctrine du sang du Christ dans les épîtres de S. Paul', RThPh 10 (1961), pp. 262–271; P. A. Harlé, 'L'agneau de l'Apocalypse et le Nouveau Testament', ETR 1956, pp. 26ff.

21 Jesus, to be sure, would often enough already have been alone to pray before. What is new here is the explicit assignation of a certain distance to the disciples.

22 K. Rahner, 'Probleme der Christologie heute', *Schriften* I (Einsiedeln 1954), pp. 165ff, and especially 190ff. On this see the critical and complementary observations of A. Grillmeier, 'Zum Christusbild der heutigen katholischen Theologie', FThh, pp. 293–296, and of F. Malmberg, *Über den Gottmenschen* (Freiburg 1959), pp. 89–114, especially pp. 113–114. On the second, cf. Karl Barth's doctrine of predestination in *Kirchliche Dogmatik* II/21 (1942).

23 Lamentations 4, 2. *Sententiae Divinitatis* ed. by B. Geyer (Munster 1909), p. 77.

24 *Sententiarum Libri* VIII., lib. 4, c. 7–8 (PL 186, 814–815ff). The continuation of these ideas in (ch. 10) becomes wholly aberrrant, because of a unilateral doctrine of predestination.

25 *Summa Theologiae* IIIa (Quaracchi IV., n. 141, p. 197).

26 *In III Sententiarum Libros*, d. 16, a. 2, p. 2, conclusio (Quaracchi III., p. 356).

27 Ibid., p. 3, conclusio (p. 358).

28 This limits the bearing of the texts assembled by E. Schweizer on the obedience

of Jesus in *Erniedrigung und Erhöhung bei Jesus und seinen Nachfolgern* (Zurich 1955, pp. 44–60).

29 W. Wichmann, *Die Leidenstheologie. Eine Form der Leidens=deutung im Spätjudentum* (Stuttgart 1930); E. Lohse, *Märtyrer und Gottesknecht* (Gottingen 1963⁴), with bibliography.

30 As U. Wilckens, op. cit., has shown, I Corinthians 2, 8 is a purely 'literary' *reprise* of a Gnostic view held by Paul's Corinthian opponents.

31 W. Popkes, *Christus traditus. Eine Untersuchung zum Begriff der Dahingabe im Neuen Testament* (Zurich 1967).

32 Ibid., pp. 23ff.

33 Ibid., pp. 25, 41.

34 Ibid., pp. 37–74.

35 Ibid., p. 79: 'It belongs to the essence of the true righteous man that God's actions and his own become one'.

36 Ibid., p. 46.

37 Ibid., pp. 127–129.

38 E. Schweizer, *Erniedrigung und Erhöhung*, op. cit., p. 36.

39 Deriving doubtless from the tradition of the Supper (Wellhausen, *Markus*, p. 91), with a retrospective reference to Isaiah 53.

40 Galatians 1, 3; Ephesians 5, 2 and 25; I Timothy 2, 6; Titus 2, 14; H. Schlier, *Galaterbrief*, p. 32. On these particles, see K. H. Schelke, *Die Passion Jesu* (Heidelberg 1949), pp. 131ff.

41 On human beings delivered up by their fellows: in the Old Testament (as betrayal): II Kings 6, 11; in the rabbinic tradition, W. Popkes, op. cit., pp. 59ff; in Hellenism (as betrayal), ibid., pp. 90ff.

42 K. Lüthi, 'Judas Iskarioth in der Geschichte der Auslegung von der Reformation bis zur Gegenwart' (Dissertation, Zurich 1953).

43 W. Popkes, op. cit., pp. 174ff.

44 It is better to say 'role' than 'substitution', as K. Lüthi rightly objects to the grand synoptic vision of Karl Barth, gathering up all the texts which contain the idea of 'delivering up' in his doctrine of election (*Kirchliche Dogmatik* II/2.2), op. cit., p. 174.

45 Strongly emphasised by P. Althaus, 'Das Kreuz Christi', *Theologische Aufsätze* I (Gütersloh 1929), pp. 1–50.

46 That Paul knows a 'delivering up' of the sinner to Satan and practises it (I Corinthians 5, 5; I Timothy 1, 20) should not be forgotten in this context, although, as has been said, satanic powers do not belong directly to the history of the Passion.

47 W. Popkes, op. cit., pp. 286–287.

48 J. Blinzler, *Der Prozess Jesu. Das jüdische und römische Gerichtsverfahren gegen Jesus Christus auf Grund der älteren Literarur*; T. Innitzer, *Kommentar zur Leidens- und Verklärungsgeschichte Jesu* (Vienna 1948⁴); W. Hillmann, *Aufbau und Deutung der synoptischen Leidensberichte* (Freiburg 1941); K. H. Schelkle, *Die Passion Jesu in der Verkündigung des Neuen Testaments* (Heidelberg 1949).

49 K. L. Schmidt, *Der Rahmen der Geschichte Jesu* (Berlin 1919), pp. 305ff. L. and G. Schille, 'Das Leiden des Herrn. Die evangelische Passionstradition und ihr

"Sitz im Leben"', ZThK 52 (1955), pp. 161–204 see the framework as given by the Liturgy. M. Dibelius, 'Das historische Problem der Leidensgschichte', ZNW 30 (1931), pp. 193–201, and, essentially, R. Bultmann, *Geschichte der synoptischen Tradition* (Göttingen 1933²), pp. 297ff recognise the unity of the original narrative.

50 N. A. Dahl, 'Der gekreuzigte Messias', in H. Ristow – K. Matthiae (eds.), *Der historische Jesu und der kerygmatische Christus* (Berlin 1961), pp. 149–168.

51 This is why W. Trilling's position could be described as somewhat minimalistic, and dictated by his own fundamental thesis that such a coincidence between 'faith' and 'history' would compromise the free venture of faith: see his *Fragen zur Geschichtlichkeit Jesu* (Düsseldorf 1966), pp. 134ff.

52 On Judas' end, see P. Benoit, *Exégèse et Théologie* I (Paris 1961), pp. 340–359.

53 H.-W. Bartsch, 'Die Bedeutung des Sterbens Jesu nach den Synoptikern', ThZ 20 (1964), pp. 85–102. The biblical references form part of the primitive condition of the account: thanks to its intimate relation with the Old Testament, the shocking character of the events became tolerable. Cf. J. Schmid, *Markus* (Regensburg 1954³), pp. 304ff.

54 W. Bauer, ThW 168.

55 Cf. P. Benoit's reference of this in his *Passion et Résurrection du Seigneur* (Paris 1966), p. 53, to the eschatological combat as represented at Qumran.

56 Ibid., p. 107.

57 *Cur Deus Homo?* I. 21 (Schmitt II. 88).

58 K. Barth, *Kirchliche Dogmatik* IV/1 (Zurich 1953), p. 602, and the whole chapter 'Gottes Gericht'.

59 S. Lyonnet, 'De iustitia Dei in epistolem ad Romanos', VD 25 (1947), pp. 23–34; 118–121; 129–144; 193–203; 157–263; VD 42 (1964), pp. 121–152. On the history of interpretation, A. Schlatter, *Gottes Gerechtigkeit: Romerbrief= kommentar* [Stuttgart 1935]; for a survey of the interpretations, P. Stuhlmacher, *Gerechtigkeit Gottes bei Paulus* (Göttingen 1966²).

60 K. Barth, op. cit., p. 612.

61 For what follows see above all: W. Thüsing, *Die Erhöhung und Verherrlichung im Johannesevangelium* (Münster 1960); J. Blank, *Krisis. Untersuchungen zur johanneischen Christologie und Eschatologie* (Freiburg 1964).

62 Compare the interpretations of John by Bultmann and Käsemann.

63 'The *onoma* of the Father designates the Father himself, and that because the Father is glorified when he is recognised, named *as* Father', R. Bultmann, *Johannes*, p. 357, n. 6.

64 W. Thüsing, op. cit., pp. 79ff.

65 Ibid., pp. 8off.

66 J. Blank, op. cit., p. 282.

67 See on this, H. Schlier, *Mächte und Gewalten im Neuen Testament* (Freiburg 1958).

68 J. Blank, op. cit., p. 285; cf. I John 3, 8: 'The reason the Son of God appeared was to destroy the works of the devil'.

69 Ibid., pp. 289ff; 291ff.

70 G. Jouassard, 'L'abandon du Christ par son Père durant sa Passion d'après la

tradition patristique et les Docteurs du XIIIe siècle (dactylographed thesis of the Institut Catholique de Lyon, 1923); idem., 'L'abandon du Christ en croix chez S. Augustin', RSPhTh 13 (1924), pp. 316–326; idem., 'L'abandon du Christ en croix dans la tradition grecque', RSPhTh 14 (1925), p. 623; idem., 'L'abandon du Christ en croix dans la tradition', RSR 25 (1924), pp. 310ff; 26 (1925), pp. 609ff. The author shows that, since Origen, two traditions predominate: the spiritual distress of Jesus because of sinners (no direct abandonment by the Father), and the suffering of the Head in his ecclesial members. A relation between the mystical experiences of God-abandonment and the cry from the Cross would not have been established until the Rhenish mystics. In his study, 'L'abandon du Christ sur la croix', L. Mahieu seeks to demonstrate this positively, making Tauler responsible for the 'sombre' theology of the Cross developed in later centuries, in which, from Jansen to Bossuet, the Father would appear, at the moment of the sacrifice of the Cross, as the 'God of vengeance' of the Old Testament. One must agree that Tauler, especially in his sermon on spiritual 'winter' sets out from the mystical experience of God-abandonment in order to illuminate (as the archetype of this latter) the abandonment on the Cross, and from that to return, in parenetic fashion, to the behaviour of Christians in God-abandonment. But psychological occasion and theological justification are in all cases two quite different things. This is why it is superficial, to an impardonable degree, to write, as does Carra de Vaux Saint-Cyr, 'The abandonment in question here (on the Cross) has nothing to do with a mystical testing, it is the distress (!) of the just man handed over to his persecuting enemies ... which God, it seems, no longer remembers, since he does not protect him', 'L'abandon du Christ en croix', in H. Bouëssé – J. J. Latour (eds.), *Problèmes Actuels de Christologie* (Bruges 1965), pp. 295–316, and here at p. 305. The under-estimate made by patristic and Scholastic theology and the partial disfigurement operative in Gothic and Baroque sensibility (the Father as God of vengeance rather than the God of justice) would have to be balanced, ultimately, by an objective interpretation, one resting on the whole Bible. Moreover, this development can only be successfully carried out theologically, not in a purely exegetical fashion. See further B. Botte, 'Deus meus, Deus meus, ut quid dereliquisti me?', QLP 11 (1926), pp. 105ff; W. Hasenzahl, *Die Gottverlassenheit des Christus nach dem Kreuzwort bei Matthäus und Markus and das christologische Verständnis des griechischen Psalters* (Gütersloh 1937); D. H. C. Read, 'The Cry of Dereliction', ET 68 (1956–7), pp. 260–262; M. Rehm, 'Eli, Eli, lamma sabachthani', BZ 2 (1958), pp. 275–278; J. Gnilka, 'Mein Gott, mein Gott, warum hast du mich verlassen? (Mark 15, 34, par.)', BZ 3 (1959), pp. 294–297; F. W. Bückler, 'Eli, Eli, lamma sabachthani?', AJSL 55 (1933), pp. 378–391.

[71] *Adversus Haereses* III. 18, 5–6.

[72] Bernard, *Sermo Diei Dominicae infra Octavam Ascensionis* (PL 183, 438A).

[73] For the various views taken by exegeis on this, see J. Heer, *Der Durchbohrte* (Rome 1966), p. 212, notes 108–110.

[74] G. Lindeskog, 'The Veil of the Temple', in *Mélanges Fridrichsen* (Lund 1947), pp. 132–137; A. Pelletier, 'La Tradition synoptique du "Voile déchiré" à la lumière des réalités archéologiques', RSR 46 (1958), pp. 161–180.

75 A. Pelletier, art. cit., pp. 167ff. Later theology and iconography have chiefly portrayed the theme of the *perturbatio naturae* as a participation in the death of the Redeemer. Already clear and with a certain grandiloquence in the pascal homily of Pseudo-Hippolytus: P. Nautin, *Homélies pascales* I (Paris 1950), pp. 103, 182: see n. 56, 'O Crucifixion which extends through all things!'.

76 E. Lohmeyer, *Matthäus*, p. 396, n. 1.

77 For this in its entirety: see H. Zeller, '"Corpus Sanctorum". Eine Studie zu Matthäus 27, 52–53', ZKTh 71 (1949), pp. 385–465.

78 G. Ziener, 'Weisheitsbuch und Johannesevangelium', *Biblica* 38 (1957), pp. 396–418; 39 (1958), pp. 37–60; F. M. Braun, *Jean le Théologien* III. 1 (Paris 1960), pp. 173ff.

79 Cf. E. Schweizer, *Erniedrigung und Erhöhung* op. cit., p. 58; J. Heer, *Der Durchbohrte*, op. cit., pp. 140–142.

80 On the rabbinic theories about the most perfect possible integrity even of those who are to be stoned if they are to share in the resurrection of the dea, see E. Lohse, *Märtyrer und Gottesknecht* op. cit., pp. 43ff.

81 N. Füglister, *Die Heilsbedeutung des Pascha* (Munich 1963), p. 63. Furthermore, the lambs were roasted on a wooden spit with a transverse bar (which seemed to have the form of a cross), ibid.

82 16, 6 (Funk I, 36, line 12); cf. E. Stommel, 'Sēmeion epektaseōs', RQ 50 (1955), pp. 1ff.

83 *Catecheses* 13, 28 (PG 33, 805B).

84 *Institutiones Divinae* IV. 26, 36 (CSEL, 19, 383).

85 *Oracula Sibyllina* VI. 26–28 (GCS 132).

86 *Apologia* I. 55 (Otto I., pp. 150ff).

87 *De Incarnatione* 25 (PG 25, 139AC).

88 From the enormous literature on this subject (cf. J. Heer, *Der Durchbohrte*, op. cit., pp. 277ff), we will cite only a few works. For the interpretation of John 7, 38, see the three contributions of P. Grelot, M.-E. Boismard and J.-P. Audet, '"De son ventre couleront des fleuves d'eau": Jean 7, 38', RB 66 (1959), pp. 369–386; (bibliography); J. E. Ménard, 'L'interprétation patristique de Jean 7, 38¹, *Revue de l'Université d'Ottawa* 25 (1955), pp. 5–25; M. Zerwick, '"Flumina de ventre eius fluent aquae"', VD 21 (1941), pp. 323–337; C. Stein, '"Ströme lebendigen Wassers"', *Bibel und Liturgie* 24 (1957), pp. 201–202; A. M. Dubarle, 'Les Fleuves d'eau vive', *Vivre et Penser* 3 (1921), pp. 238–241; J. Heer, op. cit., pp. 57ff. More particularly, on the topic of the opening of the heart, see H. Rahner, 'Flumina de ventre Christi', *Biblica* 22 (1941), pp. 269–302; 367–403; idem., 'Fons Vitae' (dactylographed dissertation, Innsbruck 1930); idem., '"Ströme fliessen aus seinem Leib"', ZAM 18 (1943), pp. 141–149; on John resting on Jesus' breast: idem., 'De dominici pectoris fonte potavit', ZKth 55 (1931), pp. 103–108.

89 For the philosophy of the heart, see A. Maxsein, *Philosophia cordis* (Salzburg 1966); D. von Hildebrand, *Über das Herz* (Regensburg 1967); G. Siewerth, *Der Mensch und sein Leib* (Einsiedeln 1963²). For the biblical theology of this, N. Adler, 'Herz', LThK V. 285ff (with bibliography).

90 RB 66 (1959), pp. 382–386. This is preferable to drawing in the Targums with

their mention of cisterns travelling with the people in the desert, then identified with the water springing from the rock of Exodus 17, 1–7: thus P. Grelot, art. cit., pp. 369–374.

91 *The People and the Presence. A Study of the Atonement* (Oxford 1942). Discussion, unfortunately without mention of this author, in P. Grelot, 'Jean 7, 38: Eau du rocher ou source du temple?', RB 70 (1963), pp. 41–43. Grelot infers that John marks the confluence of two traditions.

92 O. Cullmann, 'Der johanneische Gebrauch doppeldeutiger Ausdrücke als Schlüssel zum Verständnis des 4. Evangeliums', ThZ 4 (1948), pp. 360–374; idem., *Les sacrements dans l'évangile johannique* (Paris 1951).

93 P.-T. Dehau, *Le contemplatif et la Croix* (Paris 1956²), pp. 32, 68.

94 S. Tromp, 'De nativitate Ecclesiae ex corde Jesu in Cruce', Greg-13 (1932), pp. 489–527; H. Rahner, 'Die Kirche aus dem Herzen Jesu', *Korrespondenzblatt der Innsbrücker Priestergebetsvereinigung* 69 (1935), pp. 98–103; S. Tromp, *Corpus Christi quod est Ecclesia* I (Rome 1946), pp. 26ff; II 'De Christo Capite' (Rome 1960), pp. 193ff; III 'De Spiritu Christi Anima' (Rome 1960), pp. 62ff; idem., *Kommentar zu 'Mystici Corporis'* (Heidelberg 1958³)

95 Augustine, *In Joannem Tractatus* 9, 10 (PL 35, 1463–1464); *De Genesi ad Litteram* 9, 19 (PL 34, 408); Ambrose, *In Lucam* 4, 66 (PL 15, 1632BC), and often elsewhere.

96 Thomas, *Summa Theologiae* IIIa, q. 30, a. 1. c.

97 The deepening of this point turns on Mariology; cf. our *Sponsa Verbi* (Einsiedeln 1960), pp. 148–202; A. Müller, *Ecclesia-Maria* (Freiburg 1951).

98 That has been shown most clearly by P. Althaus, 'Das Kreuz Christ', art. cit.

99 On this, see J. Heer, *Der Durchbohrte*, op. cit., p. 49, n. 149; the distinction of the terms is supported by C. Spicq, *Agape* III (Paris 1959), pp. 219ff.

100 'Ecclesia ... fidei sui soliditate in cruce Christi *suspensa* ... firma et stabili perseverantia in arboris sua natura, i.e. in crucis ligno perdurat: Gregory of Elvira, *Tractatus* 11 (PL Supplementum I. 426–427).

101 '... ut susceptus a Christo Christumque suscipiens non idem sit post lavacrum quod ante baptismum fuit, sed corpus regenerati fiat caro crucifixi'; Leo the Great, *Sermo* 63 (62), 6 (PL 54, 357).

102 Thus correctly P. T. Dehau, op. cit., pp. 33–37. Cf. A. Feuillet, 'Mort du Christ et mort du chrétien d'après les épîtres de S. Paul', RB (1959), pp. 481–513.

103 G. Delling, 'antanaplēroō', ThW VI. 305.

104 J. Kremer, *Was an den Leiden Christi noch mangelt* (Bonn 1956), pp. 164ff. *Husterēmata*: not so much that which is 'lacking' as what is left open for complementation, and which is closed and completed by the response coming from the apostle (the *anti* est underlined) and from the Church in its entirety. E. Lohse's interpretation, whereby Christ's Passion only introduces the 'eschatological sufferings of the Messiah' which the Church must then take further is, at least in the context of the Letter to the Colossians, rather artificial (*Märtyrer und Gottesknecht*, op. cit., p. 202).

105 And so E. Güttgemanns is correct in *Der leidende Apostel und sein Herr* (Göttingen 1966), pp. 323–328.

106 It is to these aspects that K. Rahner in his *Theologie des Todes* (Freiburg 1958),

and after an assuredly justified criticism of all 'extrinsicism' in the doctrine of reconciliation, seems to limit Christ's solidarity with us. Thereby there arises at any rate the suspicion that 'the darkness of this night of the Cross, in which the everlasting Life reached down to the depths of the universe' (p. 51) is simply identified with 'what is empty, without issue, vanishing, insubstantial', attached (after the Fall) to the general phenomenon of death. This suspicion is strengthened when Rahner says, further, that, in the doctrine of redemption, one must not pay attention so much to the 'bitter suffering' of Christ as to the manner in which he posits the act of dying (*Schriften* IV, pp. 165–166). Precisely through its ambiguity does the death of Christ become the expression, the bodily manifestation of his obedience and love, the free giving over of his entire created being to God (p. 57). There may well be here a minimalist interpretation of such texts as Romans 8, 3; II Corinthians 5, 21; Galatians 3, 13 etc., where *all* the *hamartia* of the world is imposed on one single man who, for this reason, first experiences suffering and death in a way which has no analogy. Correlatively, the (purely philosophical) interpretation of the descent into Hell, which considers it as the 'foundation' of a new existential dimension in the radical depths of cosmic being, is neither biblically justified, nor theologically sufficient: that appears with all possible clarity in L. Boros, *Mysterium Mortis* (Olten 1964²) where the author, in taking up Rahner's ideas, develops what are no doubt some interesting and pertinent theological thoughts about death as a situation of decision, but where the understanding of the eschatological aspect, as of the Cross and the descent into Hell, is totally deficient. Instead, the descent into Hell becomes a 'cosmic Spring-time' for the whole world (p. 159), and we are 'carried towards God on a boundless flood-movement of the All' (p. 160). A Teilhard de Chardin might perhaps express himself thus, but hardly the Word of God.

[107] E. Riggenbach, *Das Geheimnis des Kreuzes Christi* (Stuttgart-Basle 1927³), pp. 16ff. Cf. the statement that 'The negativity of God against negation is indeed nothing other than love. For he repulses evil in the creation only because this evil is the obstacle placed over against the union of the creature with him, who is the source of life', F. von Baader, *Werke* 13, p. 62.

[108] Kattenbusch, 'Deus absconditus bei Luther', in *Festgabe für J. Kaftan* (Tübingen 1920), pp. 170–214; J. Blanke, *Der verborgene Gott bei Luther* (Berlin 1928); E. Seeberg, *Luthers Theologie I: Die Gottesanschauung* (Stuttgart 1929); O. Michel, '*Luthers Deus absconditus und der Gottesgedanke des Paulus*', ThStK *163* (1931), pp. 181–194; W. von Loewenich, *Luthers theologia crucis* (Munich 1954⁴); H. Brandt, *Luthers Lehre vom verborgenen Gott* (Berlin 1957); G. Ebeling, *Luther. Einführung in sein Denken* (Tübingen 1964), pp. 259ff.

[109] On this, see our article 'Zwei Glaubensweisen', *Hochland* 59 (1967), pp. 401–412; also in *Spiritus Creator* (Einsiedeln 1967), pp. 76–91.

4

Going to the Dead: Holy Saturday

(1) Preliminaries on Method

The more eloquently the Gospels describe the passion of the living Jesus, his death and burial, the more striking is their entirely understandable silence when it comes to the time inbetween his placing in the grave and the event of the Resurrection. We are grateful to them for this. Death calls for this silence, not only by reason of the mourning of the survivors but, even more, because of what we know of the dwelling and condition of the dead. When we ascribe to the dead forms of activity that are new and yet prolong those of earth, we are not simply expressing our perplexity. We are also defending ourselves against a stronger conviction which tells us that death is not a partial event. It is a happening which affects the whole person, though not necessarily to the point of obliterating the human subject altogether. It is a situation which signifies in the first place the abandonment of all spontaneous activity and so a passivity, a state in which, perhaps, the vital activity now brought to its end is mysteriously summed up.

That Jesus was really dead,[1] because he really became a man as we are, a son of Adam, and that therefore, despite what one can sometimes read in certain theological works, he did not use the so-called 'brief' time of his death for all manner of 'activities' in the world beyond – this is the first point we must consider. In that same way that, upon earth, he was in solidarity with the living, so, in the tomb, he is in solidarity with the dead. One must allow to this 'solidarity' an amplitude and an ambiguity, even, which seem precisely to exclude a communication on his part as subject. Each human being lies in his own tomb. And with this condition, seen here from the viewpoint of the separated body, Jesus is at first truly solidary.

This is why we shall provisionally place within parentheses the action word *descendere*, 'to descend', which, as a possibly indispensable interpretation of the same, was made use of by the primitive Church and later on, (officially speaking, from the end of the fourth century) was inserted into the Apostles' Creed. Both theological defenders and adversaries of a *descensus ad infera* (or *inferna*), a *descendus ad inferos* (or *infernos*) give to this concept the unintended and unexamined meaning of an action such as, at root, only a living man, not a dead one, can perform. In the Creeds there appeared at first only the affirmation of a 'burial for three days'[2] along with that of the resurrection *ek tōn nekrōn*,[3] *a mortuis*,[4] *vivus a mortuis*,[5] which indicates the sojourn (and solidarity) with the dead. Long prepared theologically and used by the Semi-Arians at the Council of Sirmium of 359,[6] the addition *descendit ad inferna* appears for the first time in the commentary on the Creed of the church of Aquileia given by Rufinus who remarks:

> Sciendum sane est quod in ecclesiae romanae symbolo non habetur additum: descendit ad inferna. Sed neque in orientis ecclesiis habetur hic sermo.[7]

After Rufinus' time, the formula crops up in different places. From Gaul it entered, in the ninth century, into the *Credo* of the Roman church. Popes and councils had utilised it long previously.[8]

We must now examine the biblical data to see in what degree the expression *descendit ad inferna* can be considered as a valid interpretation of the affirmations of the Bible. To begin with, one might note that the word *katabainein* is here formed in exact correspondence with the term *anabainein*, used for the Ascension or, more generally, the return to the Father, and that, in both cases, this usage does not imply any necessary relationship to a 'mythical three-storey world-picture' (which would have to be excluded unconditionally from the Church's *Credo*). It had to do, simply, with the ordinary man's sense of the world, for which light and heaven are situated 'above', darkness and the world of graves 'below'. The Church's confession of faith would not in any case want to express a 'scientific picture of the world' (which is ever an artificial product of human effort), but rather the natural picture (both sensuous and spiritual) entertained by human beings in their everyday lives. Yet does not the word *descendit* give clear expression to an activity, the more so if it be taken as the context-giving concept for certain other activities of Jesus in the realm of the dead, regarded as given immediately with it? Should we not be content, rather, to speak of a 'being with the dead'? The title of this chapter, which deliberately avoids the word 'descent' speaks of a 'going to the dead', an expression justified, in our opinion, by I Peter 3, 19: 'he went, *poreutheis*, and preached to the spirits in prison' – preached, that is, the 'good news' as I Peter 4, 6 adds by way of a self-evident clarification. At the end of the passage, this 'going' is placed in unmistakable parallelism with the Resurrection, which is the departure point of the 'going to heaven', *poreutheis eis ouranon* (I Peter 3, 22). It should not be overlooked that both Resurrection and Ascension are first described as a passive event: the active agent is God (the Father).[9]

There is no difficulty about understanding this 'going to the souls in prison' as, first and foremost, a 'being with', and the 'preaching' in the same primary fashion as the publication of the 'redemption', actively suffered, and brought about by the Cross of the living Jesus – and not as a new activity, distinct from the first. For then the solidarity with the condition of the dead would be the prior condition for the work of redemption, whose effects would be deployed and exercised in the 'realm' of the dead, though that work itself would remain fundamentally finished (*consummatum est!*) on the Cross. In this sense the actively formulated term 'preaching' (I Peter 3, 19; in 4, 6 it is passive, *evēngelisthē*) should be conceived as the efficacious outworking in the world beyond of what was accomplished in the temporality of history.

If one maintains this restrictive interpretation, many of the mythological traits deriving from the historically formed religious environment can be accepted unproblematically as the interpretation of such an outworking, and given their due place. They are nothing other than the imagistic and rhetorically embellished linguistic raiment which clothes a thoroughly non-mythical body. For, behind the myth, there is above all the idea of a *struggle* between the divinity which descends into the underworld, and the power hostile to God which is vanquished there and must yield up either the menaced or imprisoned divinity itself, or some other prey.[10] That subsequent interpretation of the *descensus* (right down to the great rhetorical tableaux of the Gospel of Nicodemus at the start of the fifth century,[11] of Cyril of Jerusalem,[12] of the Pseudo-Epiphanius[13] and Caesarius[14] and the Passion Plays which developed from these) evolved from the meagre information of Scripture an entire drama with the underworld as its *mise-en-scène* is undeniable, and it has led to such positions as that of W. Bieder,[15] who denies each and every dramatic interpretation of the Descent in Scripture, and claims to find the idea of a 'journey into Hell' for the first time in the Apocrypha (including the Jewish Apocrypha as interpolated by Christians), in Justin and Irenaeus with reference to a Jeremiah apocryphon (fabricated by Christians and the origin of a rigorously pre-determining, not otherwise traceable 'prediction' of the event),[16] in the *Shepherd* of Hermas, in the *Odes of Solomon*, and so forth. With that, the door was opened for the influence of the other historical religions in the surrounding world.[17] This thesis has far more arguments to commend it than the contrary thesis of W. Bousset,[18] who postulated an original representation (conditioned by the religious-historical milieu and transposed on to the person of Christ as a Redeemer-figure) of a descent *struggle* – a representation which, at a second stage, underwent considerable divesting of its mythological features thanks to the work of theological reflection: this Bousset found in, for example, Apocalypse 1, 18; Matthew 16, 18; Ephesians 4, 8ff, and, above all, I Peter 3. Over against his position, C. Schmidt was correct in denying the presence within the New Testament of any reference to a combat in the underworld: that corpus speaks only of a preaching to the dead.[19]

If the reduction here proposed of this entire set of questions – a reduction which regards the expression *descensus* as a secondary stage of interpretation of the affirmations of the New Testament – is found acceptable, then a middle way can be traced between an exegetically unfounded accumulation of New Testament texts allegedly concerning the *descensus* – to which can be added, of course, a multitude of early Christian and later theological affirmations[20] – and the other extreme, represented by Bieder. By excluding from the outset all mythological motifs in Christ's going to the dead, we answer, implicitly, those who reject this whole theologoumenon as completely unsustainable within the modern picture of the world.[21] And yet we do not need to take fright when we see how comparable material from the history of religion – for the most part, used consciously in an illustrative way[22] – is brought into service for the unique event of revelation.

(2) The New Testament

It is true that the Old Testament knows of no 'commerce' between the living God and the realm of the dead. It knows very well, however, the power of God over that realm: God can as well slay as make alive, lead down to Sheol as bring up again (I Samuel 2, 6; Deuteronomy 32, 39; Tobit 13, 2; Wisdom 16, 13). Buoyed up by this conviction, the Psalmist sang the verses cited by Peter in his Pentecost sermon (Acts 2, 24; 28) to prove that they were not fulfilled in David (who was buried, and whose tomb is found among us until this day), but in Christ. It is not the *going* to the dead which is important here – that is taken for granted, and identified, simply, with what it is to be genuinely dead – but rather the *return* from that bourn. God has not 'left' (or 'abandoned') Jesus 'in Hades' where he tarried; he has not let his Holy One see corruption. The accent is placed on the *whence* – the phrase *ek nekrōn* occurs some fifty times in the New Testament – a whence which implies a point of departure, namely, being with the dead. Death here is characterised[23] by 'pangs', by 'pains' (*ōdines*),[24] and by its lust to seize and hold (*krateisthai*): but God is stronger than death. The only thing that matters is the facticity of the 'being' of the one who is dead in 'death' or – for this amounts to the same thing – in Hades, whose character is (objectively) referred to by the term 'pains'. It is from thence that Jesus is 'awoken'. That Hades itself is undergoing (eschatological) 'birth-pangs', in order to give up this dead One, is not at this point a topic of discussion.

Matthew interprets the *Sign of Jonah* in terms of the *Triduum Mortis*

> For as Jonah was three days and three nights in the belly
> of the whale, so will the Son of man be three days and
> three nights in the heart of the earth (Matthew 12, 40).

It may be left undecided whether this 'heart of the earth' is the grave or is Hades, for, once again, it designates only the reality of being dead, under the image of the then current localisation. The parallel between the sea-monster and the heart of the earth was a natural one, and where the 'sign of Jonah' was spoken of, this particular association was inevitable.[25] Jonah calls on God in his prayer to him:

> Out of the belly of Sheol I cried,
>   and thou didst hear my voice (Jonah 2, 3).

The Old Testament 're-calling' is fulfilled, once again, in the Resurrection of Christ from the dead. And, once again, a voracious power is obliged to recognise its impotence to hold its prey.

Before any further consideration of this theme, which will recur more than once, those expressions should be mentioned which cast a clearer light on the dimensions of Christ's mission and, via that mission, of the power which he can claim. In Romans 10, 7ff, Paul (combining Deuteronomy 30, 12 with Psalm 107, 26) addresses the believer in these terms:

> Do not say in your heart, 'Who will ascend into heaven?' (that is, to bring Christ down) or 'Who will descend into the abyss?' (that is, to bring Christ up from the dead).[26] But what does it say? The word is near you . . .

The alteration in the text of Deuteronomy (which, in place of searching in the abyss, speaks of a going in search beyond the seas) enables Paul to refer to Christ's death and Resurrection: being dead is, however, *eo ipso*, a being in the abyss. The full dimensions of his mission and the outreach of his power are already surveyed in all their objectivity and the result offered to the believer, whose only contribution is to take it up. The fact that the depths of the ocean (the *Tehom*) are seen together with Sheol, yet no explicit identification of the two follows, is typical of the imagistic thinking of the Bible.

The bringing–down (*katagagein*) and bringing–up (*anagagein*) are also registered in Ephesians 4, 8ff as something realised: the crowning 'ascent' is mentioned first, and the 'descent', 'into the lower parts of the earth', only subsequently as the ascent's presupposition. In ascending, however, he 'led a host of captives' (Psalm 68, 19): the same powers which henceforth no longer have power to hold men prisoner and among which is certainly included 'the last enemy . . . death' (I Corinthians 15, 26). It is possible that in the phrase 'the lower parts of the earth' the realm of the dead is not expressly intended, yet no more is it simply a question of the Incarnation *tout court*,[27] but of an Incarnation whose internal logic led Christ to the Cross, where, by dying, he triumphed over the deathly powers.[28] So much is made explicit in Colossians 2, 14f, which speaks of the total disarming of the principalities and powers, their putting on public show and the spectacle at their expense. God who did this through the

Cross of Christ is the Subject here: he it is who stripped them of their weapons and their power. But to the powers is linked, so the context tells us (2, 12ff) the interior death of sin: it is the *terminus a quo* of the common Resurrection, both Christ's and that of those who are dead 'because of their misdeeds'. Here too, then, a background solidarity of the One who died on the Cross with those who were submitted to the power of death is presupposed.

This gives us the right precisely *not* to distinguish between physical and spiritual death in such a text as Romans 14, 9:

> For to this end Christ died and lived again, that he might be Lord both of the dead and of the living.

If here too the state of being physically dead occupies the foreground (cf. 14, 7ff), and with it, accordingly, Christ's solidarity with those who have died, nevertheless, in the background, the thought of the inter-relation of sin and death (Romans 5, 12; James 1, 15) is ever-present. An adequate division of the texts into those that concern 'physical death', and those treating of 'spiritual death' is therefore excluded from the start. John 6, 25, 28, 29 throws light on the passage from the second to the first.

That leads us back to the texts that speak of Jesus' power (acquired on the Cross) to 'bind the strong man' so as then to 'enter his house' and 'plunder his goods': the context speaks of the expulsion of Satan (Mark 3, 24–27 and parallels). The succession of images – the binding, the crossing of the threshold of the enemy's house, its plundering – certainly has no need to be shared out among the different phases of Christ's redemptive work (Incarnation, Passion, Descent into Hell). Nevertheless, it shows clearly that the total de-potentiation of the enemy coincides with a forcible entry into the innermost terrain of his power. That is why we would bring into relation with this text Matthew 16, 18 which speaks of the impotence of the gates of Hell to prevail against the Church, as also all those other passages where we hear of the *exousia* of binding and lossing. Without divine 'deliverance' from the 'pangs of death' (Acts 2, 24), Christ has no possibility of communicating a share in his own *exousia* to 'unbind' (to forgive sins, Mark 2, 10) in a way that will be recognised 'in heaven' (Matthew 18, 18; John 20, 22ff).

And here the word of the Lord of the Apocalypse must be added to our collection:

> I died, and behold, I am alive for evermore, and I have the keys of Death and Hades (Apocalypse 1, 18).

Once again, it is neither a question of a 'struggle' nor of a 'descent', but of absolute, plenary power, due to the fact that the Lord was dead (he has experienced death interiorly) and now lives eternally, having vanquished death in itself and for all, making it something 'past'. The apocalyptic tableau of Matthew 27, 51–53 describes the upshot of this de-potentiation in visionary and imagistic terms: such a shaking of the earth and of the rocks was there that graves broke open and those lying there in were made ready, after Christ's resurrection from his own grave, to accompany him out of their own state of death, and to appear in the holy city. The legendary mode of the narrative gives the opportunity to articulate in a very precise form the realities involved: in the Cross the power of Hell is already broken (down), the locked door of the grave is already burst open, yet Christ's own laying in the tomb and his 'being with the dead' is still necessary, so that, on Easter Day, the common resurrection *ek tōn nekrōn* – with 'Christ the first-fruits' – can follow. One cannot, therefore, say (for example, by reference to Philippians 2, 8–9), that between the dying and the rising again there is no room left for a special condition of being dead. The logion of the Sign of Jonah places precisely this condition at the centre.

There remains the controversial text of I Peter 3, 18–20; 4, 6, whose turbulent exegetical history cannot be set forth here. Since the criticism offered by K. Gschwind,[29] weighty voices have spoken out against any interpretation in terms of a *descensus*.[30] C. Spicq advises the greatest caution yet, despite all the counter-arguments, retains a 'descent' interpretation.[31] The linguistic manner of the passage is highly elliptic, presupposing a knowledge of contexts with which we are no longer familiar. Only *en passant*, in a parenetic context and by way of allusion to the baptismal commitment (*eperōtēma*) of the Christian does it speak of Christ's 'going away' 'in the Spirit' (*en hōi = pneumati*) 'to the souls in prison', with the aim of making a proclamation (*ekēruxen*): these souls are, however, the same who:

> formerly did not obey, when God's patience waited in the days of Noah, during the building of the ark, in which a few, that is, eight persons, were saved through water. Baptism, which corresponds to this, now saves you, not as a removal of dirt from the body but as an appeal to God for a clear conscience, through the resurrection of Jesus Christ, who has gone into heaven and is at the right hand of God, with angels, authorities, and powers subject to him.

Then follows a parenetic section which, in 4, 1, again takes as departure point the Passion of the Christ in the flesh, so as to urge the renunciation of all pagan sensuality, even though the pagans would find such abstention strange.

> They will give account to him who is ready to judge the living and the dead. For this is why the gospel was preached even to the dead, that though judged in the flesh like men, they might live in the spirit like God (4, 5–6).

We would like: first, to maintain (against Gschwind) that 4, 5 (in conformity to what we have said above about the fluidity of the transition between spiritual death and its physical counterpart) cannot treat only of the spiritually dead – the more so as the eschatological formula ('to judge the living and the dead') constitutes a title of sovereignty for the exalted Lord and signifies the definitive judgment of the world.[32] But then, secondly, the preaching of the Good News to the dead in 4, 6 is an event in the world beyond, producing there the effective fruits of Christ's suffering in the flesh –

whatever idea of conversion after death may be involved. The Corinthians too had themselves baptised representatively for the departed (I Corinthians 15, 29). The efficacy of the redeeming death for the final judgment is expressed in the paradox that the dead are doubtless 'judged' (by dying) conformably to the general human lot, but, despite this, can live in the Spirit (that is, thanks to Christ's Resurrection: 3, 18c, 21c). Thirdly, these inter-connexions make it appear in the highest degree probable that the preaching of the Good News to the dead in 4, 6 and the proclamation to the spirits in prison in 3, 9 are the same event, and one may, with B. Reicke, still see in these 'souls' the world powers of the age before the Flood, *including* those human beings whose lords they were.[33] That, where this 'prison' is concerned, one should not think of a sub-terranean Hades, but rather of a prison in the realm of the air (cf. Ephesians 6, 12), between heaven and earth (Gschwind, cf. Schlier)[34] and that, on this account, the *poreuthis* should not be interpreted as a *descensus* but as an *ascensus* instead, as a process within the movement of the Ascension (4, 22), seems to me highly improbable. Fourthly, the principal stress lies on the opposition between the time of the Deluge and the present eschatological time of the Resurrection, something which necessitates a sideward glance at II Peter 3, 5ff. A first and total judgment of the world made the 'world that then existed' to perish, 'deluged with water'. But that judgment belongs to the past. We are nonetheless moving towards the fire that is to come, which, for the Godless, will be a day of ruin. Yet God's longsuffering patience reigns: he does not wish that 'any should perish, but that all should reach repentance'. The longanimity of which Second Peter speaks when thinking of the final judgment, First Peter mentions in relation to the first judgment (that of the Flood). In the presence of that sign of salvation, the ark, it was a time of salvation conceded to the decision of faith, and yet, like the first judgment by water, it was, thanks to the longanimity of God in Jesus Christ, a provisional time, destined to be transcended. Fifthly and lastly, that makes it clear that the 'proclamation' in I Peter 3, 19 cannot be anything other than a preaching of salvation to the dead of 4,

6 (the particle *gar* is noticeable here). Furthermore, one should not present this as a subjective kind of preaching, meant to move others to conversion: it is the objective announcement (like a herald's signal) of a fact – the fact, namely, that what appeared to be definitive judgment (a 'prison') on the unbelief which greeted the first sign of salvation is overcome by the grace of Christ, which has turned the sign of judgment (the Flood) into a sign of salvation (baptism), and created from the 'tiny remnant' ('eight souls') who survived the great catastrophe an entire redeemed people (I Peter 2, 9). Bieder is right: what is in question in 3, 19 is not

> a victory obtained by means of a descent, but a triumphant making known of a victory already won. There is no question but that the First Letter of Peter, like the rest of the New Testament, is thinking here of the death of the Cross and the Resurrection of Christ.[35]

And yet this proclamation is introduced by the first *poreutheis*: it happens in the going to the dead 'in prison'. This 'going to' has a two-fold content (with nothing further to be added): first, the solidarity of the dead Christ with those who have died, among whom, symbolically, those who did not believe at the time of the first judgment on the world are given, specifically, a prominence of their own, and, secondly, the proclamation of the reconciliation of God with the world as a whole (II Corinthians 5, 19; Colossians 1, 23), achieved in Christ as a finished (factum) event.

> For the understanding of the text about the journey into Hades it is of decisive importance to know that it has an antithetical model in the Ethiopian book of Enoch, which received its present form after the Parthian invasion of 37 B.C. Chapters 12 to 16 describe how Enoch was commissioned to go to the fallen angels of Genesis 6, and to disclose to them that 'they will find no peace and no pardon' and that God will reject their plea for peace and mercy. Seized by fear and trembling, they ask Enoch to compose a written request for

indulgence and pardon. Enoch is carried away to the flame-surrounded throne of God and receives the reply which he is to communicate to the request of the fallen sons of God. The decision consists in one short, shocking statement, 'You will have no peace'. It is scarcely to be doubted that the theologoumenon of the Hades journey of Christ has as its model the myth of Enoch as just described. On the disobedient spirits in the darkest dungeon of the infernal fortress there advances once more a divine messenger with a divine message. But whereas Enoch has to announce to them the impossibility of pardon, the new message reads quite differently: it is the Good News (4, 6). Thus the doctrine of Christ's preaching in Hades gives expression to the fact that the Righteous One died for the unrighteous (3, 18); even for those who were lost and without hope, his atoning death has brought salvation.[36]

(3) Solidarity in Death

What we have said up to now leads us to undertake a critical examination of the theological tradition, as that has developed from the end of the first century until our own day, without for all that rejecting it completely. We must not only grade the differing value of its affirmations but examine each one in particular in order to re-compose the set in a new way. Certain elements will find themselves definitively laid to one side (such as the mythical accoutrements of a combat in Hades). Others, and above all the soteriological explorations excluded by recent dogmatics in favour of a rigid systematisation, will be once again placed in the limelight.

A first vantage point to be taken up is that of the solidarity of the Crucified with all the human dead. The careful description, free of all apologetic tendencies, of the taking down from the Cross, of the treatment bestowed on the cadavre, and of the burial testifies in simple fashion to this solidarity. The body simply *must* be put into the earth. (There is no question here of making an exception, for example, by reason of 'incorruptibility' cf. Acts 2, 27 and 31.) It is thereby implicitly affirmed that the soul of Jesus is 'with' the dead.[37]

(a) Sheol

The fact of being with the unredeemed dead, in the Sheol of the Old Testament, signifies a solidarity in whose absence the condition of standing for sinful man before God would not be complete. This is why Sheol must be understood in the classic Old Testament sense, putting between parentheses the speculations of later Judaism, influenced as these were by Persia and Hellenism, about the difference of destiny which distinguishes men by way of reward and penalty after death. This is so even if such representations do occur occasionally in the New Testament, notably in Luke, in the parable of Lazarus (16, 19–31) and the address to the Good Thief (23, 43). 'Paradise' (a polymorphous term)[38] and 'Gehenna'[39] remain therefore included within the englobing and determining concept of Sheol. This is the Hades whose keys the Risen One holds (Apocalypse 1, 18); it is Tartarus (II Peter 2, 4), the 'Pit' (Isaiah 24, 22), as also the prison wherein the evil angels are 'kept in eternal chains in the nether gloom until the judgment of the great day' (Jude 6). The Pentateuch, the book of Joshua, the books of the Kings know of no distinction between men in what concerns their lot in the beyond, recognising at most a personal responsibility before Yahweh. To existence in death there belong darkness (Job 10, 21ff 17, 13; Psalm 88, 7 and 13; 143, 3; and even eternal darkness: Psalm 49, 20), dust (Job 17, 16; Psalm 30, 10; 146, 4; Isaiah 26, 19; Daniel 12, 2), silence (Psalm 94, 17; 115, 17). From Sheol one does not return (Job 7, 9; 10, 21; 14, 12). No activity goes on there Qoheleth 9, 10), there is no joy (Sirach 14, 11–17), no knowledge of what happens on earth (Job 14, 21ff; 21, 21; Qohelet 9, 5; Isaiah 63, 16). There is no more praise of of God (Psalm 6, 6; 30, 10; 115, 17; Sirach 17, 27; Isaiah 38, 18). Deprived of all strength and all vitality (Isaiah 14, 10), the dead are called *refa'im*, the powerless ones. They are as if they were not (Psalm 39, 14; Sirach 17, 28). They dwell in the country of forgetfulness (Psalm 88, 13). 'And to there even the Christ descended after his dying.[40]

Of this comprehensive character of the reality of Sheol *vis-à-vis* all the places of the world beyond in the Old Testament, Augustine offers a testimony which is exegetically weak but theologically strong in his celebrated letter to Evodius.[41] There Augustine distinguishes between a lower *infernum* (where the 'rich man' lives) and a higher (where Lazarus dwells, in the bosom of Abraham). The two are separated by a *chaos magnum*, yet both belong equally to Hades. That Christ descended even to the lower *infernum*, in order to 'deliver from their sufferings tortured souls, that is, sinners' (*salvos facere a doloribus*) Augustine regards as certain (*non dubito*). The grace of Christ redeemed all those who tarried there: *adhuc requiro*. We this we may compared his *De Genesi ad Litteram* 12, 63

> Et Christi quidem animam venisse usque ad ea loca in quibus peccatores cruciantur, ut eos solveret a tormentis, quos esse solvendos occulta nobis sua justitia judicabat, non immerito creditur.[42]

One should note that what is in question here, for Augustine, is delivery from Sheol, and not from the Hell of the New Testament.

Robert Pullus, who, in his *Sententiae*, reflected in the profoundest and most original manner on the problems of Hades, and whom we shall meet often enough later, follows, in all fundamental matters, the line of Augustine here, declaring that the *chaos magnum* between the place of punishment and that of reward does not foreclose the possibility of a dialogue between the wastrel and Lazarus. It is this very conversation which, for him, makes it certain that both places are situated in the *infernum*.[43]

(b) The condition of Sheol

The Old Testament descriptions are so existential in their tenor that the accent falls much more on the condition of the dead than on the place where they find themselves. It is not, then, a matter for surprise that, in Christian theology, the theme of places (*receptacula, promptuaria*)[44] and that of conditions are set side by side with little or no reciprocal influence, and that the second can sometimes appear without the former. It is highly significant that Bede who, no doubt, believed in a local Hell, is able with equal facility to consider Hell as an 'act'. In this sense, the Devil, even when he leaves the Hell which is a place, carries his Hell everywhere he goes.[45] This view is shared by the *Summa* of Alexander of Hales.[46] In accordance with a tradition deriving from Plato and Plotinus, Augustine, in his *Literal Commentary on Genesis* admitted the purely spiritual character of Hell.[47] If the soul is spiritual, it can nevertheless experience the play of mental images, conjuring up the reality of bodies, and by them (for example in dreams) be either tormented or rendered blessed. 'Hell' would be the condition where one is so affected in the intensest way possible.

> One may reasonably ask why they say of Hades that it is exists beneath earth, when it is no physical place, or why it must be called the underworld, if it is not under the earth.

John Scot Eriugena,[48] Nicholas of Cusa[49] and, finally, Marsilio Ficino[50] maintain that where the soul is attached by a preferential love for the sensuous (rather than for the spiritual), it is rightly plagued by imaginative representations of the sensuous order after death. Pulleyn – here as elsewhere – goes his own way and, after lengthy mulling over the subject arrives at a concept of Hades more spiritual than local. This enables him to avoid the admission of a localised *chaos magnum* between the evil Rich Man and Lazarus. In reality, what separates them is their inner spiritual state: 'poena atque quies (sunt) insimul, praetermissa divisione locorum.'[51] Though a de-mythologisation so radical as this is not common, it opens the way to a psychic solidarity between the dead Christ and those who dwell in the Hades of the spirit.

(c) Solidarity

This ultimate solidarity is the final point and the goal of that first 'descent', so clearly described in the Scriptures, into a 'lower world' which, with Augustine, can already be characterised, by way of contrast with heaven, as *infernum*.[52] Thomas Aquinas will echoe Augustine here.[53] For him, the necessity whereby Christ had to go down to Hades lies not in some insufficiency of the suffering endured on the Cross but in the fact that Christ has assumed all the *defectus* of sinners.[54] And since soul and body are adapted one to the other (*proportionalia*), Christ had to remain, with his soul, in Hades for as long as his body lay in the tomb, 'ut per utrumque fratribus suis similaretur'.[55] Of the four reasons which Thomas gives for the descent among the dead, the one he places first is 'ut sustineret totam poenam peccati, ut sic totam culpam expiaret'. Now the penalty which the sin of man brought on was not only the death of the body. It was also a penalty affected the soul, for sinning was also the soul's work, and the soul paid the price in being deprived of the vision of God. As yet unexpiated, it followed that all human beings who lived before the coming of Christ, even the holy ancestors, descended into the *infernum*. And so, in order to assume the entire penalty imposed upon sinners, Christ willed not only to die, but to go down, in his soul, *ad infernum*.[56] As early as the Fathers of the second century, this act of sharing constituted the term and aim of the Incarnation. The 'terrors of death' into which Jesus himself falls are only dispelled when the Father raises him again.[57] According to Tertullian, the Son of God adapted himself to the whole law of human death:

> Huic quoque legi satisfecit, forma humanae mortis apud inferos functus.[58]

The same affirmation is found in Irenaeus:

> Dominus legem mortuorum servavit, ut fieret primogenitus a mortuis.[59]

He insists on his own grounding principle, namely, that only what has been endured is healed and saved.[60] Since above all this is a matter of penetrating into the realm of the *inferi*, so for Ambrosiaster in the *Quaestiones ex Novo Testamento*, Christ had to die so as to be capable of this step.[61] Christ willed to be like us, says Andrew of Crete, in 'walking amidst the shadows of death, in that place where souls had been bound with chains unbreakable'.[62] All that only expresses the law of human death, thought through to its logical conclusion. It tells us nothing about a 'descent', much less a 'combat' and least of all a 'triumphant victory procession' by Christ across Hades. To the extent that the experience of death was objectively capable of containing an interior victory and thus a triumph over hostile powers, to that extent it was in no way necessary that this triumph be subjectively experienced. For precisely that would have abolished the law of solidarity. Let it not be forgotten: among the dead, there is no living communication. Here solidarity means: being solitary like, and with, the others.

(d) The indefinability of the Sheol condition

Behind this solidarity there lies hidden a grave theological problem whose inner disagreement our thinking, limited as it is by time, cannot resolve. The penalty which weighs on 'pre-Christian humanity' by reason of 'original sin' – if we abstract here from personal sin – is *de jure* definitive: it is *poena damni*, deprivation of the vision of God. On the other hand, before Christ there was already – in manifest form among the Jews, but in hidden form, surely, among other peoples – an order of salvation oriented towards Christ which in some way makes it possible, in co-operation with the grace of God, to be 'just' and thus, in the midst of the *poena damni*, to await 'redemption'. This dialectic loses its bite if one naively ascribes to the pious men of the Old Testament the 'light of hope' amid the darkness of the *poena damni*. For hope in the theological sense is a participation in the divine life and therefore contradicts the *poena damni* –and, in thorough-going fashion, the classical Old Testament texts on the concept of Sheol as well. When Thomas says that Christ has friends not only on earth but also in Hell, since 'in inferno multi erant qui cum veritate et fide Venturi decesserant',[63] this naive, non-dialectical conception dominates his thought too. The dialectical element appears in a proposition in the *Summa* of Alexander of Hales:

> Nullius hominis caritas potest mereri vitam aeternam post peccatum nisi interveniente merito Christ, quia omnes sunt originali reatu obligati ad satisfactionem.[64]

And Ambrosiaster can remark that

> The man who is already reconciled with God cannot yet ascend towards God. That is why Christ descends to snatch away from death the prey which death retained unjustly.[65]

But Hades, seen christologically, takes on thereby a certain character of *conditionality*: the man who is already reconciled with God, who has faith, hope and charity, cannot, to be sure, theologically speaking, be reconciled except through Christ, and so, to possess this grace, he cannot really be waiting for Christ, since he already has something of the Christ-life in himself. Richard of Saint-Victor sees the difficulty: the just before Christ have *caritas*, and yet, despite that, they have to dwell in the *infernum* and wait for Christ's Hades journey:

> Tenebantur debito damnationis aeternae, non quod eis aeterna fuerit, sed quod eis aeterna *fuisset*, nisi mors Christi eos ab hoc debito absolveret.[66]

On the one hand, one must point out here that concepts of time taken from the world are no longer valid after death and so we cannot determine in temporal terms the taking on of the experience of Sheol by the Redeemer (nor, consequently, the waiting of the unredeemed for him).[67] We are forced to the paradoxical and self-annulling concept of a 'provisional *poena damni*'.[68] But another thought leads further: if through the grace of Christ, working by anticipation, those who lived before Christ in love did not experience the entire, truly merited, *poena damni* (since they waited for him in the light of faith, hope and charity), who then did really experience it save the Redeemer himself? Is not precisely this inequality the final consequence of the law of solidarity? Does not God, as Gregory the Great so justly saw, englobe, by his own ever greater depth, all the deep places of the underworld? He who is higher than heaven is also 'inferno profundior, quia transcendendo subvehit'.[69] It is Christ who through *compassio*, has taken upon himself the *timor horroris*:

> verum timorem, veram tristitiam sicut et veram carnem

not because he *had* to suffer but rather 'miserationis voluntate' as Alain of Lille puts it.[70]

But in that case it is *he* who sets the limits to the extension of damnation, who forms the boundary stone marking the place where the lowest pitch is reached and the reverse movement set into operation. This is what the Canon of Hippolytus says in a mysterious expression of its own:

> Qui cum traderetur voluntarie passioni ut mortem solvat
> et vincula diaboli disrumpat et infernum calcet et justos
> inluminet et *terminum figat* . . .[71]

Gregory of Nyssa concurs when he makes the light of Christ shine forth from the uttermost end of darkness.[72]

> The Lord has touched all parts of the creation . . . so that each might find the Logos everywhere, even the one who has strayed into the world of demons (Athanasius)[73]

Christ descended, therefore, to where one is in death:

> in order to bear our guilt, As it was fitting that he should die in order to redeem us from death, so was it

also fitting that he should go down into Hades, to redeem us *from descent* into Hades ... according to the word of Isaiah, 'Truly, he has taken upon himself our malady, he has born our pains' (Thomas).[74]

(4) The Being Dead of the Son of God

On the basis of what has just been said, we cannot avoid the following thought: given that the Redeemer, in his solidarity with the dead, has spared them the integral experience of death (as the *poena damni*), so that a heavenly shimmer of light, of faith, love, hope, has ever illuminated the 'abyss' – then he took, by substitution, that whole experience upon himself. The Redeemer showed himself therefore as the only one who, going beyond the general experience of death, was able to measure the depths of that abyss. Once again, and this time retrospectively, one can reject as incomplete a 'theology of death' which limits Jesus' solidarity with sinners to the act of decision or some self-gift of existence in the moment of dying. Rather must we say, with Althaus: for the death of Christ to be inclusive, it must be simultaneously exclusive and unique in its expiatory value. This aspect of Christ's death – to which the present section is devoted – can be developed in three directions: as experience of the 'second death' (where for the first time the New Testament concept of Hell makes its appearance); as experience of sin as such (which allows us to give its proper place to the theme of '*descensus* as triumph'); and lastly as Trinitarian event, since each and every saving situation in the life, death and resurrection of Jesus Christ can only be interpreted, ultimately, in a Trinitarian way. Here too, and here especially, it is important to examine critically the many fragments of tradition and to re-assemble them in a manner different from that long customary.

(b) The experience of the second death

The *Sententiae Parisinenes* formulate a principle in simple terms: 'Anima Christi ivit ad infernum, id est sustinuit passiones, ut liberaret suos de inferno'.[75] What these 'passions' might be is not here stated. But we can recall the fundamental thesis of Bonaventure, whereby spiritual *compassiones* surpass in intensity bodily *passiones*.[76] The explicit subject of this text is, in fact, *compassio* in death, and no longer the *compassio* of Good Friday at the foot of the Cross.[77]

And here we encounter the well-known view of Luther, and above all of Calvin, according to which Jesus experienced on the Cross Hell's tortures in place of sinners, thus rendering superfluous a similar experience of Hell on Holy Saturday. Luther remarks of the Mount of Olives and the Cross: 'vere enim sensit mortem et infernum in corpore suo',[78] but he can admit an experience of Hell even for the dead Christ. Christ would have truly gone down into Hell, so as to undergo the 'dolores post mortem'.[79] But just this suffering is his triumph over Hell, so much so that one can speak of a *victrix infirmitas*.[80] Melanchthon stresses in a unilateral way the aspect of triumph, determining thereby the interests of later Lutheranism.

Calvin is aware of the soteriological meaning of the *descensus*, but for him it is more important to establish that Christ had to suffer the 'divinae ultionis severitatem'; 'diros in anima cruciatus damnati ac perditi hominis'. 'Nothing would have been achieved if Jesus Christ had not undergone physical death'. In order to liberate us, he had to engage, rather, in a direct struggle with the horror of everlasting death'. Yet he could not be held by the *dolores mortis*. Calvin cites Hilary on this point: 'The Son of God is in Hell, but man is raised to heaven' (Trin. 3, 15). He defends himself, however, against the charge of interpreting the abandonment by God in Hell as the 'despair of not believing':

The weakness of Christ was pure of all stain, since it was enclosed within obedience to God.

And precisely in that did his mortal anguish and God-abandonment differ radically from the habitual anxiety of the sinner. Thus for Calvin the God-abandonment which 'began' on the Mount of Olives, continued on Calvary and came to its climax on Holy Saturday is a unique event.[81] The Heidelberg Catechism follows him here in its forty-fourth question.[82] These texts underline the continuity and homogeneity between the God-abandonment before death and that same abandonment after death, rather than the difference between them which is our concern at the moment. To this hesitation of the Reformers in regard to the kenotic and triumphant aspects of Holy Saturday later Protestant theology added endless discussions and distinctions (whether consummationist or infernalist) which we shall here ignore.[83]

Nicholas of Cusa accepted the existence of a passion of Holy Saturday in clear terms, and regarded it as forming part of the vicarious Passion properly so called. Let us hear him:

> The vision, *visio*, of death by the mode of immediate experience, *via cognoscentiae*, is the most complete punishment possible. And since the death of Christ was complete, since through his own experience he saw the death which he had freely chosen to undergo, the soul of Christ went down into the underworld, *ad inferna*, where the vision of death is. For death is called 'underworld', *infernus*, and it has been loosed from out of the deeper underworld, *ex inferno inferiori*. The lower or deeper underworld is where one sees death. When God raised Christ he drew him, as we read in the Acts of the Apostles, from out of the lower underworld, after delivering him from the torture of that underworld, *solutis doloribus inferni*. That is why the prophet says, 'He did not leave my soul in the underworld'. Christ's suffering, the greatest one could conceive, was like that of the damned who cannot be damned any more. That is, his suffering went to the length of infernal punishment (*usque ad poenam infernalem*) . . . He alone through such a death entered into glory. He wanted to experience the *poena sensus* like the damned in Hell for the glorifying of his Father, and so as to show that one should obey the Father even

to the utmost torture (*quod ei obediendum sit usque ad extremum supplicium*). That means: praising and glorifying God in every possible way for our justification – which is what Christ has done.[84]

This constitutes the logical consequence of what we have said about a substitutory 'being with the dead' and permits an understanding of how Sheol, or the Old Testament Hades, can pass theologically into the New Testament Hell. The Jewish Gehenna represents here only a mediation of an exterior kind. Despite all other considerations, the passage is, theologically, a leap, and it can only be grounded on Christology.

It is in the Letter to the Hebrews that we are really present at the birth of the concept. Before the Christological *hapax*, nothing, either in this world or in the world to come, is absolutely definitive. But, thanks to the uniqueness of Christ, man comes to the unique and definitive decision. For those who have received and tasted the richness of the eschatological good things, 'and nevertheless have fallen away', 'it is impossible to restore (them) again to repentance'. They will end by being 'burned' (Hebrews 6, 4–8).

For if we sin deliberately after receiving the knowledge of the truth, there no longer remains a sacrifice for sins, but a fearful prospect of judgment, and a fury of fire which will consume the adversaries.

The transgressing of the Law was punished with death.

How much worse punishment do you think will be deserved by the man who has spurned the Son of God, and profaned the blood of the covenant by which he was sanctified, and outraged the Spirit of grace? (10, 26–29).

Esau likewise was only an earthly figure: he lost the blessing, and

when he desired to inherit the blessing, he was rejected
. . . though he sought it with tears (12, 16–17).

And so, with a perfect lucidity of expression, 12–25
following:

> See that you do not refuse him who is speaking. For if
> they did not escape when they refused him who warned
> them on earth, much less shall we escape if we reject
> him who warns from heaven.

The author twice speaks of God as of a devouring fire.

It is theologically mistaken to retroject the concept of the
New Testament (Christological) Hell into the Old Testament,
and, on that basis, present Holy Saturday with questions
which are insoluble since ill posed. Augustine is capable of
expressing himself very clearly on the theological replacement
of Hades by Hell.[85] Hell in the New Testament sense is a
function of the Christ event. Now, if Christ has suffered, not
only for the elect but for all human beings,[86] he has by this
very fact assumed their eschatological 'No' in regard to the
event of salvation which came about in him. And therefore,
however one describes the experience of Holy Saturday, one
must grant that Nicholas of Cusa was fundamentally right.
This experience has no need to be anything other than what
is implied by a real solidarity with the inhabitants of Sheol
that no redemptive light has brightened. For all redemptive
light comes uniquely from the one who was in solidarity
until the end. And he can communicate it because he,
substitutionally, renounced it.

(b) The experience of sin as such

Nicholas of Cusa spoke with great exactitude in the passage
cited above of a vision of the (second) death, a *visio mortis*.
This contemplative and objective (passive) moment is what
distinguishes Holy Saturday from the subjective and active
experience of suffering in the Passion. Christ belongs now
with the *refa'im*, with those 'deprived of strength'. He cannot

conduct an active struggle against the 'powers of Hell'. No more can he 'triumph' subjectively over them, which would pre-suppose new life and strength. And yet this extremity of 'weakness' certainly can and must be one with the object of his vision: the second death which, itself, is one with sheer sin as such, no longer sin as attaching to a particular human being, sin incarnate in living existences, but abstracted from that individuation, contemplated in its bare reality as such (for sin *is* a reality!).

In this amorphous condition, sin forms what one can call the second 'chaos' (generated by human liberty) and that, in the separation between sin and the living man, is then precisely the product of the active suffering of the Cross. In this respect, the dead Redeemer in the infernal Sheol does not really contemplate anything other than his own triumph, though he sees that triumph not in the shining forth of the life of the Resurrection − for how could he who was awakened to eternal life still possess a point of contact with this chaos? − but in the one and only condition which allows such immediate contact, namely, the absolute emptying of life which he knew as the Dead One?[87] The object of this *visio mortis* cannot be a populated Hell, for then it would be the contemplation of a defeat; nor an inhabited Purgatory, for theologically there could be no such Purgatory 'before' Christ, as we shall show; nor a populated 'Pre-Hell', which is rightly represented symbolically as de-populated by the 'descent of Christ'. The object of the *visio mortis* can only be the pure substantiality of 'Hell' which is 'sin in itself'. Plato and Plotinus created for this the expression *borboros* (mud, ordure) which the Church Fathers (and notably the Cappadocians) gratefully took up.[88] Likewise the image of chaos is a natural one here.[89] In another image still, Eriugena says that, in our redemption, 'all the leprosy of human nature was thrown to the Devil'.[90] And when the great harlot of Babylon, as quintessence of the sin of the world, 'has fallen', and 'has become a dwelling place of demons, a haunt of every foul spirit', when she has been abandoned on all sides to be 'burned with fire' in 'pestilence and mourning and famine' (Apocalypse 18, 2, 8), when men see, at first only from 'far off' the 'smoke of her burning' (18, 9 and 17), when she is 'thrown down' and is 'found no more' (v. 21), when the smoke arising from her 'goes up for ever and ever' (19, 3), we have beneath our eyes the ultimate image to which Scripture has recourse in the representation of pure evil's self-consumption. Of that self-consumption, A. Gügler, the disciple of Herder and Sailer, painted a great tableau, using the palette of the Romantic philosophy of nature. He describes Hell as the final 'residue and phlegm which it is absolutely impossible to restore to life' and where the 'hate which belongs to enemies is absolutely objectified'. For what is consumed can no longer be kindled again by contact with a Living One. It can no longer do anything more than consume itself eternally like a flame that is darkly self-enclosed, 'to engulf for ever in the empty abyss the final burnt out relics of all that can be burned'.[91]

In this presentation, Hell is a *product* of the Redemption, a product which henceforth must be 'contemplated' in its own 'for itself' by the Redeemer, so as to become, in its state of sheer reprobation that which exists 'for him': that over which, in his Resurrection, he receives the power and the keys. This is why every dramatic representation, of the style of the 'theory of ransom', in either its grosser or its more subtle form, is here superfluous.[92]

(c) *Trinitarian character of the event*

That the Redeemer is solidary with the dead, or, better, with this death which makes of the dead, for the first time, dead human beings in all reality – this is the final consequence of the redemptive mission he has received from the Father. His being with the dead is an existence at the utmost pitch of obedience, and because the One thus obedient is the dead Christ, it constitutes the 'obedience of a corpse' (the phrase is Francis of Assisi's) of a theologically unique kind. By it Christ takes the existential measure of everything that is sheerly contrary to God, of the entire object of the divine eschatological judgment, which here is grasped in that event in which it is 'cast down' (*hormēmati blēthēsetai*, Apocalypse

18, 21; John 12, 31; Matthew 22, 13). But at the same time, this happening gives the measure of the Father's mission in all its amplitude: the 'exploration' of Hell is an event of the (economic) Trinity.

> Patiens vulnerum et salvator aegrorum, unus defunctorum et vivificator obeuntium, ad inferna descendens et a Patris gremio non recedens.[93]

If the Father must be considered as the Creator of human freedom – with all its foreseeable consequences – then judgment belongs primordially to him, and thereby Hell also; and when he sends the Son into the world to save it instead of judging it, and, to equip him for this function, gives 'all judgment to the Son' (John 5, 22), then he must also introduce the Son *made man* into 'Hell' (as the supreme entailment of human liberty). But the Son cannot really be introduced into Hell save as a dead man, on Holy Saturday. This introducing is needful since the dead must 'hear the voice of the Son of God', and hearing that voice, 'live' (John 5, 15). The Son must 'take in with his own eyes what in the realm of creation is imperfect, unformed, chaotic' so as to make it pass over into his own domain as the Redeemer. This is what Irenaeus tells us:

> Propter quod et descendit ad inferiora terrae, id quod erat inoperatum conditionis visurus oculis.[94]

This vision of chaos by the God-man has become for us the condition of our vision of the Divinity.[95] His exploration of the ultimate depths has transformed what was a prison into a way. And so Gregory the Great can say:

> Christ went down into the deepest abysses of the sea, when he went into the Lowest Hell, to fetch forth the souls of his elect. Before the redemption, the depth of the sea was a prison, not a way ... But God made of this abyss a road ... It is also called 'the deepest abyss' on the grounds that, just as the depths of the sea cannot

be fathomed by any human gaze, so too the secret of Hell is impenetrable to all human knowledge.

Yet the Lord can cross (*deambulare*) this deepest Hell, since he is not bound by any of the bonds of sin, but is, rather, 'free among the dead'. Gregory now turns, from the depths of Holy Saturday, to consider the spiritual descent of the Redeemer into the lostness of the sinful heart: the very same *descensus* is repeated each time that the Lord goes down into the depths of the *desperata corda*.[96] In Gregory's footsteps, Isidore of Seville too speaks of the *via in profundo maris*, which opens to the elect the way of heaven.[97] Inasmuch as the Son travels across the chaos in virtue of the mission received from the Father, he is, objectively speaking, whilst in the midst of the darkness of what is contrary to God, in 'paradise', and the image of triumph may well express this.[98]

> Today he is, as king, come to the prison; today he has broken down the doors of bronze and has snapped the bolts of iron. He who, a dead man like any other, was swallowed up, has laid Hell waste in God.[99]

In any case, it is, as Thomas Aquinas underlines, a 'taking possession'.[100] Henceforth Hell belongs to Christ, and Christ in rising with the knowledge of Hell can communicate that knowledge to us also.[101]

(5) Salvation in the Abyss

As Trinitarian event, the going to the dead is necessarily also an event of salvation. It is poor theology to limit this salvific happening in an a priori manner by affirming – in the context of a particular doctrine of predestination and the presumed identification of Hades (Gehenna) with Hell – that Christ was unable to bring any salvation to 'Hell properly so called', *infernus damnatorum*. Following many of the Fathers, the great Scholastics set up just such a prioristic barriers. Once agreed that there were four subterranean 'reception areas' – pre-Hell,

Purgatory, the Hell of unbaptised infants and the true Hell of fire — theologians went on to ask just how far Christ had descended and to just what point his redemptive influence extended, whether by his personal presence, *praesentia*, or merely by a simple effect, *effectus*. The most frequent reply was that he showed himself to the damned in order to demonstrate his power even in Hell; that in the Hell of infants he had nothing to achieve; that in Purgatory an amnesty could be promulgated, its precise scope a matter of discussion. The Pre-Hell remained the proper field of play of the redemptive action.[102] In the light of our remarks above, this whole construction must be laid to one side, since before Christ (and here the term 'before' must be understood not in a chronological sense but in an ontological), there can be neither Hell nor Purgatory — and as for a Hell of infants, of that we know nothing — but only that Hades (which at the most one might divide speculatively into an upper and a lower Hades, the inter-relationship of the two remaining obscure) whence Christ willed to deliver 'us' by his solidarity with those who were (physically and spiritually) dead.

But the desire to conclude from this that all human beings, before and after Christ, are henceforth saved, that Christ by his experience of Hell has emptied Hell, so that all fear of damnation is now without object, is a surrender to the opposite extreme. We shall have cause to speak of this again later, but even at this stage we have to say that precisely here the distinction between Hades and Hell acquires its theological significance. In rising from the dead, Christ leaves behind him Hades, that is, the state in which humanity is cut off from access to God. But, by virtue of his deepest Trinitarian experience, he takes 'Hell' with him, as the expression of his power to dispose, as judge, the everlasting salvation or the everlasting loss of man.

Certainly, this was above all a *saving* event: the deployment of the effects of the Cross in the abyss of deadly perdition. On that point, K. Rahner and L. Boros are right. Their thinking is not new. It has often been expressed in the period after Schleiermacher and Hegel. E. Güder drew attention to the 'soteriological consequence' of the Holy Saturday event:

from now on, salvation is offered to all men, in such a way that the dead will decide on their response to that offer, in conformity to what that author calls 'the human possibility of deciding for or against God's revelation in Christ', under the influence of the 'fundamental orientation of the soul's desire' as shaped during this life. And this concerns the dead before Christ's appearing, as well as after.[103] The intimate interest which the nineteenth century took in the theological motif of the *descensus* has to do with this insertion of salvation into the fundamental construction of the world and so with the universal offer of salvation with results therefrom. Accordingly, the question as to whether the *descensus* forms part of the *status exinanitionis* or of the *status exaltationis* receives a new answer. The descent is treated as a 'dialectical reversal of defeat and victory' (P. Marheineicke), a 'passage' from the first to the second (G. Thomasius), a process which generates 'movement in the inter-mediate state of the departed', since Christ makes himself thereby a 'mid-point overtopping all natural barriers' (J. A. Dorner).[104]

(a) Purgatory

Seen theologically, Purgatory cannot take its rise elsewhere than in the event of Holy Saturday. Even if, in First Corinthians 3, 12–15, Paul makes use of an Old Testament language and draws in the eschatological judging fire of the 'Day of the Lord' for the 'probation' of man, the criterion for that judgment is none other than the 'foundation', Jesus Christ. The eschatological fire can, no doubt, test the works raised on this foundation and in certain circumstances burn them up totally, but it saves the human being himself 'as through fire'.[105] What is in question is not purification but putting to the test. The fire is the instrument of an eschatological judgment, but that judgment is not exercised by, simply, the devouring wrath of God. On the contrary, indeed, it is exercised by him who is solidary with us, Jesus Christ. The Pauline text, whose background is the fire of the Day of Yahweh, has nothing in common with the language of Matthew 25, 41 whose backcloth is the Jewish representation of Gehenna. Despite all the exegetical objections that Origen's account may arouse,[106] he was theologically correct: in 'being with the dead', Christ brought the factor of mercy into what is imaged as the fire of the divine wrath.[107]

> Once Hades engulfed us all and held us firm. That is why Christ did not only come down to earth, but also under the earth . . . He found us all in the nether world . . . and brought us out from there not onto earth but into the Kingdom of heaven.[108]

Catholic dogma must, in any case, speak of a 'universal purpose of redemption' (ever against the restrictions of a doctrine of double predestination).[109] A negative confirmation of the theological rectitude of this approach is furnished by those Scholastic speculations which, by postulating a pre-Christian 'Purgatory' in Hades, find themselves involved in insoluble contradictions. Once again, that appears with great clarity in Pullus, who thought through these matters in the most rigorous way.[110]

(b) The 'loosing of the bonds'

If one asks about the 'work' of Christ in Hades, or, better, since we have described that work as a purely passive 'vision' of sin in all its separateness, about the 'fruit' Christ brought forth there, we must, in the first place, guard against that theological busyness and religious impatience which insist on anticipating the moment of fruiting of the eternal redemption through the temporal passion – on dragging forward that moment from Easter to Holy Saturday.

To be sure, one can, as the Eastern Church customarily does, see the decisive image of the redemption in the *descensus*, that is, in the breaking down of Hell's gates and the liberation of the prisoners.[111] Times innumerable the icon-painters depicted that scene, the true Easter image of the East.[112] Here the entire work of the *Triduum Mortis* is perceived as a single movement which on Holy Saturday reaches its supreme dramatic intensity. Whereas the Western images of Easter always show the risen Christ alone, the East makes us see the soteriological and social aspect of the redemptive work. That is only possible by an anticipatory interpolation of the Easter event into the time of Holy Saturday, and by the transformation of a victory which was objective and passive into one that is subjective and active. The preaching of the first centuries, itself superseded to some degree by the Easter mystery plays of the Middle Ages, yielded more and more to this understandable need. That preaching, and those plays, preserved an important theological theme increasingly lost to view in systematic theology. But in preserving one theme they obscured another, which only recent liturgical directives have revalidated in excluding from Holy Saturday the alleluia chant.

I Peter 3, 19 speaks in the active mood of *kērussein*, 4, 6 in the passive mood of *euangelizesthai*, Acts 2, 23 of *luein*, the sufferings or bonds of death, with God as subject. Accordingly, two themes compete for predominance: the theme of preaching or proclamation, and that of liberation or redemption.

The *proclamation*, in its sheer objectivity, and inasmuch as it is *evangelion* or good news, should be understood as an action which plants within eternal death a manifesto of eternal life – no matter how that proclamation is made,[113] or which persons are its heralds,[114] or what the positive, or less positive dispositions of those whom the proclamation concerns. This removes at a stroke the problem, so pre-occupying for the Fathers, of how those already dead can be subsequently converted, and not only of the possibility of such a post-mortem conversion[115] but also of the number of those thus converting.

The theme of *liberation*, that is, of the salvation offered to the dead, as the content of this proclamation, must be understood no less objectively. Just as Jesus' condition in death is scarcely described in its subjective aspect, so here too the subjective effect of the proclamation on the 'spirits in prison' hardly enters into the reckoning. The dramatic portrait of the experience of triumph, of a joyful encounter between Jesus and the prisoners,[116] and in particular between the new Adam and the old, is not prohibited as a form of pious contemplation, but it does go beyond what theology can affirm. It is here most particularly that the exigence for system-building must be checked. Otherwise it would move forward unhindered to the construction of a doctrine of apokatastasis.

On Holy Saturday the Church is invited rather to follow at a distance. Gregory of Nyssa exhorts us to participate in spirit in the Lord's descent: *an eis hadou katiēi, sunkatelthe, gnōthi kai ta ekeise tou Christou mystēria.*[117] Thomas Aquinas repeats the exhortation:

Nam Christus descendit ad inferos pro salute nostra, et nos frequenter debemus solliciti esse illuc descendere . . .[118]

It remains to ask how such an accompanying is theologically possible – granted that the Redeemer placed himself, by substitution, in the supreme solitude – and how, moreover, that accompanying can be characterised if not by way of a genuine, that is, a christianly imposed, sharing in such solitude: being dead with the dead God.

References

1 Rightly, Athanasius attaches a good deal of importance to the official burial of Jesus. His state of death is definitive, and it is officially certified: *De Incarnatione Verbi* 23 and 26 (PG 25, 136; 141). In Mark 18, 45 it is a matter of the *ptōma* (cadavre). The burial of Jesus forms part of the most ancient confession of faith, I Corinthians 15, 3–4: see J. Kremer, *Das älteste Zeugnis von der Auferstehung Christi* (Stuttgart 1966), pp. 36ff. Who finally buried Jesus is not clear in the sources, themselves many times re-worked. Cf. Acts 13, 29.

2 Short Armenian baptismal creed, D-S 6.

3 Marcellus of Ancyra, D-S 11.

4 *Codex Laudianus*, D-S 12; Ambrose, D-S 13; Augustine, D-S 19 etc.

5 *Traditio Apostolorum* (Latin recension), D-S 10; Nicetas of Remesiana, D-S 19 etc.

6 'The One who had died and gone done into the underworld, he has put in order what he found there (*ta ekeise oikonomēsanta*), and the gates of Hell

trembled on seeing him!' (the last words refer directly to Job 38, 17 in the Septuagint version). Similarly: the synods of Nicaea (359) and Constantinople (360).

7 *Commentarium in Symbolum*, 18 (PL 21, 356).

8 For the details, see DTC IV/1, cols. 568–574 ('Descente de Jesus aux enfers').

9 Matthew 14, 2; 16, 21 and parallels; 17, 9; 27, 6ff and parallels; John 2, 22; 5, 21; Acts 3, 15 etc.; Romans 4, 24ff; 6, 4 and 9, etc.; I Corinthians 15, 12ff; 29, 32 and 35 etc.; II Corinthians 4, 14; Galatians 1, 1; Ephesians 1, 20 etc. For the Ascension, the term is *anealēmphthē*: Mark 16, 19; Acts 1, 2–11 and 22; I Timothy 3, 16.

10 For an analysis of the relevant myths, from Sumer, Assyria, Babylon, Egypt, Greece, Rome and among the Mandaeans, see DBS II, cols. 397–403.

11 W. Schneemelcher, *Neutestamentliche Apokryphen*, op. cit. pp. 348–356.

12 *Catecheses* 14, 19 (PG 33, 848–849).

13 *Homily for Holy Saturday* (PG 43, 452–464): extracts translated in H. de Lubac, *Catholicisme* (Paris 1941), pp. 336–337.

14 *Homilia 1 de Paschate* (PL 47, 1043), = Pseudo-Augustine, *Sermo 160 de pascha* (PL 39, 2059–2061).

15 *Die Vorstellung von der Höllenfahrt Christi* (Zurich 1949).

16 Ibid., pp. 135–153, where the use of different New Testament concepts for the text in question is patent. It reads, 'The Lord God (the Holy One) of Israel has remembered his dead, those who slept beneath the earth. And he went down (*katebē*) to them in order to announce to them (*euangelisasthai*) his salvation!'

17 Ibid., p. 204.

18 *Kyrios Christos* (Göttingen 1921²); idem., 'Zur Hadesfahrt Christi', ZNW 19 (1920), pp. 50–66.

19 *Der Descensus ad inferos in der alten Kirche* (Leipzig-Berlin 1919), pp. 453–576.

20 Thus J. L. König, *Die Lehre von Christi Höllenfahrt nach der Heiligen Schrift der ältesten Kirche, den christlichen Symbolen und nach ihrer vielumfassenden Bedeutung* (Frankfurt 1842).

21 Radically: F. Huidekopper, *The Belief of the First Three Centuries concerning Christ's Mission in the Underworld* (Boston 1854), but the theology of the Enlightenment age had already reached the same viewpoint.

22 Cf. the great collection of texts of J. Kroll, *Gott und Hölle. Der Mythos vom Descensuskampf* (Leipzig 1932).

23 'The pangs of death' in Acts 2, 24, influenced by Psalm 18, 6 in its Septuagint version, but the Hebrew term *hebel* signifies 'bonds' (cf. Psalm 119, 61; 140, 6): what is intended are the bonds of death which were unable to hold Christ fast.

24 It cannot be a matter of the suffering of the Crucified, since, for a dead man, his suffering is past. He is delivered by God from the 'bonds of death': death is here a personification for the domain of the dead, Sheol.

25 Rightly, K. Gschwind, op. cit., p. 159, writes, 'The saving of Jonah from the fish's stomach ... seems to me quite certainly to have been comprised within the authentic meaning of the Sign of Jonah' – despite Luke 11, 30.

26 S. Lyonnet, 'S. Paul et l'exégèse juive de son temps. A propos de Romains 19, 6–8', in *Mélanges bibliques A. Robert* (Paris 1957), pp. 494–506, cites a fragmentary

targum from Jerusalem chamber II on Deuteronomy 30, 12–13: 'If only we had someone like the prophet Jonah, who would descend into the depths of the sea in order to restore it (the Law) to us, and who would bring us his prescriptions so that we may accomplish them!'. It was not Paul, then, who took the initiative in changing the horizontal line of the sea into the vertical line of its depths. The presence of such an idea can also throw new light on the Jonah logion in Matthew.

27 H. Schlier, *Epheser*, p. 192, with many other writers.

28 W. Bieder, *Höllenfahrt*, p. 89.

29 *Die Niederfahrt Christi in der Unterwelt* (Munich 1911).

30 Above all: B. Reicke, *The Disobedient Spirits and Christian Baptism* (Copenhagen 1946); also on this topic, W. Bieder, ThZ 6 (1946), pp. 456–462; idem., *Die Vorstellung von der Höllenfahrt Jesu Christi* (Zurich 1949); W. J. Dalton, *Christ's Proclamation to the Spirits* (Rome 1965).

31 'That is to say that our opinions are only probable, that the best exegesis will be that which denies itself any soliciting of text or philology, and that finally, whatever some may say, it is impossible to speak of a common teaching of the Church today on this theme': *Les Epîtres de S. Pierre* (Paris 1966), p. 147.

32 Acts 10, 42; 17, 31; I Corinthians 4, 5, 2; II Timothy 4, 1; I Peter 5, 4.

33 Op. cit., pp. 70ff.

34 *Epheser*, pp. 15ff.

35 Op. cit., p. 116.

36 J. Jeremias, *Der Opfertod Jesu Christi* (Stuttgart 1963), p. 8.

37 The most complete work on the tomb of Jesus is that of the Oratorian, somewhat tainted with Jansenism, J. J. Duguet, *Le tombeau de Jésus-Christ* (Paris 1731–2; 1735) with all the patristic data. According to H. Bremond, *Histoire du sentiment religieux en France* 9, it is Duguet's master-work. See D-S 1759ff. On the placing in the tomb, cf. J. Blinzler, op. cit., pp. 282ff.

38 There is a 'paradise of Adam', a 'paradise of the sleeping righteous' (the 'bosom of Abraham', 'Eden', corresponding to the Hellenic Elysium) and an eschatological paradise: cf. W. Bousset – H. Gressmann, *Religion des Judentums* (Tübingen 1925²), p. 282; P. Volz, *Eschatologie der jüdischen Gemeinde* (Tübingen 1934), pp. 417ff.

39 J. Nelis, 'Gehenna', art. cit., pp. 529–531.

40 Idem., 'Totenreich', in *Bibel-Lexikon* (Einsiedeln 1968²), pp. 1773–1774: we have borrowed from him the foregoing texts. The same article offers a bibliography.

41 *Epistolae* 164, 3; PL 33, 170.

42 PL 34, 481; similarly, Fulgentius, *Ad Thrasymundum* 3.30 (PL 65, 294); DTC IV.1, col. 602.

43 *Liber Sententiarum* IV. 19–20m (PL 186, 824–825).

44 This representation already appeared in late Judaism: cf. P. Z. Volz, op. cit., p. 257.

45 *In Epistolam Jacobi* 3 (PL 93, 27).

46 IIIa., tr. 5, q. 2, c. 4 (Quaracchi IV. 233).

47 12, 32–33, lx–lxiv (PL 34, 480–482). In his old age, he regretted his boldness and half-retracted in the *Retractationes* (12, 24, 2; PL 32, 640) what he had said.

48 *De Praedestinatione* 17 (PL 122, 417ff); *De Divisionibus Naturae* V. 949ff; 971ff.

49 *Docta Ignorantia* III. 9–10 (Petzelt I, 107–112).

50 R. Klein, 'L'enfer de Ficin', in E. Castelli (ed.), *Umanesimo e Esoterismo* (Padua 1960), pp. 47–84. The same article deals with Arab influences. Following Ficino, the identical idea was taken up by Francesco Giorgi in his *Harmonia Mundi* III. 7, 14–17, and by Giordano Bruno in the *De Vinculis in Genere*. For a general view, see also P. Courcelle, 'Les Peres devant les Enfers virgiliens', AHD 22 (1955), pp. 5–74.

51 *Liber Sententiarum* IV. 24 (PL 186, 828).

52 'Propter ista duo inferna missus est Dei Filius, undique liberans: ad hoc infernum missus est nascendo, ad illud morinedo', *Enarrationes in Psalmos* 85, 17; PL 37, 1093ff. With its misery and mortality, its comings and goings, its *timores, cupiditates, horrores, laetitiae incertae*, and *spes fragilis*, the earth can already be called an *infernum* – and resoundingly so. That is why even here below one can pray, 'Quoniam non derelinques animam meam in inferno?', Psalm 15, 10; 85, 12–13; cf. Acts 2, 27. Irenaeus, it is true, had blamed the Gnostics for calling this world a hell: *Adversus Haereses* V. 31, 2.

53 Thomas distinguishes therefore in *Summa Theologiae* IIIa., q. 57. a. 2, ad ii between a first *descensus secundum exinanitionem* whose subject is God, and a second *descensus* to Hades, which he calls a *motus localis*, whose subject is man.

54 *In Libros Sententiarum* III.d . 22, q. 2, a. 1, qla. 3.

55 Ibid.

56 *Expositio Symboli* 5 (Spiazzi 926): 'Descenditque cum illo in foveam' (ibid. 930).

57 Polycarp, *Epistola II ad Philippenses* 1, 2 (Fischer 248).

58 *De Anima* 55 (PL 2, 742).

59 *Adversus Haereses* V. 31, 2 (PG 7, 1209); Cf. Hilary *In Psalmum* 53, 4 (PL 9, 339A); *In Psalmum* 138, 22 (803c–804A).

60 *Adversus Haereses* III.23, 2 (PG 7, 961).

61 PL 35, 2277.

62 *Oratio 12 de Dormitione* 1 (PG 97. 1048).

63 *Expositio Symboli* 5 (927); cf. *In Libros Sententiarum* III.d, 26, q, 2, q 5, qla. 1, sol, 3; *Summa Theologiae* IIIa., q. 52, a. 1, c.

64 *Summa* III (Quaracchi IV. 161, p. 223, a.). This is also the teaching of Thomas: original sin keeps the just in the *infernum*: 'ad vitam gloriae propter peccatum primi parentis aditus non patebat', *Summa Theologiae* IIIa., q. 52, a. 5, c.

65 *In I Timotheum* (PL 17, 467).

66 *De Potestate Ligendi atque Solvendi* 19 (PL 196, 1171).

67 Cf. my study 'Umrisse der Eschatologie', *Verbum Caro* (Einsiedeln 1960), p. 285.

68 Pohle-Gierens, *Dogmatik* III (Paderborn 1937⁹), p. 660.

69 *Moralia* 10, 9 (PL 75, 928D).

70 *Sermo* 3 (PL 210, 204).

71 Text as given in A. Jungmann, *Missarum Sollemnia* I (Paris 1964), p. 55. Cf. Peter Chrysologus, *Sermo* 74: 'sistuntur inferna', PL 52, 409C.

72 'Cum igitur malitiae vis se totam effudisset, . . . quando conclusa erant omnia sub peccato, . . . quando vitiorum tenebrae ad summum usque terminum venerant: tunc apparuit gratia . . ., tunc in tenebris et umbra mortis sedentibus ortus est justitiae sol', *In Diem Natalem Christi* (PG 46, 1132 BC).

73 *De Incarnatione* 45 (PG 25, 177).

74 *Summa Theologia* IIIa., q. 52, a. 1, c.

75 Edited by A. Landgraf, in *Ecrits théologiques de l' école d'Abélard* (Louvain 1936), p. 16.

76 See above.

77 Fulgentius sees, at least, this *compassio*: *Ad Thrasymundum* 3, 30, even if, following Augustine, he does not really take it seriously, PL 65, 294ff.

78 Commenting on Genesis 42, 38 (WA 44, 523). E. Vogelsang, 'Weltbild und Kreuzestheologie in den Höllenfahrtsstreitigkeiten der Reformationszeit', *Archiv für Reformationsgeschichte* 38 (1941), pp. 90–132.

79 Commenting on Psalm 16, 10 (WA 5, 463).

80 Cf. W. Bieder, *Höllenfahrt*, op. cit., pp. 6–7.

81 *Institutio* II. 16, 10–12.

82 *Bekenntnischriften* (1938), p. 159.

83 W. Bieder, op. cit., pp. 6–13, M. Waldhäuser, *Die Kenose und die moderne protestantische Christologie* (Mainz 1912).

84 *Excitationes* 10 (Basle 1565), p. 659.

85 'Cum vero Deus et dicendo, "Adam, ubi es?" mortem significaverit animae, quae facta est illo deserente, et dicendo, "Terra es, et in terram ibis" mortem significabat corporis, quae illi fit anima discedente, propterea de morte secunda nihil dixisse credendus est, quia occultam esse voluit propter dispensationem Testamenti Novi, ubi secunda mors apertissime declaratur, ut prius ista mors prima, quae communis est omnibus, proderetur ex illo venisse peccato, . . . mors vero secunda non utique communis est omnibus, propter eos "qui secundum propositum vocati sunt" . . . quos a secunda morte per Mediatorem Dei gratia liberavit', *De Civitate Dei* XIII.23, 1: PL 41, 396–397.

86 D-S 901 and fairly often elsewhere; I Timothy 2, 4–6; 4, 10; Titus 2, 11; Romans 12, 32; I Corinthians 10, 33; Philippians 2, 11; Hebrews 9, 28; II Peter 3, 9; John 12, 32.

87 On all this, A. von Speyr, *Kreuz und Hölle* (privately printed, Einsiedeln 1966).

88 M. Aubineau, 'Le thème du "bourbier" dans la littérature profane et chrétienne', RSR 50 (1959), pp. 185–214. Origen spoke of a latrine of the world, *Homilia super Librum Numerum* 14, 2: Baehrens 7, 124). The image returns in Swedenborg, Oetinger, von Baader.

89 L. Eizenhöfer, 'Taetrum chaos illabitur', ALW 2 (1952), pp. 94ff; Peter Chrysologus, Sermo 74, 'Movetur chaos' (PL 52, 409C).

90 *De Divisionibus Naturae* V. 6 (PL 122, 873C). For Cyril of Alexandria, *Homilia Paschalis* 7 (PG 77, 552). Jesus at the moment of the redemption of Hades, strips the Devil so totally that the latter comes away alone and empty-handed.

91 'Die Hölle', in *Nachgelassene Schriften* V (Lucerne 1836), pp. 545–569.

92 The Devils' right over souls; the blood of Christ as ransom made over to the Devil; the Devil duped by Christ's entry into his realm, since he had no power to retain him, etc.: texts in Diekamp-Jussen, *Katholische Dogmatik* II (Münster 1959¹²), pp. 323–324.

93 Hormisdas, *Epistola 'Inter Ea Quae' ad Justinum Imperatorem*, in D-S 369.

94 *Adversus Haereses* IV. 22, 1 (PG 7, 1047A).

[95] *Summa Alexandri* III., tr. 7, q. 1, a. 1 (Quaracchi IV, 205).

[96] *Moralia* 29 (PL 76, 489). For the descent into the ultimate depths of Sheol, see already *The Odes of Solomon* 42, 13ff.

[97] *Sententiae* I, 14, 1 (PL 83, 568A).

[98] Philo Carpasius, *Commentarium in Canticum Canticorum* (on the 'going down of the Spouse into his garden', 6, 1): 'Thereby is signified, it would seem, the descent of the Lord into Hell'; Philo justifies his opinion by re-calling the word addressed to the good thief (PG 40, 112–113).

[99] Proclus of Constantinople, *Sermo*, 6, 1 (PG 65, 721).

[100] *Expositio Symboli* 928.

[101] Ibid., 935.

[102] Thomas Aquinas, *In Libros Sententiarum* III, d. 22, q. 2, a. 2; *Summa Theologiae* IIIa., q. 52, a. 2, a. 8.

[103] *Die Lehre von der Erscheinung Jesu Christi unter den Todten* (Berne 1853), p. 357, cited from W. Bieder, op. cit., p. 17.

[104] Proposed justifications in W. Bieder, op. cit., pp. 22–25. The same ideas, moreover, can already be found in Herder, for whom the 'descent into Hell' constitutes the 'development' from the purely sensuous concept in the Old Testament to the spiritual in the New Testament: see his 'Erläuterungen zum Neuen Testament', III.1 in *Werke* (Cotta 1852) VII. p. 131.

[105] J. Gnilka, *Ist I Korinther 3, 10–15 ein Schriftzeugnis für das Fegfeuer?* (Dusseldorf 1955).

[106] Ibid., p. 20ff.

[107] The question of when this fire enters into act, whether after the death of the individual or at the 'Last Judgment' forms part of eschatology, and need not be elucidated here.

[108] *Homiliae in Librum Exodi* 6 (Baehrens VI. 197–198). Cf. Pseudo-Augustine, *Sermo*, 37: 'tunc leonem et ursum strangulavit quando ad inferna descendens omnes de eorum faucibus liberavit' (PL 39, 1819).

[109] Cf. M. Scheeben, *Dogmatik* III, para. 266 (Freiburg 1961), pp. 356ff.

[110] He is forced to admit that Purgatory is an event situated between the two levels of Hell: the lower level, where the evil rich man is tortured, and the upper, where Lazarus is restored, at Abraham's bosom. But, first, the assertion of the existence of a *chaos magnum* between the two 'places' causes him difficulty, while, secondly, the process of purification does not lead the *purgandi* to God, but only to another form of the *poena damni*. It is only after Christ's going through Hell that the 'exit' from Purgatory is no longer the upper Hades but heaven *Sententiae* IV, 21–26 (PL 186, 825–30). Cf. also Ludolph of Saxony, *Vita Christi* II. 68, and *De Sabbato Sancto* 5.

[111] J. Monnier, op. cit., pp. 183–192; B. Schultze, 'La nuova soteriologia russa', OrChrP 12 (1946), pp. 130–176; H. J. Schulz, 'Die "Höllenfahrt" als "Anastasis"', ZKTh 81 (1959), pp. 1–66.

[112] M. Bauer, 'Die Ikonographie der Höllenfahrt Christi von ihren Anfängen bis zum 16. Jahrhundert' (dactylographed dissertation, Göttingen 1948); G. Cornelius, *Die Höllenfahrt Christi* (Munich-Autenried 1967); H. Rothemund, 'Zur Ikonographie der Höllenfahrt Christi', *Slavische Rundschau* II (1957),

pp. 20ff; O. Schönwolf, *Die Darstellung der Auferstehung Christi, ihre Entstehung und ihre älteste Denkmäler* (Leipzig 1909); J. Villette, *La résurrection du Christ dans l'art* (Paris 1947); E. Völter, *Darstellung der Auferstehung Christi bis zum 13. Jahrhundert* (Freiburg, n.d.); R. B. Green, 'Höllenfahrt Christi (in der Kunst)', RGG III. pp. 410ff; *Handbuch der Ikonenkunst* (Munich 1966², published by the Slavonic Institute of Munich), p. 308.

[113] It is not a question of 'exhortations' or attempts at conversion, as for example Hilary (*In Psalmum* 118, 11, 3; PL 9, 572–3) lets one suppose.

[114] Hermas thinks in terms of a continuation of this work of preaching in the beyond by the apostles and doctors: *Similitudines* 9, 16, 5 (Funk I. 532). According to Origen, the prophets and above all the Baptist are, even in Hades, the precursors of Jesus' preaching: *Contra Celsum* 2, 43 (PG 11, 865); idem., *Homilia in Libros Regum* 2 (865). Clement follows Hermas' view, for which this preaching is continued, after the resurrection of Jesus, by his disciples: *Stromateis* 6, 6 (PG 9, 265); 2, 9 (PG 8, 980).

[115] Speculation oscillates between, on the one hand, a complete emptying out of Hades in the sense of a redemption of everyone: cf. Cyril of Alexandria, *Homilia Paschalis* 7 (PG 77, 657), and Pseudo-Ambrose, *Homilia de Paschate* 3ff – in Adam all have fallen into Hell and are in torment there until Christ comes, gains the victory over Hell and delivers all men; and, on the other hand, a redemption of only those souls (Jewish, perhaps also pagan?) who possessed the merit of a certain faith and a good life or a conversion *in ultimis*: Irenaeus, *Adversus Haereses* IV. 22 and 27, 1 (PG 7, 1047 and 1056–8); Origen, *Contra Celsum* 2, 43 (PG 11, 865); Ambrosiaster, *In Ephesios* 4, 9 (PL 17, 387: 'quotquot cupidi eius essent'); idem., *In Romanos* 10, 7 (PL 17, 143: 'quicumque, viso Salvatore apud inferos, speravit de illo salutem'); with hesitation, Gregory Nazianzen, *Oratio* 45, 24 (PG 36, 657: everyone, or at least those who believed in him); John Chrysostom, *In Matthaeum, homilia* 26, 3 (PG 67, 416): even those pagans who did not hope in Christ, if they have not adored idols, but honoured the true God); Philastrius of Brescia, *De Haeresibus* 125 (PL 12, 1251–2) wants to include also poets, philosophers and other pagans, though with the reservation suggested by Chrysostom. The most severe is Gregory the Great: *Epistola* 1, 7, 15 (PL 77, 869–870): not 'omnes qui illic confiterentur eum Deum' but 'solos illos . . . liberavit, qui eum et venturum esse crediderunt et praecepta eius vivendo tenuerunt'. For, in the same way that today faith and good works are needful for redemption, so it was then also. Augustine, *Epistola* 164, 14 (PL 33, 715: 'recte intelligitur solvisse et liberasse quos voluit'), leaves the question open. Thus a whole spectrum of opinions unfolds, from the widest to the narrowest.

[116] There is first the theme, often treated, for which Christ by his entry into gloomy Hades plunges everything into light: cf. F. Dölger, *Sol Salutis* (Münster 1925²), pp. 336–364, and already, in the same sense, the *Gospel of Nicodemus*: 'At the hour of midnight, something like sunlight penetrated into the darkness which reigned there and shone out . . . all the dark corners of Hades became luminous' (Schneemelcher, op. cit, I., pp. 349, 351). In the same sense, the Pseudo-Augustine, *Sermo* 160, 2 *De Pascha* (PL 39, 2060): 'Quisnam est iste terribilis et niveo splendore coruscus?'; and again, Caesarius: *Homilia* 1 *in Paschate* (PL 67,

1043); and right down to the Easter plays where the Paschal fire, lit in front of the darkened church, is introduced into church as *Lumen Christi* and symbolises the entry of Christ into Hades which, by that entry, is transformed into paradise: thus the Redentine Easter play (composed c. 1464), Golther, p. 492. Next, there appears the theme of a struggle with the Devil who is constrained by the higher power of Christ to open the 'gates of bronze' and let the triumphant victor enter. The first victory of Christ over Hell proclaims a second and definitive such victory at the Last Judgment, when Hell will be finally destroyed. Thus the Redentine play, and down to the work of Ayrer, *Historischer Processus juris in welchem sich Luzifer über Jesum, darüber, dass er ihm die Höllen zerstöret, beklaget* (Frankfurt 1680). Lastly, we have the themes of the encounter with Adam, and the dialogues which accompanied that meeting, (as early as the *Gospel of Nicodemus*, and, in a most beautiful form, in the sermon of Pseudo-Epiphanius PG 43, 452–464), deployed in the Passion plays. Cf. the Passion Play of *Palatinus*: 'Issiez hors de ceste prison/ Mi ami, mi cousin, mi frere./ Je vieng de la destre mon pere/ Pour vous sauver ai morte soufferte./ Maintenant vous sera ouverte/ La porte d'enfer e li huis', in *Jeux et sapience du Moyen-Age*, ed. Pauphilet, p. 257; *St Galler Passionspiel*, ed. Hartl, 1952, verses 1509–1529; *Das Osterspiel von Muri*, ed. Ranke, 1944, pp. 45ff; *Donaueschinger Passionspiel*, ed. Hartl, 1942, verses 3949 and ff. Already in Ephraim, we find, 'Ramus se inclinavit usque ad Adamum in infernum, deinde se erigens assumpsit eum atque reduxit in Eden', *Hymni*, ed. Lamy, IV. 678; cf. 758 and 762–764; Cassian, *Institutae* III.3, 6; the sermon of the Pseudo-Thaddaeus at Edessa as given in Eusebius, *Historia Ecclesiastica* I. 13, 3. In our time, P. Claudel, who often reflected and wrote about Hades (cf. his drama of the *descensus*, *Le repos du septième jour*, written in 1896) has also spoken of an interior Holy Saturday procession, from Hell to Heaven: 'La Sensation du divin', in *Présence et Prophétie* (Paris 1942), pp. 113ff.

[117] *Oratio 45 in Sanctum Pascha*, (PG 36, 657A).

[118] *Expositio Symboli 932.*

5

Going to the Father: Easter

The whole New Testament is unanimous on this point: the Cross and burial of Christ reveal their significance only in the light of the event of Easter, without which there is no Christian faith. We place this event under the title 'Going to the Father', a Johannine phrase (John 16, 28), which needs to be enriched by the other available descriptions in order to be fully grasped. The Father is the Creator who, acting at Easter in the Son, brings his work to completion; the Father, in exalting his Son, also brings the Son's mission to its conclusion, and makes the Son visible to the world, spreading abroad there the Spirit which is common to them both. That this event which includes everything within its embrace at one and the same time withdraws itself from our gaze (inasmuch as it happens in the form of a return to the Father, to eternity) and also reveals itself to us (so that we may grasp by faith the meaning of the history of salvation), that it must needs be simultaneously 'meta-historical' or 'pre-historical'[1] and also historical; that it can both possess the highest theological certitude and, despite that, by the manner in which it is formulated and presented, burst apart the form of profane narration, so confronting exegetes with problems never fully soluble (hence the sparking off of a 'continuous critical dialogue between historical analysis and theological understanding')[2] – all of this belongs to the a priori structure of the phenomenon. But, because the certitude of faith attaching to the achieved event engenders a multiplicity of human attempts to express it (on which exegesis can use its critical methods), this multiplicity is, in its very contrasts and even oppositions, filled with theological content of the highest consequence. And this brings us to the three chief perspectives which will give our exploration its bearings: 1. The fundamental theological affirmation, something whose unity, and main convergent outlines, we can sketch; 2. the exegetical structure, whose *aporiai* derive, in large measure, from the structure of the Easter event itself – and this leads exegetes looking for the clarification of these difficulties to confront certain options, which pre-determine how their investigations will proceed; 3. the development of the theological themes contained in the divergent presentations of the event – aspects, these, whose richness and importance may form the unique rationale for the way in which the dissonances between the narratives have been left juxtaposed, unresolved.

(1) The Fundamental Theological Affirmation

The fundamental theological affirmation must in its turn be exhibited from three angles: in its uniqueness (together with the problematic which considers how that which is absolutely without analogy, and cannot be reduced to any component elements, can and must be expressed, nonetheless, in categorial forms and on the basis of determinate principles of understanding in its background); next, in its Trinitarian structure (for the initiative is ascribed throughout to the Father, yet the Son appears in a self-activating way as the Living One, while the Spirit is 'freed into' the world precisely from Easter onwards); and lastly in the – concordantly described – main ways wherein the Risen One manifests and gives himself and which form the very foundation of the unshakeable edifice of Easter faith.

(A) The uniqueness of the affirmation

(aa) Every philology holds for valid, and, indeed, as its supreme law, the principle that one should let the texts say what, of themselves, they wish to say.[3] The question as to whether what they say possess any validity for us comes second.[4]

What is decisive, however, is the complete accord found in the universal faith-recognition of the resurrection of Jesus itself.[5]

The phrase 'faith-recognition' implies, on the one hand, that the affirmation concerned takes as its subject an objective reality, expressed in the brief formulae and acclamations of the early Church: 'The Lord has risen indeed (*ontōs*) and has appeared to Simon' (Luke 24, 34); 'This Jesus God raised up' (Acts 2, 32, 3, 15; 4, 10), etc.; but on the other hand the phrase also intends to say that this affirmation can only be made in faith:

> The Church has never spoken of the Resurrection of Jesus Christ in distant or uncommitted terms but gripped and confessing.[6]

This confession is what founds the Church. Had Christ not arisen, there would have been neither Church nor faith. 'Whether then it was I (Paul) or they, so we preach and so you believed' (I Corinthians 15, 11). The unanimity of the proclamation must not be understood as a mere summation – a certain number of individuals were, on this point, of the same opinion. Rather is it insofar as the witnesses accord that they form, themselves, the Church. It is the Church who is the real subject of Easter faith, just as that faith is the real object whereby the Church, as believing subject, is constituted for the first time. Without the living presence of the Lord, initiated by Easter, there is no Church.[7] That is why we shall not be following Schleiermacher and his school in removing the Resurrection of Christ from its position at the centre of the Christian faith.[8] On the contrary: it is in the Resurrection that all ecclesial theory has its starting-point, the only one which grants the earthly existence of Jesus, and his Cross, their momentous consequences.[9]

The most ancient testimony[10] to the Resurrection is the credal formula of which Paul reminds the Corinthians, First Corinthians 15, 3–5:

> That Christ died for our sins in accordance with the
> Scriptures, that he was buried, that he was raised on the
> third day in accordance with the Scriptures, and that he
> appeared to Cephas, and then to the Twelve . . .

Where this antique, rhythmic, many-membered formula
stops short is a disputed question: doubtless, it cannot end
before 'Cephas', since 'appeared to' requires a predicate; the
Twelve too belong to the formula's primitive state. Paul
continues the list:

> Then he appeared to more than five hundred brethren
> at one time . . . Then he appeared to James, then to all
> the apostles. Last of all, as to one untimely born, he
> appeared also to me.

The basic formula here contains what Paul had himself
'received' from the apostles at Jerusalem after his conversion
(in 33 or shortly after). The text presents numerous non-
Pauline[11] and most probably Semitic traits.[12] Its origin is
Jerusalem, or at any rate Antioch. The parallel between
'Cephas and the Twelve' and 'James and all the apostles' does
not oblige us to posit separate and rival currents of tradition
– as, since Harnack's time, has frequently been admitted. Nor
is there any need to regard it as, first and foremost, an
apostolic 'legitimation formula' (what would be the point in
that context of the appearance to the five hundred
brethren?).[13] That Paul wanted to arrange the appearances, at
least to some degree in their chronological order, ought not
to be contested.[14] Even more misleading would be the
attempt to render *ephapax* (in the phrase 'five hundred
brethren at one time') as 'once for all', and so reduce all the
other appearances to this one and only occurrence.[15] On the
other hand, it would not be right to read into the formula an
entire theology of the primitive Christian mission.[16]

The two essential affirmations of the formula are: 1. There
are a great many witnesses to the Resurrection. That these
were still in Paul's time 'available for questioning' (verse 6) in
no way means that Paul wished to 'prove' the Resurrection.

Rather is he referring to the 'chosen ... witnesses' (Acts 10, 41) among whom he counts himself. 2. Already in this most ancient formula the death on the Cross and the burial are bound together with the Resurrection and the appearing of the Risen One in a single profession of faith. Even so early – and this is important – the Cross is understood within the horizon of the Resurrection as an atoning death 'for our sins', while the two realities, the death and the Resurrection, become intelligible within the total horizon of Scripture just as they provide Scripture with its definitive illumination.[117] The two events are clearly distinguished from each other (the Cross is, moreover, underlined by the mention of the burial – for someone who is buried, the state of being dead is finally signed and sealed).[18] The repeated formula 'according to the Scriptures' indicates that the death and Resurrection belong together, even though they are signalised as distinct. And so, over against Bultmann, one must agree with Barth when the letter affirms that in the Resurrection we are dealing with a specific divine act,[19] and not merely with an awareness of the meaning of the Cross.[20] The pre-Pauline formula found in Romans 4, 25 connects the process of our justification, primarily and essentially, not to the Cross but to the Resurrection.[21] On the basis of these texts there can be no doubting the objectivity of the prior deed of God in Christ, a deed which has in the aftermath its secondary, and certainly decisive, effect in the world as a whole and in each human being in particular. The destruction of this objective character, from Schleiermacher to Herrmann and the latter's pupil Bultmann, on the grounds that such objectivity would neutralise the existential relationship with the believing 'I' and would 'dogmatise' or 'mythologise' the event, leads to the suppression of the significance of the Cross itself for our redemption. Between the gracious God and the 'I' who receives the grace of God the objective mediation of Christ disappears from the picture.[22]

(bb) That a dead man should begin to live again is not, in the world of the Bible, an entirely unique occurrence. But it is not, in any case, what the Resurrection of Jesus expresses.

The meaning of the Resurrection lies, rather, in Jesus' passage
to a form of existence which has left death behind it once for
all (Romans 6, 10), and so has gone beyond, once for all, the
limitations of this aeon in God (Hebrews 9. 26; 1 Peter 3, 18).
In contrast to David, but also to those whom he himself
raised from the dead, Jesus is withdrawn from corruption
(Acts 13, 34), he lives for God (Romans 6, 10), he lives 'for
evermore' and has 'the keys of Death and Hades' (Apocalypse
1, 17ff). This event is, as has rightly been said time and again,
without analogy.[23] It pierces our whole world of living and
dying in a unique way so that, through this breakthrough, it
may open a path for us into the everlasting life of God
(I Corinthians 15, 21ff). However, in this unique movement
from one *aeon* to the other, both termini are important: not
only our being taken up into the new aeon (which would
then be represented falsely, as the contrary of the temporality
of the old, and so as an abstract and non-temporal eternity),[24]
but also designation of the *terminus a quo*, that point of history
where history itself is decisively transcended. That is why one
must without demur call the Resurrection

> in terms of this world and what it contains a true event
> . . . since it *happened* in the midst of time as a special
> history within the general history of man.[25]

One can even venture the attempt to embed the Resurrection,
considered as an historical event, in the total chain of events
of history as a whole.[26] But one can also speak of an 'historical
border' to the Resurrection,[27] or of an aspect in which that
'meta-historical event' 'opens up towards history'.[28] And in
the latter respect it is easy to see how the historical signs
become ambiguous once separated from the event of faith.
For this reason, enforcing a choice between the alternatives of
'historical' and 'non-historical' has rightly been rejected as
perilous:[29] the cataclysm which orders the history of man,
and of the world, towards God can only be made known
historically (that is, within history) inasmuch as the God who
transcends history acts in the One who has died, and enables
the living Son to disclose his transcendence in history's regard

in history's midst. That is why, as will be shown later, there are no witnesses to the Resurrection as such,[30] and why, right from the start, the empty tomb has not been conceived as a 'proof' of the Resurrection: in the last analysis, no one could be a disinterested observer of the Lord's self-manifestation. But precisely here the question of how an understanding of this unique event can be possible arises in an acute form. Such an understanding is only possible if categorical principles of understanding are present in the background, principles which, however, must necessarily then be transcended in the presence of this unique event, and be so, indeed, in their converging upon it. Of such principles of understanding Scripture offers us, in the main, three: 1. The representation (increasingly important) of the living God, who is, in his Covenant, a God of the living. 2. The horizons opened by pre-Christian, Jewish apocalyptic. 3. The claim of the historical Jesus to be, for those who met him, the occasion of a decision drawing in its train everlasting salvation or everlasting loss.

In all periods, the God of the Covenant was not only the Living One but also the Giver of life. 'There is real life, for the Israelites, only in community with the living God.'[32] 'For with thee is the fountain of life' (Psalm 36, 9). And, for Jesus, God 'is not God of the dead, but of the living' (Matthew 22, 32). Already in the Old Testament itself, levitical piety, thanks to this idea of the living God, went beyond that boundary of death so inexorably imposed on man: it developed a

> confidence which issued only from the certainty of an indestructible community of life, offered by God.[33]

But Jesus, as the living and incarnate Word of God, is the real Living One (John 14, 19 etc.); he is, indeed, the One who has life in himself through the Father (John 5, 26). Thus it is logical enough, when the Lucan angels ask of the women at the tomb: 'Why do you seek the living among the dead?' (24, 5); cf. 24, 23; Acts 1, 3; 25, 19). The unique event, the absolutely unexpected – that a dead man should rise again into a life that is definitive and immortal – appears as a step beyond something already known, and in some sense already awaited.

The apocalyptic (and prophetic) horizon of Late Judaism offers different categories which can aid in understanding the uniqueness of the mystery of Easter. No one such category will suffice; and all indeed will fail us at the decisive point. Since the writing of Daniel 12, 2 and the Apocalypse of Isaiah 24–27, the idea of a resurrection of the dead at the end of time had become familiar in a certain segment of Judaism (Acts 23, 8; cf. Mark 9, 10). On the other hand, for such Judaism there could be no question of an individual anticipation of the general resurrection of the dead.

> The Resurrection, a new bodily existence, is expected only with the advent of a coming new world. When the disciples speak of Jesus' Resurrection, what they are doing is, quite simply, to speak of this same, single eschatological event. Paul is of the same meaning when he puts together the Resurrection of Jesus with the eschatological resurrection of the dead, and calls the Risen One the first-fruits of the new world (I Corinthians 15, 20–58). So the Easter kerygma is, for the Jewish world, a unique, and unheard of, proclamation, whilst in relation to the Hellenistic world, it lies far away.[34]

But before we bump up against that obvious boundary wall for thought which is the category of the 'resurrection of the dead', we must for a moment, ponder the fact that, to a Jewish understanding and sensibility, once the certitude of Jesus' real Resurrection was obtained, the ancient *aeon* and temporality must appear as in some way reaching their end. This is why, in the earliest strata of the Resurrection accounts, there is a kind of coincidence of Resurrection and Parousia, an experience, as it were, of the pure presence of the final action of God, beyond which there is nothing more to be expected. Only the reflection that the witnesses of this event continued to live in a time-bound condition, led to a dismantlement of the eschatological present into a now and a later, a possession and a renewed hope and (imminent) expectation. H. W. Bartsch, recognising the formal relatedness of Matthew 28, 2–4 and the christology of Apocalypse 1, 13ff, suspects that behind the Matthaean angelophany there lies an original appearing of Christ. Unequivocally apocalyptic is, moreover, Matthew 27, 51ff with the earthquake, the splitting of rocks, the opening of graves and the co-resurrection of many of the bodies of the saints who had fallen asleep, on Easter Day. To this belongs the darkness stealing out over the whole earth (Mark 15, 33 and parallels) as a sign of the now commencing end of the world (Amos 8, 9). And the Danielic text about the appearing of the Son of Man who sits at the right hand of the power and comes upon the clouds (Mark 14, 62) may very well have been applied at first to the presence of the eschatological event.[35] P. Seidensticker adopts the same perspective in seeking to gather together the fragments of 'Easter reporting in apocalyptic style' (above all, in the line of descent from Daniel 7). For instance, he interprets 'the power and coming of our Lord Jesus Christ' (II Peter 1, 16) not in terms of the eschatological return but in relation to the power-filled coming of the Lord in the Church's present.[36] Furthermore, he takes Matthew 28, 16–20 to be an apocalyptic scene depicting the investiture of the exalted Christ with 'all authority' (*edothē moi pasa exousia*) as well as the homage and adoration of the disciples.[37] And yet all of this hardly involved more than an attempt of thought to render credible in preaching the meaning of the Easter event, an attempt, moreover, whose defects soon became obvious.[38] The same is true of W. Pannenberg's effort to make the apocalyptic background ideas the *sine qua non* for an understanding of Christ's Resurrection.[39]

The third line of thinking we have to consider here has also received its most radical treatment at the hands of Pannenberg. Pannenberg followed in the paths marked out by, on the one hand, Albert Schweitzer with his radically eschatological Christology, and, on the other, by Eduard Schweizer who tried to throw light on the way, and the self-understanding, of Jesus by investigating that background which is the prophetic, and Jewish, schema of the Just Man Humiliated and Exalted.[40] For A. Schweitzer, Jesus lived proleptically, in anticipation of the coming Kingdom and his own investiture as Messiah and Son of Man; on the Cross, his aspirations had been shattered into smithereens. Pannenberg also has Jesus live 'in anticipation of an expected confirmation which only the future can bring' – that is, from God the Father. That confirmation corresponded to the vision of history which the apocalyptic authors entertained, but, since Jesus lived in expectation of the 'imminent general resurrection of the dead' could not be brought to fruition by him alone. However correct this view of the proleptic nature of the claim to Messiahship may be, it depends on a two-fold background of ideas whose combination is impossible, and thus itself comes to grief. The suffering righteous man (even the suffering prophet) is never the Messiah. Such an idea did not exist in the time of Jesus.[41] Not even Isaiah 53 is linked with the idea of the Messiah. That is why Jesus' 'anticipation' of his 'justification' by the Father may bear, no doubt, an analogy with the believing trust of the humiliated righteous man, but no more than that. For Jesus' claim is, (at any rate formally) messianic in its intensity and implications whilst the category of Messiahship available to him knew no such claims-by-anticipation.

In the event of the Resurrection all previous schemata come to their fulfilment and suffer their breakdown at one and the same time. They have to be used in preaching, but the very fact of their cumulative employment shows that each is powerless to contribute more than a fragment to a totality of a transcendent kind. 'What the disciples proclaimed goes beyond the limits of the thinkable.'[42] For the assured self-understanding of the Church new schemata had first to be created. In this way the imminent expectation of the early Church differed profoundly from that of the prophets or even of Jesus himself. With the Resurrection, the End is, fundamentally, already inaugurated, and what is still to be awaited is merely its definitive entry into vigour. Earlier categories sink down to the level of images and media of expression which, for this reason, may be used simultaneously but without rivalry. Thus in the earliest strata of the texts, it is already impossible to separate out the death-Resurrection schema from that of humiliation-exaltation.[43] To the first background of ideas described above there must be added the category of 'life' as well, though it would be undesirable to sunder it from the others and erect it into the only one that still possesses validity for us today.[44] Luke introduces the category of *analēmpsis* (a taking up through death and ascension into heaven), probably in dependence on those Old Testament figures who were carried away out of human sight.[45] For John, both the 'exaltation' and the 'glorification' bear a double sense: they signify the raising up on the Cross and in the Resurrection, for the two are alike aspects of the same 'passage', the same 'ascent' to the Father. Not only the Cross and the Resurrection but Resurrection, Ascension and Pentecost are, in that transit, 'closely linked one with another'.[46] Besides, in the earliest reflection on the Easter mystery, the form of the Servant of God and his substitutory suffering is already in use as an interpretative model, as the pre-Pauline formulae of Romans 4, 24ff and 10, 9[47] show (compare I Corinthians 11, 26 and a formula commented above, namely I Corinthians 15, 3–5. It should be clear that in the latter, the reference to 'the Scriptures' points chiefly to Isaiah 53.[48]

All of these categories come from within the Bible. It is generally recognised nowadays that, for the original interpretation of Jesus' Resurrection, the pagan parallels known to us from the history of religion (the dying and rising gods) are barely pertinent at all.[49] At the most, they might be adduced in a secondary, and purely illustrative, way. It was not, then, easy to preach the Resurrection of Jesus to the pagans, for whom the biblical categories were alien. The analogies drawn by Paul from the world of nature in I Corinthians 15, 35–41 are not very illuminating – which is why he soon starts referring once again to Jewish and apocalyptic images. The *graphai* need to be considered as a whole by the pagans too: decisive access to the understanding of the Resurrection results from the convergence of all the images of ancient Scripture. Even if, in the cultic hymn of Philippians 2, 5–11, a mythic scheme (that of a god who descends and re-ascends) has been employed, the central thought of the hymn-writer – that the descent was obedience towards the Father until death – hollows out the entire myth in order to fill it with sheerly biblical, and in the last analysis, sheerly christological material. It is not the One who descends who is the author of his own exaltation; rather does the Trinitarian Father raise up the Son who obeyed to the lengths of the Cross.[50]

This ample collection of images used for the presentation of the mystery of the Resurrection – and here there is nothing save images, for 'Resurrection' and 'restoration to life' are images too – leads us to the conclusion that the mystery is, in its uniqueness, in no way a comstruct. The images surround an inaccessible mid-point which alone has the magnetic force to arrange around itself, in concentric fashion, this image-garland.[51] And if the images cannot be added together to form of themselves an objective unity, no more (as we shall have occasion to show) do the subjective experiences of the witnesses come together to constitute the content of their testimony in a fully integrated way.[52]

This is by no means to say, however, that we cannot pursue any gradual enrichment of the theological understanding of the Resurrection – that, in whose light, everything becomes clear. It is not to be wondered at, but rather considered normal, that the theological synthesis which gathers around the mid-point of the Resurrection was only realised in stages. Nothing was pre-prepared. The Gospels are unaninimous in their report that

> Jesus' Resurrection took his disciples completely by surprise. They also lead us to understand that Jesus' Resurrection lay entirely outside what could justly have been expected of the disciples. There was no place for a Resurrection of Jesus in the representations which they had at their disposal.[53]

If we prescind from the fragmentary outlines of the

apocalyptic images mentioned above, the first reflection had to be that God had taken Jesus' part against his murderers and lifted up his servant to be Lord and Messiah (Acts 2, 36). And since Jesus was 'justified' by God, his disciples must be also. The earliest idea of justification, and so of the forgiveness of sins, is linked to the Resurrection, not (yet) to the Cross (Romans 4, 25; cf. Luke 24, 46ff).[54] And, just as (probably on the basis of Isaiah 53, as shown above) the saving significance 'for us' of the death of the Cross was disclosed by the Resurrection – something clear enough even before Paul[55] who takes it deeper still in making it his own, so there remains in Pauline thought a tendency to enhance the saving power of the Resurrection in comparison with that of the Passion (Romans 5, 10 and 17; 8, 34). and yet, henceforth, Cross and Resurrection are for Paul, and afterwards for the gospels, inseparable. They are the darkling question and its luminous response, or again, the decisive, hidden acting and its publicly manifest result. Moreover, the acting is no longer initiated primarily by the men who did the crucifying (Acts 2, 36; 3, 14; 4, 10), albeit according to the design and foreknowledge (Acts 2, 23) and the explicit plan of God (Acts 3, 18ff; Luke 24, 7 26 and 45). Rather is the true actor God who handed over his Son out of love (Romans 8, 32; II Corinthians 5, 21), and it is the Son who, by an active love of his own, takes up our sins (Romans 8, 32; Galatians 2, 20) and our curse (Galatians 3, 13; Colossians 2, 13ff). And if already Paul, in his account of the redemptive work of Cross and Resurrection, presents the love of God the Father and that of the Son become man as inter-penetrating (Romans 8, 32–35 & 39), just as he speaks of one single Spirit which is that of Father and of Son (Romans 8, 9 and 11), so John can see the indivisible love of Father and Son finally glorified in the indivisible unity of the Cross and the Resurrection. At the same time, the implicit recognition of the divinity of Jesus (who, exalted as Kyrios, already receives the Old Testament title of Lord, which belonged to YHWH)[56] likewise develops into explicit recognition at the end of the gospel of John[59] (John 20, 28; cf. 1, 1), and the idea of the real pre-existence of the Son then makes its appearance by virtue of an internal

logic and not merely, for example, on the basis of an already
existing mythical schema (such as might be presumed in
Philippians 2, 6–11). In the course of reflection, there is an
enrichment (taking place, perhaps, in two opposite directions)
of the christologically determined experience of time, since
the Christ who made himself present at Easter then
disappeared in order to be the eschatological Son of Man
who is to come, while, in contrast, the futurity of the Danielic
figure is perceived by faith, thanks to the Easter experience,
not just as apocalyptic hiddenness in God (as in the Book of
Enoch, cf. Acts 3, 21), but as a presence in human history
'always, to close of the age' (Matthew 28, 20; John 14, 19).
Gradually, the whole life, activity and speech of Jesus in his
days on earth had also to be slowly thought out afresh on the
foundation of the Resurrection and drawn into the light that
would illuminate them once and for all. That is an event
which we can to some degree follow in the redactional stages
traceable in the gospels. Finally, the anthropological,
theological-historical and cosmic dimensions and consequences
must themselves become the object of a reflection proper to
them. That will bear, first of all, on the transformation
wrought in the believing man through the saving event of
the Cross and Resurrection: dying, being buried, and rising
again with Christ (Romans 6) – and that not, indeed, as a
once and for all happening but rather as a permanent being
'in Christ'.[58] Next, it will have to do with the theology of
history (on the one hand, the global meaning of history as in
Romans 8, 18–25, and, on the other, its dialectic as in
Romans 9–11). Lastly, it will concern cosmology, as in the
Letters to Ephesus and Colossae (and compare the Letter to
the Hebrews), and this opens up ultimately 'the possibility of
a Christian ontology, in the perspective of a theology of the
Resurrection'.[59] This whole development is not, however, a
speculation which grows up anyhow, in the wild, but remains
enclosed within the space of the Word which the Church
proclaims and so of the faith that does not see (Romans 10,
9; John 20, 29).

(B) The affirmation's Trinitarian form

The impression of a confusing multiplicity of images which the kerygmatic assertion of the Resurrection gives is dispelled when we turn our attention to the Trinitarian character of its fundamental structure. The Resurrection of the dead Son is consistently ascribed to the action of the Father, and in the closest possible connexion with the Resurrection there is presented to us the outpouring of the divine Spirit. Only because 'God has sent the Spirit of his Son into our hearts' (Galatians 4, 6) does the objective event become something that touches our own existence. Here we must once again recall that the texts forbid a simple identification of the saving event with the actuality of the message concerning that event. The message transmits the testimony to an encounter with the living Christ; but that encounter itself points back to a prior, presuppose event, to that 'blessed night' of which no human being was the experiencing witnesses.[60] H. Schlier remarks that the thesis of Bultmann, according to which Christ rose into the kerygma would mean no less astonishing a miracle than the affirmation of his objective Resurrection whose dogmatic objectivity Bultmann's theory tries to avoid.[61] It is only when, first of all, we grant this event its Trinitarian dimension that we can go on to speak appropriately of its being *pro nobis* and *pro mundo*.

On the one hand; in the contrast between the two wills of the Father and the Son on the Mount of Olives, and in the abandonment of the Son by God on the Cross, the drastic counterposing of the divine Persons in the economy became visible. On the other hand: for the individual who thinks this out more deeply, this very opposition appears as the supreme manifestation of the whole, integrated saving action of God whose internal logic (*dei*: Mark 8, 31, and parallels; 9, 31 and parallels; 10, 34 and parallels) is once again disclosed in the inseparable unity of the death of the Cross and the Resurrection. John gives this Trinitarian mystery its most concise expression, by coining, from the materials of the Old Testament,[62] the phrase, 'The Word became flesh'. This formula allows us to understand the man Jesus – his life, death and resurrection – as the fulfilment of the living Word of God of the old covenant, shows the event of Jesus to be the definitive, superabundant consequence of the event of God himself, and interprets the Son's Resurrection as God's take-over of power in his own world, the fundamental break-through of the Kingdom.[63]

It is, then, to the Father that the initiative in the Son's Resurrection is ascribed. It is he who acts, and he acts precisely as who he is for the world, namely, its Creator who brings his creative action to its completion in the resurrection of the dead. The affirmation recurs in a stereotyped way:

for example, in the parallel antitheses of Acts: '(You) killed the Author of life, whom God raised from the dead' (Acts 3, 15; cf. 2, 24; 5, 30, and elsewhere). The formulation allows the reader to recognise thereby that the Resurrection of Jesus Christ is an act of the divine power, a deed wrought by the 'working of his great might' as Ephesians 1, 19 puts it in an impressive pleonasm (compare Colossians 2, 12). In place of speaking of God's *dunamis*, there is also mention, in this context, of his *doxa*: '"Christ was raised from the dead by the glory of the Father (Romans 6, 4) – that is, by his transfiguring power ... Lastly, it is in the strength of the Spirit of God, his *pneuma*, that the Resurrection of Jesus Christ is accomplished, as Romans 8, 11 and I Peter 3, 18 indicate. In this powerful, transfiguring action of his Spirit, God shows himself so much, and so definitively, the God who raises the dead that participial or relative forms – 'he who raised Christ Jesus from the dead' (Romans 8, 11; II Corinthians 4, 14; Galatians 1,1; Ephesians 1, 20; Colossians 2, 12) – become, as J. Schniewind once remarked, God's 'honorific names'.[64]

In this action, God (the Creator and Father) furnishes at the same time the supreme justification of the truth of his Word and of the truth of the life of his obedient Son who himself is identical with the Word.

He thus demonstrates that he is the true and living God in whom Abraham already believed: Abraham believed in the God 'who gives life to the dead ... (and) raised from the dead Jesus our Lord' (Romans 4, 17 and 24). And he seals his final covenant with the world, inasmuch as 'in Christ, God was reconciling the world to himself' (II Corinthians 5, 19), for 'in him all the fullness of God (in gracious activity) was pleased to dwell, and through him to reconcile to himself all things, whether on earth or in heaven, making peace by the blood of his Cross' (Colossians 1, 20). One can say, therefore, that the entire action of the living God in all ages has had as its goal the Resurrection of the Son,[65] that the completion of Christology found in the Father's act is at the same time the fulfilment of the act of creation itself.[66] But insofar as God's Word became flesh and died so as to show the faithfulness of God, the Resurrection of the Word does not amount to, let us say, his withdrawal from the world but rather to his glorification before the world, his justification in the presence of all, his enthronement as the definitive All-ruler, and lastly, since the death of Jesus was a sacrificial death for the world, the solemn acceptance of his sacrifice. These various aspects form a constellation around the same event. It has often been remarked that God, with Christ's Resurrection, showed forth in a definitive way his *doxa*, that glory which, in the Old Testament, never ceased to render itself visible in act.[67] The term *ōphthē*, used for the Resurrection appearances, points back to just this manifestation of the divine *kabod*.[68] That God in this way justified both himself and his Son is the message of the hymn found in I Timothy 3, 16: *edikaiōthē en pneumati*, 'he was vindicated in the Spirit', namely in his risen existence). This is the 'judgment of the Father' (K. Barth) in the trial which the world mounted against the Word of God and seemed to win, but which it now loses thanks to the Advocate of Christ and God (John 16, 8–11). If one wishes to speak of an anticipatory vindication of the Son, then this vindication is confirmed by the Father in the Resurrection.[69] The justification of the crucified Word is simultaneously his enthronement as Kyrios, as the Philippians hymn so solemnly portrays it (Philippians 2, 9–11), comprising the presentation of the 'new' Lord before the angels; *ōphthē angelois* (I Timothy 3, 16).[70] If the sacrifice of the Cross is interpreted in a cultic context (as the Letter to the Hebrews so interprets it, and with what grandeur) then the Resurrection becomes the acceptance of the sacrifice by the Godhead. That point of view, strongly emphasised by F. X. Durrwell, corresponds above all to the French theological tradition from Bérulle and Condren down to De la Taille.[71] The sacrificial mentality demands a real taking hold of the victim of the holiness of God.'[72] When Jesus, prior to his passion, pronounces the words *hagiazō hemauton* 'I consecrate myself' (John 17, 19), he withdraws from the profane world and surrenders himself to the consuming holiness of God, to undergo that 'slaying' (Apocalypse 5, 6, 9 and 12), as 'a fragrant offering' (Ephesians 5, 2), for he is the 'lamb without blemish or spot' (I Peter 1, 19), given up 'for many' (Matthew 20, 28; Mark 10, 45), 'that they also may be consecrated in truth' (John 17, 19). This is no sin-bearing Lamb (John 1, 29), climbing up on to the heavenly altar, there to reign for ever with the Father, and to receive the songs of praise of all eternity. The Lamb's action consists only in giving himself, in delivering himself over (Galatians 1, 4; 2, 20; Ephesians 5, 25; Titus 2, 14; Hebrews 9, 14), in the 'hands' (Luke 23, 46) of him who alone can and must receive this sacrifice and make it not just full of meaning but also full of fruit. Only by means of this acceptance does the thought which lies behind the question, 'Are not those who eat the sacrifices partners in the altar?' (I Corinthians 10, 18) make sense. For this acceptance by the Father the Son's prayer urges: 'Father, glorify thou me . . .' (John 17, 5).

In bringing to their climax, in the Resurrection of the Son, all these lines of meaning, the Father *shows* to the world his risen and glorified Son. 'God shows Jesus *as* his Son.'[73] This showing is a gift, an act of benevolence , as the Lucan formula makes clear: *Theos . . . edōken auton emphanē genesthai* (Act 10, 40). In raising from the dead, that is, in raising bodily his Word made man, God takes no backward step in relation to the Incarnation of his Word. We are not to believe that Jesus had to disappear in his bodiliness and become spirit, so that faith in him might be liberated from the obstacle which his personality set up and in that way achieve for the first time its own perfect purity as faith in the invisible – which is what G. Ebeling thinks.[74] To infer this from John 16, 7 is implausible, if only because of such other Johannine texts as

16, 22 and 14, 2. The Father does not conceal his now completed Word by making him pass over into the realm of the invisible, but bestows on him the quality of being his own eschatological revelation (*apokalypsis:* Galatians 1, 12, and 16). No doubt that 'apocalypse' is not unveiled before 'all the people, but before the witnesses that God had chosen beforehand' (Acts 10, 41), but this accords with the fact that God never reveals himself except in his own essential mystery.[75] And yet, since the Son is the Word of the Father, the Father, in disclosing the Son as the justified and glorified One, *also discloses himself.* The appearances of the risen Christ are 'self-presentations of God through him',[76] and they are, furthermore, 'the goal of the earlier self-revelations of God'.[77] This is so much so that, with the Resurrection, 'the Scriptures' (I Corinthians 15, 3f) in their entirety, and not merely a handful of prophetic passages within them, come to their fulfilment.

The Father, in showing the world his Son as the One who became through him definitively *living*, gives the Son an utter spontaneity in his own self-showing. If this were not so, it would only be an image that is shown to us, and not a living person. The Father's freedom, whereby he raises the Son in a sovereign act of lordship, is manifested in the freedom with which the Son shows himself of his own accord in a perfect sovereignty entirely his own. We will have a further occasion to speak of this later. What is decisive at this point is the revelation of the mystery of the Trinity which takes place in that it is precisely the *person* of the Son who manifests the person of the Father, the latter appearing in him. If it belongs to the supreme obedience of the Son that he lets himself be raised by the Father,[78] it belongs no less to the completion of his obedience that he lets it be 'granted' him by the Father to 'have life in himself' (John 5, 26) – and even, indeed, to *become* clothed in all the apparel of his own divine sovereingty, despite the fact that the apparel in question was already his own 'before the world was made' (Philippians 2, 6; John 17, 5). That Jesus thus *became* what he already was, both before the world's foundation and during his earthly ministry: this must be taken with absolute seriousness by every Christology. Whoever regards that as a contradiction in terms will necessarily mishear and misunderstand the preaching of the Gospel. Whether one stresses the distinction between Jesus and the eschatological Son of Man, and so underlines the element of becoming (conformably to Mark 8, 38 and parallels), or whether, with Matthew 10, 33, one affirms their identity, and so emphasises the element of being, neither aspect may be isolated from the other. A dynamic Christology must not be sundered from its ontological counterpart.

In other words, the renunciation of the 'form of God' and the taking on of the 'form of a slave' with all their consequences do not entail any alienation within the Trinitarian life of God. God is so divine that by way of the Incarnation, death and Resurrection, he can truly and not just in seeming become that which as God he already and always is.[79] Without under-estimating the depth to which God stooped down in Christ, but perceiving that this 'supreme' abasement (John 13, 1) formed, with the exaltation, one single reality, for the two movements express the self-same divine love, John was able to apply to both the categories of 'exaltation' and 'glorification': yet in a way which is, (to use the language of the Chalcedonian Definition) *asynchytōs, achōristōs;* 'without confusion', 'without separation' (DS 302). In this integrated vision, it is no longer contradictory for John to ascribe to the Son who died and was raised by the Father the power not just to give his life but also to take it up again (10, 18; 2, 19), as well as, through this power, to raise up (11, 25) the dead both in time (12, 1, 9 and 17) and at the end of time (5, 21; 6, 39, etc., *auto-anastasis* 'the Resurrection itself' one might call him, imitating Origen's celebrated neologism). In fact, the Son's absolute obedience 'even unto death, the death of the Cross' is intrinsically oriented to the Father (otherwise, it would be meaningless, and not in any case an absolute, divine obedience). Resting on the Father's power, which is itself identical with the Father's sending of his Son, the Son allows himself to be reduced to the uttermost weakness. But this obedience is so thoroughly love for the Father and by that very fact is so altogether one (John 10, 30) with the Father's own love that he who sends and he who obeys act by virtue of the same divine liberty in love – the Son, inasmuch as he allows the Father the freedom to command to the point of his own death, the Father inasmuch as he allows the Son the freedom to obey right down to the same point. When, accordingly, the Father grants to the Son, now raised into eternal life, the absolute freedom to show himself to his disciples in his identity with the dead Jesus of Nazareth, bearing the marks of his wounds, he gives him no new, different or alien freedom but that freedom which is most deeply the Son's very own. It is precisely in this freedom of his that the Son reveals, ultimately, the freedom of the Father.

We misinterpret the testimonies to the Resurrection in the grossest fashion if we reduce them to the literal sense of the word 'appearances' (because in any case we must make a certain allowance for the rôle of imagination here), rather than let them witness to the encounter with the living person of Jesus Christ – a person to whom one prays,[80] whom one adores (John 20, 28), and with whom one has a 'personal relationship': 'I belong to him' (Schniewind).[81] When the Risen One comes personally to meet his disciples, they are able to recognise him because, essentially, of his identity with the Crucified. Even Paul, who had not known Jesus as a mortal being, had not the slightest hesitation, when writing to the Corinthians, in identifying the Crucified One with the Risen Lord. If this identification be abandoned, whether in a Gnostic or an Ebionite direction, then the Christian faith collapses.[82] It is precisely this unity which God the Father, the Creator and the Founder of the Covenant, presents to the world as his definitively realised Word, as really and truly the completed Covenant between God and man, and as the perfect *dikaiosunē Theou*, 'righteousness of God'. The Crucified One in rising has become the Covenant in person: that is why he is represented as taking his place at God's right hand, 'seated' (Psalm 110, 1) or 'standing' (Acts 7, 56) there, invested with all authority (Matthew 28, 18). Owing to this identity, the disciples' encounters with Christ become testimonies to the central event which unites heaven and earth.

Lastly, the Resurrection of the Son is the revelation of the *Spirit*. To see this as it originally was, it is best not to begin from the temporal division into periods found in the Acts of the Apostles, where the Easter event and that of the Ascension are separated by an interval of forty days and the Ascension is made into a presupposition for the sending of the Spirit at Pentecost. If we leave the question of the forty days provisionally to one side, the Lucan idea[83] of how the Son, ascending to the Father, receives from him for the first time the promised Spirit so as to pour him forth upon the Church (Acts 2, 33; 1, 4ff) can take on a theologically deeper meaning – especially if we relate this event to the promise of the departing Lord in the Fourth Gospel. He must depart so that the Spirit may come (John 16, 7); he will ask the Father (that means, of course, when he is exalted) to send to the disciples another Paraclete, who will abide with them for ever (14, 16), and, more than that, will himself send this Spirit from the Father (15, 26; cf. Luke 24, 49). If one holds together these aspects of the Johannine teaching with the message of Luke then what transpires is the reunion with the Father of the Son who was sent to the world, and to the Cross, a reunion which takes place after the complete fulfilment of his mission (John 19,30). In the tones of speculative theology we might say that the reunion of the Father and the Son (in his human nature) as a single principle of aspiration (in the economy) appears as the condition for the sending forth of the Spirit to the Church and to the redeemed world. Luke offers his own interpretation of this idea by extending the temporal and festal cycle, spacing out his material in a way which is at once pedagogical but also, certainly, cultic in character. John, on the other hand, in no less essentially theological a manner, compresses Easter, the Ascension and Pentecost so that they inter-penetrate one another. As early as the evening of Easter Day, the Risen One, as John presents him, breathes out the Spirit upon the Church (20, 22), which is not to deny that John knows, at least by allusion, the 'ascending to the Father' (20, 17) which precedes the breathing forth of the Spirit. Even Luke, in Acts 2, 33, in no way implies that Jesus had to await the Ascension in order himself to 'receive from the Father the promise of the Holy Spirit': what is at stake here is a promise made by Jesus to his disciples, a promise whose content is meant for them (Luke 24, 49): in other words, the great promise of the prophet Joel that the Spirit will be poured out eschatologically 'upon all flesh' (Acts 2, 17). What was essentials in Luke's eyes is that:

> one can only receive the Spirit from Jesus, just as, in general, one can only participate in the present epoch of saving history which is the time of the Spirit on the condition that one shares, by the Spirit, in the time of Jesus.[84]

Paul's contribution here was decisive in that, for him, all the problems concerning the lapse of time between the Resurrection and the sending of the Spirit fall away, since he sees the two events in the closest possible unity. We have already noted that the Father raises the Son by his Spirit (Romans 8, 11), and that the terms *dynamis*, *doxa* and *pneuma*, which alternate as principles of resurrection, are to a considerable degree interchangeable. But the Spirit is not only the instrument of the Resurrection. He is also the milieu in which the Resurrection takes place: *zōopoiēstheis de pneumati*, 'he was made alive in the Spirit' (I Peter 3, 18); *edikaiōthē en pneumati*, 'he was vindicated in the Spirit', (I Timothy 3, 16; cf. Romans 1, 4). This milieu is not, however, one which Christ enters as into an environment strange to him. Rather is it an inheritance that belongs to him, since he is beforehand, as 'second Adam', the *pneuma zōopoioun*', 'life-giving Spirit' (I Corinthians 15, 45); rises again as *sōma pneumatikon*, 'a spiritual body' (I Corinthians 15, 44); and is wholly identified with the realm of the Spirit ('The Lord is the Spirit', II Corinthians 3, 17). Whoever wishes to live in the Lord must live in the Spirit and by him (Galatians 5, 16, 22 and 25). John puts into words the same idea when he makes the earthly Jesus one to whom the Father gives the Spirit 'without measure' (John 3, 34) and (as the true 'rock in the desert') the dispenser *par excellence* of water and the Spirit (7, 38). Yet the rock must first be struck by the lance of the Passion before he can pour out, with his blood, this water (and that Spirit) which, before his glorification is only promised (7, 39; 4, 10 and 14), but which afterwards is both the foundation and the testimony – in the unity of the Spirit with the water and the blood – of the faith of the Church (I John 5, 6ff; John 3, 5 and 8). When Jesus on the Cross gives over his *pneuma*, he also, doubtless, breathes forth the Spirit who is sent on mission, 'given without measure' (*pneuma aiōnion*, Hebrews 9, 14), – the Spirit whom the Father, in raising Jesus, returns to him as in the highest possible manner personally his own, but who is henceforth also the divine Spirit, identical with *dynamis* and *doxa* and now made known openly to the world (Romans 1, 4).

This explains why for Paul, as for the author of the Acts of the Apostles, and indeed 'for the witness of all the New Testament writers',[85] the action of the Holy Spirit, manifesting himself in the Church, remains the real proof of Christ's risen being. For that Resurrection was nothing less than Christ's taking possession of God's Spirit and power, access to which he had promised to those who believe in him. Luke for his part provides for the Church, aware as she is of her living possession of the Spirit, a central moment of a cultic kind, and one capable of being dated – namely, the event of Pentecost. Such possession of the Spirit is expressed not only in the continuation of the 'signs and wonders' on whose basis Jesus had been 'attested . . . by God' (Acts 2, 22), but also in the inner dispositions of the community: its prayer, its living faith, its brotherliness of common life, concern for the needy and so forth.[86] Last but not least to be mentioned among these indices of the ownership of the Spirit comes: being found worthy to share in the sufferings of Christ, something only possible through the inner incorporation of believers into the realm of Christ and the Spirit.[87]

The decisive revelation of the mystery of the Trinity is not, therefore, something which precedes the *Mysterium Paschale* itself.[88] As has been shown above in discussing the Passion, that revelation is prepared in the counter-position of the wills on the Mount of Olives and by the divine abandonment on the Cross, yet only with the Resurrection does it come forth openly into the light. D. M. Stanley concludes his analysis of the place of the Resurrection in Pauline soteriology with these three theses: 1. 'Christian salvation, that of Christ as well as of Christians, starts out from God the Father. 2. It has been perfectly realised by Jesus Christ, the Son of God, in his sacred humanity; through this now glorified humanity the process of its realisation in Christians is begun. 3. Its present reality and future realisation in Christians depends on the Holy Spirit who inhabits them as the principle of their adoption as children of God.'[89] We cannot here investigate the soteriological and ecclesiological perspectives which these theses at once open up in all directions. It must suffice to show that:

> for the New Testament, not only does the Christian Church have its roots in the Resurrection of Jesus. That Resurrection also provides the origin for specifically Christian theology – that is, for Trinitarian theology – which is a development of belief in the one God on the basis of the central revelatory event of Jesus' Resurrection from the dead.[90]

This serves as a negative demonstration that 'Christian faith in the Trinitarian God disappears wherever the New Testament message about the Risen One is, under whatever form, modified, corrected, or erroneously interpreted'.[91]

But precisely this sheds light on something of importance. When God the Father, in his Word, made a covenant with Israel (and even earlier, through the Noahide covenant, with humanity at large), issuing his promises in Abraham, giving the Law on Sinai, and through the prophets declaring his judgments and turning his people towards the Covenant's definitive form, what was at stake in this entire history was God's being for us and with us. That stands out once again in the Incarnation of the Word of God: in the Resurrection of Jesus it cannot be brought into question but be brought rather – and how much more! – to its conclusion. Since the

Resurrection of Jesus by the Father and the gift of their common Spirit, God is wholly and definitively present for us. He is disclosed to us in the depths of his triune mystery, even if this depth which has been revealed to us (I Corinthians 2, 10ff) manifests in a wholly new and quite overwhelming fashion the abyssal and hidden character of his being (Romans 11, 33).

This is why great care must be taken in giving a dominant position to the Johannine scheme of the Redeemer who descends and re-ascends, coming from the Father into the world and leaving this world again in order to return to his Father (John 16, 28). In John himself, this scheme is complemented (for instance, in the farewell discourse and the Resurrection appearances at 20, 19ff) by another perspective. It is not, indeed, suppressed – for 'it is to your advantage that I go away' (16, 7); the disciples had to be transformed and raised up from a *carnalis amor ad Christi humanitatem*, that Christ who *videbatur esse quasi homo unus ex eis*, by being carried, entranced, into the sphere of the Spirit, to a *spiritualis amor ad eius divinitatem*.[92] The Resurrection appearances are themselves a training in just such a transformation. 'The Risen One appears in withdrawal', above all in Matthew, where the single appearance before the eleven disciples is 'simultaneously a farewell'.[93] The disciples on the road to Emmaus recognise the Lord in the moment when he 'vanished out of their sight': Luke emphasises this disappearance theme on more than one occasion subsequently (Luke 24, 51; Acts 1, 9ff). In John, it will receive a thoroughgoing 'theological thinking through', inasmuch as, for him, every earthly appearance of Jesus was, from the start, 'already in each case a farewell'. And yet there is a complementary truth which is equally important, nay more important still: the disappearance is at the service of a deeper and more definitive presence – not that of a distant God, hiding himself anew from men, but, rather, that, in express terms, of him who became man and is the 'heir' of all the Father's creating work, reflecting the 'glory of God' and bearing 'the very stamp of his nature' (Hebrews 1, 3). 'I am with you' (Matthew 28, 20); 'I will not leave you desolate; I

will come to you ... you will see me; because I live, you
will live also' (John 14, 18ff). Jesus speaks here of his presence
in the Church. The appearances of the Risen One are a kind
of down-payment towards this abiding presence, and indeed
of the ceaselessly self-renewing advent (parousia) of the
definitive Word of God in the Church. In this respect,
Bultmann's assertion that Christ rose into the kerygma has a
justified sense; and no less is true of the thesis of Gerhard
Koch,[94] for whom Christ rose directly into the history of
humanity, and more precisely into that of the Church, above
all in its cultic assembly, and is even in continuous course of
rising again there.

A word should be said about the passionate and
intellectually powerful undertaking of G. Koch: the most
original theology of the Resurrection produced in our time.
Starting out from a recognition of the failure both of a
subjectivist theology (where Jesus' interiority becomes my
interiority) and of its objectivist counterpart (the old dogmatic
approach of saving events, but also the question of the
historical Jesus, or, with Barth, the idea of the objective acting
of the Father in the Son before the latter's appearing as the
Risen One),[95] Koch leads everything back to the personal
encounter with the living Christ of the human being who is
to be his partner. Presence as being-with,[96] and indeed as
bodily being-with,[97] of such a kind that it invites the
participation of others;[98] a being-with which embraces within
itself (something that can only happen here) the whole
biography of Jesus,[99] and the entire history of Israel,[100] and
in the end lights up the total history of God with his
world:[101] – that is what the Easter event is: something
personal, something that cannot be reduced to the status of
an object, something which as 'an event of presence'[102] will
not let itself be pushed into the past, but rather makes itself
incessantly actual now. The decisive factor here is the
identification of Resurrection with appearing;[103] Resurrection
does not lie beyond history;[104] one cannot, therefore, speak
of an 'historical pole' in the event.[105] Rather is 'Jesus risen
into history'.[106] In that event, God acquires a definitive *figure*
in which he appears to men, but this figure consists in the

indissoluble reciprocal relationship which joins the God who gives himself in Christ to man who receives that gift, and entrusts himself to it. This is an originating relationship (like the *noēma* and *noēsis* of Husserl), existing only as personally actualised, which means to say in mutual encounter.

> The figure takes on form! It appears in the relation between epiphany and faith, between appearing and seeing, between perceiving and confessing.[107]

That this figure will then have to be 'reproduced' for the purposes of communication makes it already questionable,[108] since in Jesus it is God himself who appears in all his livingness, and yet, at the same time, in a normative form – [109] and who would claim to be able to copy that, when even among men significant gestures only preserve their meaning insofar as they possess a transparency for the partners to the encounter, as the latter exteriorise themselves and bestow themselves on each other, or refuse to make that act of bestowal?[110] The distance between heaven and earth must shrink into the space of this event which reconciles God and the world, as well as illuminating in Jesus what the being of the world is.[111] The coming to be of the (Resurrection) figure is the decisive expression of being itself,[112] and as such it is the supreme centre, placed mid-way between factual history (objectivity) and faith (subjectivity).[113] From the side of God, the name of being, thus disclosed, is love;[114] from the side of man, it is responsive, trusting self-donation which determines in the sequel all man's problematic being-in-the-world.[115]

It is impossible to ignore Koch's synthesis, worked out as this is by way of precise thinking about the entire state of recent theology. Yet the price he would exact is high. The Risen One who makes himself present (in each 'now') can take no different form when the appearances of the so called Forty Days are compared with the ever new actualisation of Jesus' presence in the cultic Meal of the community (and the word uttered there).[116] The Lucan passage on the Ascension is, in this perspective, no more than a necessary reaction to the accelerating 'materialisation' of the New Testament Resurrection appearance reports.[117] But this very effort to make encounter with Christ and the ongoing preaching of the original proclamation into something living is more threatened than promoted by obliterating the distinction between the 'eye-witnesses' and later believers.[118] And if, by the turn of phrase 'Resurrection into history', the theology of the Covenant receives, in a most positive sense, its own crowning, and finds its relevance to all subsequent Christian generations displayed, nevertheless, the Trinitarian form of that Covenant theology is here demolished at a fundamental level, since no room is left for what is specific in the work of the Holy Spirit. That work is replaced – ousted – by the continuing and ever actual work of the risen Christ. In Catholic ecclesiology, many of Koch's *aporiai* and exaggerations find their own proper resolutions, since here the Church is at once the presence of Christ's fulness and the work of the Spirit who is Christ's interpreter. Accordingly, the tragic opposition between 'Barth' and 'Bultmann' (taking these names as representative of two tendencies) do not exist in the Catholic world.

(C) The self-attestation of the Risen One

We remain attached here to the fundamental theological affirmation which the texts may be heard to make when they are permitted to say what they wish to say. In the first place, it has been shown that this affirmation is unique and without analogy; next, attention has been drawn to its authentically theo-logical – that is, Trinitarian – form. What must now come under consideration is its concrete content: it is a confessing report of encounters with one who was dead and buried, and who 'presented himself alive . . . by many proofs' (Acts 1, 3) to the apostles. So far as these 'proofs' are concerned, proofs which in no way can be reduced to mere 'visions', whether subjective or objective, five may be distinguished, though, naturally enough, they have links with one another. These five will be discussed here without any essential reference to those exegetical questions which tensions and contradictions between the texts raise.

(aa) The reports are unanimous in taking as their subject-matter *encounters* with the living Christ.

> The encounter which befalls the witnesses is his
> initiative. It is pure gift – in word and sign, in greeting
> and blessing, in call, address, instruction, in consolation,
> command and mission, in the founding of a new
> community.[119]

Of course, since these are meetings between human beings,
the senses of those who experience them are involved: they
see and hear, they touch, they even taste (if the Vulgate's
version of Luke 24, 43 be accurate). But it is not on the
sensuous experiences that the stress lies. Rather, it is their
object which is emphasised, and this latter, the living Christ,
shows himself *of his own volition*. That is the import of the
word *ōphthē* which crops up at a number of decisive points
(I Corinthians 15, 3ff: more than once; Luke 24, 34 in the
encounter with Simon; Acts 13, 31; for the appearances to
Paul, see Acts 9, 17; 16, 9; 26, 16). In the Septuagint the
word serves above all to indicate an appearing of God, or of
heavenly beings 'normally hidden to view',[120] for the reason
that human senses could not support such a sight, as well as
because God is only seen when, by his free benevolence, he
chooses to reveal himself. The word denotes more, then, than
a vision.[121] It implies that the bridge of knowledge has been
thrown across the subject–object divide. In the case of the
appearances of the Risen One, this is underlined by the fact
that, in the form of his appearing, he is not given up, as are
mortal men, to the knowledge of others but can manifest
himself 'in another form' (Pseudo-Mark 16, 12), while 'their
eyes were kept from recognising him' (Luke 24, 16; cf. John
20, 15; 21, 4; perhaps Luke 24, 41). Origen was particularly
successful in bringing out this spontaneity of the Risen One's
self-manifestation.[122] A step-by-step revelation, a disclosure in
what still remains a closure, is perfectly possible ('Did not
our hearts burn within us . . .? Luke 24, 32). If, then, *ōphthē* is
'the most frequently employed concept for theophanies and
angelophanies',[123] and especially for the appearance of the

Glory of God with its attendant terror, doubt, astonishment and so forth;[124] if, in the language of Scripture, it serves to 'make known the breaking-through of what is hidden and invisible into openness',[125] then its use is especially appropriate for that high-point in the covenantal action of God which the last section has described. That is why, in this appearing of the Son, the supreme livingness and spontaneity of him who appears comes to expression. The category of mere visionary seeing is not enough;[126] even 'speaking of "objective visions" remains unsatisfactory'.[127] Talk of 'encounter' is here an absolute necessity:[128] encounter, moreover, in which for the first time the quite determinate 'I' of the One encountered is recognised.[129] It is not as though the material identity of this person with the Crucified occupies the chief place of interest in the appearance; nevertheless, that identification has to be established beyond all question (hence the gesture of showing the hands and feet, and, in John, the side), so that the truth of the whole Old Testament and New Testament revelation may come into the light.[130] Only so can Abraham be proved right in his belief that 'God . . . gives life to the dead' (Romans 4, 17), and in his rejoicing to see the day of Christ, a day which he really saw (John 8, 56). It is possible to submit the words Jesus addressed to the disciples to a rigorous exegetical criticism; they will have undergone a fair measure of stylisation.[131] It is nonetheless the case that Jesus' appearing was, in a quite central way, address:

> The word, considered as event, is not just a statement; it is a manifestation of the person and a sign . . . The word of the Risen One is an address . . . It is a history, which belongs with history's own total content and emerges from it.[132]

And it is a word which reaches the heart: 'Mary!' (John 20, 16).[133]

(bb) And there we come to the second point which can only be made by using several words at once: conviction, conversion, repentance. W. Künneth speaks of a 'being subjugated in one's conscience'.[134] H. Schlier, concordantly, of an 'over-powering'. [135] In this happening, the disciples know themselves to be not only recognised but also seen through; and more, in their very own reality (which exists in him) he knows and understands them – so they now realise – much better than they know and understand themselves. Hence the broken-hearted confession of, for example, the disciples on the Emmaus road. Before, they wanted, no doubt, truly to believe, hope and love, but their faith came up against insuperable barriers and these were re-inforced by the bad conscience which their flight and denial brought about. Their faith (which was biblical faith in the living God) had been bound up by Jesus himself with his work and person, and so, at his death, their faith too seemed to have died. The idea that, despite this death, 'Jesus' cause could still have a future' (W. Marxsen) finds no echo in the texts. That is why not even the message of the women can re-awaken the lifeless faith of the disciples (Luke 24, 11). Only the Risen One himself can do that as he gives back to them, with himself, the living God.[136] With the Eleven, as with Magdalen at the tomb, something must happen of a similar kind to what befell Paul outside Damascus: a falling down on the earth (Acts 9, 4) at least in a spiritual sense of those words. That this conversion of the whole inner attitude is, in the features of human existence it involves, much like a confession; that it arouses fear (Mark 16, 8; Luke 24, 37), blame (Luke 24, 25; Pseudo-Mark 16, 14), sorrow (John 21, 17), a mixture of fear and joy (Matthew 28, 8; Luke 24, 41), and finally pure paschal joy (John 20, 21) corresponds in an archetypal way, to the sacramental event that, on Easter day, is bequeathed to the Church as the Lord's own gift (John 20, 22ff). That sacramental reality continues Jesus' activity of revealing and convincing during his days on earth, and introduces, as by a prelude, his post-Easter activity as judge of his Church, as her exalted Lord (Apocalypse 2–3). His identity is, perhaps, nowhere more deeply manifested than here, where he is at once a living person and the personified sword of judgment of God. And yet the severest words of judgment are, at

Easter, always words of salvation and healing, as the story of Thomas shows.

(cc) This power to convince and hearts bring about in the disciples, for the first time, the *confession of the divinity of the Risen One*. That such a confession could have been offered in the time before Easter is not to be thought of.[137] The bare fact that Jesus dwelt among them, alive, confirmed, for the disciples, two things at the same time: the legitimacy of the absolute claim he had made, and linked with his own person, in the years that had passed, *and* the presence in him of the living God who had finally vindicated the truth of his ancient title: he who 'brings down to Sheol and raises up' (I Samuel 2, 6; Deuteronomy 32, 39; Wisdom 16, 13; Tobit 13, 2). From now on, these two aspects no longer admit of any distinguishing: that is why the entire development of Christology from the idea of the exaltation of the servant to be Kyrios and Messiah (Acts 2, 36) right down to Chalcedon is irresistibly consistent. In the Easter texts, the adoration of Jesus is spoken of for the first time: twice in Matthew (28, 9 and 17) and twice in John (20, 16: *rabbuni* is, in this period, a divine title; 20, 28).[138]

> The predicative used (in the confession of Thomas) sends us back – beyond all that is said of the earthly Jesus (and certainly beyond, also, all that, according to John, might be said of him) to the Prologue, and so to the pre-existing Word in whose total premundane sovereignty Jesus is now, with Easter, once again installed.[139]

That Thomas' confession, in the context of the (original) ending of the gospel, thus refers back in such unmistakable terms, to the gospel's beginning makes it improbable that the episode of Thomas possessed, for the evangelist, only a peripheral significance.[140] Even the title of Kyrios is not, as has already been remarked, the subsequent taking-over, by Hellenistic communities, of a pagan title which usurped divine prerogatives for Jesus' benefit: That thesis of Bousset's overlooks the fact that

in the Galilaean Easter narratives, the power of the
Kyrios has already been experienced in his appearing,
and that faith in the Kyrios arose thereby in that Easter
time itself . . . The invocation of the Kyrios, as the New
Testament reports it, differs essentially in its structure
from what is found in the mystery cults. It refers back,
in fact, to the historical road of Israel, on whose way
Israel called out to her God . . . If God had truly revealed
his essence in Christ, then Christ is henceforth the name
of God, the openness of his being.[141]

(dd) The evangelists are united in attesting that it was only
on the basis of the Easter event that the disciples were able to
grasp the meaning of Jesus' earlier life, and, indeed,of the
Scriptures as a whole. This statement is most powerfully
confirmed by the way in which they have poured out Easter
light over their entire description of the life of Jesus.[142] What
had been hitherto at best dimly surmised – and that
presentiment itself foundered with the death of Jesus – drew
from the Resurrection a *harmonious coherence* nothing short of
fascinating for the spiritual eyes of the first communities and
leading them, in their re-reading of 'Scripture', from
discovery to discovery.

This is why projections of post-Easter understanding
into the historical life of Jesus are not to be dismissed on
the grounds of their being 'legendary formations'.
Rather do they correspond perfectly to the 'very reality'
of the Gospel, to that degree, in fact, wherein the Gospel
of the Resurrection is a reality.[143]

What is decisive is not that individual words of the Old
Testament now submit to reading and interpretation in an
innovatory way, as predictions,[144] but that the *graphai*, the
books of the entire Old Testament, have been made to deliver
a transcendent synthesis which could not have been
constructed on their basis alone.[145] Beginning from the
complete fulfilment, particular texts might legitimately be
placed in a christological light: some have remained important

(especially Isaiah 53); others (like Psalm 16, 8–11) could be used for a period and then fall out of favour. Luke disengages for us what is really important in this process. Jesus, the Risen One, himself explains the Scriptures by applying them to his own person: 'all that the prophets have spoken' (24, 25), 'everything written about me in the law of Moses and the prophets and the psalms must be fulfilled' (24, 44), and Luke already modified the message of the angels at the tomb to the women by shifting it in this direction (24, 7). The personal Word of God interprets itself, himself, and into the Church's tradition. It takes up its pre-history in the old Covenant, but also, and in a quite fundamental way, integrates the earthly story of the Word made man into this self-explication. Whether the formulation of the Passion predictions be earlier than Easter or later, they will be in any case taken up again after Easter in order to be placed in the light of salvation-historical necessity: 'Was it not necessary that the Christ should suffer these things and enter into his glory?' (Luke 24, 26). But whereas the first community needed this interpretation of Scripture in its entirety in order to recognise, on the basis of spiritual correspondences, Jesus' definitive position, and had constant recourse to the 'promise-fulfilment' relationship in its preaching and catechesis, John knows that the Lord is so much the 'fulness' (1, 16) that he *needed* no testimony, neither that of Moses nor the Baptist's, in order to have access to that plenitude. His truth is so self-evident that the testimonies of Scripture, and of the Baptist, are more in the nature of exterior supplements for those seeking faith rather than integrating parts of the truth of Christ.[146] Henceforth, Jesus alone suffices. This observation is in no way affected by the fact that the conceptual system, and the treasury of words and images, established for, and applied to, the Passion and Resurrection, not only by Palestinian, but also by Hellenistic Chistians (compare the letters of Paul) passed by way of the Old Testament.[147] John himself does not disdain to make use of the post-paschal 'remembering' of what had not been understood before (2, 22; 12, 16).[148] Mark, who writes his whole gospel in the post-paschal perspective (1, 1), seeks to make credible, by his theory of the messianic secret, how Jesus was able to remain hidden: Jesus' forbidding others to make him known, as well as the incomprehensible blindness of the disciples. Thus it is, on the one hand, correct to characterise the Easter events, with N. A. Dahl, as above all, an *interpretandum*, since, unforeseen by the disciples, they needed to be placed in the great ensemble of salvation history if they were to be understood.[149] But on the other hand, those events did not rise up before the disciples as something irrational which only subsequently called interpretations into existence. Rather did those events present themselves in a sovereign fashion as the very mid-point of meaning which ordered, like a magnet, all the fragments of significance found in the Scriptures around itself.

(ee) The fact – mentioned in the course of criticising the position of G. Koch – that the moment of Jesus' appearing is also the moment of his disappearance and departure may be taken as the reverse side of the last all-pervasive Easter motif: *mission*. Jesus appears as he who, in a definitive way, sets those who have been favoured with the sight of him – but above all with his Spirit, on the road to their brethren. 'As the Father has sent me, even so I send you': the Johannine word (20, 21) sounds no less powerfully in Luke (24, 47–49; Acts 1, 8) and Matthew (28, 18–20). The importance of the mission outweighs all other considerations: what was called before Easter 'discipleship' (and was already, on occasion, a preliminary test of mission: Luke 10, 1; Matthew 10, 5 and 16), now, after Easter, bears its definitive name, mission, and possesses those dimensions which the four times repeated 'all' of the end of Matthew's gospel unfolds. These four dimensions correspond to those of the realm where the Kyrios holds sway: 'All authority in heaven and on earth' is the enabling ground of mission; 'all nations' in space and time defines its extension; 'observe all that I have commanded you' is the catholicity of the charge now entrusted; and 'I am with you always (all days), to the close of the age' is mission's guarantee.

The apostolate of primitive Christianity does not depend on the historical sending out on mission of the disciples by the rabbi of Nazereth. Rather it is founded on the appearances of the Risen One.[150]

It rests intrinsically on the four characteristics of encounter with the risen Christ described in the foregoing, and without them would be impossible. The mission is the chief goal of the appearances which are in no sense ends in themselves but, rather, aim at the founding of the Church. Likewise, it is mission which distinguishes Paul's fundamental experience on the Damascus road from his other mystical or charismatic experiences (compare Romans 1, 5). Mission, for the 'service of the world', is the fulfilled discipleship of Christ who himself came to be, in the most comprehensive of all senses, at the service of the entire creative and salvific work of his Father (Luke 22, 27 and parallels). In order that so all-encompassing a discipleship might be possible, Jesus breathes into his disciples his Spirit, who must 'lead' them (Romans 8, 14) on all the ways of the world and the paths of its history.

(2) The Exegetical Situation

(a) The aporia *and attempts at a solution*

If it is true that all the actions of the living God in saving history since Abraham (Romans 4, 17) have as their aim the resurrection from the dead, then this final event of which Jesus Christ is the 'first-fruits', and which is set in motion through him (I Corinthians 15, 20; cf. Matthew 27, 53) cannot be of such a kind that it has no more to do with saving *history*, transcending history in every possible respect. But if, on the other hand, this event breaks open in a radical way the entire circle of human existence as bounded by birth and death, goes beyond the 'present', 'ancient' aeon, and forms the foundation of the 'future' one (Hebrews 6, 5), then one has to say a priori that the Resurrection can be no *inner-historical* event, – defining history in the sense familiar to us and judging a putative event within it in terms of the customary, or scientifically refined, means of 'ascertainability'. What we know as 'history' can at best be the *terminus a quo* of a 'journey' that can no longer be determined from within history (and is, therefore, entirely withdrawn from both time and space). It can only be described now in metaphorical terms as a 'going', a 'going away', or 'ascent' or 'being lifted up' or 'glorified' (John), a 'no longer being there' (Mark 16, 6), or a 'being carried away' (Luke 9, 51; Acts 1, 2, 11ff; I Timothy 3, 16; Pseudo-Mark 16, 19), with its *terminus ad quem* identified as 'heaven', 'the Father', 'sitting at the right hand of God', and so on. The actualisation of this history-transcending event *within* history can only ensue in a paradoxical way that escapes historical modes of expression and the methods of historical investigation. The 'way' on which the Risen One goes cannot be followed, if only because it first originates with his going upon it. He who steps out on it is himself 'the Way' (John 14, 6), just as he is himself 'the Resurrection' (John 11, 25). He designates himself in this fashion as the comprehensive category, within which further 'ways' and 'resurrections' can come to be, no less transcendent vis-à-vis the ancient aeon, and so 'eschatological'.

What is ascertainable within history is, significantly, the empty spot where he had been lain, the fact that he is 'no longer here' (Mark 16, 6). But, starting from this absence, one cannot, evidently, follow the route that leads out of our history. (It would be naive in the highest degree to interpret the final event of salvation along the lines of the ancient multi-storey building picture of the world, in inner-cosmic terms, as 'mythical': what has been said earlier about the convergence of biblical images in expressing something which transcends them already rules such an interpretation out of court.) Within history, the empty tomb remains of necessity an ambiguous affair. The 'unique', eschatological character of the Resurrection' implies that

it cannot be 'proved' in the sense in which we now speak of 'proofs' . . . What can be proved is exclusively the conviction of the witnesses and of the primitive Church.[151]

But, alongside the account of the empty tomb, there are also the more important reportings of encounters between mortal men and the Risen One, meetings which create in these men the conviction that the same Jesus, who was known to them from the old aeon had, 'by many proofs', *tekmērias*, 'presented himself alive', *parestēsen heauton*) to them 'after his Passion' (Acts 1, 3), from out of the new aeon. In other words, this self-manifestation was so vital that it possessed, for those to whom it happened, the validity of a 'proof' – not naturally, in the sense of a scientific demonstration, but rather in that of unsurpassable, objective evidence. In relation to that evidence, not only did they have to found their lives anew as witnesses of this event, but to re-interpret the world and history as a whole. Again, this being convinced on the part of the witnesses is, when considered from a purely inner-historical standpoint, a psychological phenomenon which – if on a different plane from that of the 'empty tomb' – remains ambiguous. It all depends on whether one believes the witnesses or not, whether one regards the evidence to which they bear testimony as objective or subjective (or, and this comes down to the same thing) as conditioned by their world-picture. Before the testimony of the witnesses, before the kerygma of the Church, before the Resurrection of Christ, minds find themselves divided. And if theology is a (*sui generis*) science, it belongs to its foundational structure that the division between faith and non-faith passes right through its middle, or, more precisely put, right through the middle of its concern with those data on whose basis it is built. That concern, when pursued scientifically, is exegesis, and so H. Schlier was right to call the Resurrection a 'limit-problem' for exegesis itself. In the presence of this object, exegesis sees itself

> confronted with a choice, either to reinterpret it according to those criteria implied by historical science as a *Weltanschauung* and to reduce it to what is comprehensible in its 'historical epoch',

or to yield itself to the evidence set before it, evidence which, doubtless, cannot be termed historically guaranteed', but – and this is more – can be called evidence that imposes itself historically in a convincing fashion.

It is the 'evidence of a phenomenon which shows itself disingenuously from its own resources'.[152] One can therefore say with confidence that the evidence shining forth from the testimony is 'accessible to anyone who has eyes to see',[153] all that more so in that:

> the events in which God has shown his divinity . . . are, as such, intrinsically self-evident within their historical context.[154]

And yet there is the possibility of relativising, by de-mythologisation, just that very context. Thus the eyes which can see are the 'enlightened eyes of the heart' (Ephesians 1, 18), the organs of *oculata fides*, as Thomas Aquinas calls it,[155] which alone can contemplate the form of revelation as it offers itself[156] in all its spontaneity. A relatively innocent view of the events allows the historical recognition that:

> at least in the moment of decision, when Jesus was arrested and executed, the disciples entertained no certitude of this kind (namely, of an expected Resurrection). They fled, judging Jesus' cause lost. Something must, have intervened, therefore, to provoke, in a brief space of time, not only the complete reversal of their attitudes, but also their arousal to fresh activity and the founding of the community. This 'something' is the historical kernel of the Easter event (M. Dibelius).[157]

This often cited assertion usefully locates a kind of borderline where inner-worldly historical method is invited to hold itself open, in regard to an event which its methods are fundamentally powerless to review. The concept of analogy, too, which has pride of place in its capacity to make connexions within the Bible and can, on that basis, be extended, if problematically, to general anthropology and 'fundamental ontology',[158] will not help us to cross this frontier, inasmuch as all these analogies converge, as we have seen, on a culminating point itself 'without analogy'.

This is why it is hard to qualify the Resurrection, considered as the turning point between the old *aeon* and the new, as

> a real inner-worldly event ... in human space and human time[159]

although the manifestation of the Living One is really accomplished in, and into, this world, this space and this time, and although, furthermore, the Risen One has evidently transformed our time and our space, and thus our very world, in his new mode of existence (as the *sōma pneumatikon*).[160]. G. Koch's formula, whereby Christ has 'risen into history' could express the right understanding, namely, the direct presentation of the new aeon embodied in Christ to those who still abide in mortality – had not Koch overdone his formula by identifying Resurrection with appearance. It is true, however, that all translation of such a unique meeting of the aeons in the world of images and concepts of the 'present aeon' (Galatians 1, 4) is a priori problematic. It can only be done by way of approximations, tentative evocations, rather as concentrated white light, refracted in a prism, lets itself be decomposed into, certainly, on the one hand, a continuous spectrum of colours shading into each another, while yet, on the other, this same spectrum also contains the greatest oppositions (green-red, yellow-blue). The Resurrection accounts of the gospels are as much in continuity with one another as they are in partly irreconcilable opposition. It will be the concern of our third section in this closing chapter to describe the theological meaning of the differing shades of colour (as partial reproductions of that 'white' which no colour can reach). But first of all, in the present section, a word must be said about the situation in which, owing to this 'decomposition', the exegete finds himself.

Starting at the most general level: this situation is not typified only by the fact that the accounts to be interpreted, reconcilable only with difficulty or irreconcilable as these may be, are always given some kind of unity according to a fundamental decision by the researcher – whether this unity lie in the direction of the affirmations of faith, or, contrariwise, in that of an historically conditioned anthropology. For also characteristic of the general situation is the taking of *partial prior decisions* (a necessity from the standpoint of the pure exegete) in whose light, in each case, texts are ordered after one fashion or another. Such partial prior decisions are taken within the fundamental decision just mentioned and often appear as intermediary positions between its two poles. Within the framework of the philological and historical method, such prior exegetical options to illuminate the texts in a determinate way are, doubtless, inevitable. But it may be asserted that, in terms of their theological consequences, these options are of varying degrees of significance. None of them can be a matter of wholesale theological indifference, but many are relatively peripheral[161] (for example, the question as to whether the women at the tomb 'really' experienced angelophanies), whereas others are relatively central, and touch, more or less, upon the fundamental decision (for faith or non-faith) itself. If, from the scholarly viewpoint, the greatest prudence is required in the face of these (frequently unconscious) options, yet on the kind of illumination a text receives depends, nonetheless, to a considerable extent, the context of meaning into which it is introduced, and the weight of meaning which it is ascribed. Our task here can in no way be that of examining in turn all the exegetical questions involved, and of commenting on them with exegesis' own methods. Rather is it to highlight the reciprocal dependence of exegesis and theology in some of its most important instances. This enterprise must form the transitional stage between the dogmatic affirmation *that* Christ is risen (1), and the deployment of this dogmatic affirmation in a variety of images and concepts (3).

In I Corinthians 15, 3–5, Paul offers that most ancient list of witnesses whose unitary or composite character has been a matter of controversy, but whose antiquity leaves no time for a lengthy history of composition.[162] Since Paul refers the Corinthians to witnesses (among them the five hundred brethren named in third place) who, in part, are still alive and able to be questioned, his catalogue is intended, incontestably, to offer a succession of historical testimonies – very probably a chronological succession, so that Seidensticker's theory, for which the *ephapax* of verse 6 means 'once for all' and gathers all the appearances into a single one (rather as in Matthew), contradicts Paul's affirmation. Of the six encounters that Paul enumerates, only three are known to us from the Gospels: the first, with Peter (mentioned fleetingly by Luke alone, 24, 35, but cf. John 21, 15), that to the Twelve and that to Paul himself. We do not know when or where the appearance before 'five hundred brethren at one time' happened or could have happened, nor the time and place in which the appearance to James should be situated. The hypotheses that have been suggested diverge, and lead into no solid ground.[163] Those whose, in contra-distinction to the 'Twelve' are described as 'all the apostles' (v. 7) are obscure to us.[164] Vis-à-vis the ancient formula of faith, there is, on the hand, the sermons of the apostles in the Book of the Acts, sermons which repeat the kerygmatic affirmation without amplifying it; and, on the other, the (most likely) two-fold tradition – the empty tomb, and the appearances to the disciples, two strands which seem intertwined in different fashions in the Gospels. It is clear, though, that the Resurrection of Jesus could not be proclaimed by witnesses who were not (already, from the outset) equipped to narrate something about the encounters with the Risen One – whatever the degree to which their accounts may have been re-worked in order to produce the later form which lies before ourselves. And insofar as, in the kerygma, the death and Resurrection of Jesus always appear as inter-linked, these accounts must have presented a realism corresponding to that of the events of the Passion themselves, as known to the audience ('as you yourselves know', Acts 2, 22).

The question now arises as to whether we are able, from

the texts before us, to identify the process of composition, and if, so, to what degree. There are, in the first place, numerous, doubtless, linking texts.

> When the Emmaus disciples wish to pass on their experience, the eleven forestall them with the glad tidings of the vision of Peter; but this ill befits the disciples who, in the following pericope, take fright when Jesus appears, and have to be convinced by manifold tangible proofs (cf. Luke 24, 33–42).[165]

The fact that the Matthaean angel instructs the women to tell the disciples that they are to go ahead to Galilee where they will see the Lord ill accords with the other recorded claim that the women themselves will experience *en route*, in Jerusalem therefore, an appearance of the Risen One. Moreover, it is not probable that Jesus simply repeats for their benefit words which they have already heard from the angels (28, 7–10). It is only with difficulty credible that, in John, Mary Magdalen lingers at the tomb on two occasions: on the first occasion, finding it empty and without the interpreting angel, and on the second with the same interpreting angels who appear in the Synoptics yet who here have nothing to announce prior to, finally, her experience of an encounter with Jesus.

There is, secondly, the phenomenon of enrichment in the accounts – though here we must tread with the greatest prudence since behind such asseverations of enrichment there lie hidden not infrequently concealed prior decisions (about what texts are earlier and what later). The story of the entombment seems to have undergone an enrichment: in Mark, Joseph of Arimathea is 'a respected member of the Council, who was also himself looking for the Kingdom of God' (15, 43); in Luke, he is 'a good and righteous man, who had not consented to their purpose and deed' (23, 50ff); in Matthew he has (already) become a disciple of Jesus (27, 57): that is what he is in John as well, though a secret one, like Nicodemus who becomes his auxiliary in helping at the tomb (19, 38ff). The Apocrypha further embroider this episode.[166]

In Mark 15, 47, the women look on at the laying in the tomb and, on Easter morning, wish to carry out the anointing with balsam. In Matthew, they remain sitting at the graveside until dispersed by the guard: of the care to be lavished afterwards on the body we hear nothing. In John (19, 39), the anointing takes place with the utmost extravagance ('for a hundred pounds') as early as the moment of the entombment itself.

Another *crescendo* comes in the increasingly emphatic exoneration of the disciples, who had fled, and were absent at the Cross and burial (up to the point of John 18, 8), and of Pilate.[167] It may be assumed that the theme of the disciples' doubt has been accentuated for apologetic reasons, above all in the Apocrypha, where the Risen One is obliged to have recourse to massive measures in order to break it down.[168] One can find traces of a tendency to draw together the appearances, whether in space (either Galilee or Jerusalem), or in time (in Luke, on one single day), and to present them almost as a 'closing tableau' (Matthew) of a schematic kind.[169] The extension of the time involved to forty days involves another problem which we must come to grips with later. There is perhaps – though here the highest caution is appropriate – a development which some have thought it proper to call that of an ever greater 'massive realism' about the Risen One, to the point of touching his body, and of depicting him in the act of eating, in the presence of his disciples. If one takes as criterion the apparently 'more spiritual' vision of the Damascus Road, and the assertions of Paul about the spiritual body, then the evangelists' accounts must appear as 'coarsenings' with surely (?) apologetic ends in view:[170] one then understands why Luke has limited such 'massive' scenes to the forty days. But one must be on guard against this latter theory: the Marcan first stage (in such a 'development') is lacking; Matthew, though certainly later than Luke, is not 'coarser' than Luke is; and John, without a moment's hesitation, places wholly spiritual and entirely sensuous traits side by side. Moreover, there is no reason to take the kind of appearance found at Damascus as the norm for all Easter appearances.

There are probably, in the third place, certain harmonisations between the individual accounts which, however, in no sense go so far as to want to eliminate all contradictions. Here too certain prior options determine in considerable measure the answer to the question of just which gospel served as a basis for just which other. We do not have to concern ourselves here with the view that, to the conclusion of Mark's gospel, which refers clearly enough to a promised appearance in Galilee but narrates none, there was added by the 'presbyter Arist(i)on' an 'independent epitome' of the appearances, bringing together, above all, those of Luke. It is striking that the appearance to Peter, given pride of place in Paul's account, is mentioned only once by the Synoptics, and that in a colourless and somewhat oblique fashion, in Luke 24, 34: 'no tradition ... knows how to recount what Peter experienced and saw'. Perhaps such a question is superfluous anyway if it be only a question of 'an ecclesial formula, of kerygmatic significance'[171] ('the Lord is truly, *ontōs*, risen, and has appeared to Simon') which Luke might have received from Paul, or, if one wishes, from the tradition whence Paul's formula arose. A further open question concerns Luke's report, in 24, 12, of Peter's hurrying to the tomb: when 'stooping and looking in, he saw the linen cloths by themselves; and he went home wondering at what had happened'. Are we dealing here with a *résumé* of John 20, 2–10, the race of the two disciples to the tomb, where Luke has retained, for reasons of piety, at any rate the visit to the tomb of Peter? This seems more probable than the inverse thesis, namely that John has spun his entire subtle scheme from out of a single verse of Luke's gospel.[172] The appearances to the disciples in Luke and John are so alike that 'one may ask whether the manuscripts of each have not been harmonised with those of the other'. Here too it seems more likely that Luke knew and used the Johannine tradition, rather than the opposite.[173] Hardest to decide about is the relation between the Johannine appendix with its appearance on the Sea of Tiberias, and the story of the call on the Lake in Luke 5, 1–11. It can scarcely be contested that, behind the two, stands one single event. Yet which composition lies nearer the source cannot really be decided: as with the preceding case, it all turns on an evaluation of the antiquity of the Johannine tradition. We will not stray far from the truth in seeing as the nucleus of these stories the authentic, original Galilaean appearance of the Lord to the apostles, to which the conferring of plenary power on Peter would belong. The consequence would follow that the sayings about 'fishers of men' and Matthew 16, 18–19) should be attached to this post-Easter scene. Somewhat fantastic, yet worthy of mention, is E. Hirsch's proposal that Matthew 14, 28ff should be related to John 21, 7, and the original appearance to Peter recognised in the result.[174]

In the wake of these assertions about linking texts, enrichments and borrowings, all of which carry with them their own problematic, it can also be asked whether literary criticism with any show of certainty can exclude particular accounts as without historical value. This question should only be raised *vis-à-vis* the legend of the guard at the tomb, which is a peculiarity of Matthew's gospel and betrays a late, apologetic tendency. It presupposes a tendency to ascribe to the empty tomb a certain demonstrative power, something altogether foreign to the earliest accounts, and further, a counter-blast to the Jewish polemic which would have it that the corpse was stolen or carried off, and a Christian response to this. The Apocrypha render this legend grosser still, in portraying the enemies of Jesus – the scribes, the Pharisees and the elders of the people – as witnesses to Jesus' Resurrection from a tomb sealed with a seven-fold seal.[175] Matthew's narrative mirrors, therefore, a secondary situation in the Church's life.

All the other colours of the prism can further reflect the aboriginal Easter light in differing refractions. None of these enable one to seize in a direct way the incomprehensible event: as was shown at the outset of this discussion, that would contradict its very essence. And yet there is in the very brokenness of divine revelation in the Bible an adequacy or harmony – the work of divine inspiration is glimpsed therein – arising from within the reciprocal relationship between the self-revealing Lord and the believing and meditating community (of the Old Testament as of the New). This encounter is the primordial phenomenon, which no criticism can dissolve.

(B) Options of exegesis

In what follows we shall note the most important exegetical difficulties in the Easter texts – not in order to resolve them nor even to expound them in some detail – but rather to show that the researcher, by means of 'hypotheses' (or, otherwise expressed, 'prior options'), can place them, admittedly to different degrees, in a light which shows them up in a fairly satisfying way.

(aa) The problem of the *ending of Mark's gospel* calls for sheer decision one way or the other. The abrupt breaking off of the gospel is extremely surprising.

> Either the original ending has been suppressed, or it was never there, or it has been lost accidentally.[176]

The third possibility would be the most satisfactory, if there were any evidence, however, meagre, to back it up. The loss of the last leaf, with the story of the Resurrection to which, in the closing verses, the angel refers, must have happened, in this case, very early, since neither Matthew nor Luke have read it. That is improbable. Was it suppressed, on the grounds that it contained something that impeded the proclamation of the early Church, or that was or seemed to be, irreconcilable with other traditions which aimed at dominance (above all, Luke's Jerusalem tradition)? Here we have opening up before us a field-day for endless, and groundless, speculation, in dependence of the prior options taken by exegetes when dealing with other issues.[177] Or should one accept that Mark did originally end in fact at 16, 18:

> And they (the women charged by the angels to go to the disciples with the Easter message) went out and fled from the tomb, for trembling and astonishment had

come upon them; and they nothing to anyone, for they were afraid.

Does it suffice to recall that Mark often lets miracles stories issue in an account of the fear that overcomes the witnesses? Moreover, the fact that the pericope has come to its end[178] does not mean that the work as a whole has done so. Does Mark regard the Easter appearance as no longer part of the story of the life of Jesus? But in that case, why does he describe that entire life-story in the light of Easter?[179] Is there here some reserve (E. Meyer) or discipline of the secret (J. Jeremias), – even though neither Mark, elsewhere, nor the other evangelists show any signs of it? Or again, did Mark, as W. Marxsen thinks,[180] propose to identify the Galilee appearance with the Parousia to which the Christian community was moving (which, if true, would dispose of all the other appearances narrated as legendary formulations)? H. Grass regards this thesis as 'even more deviant'[181] than that for which the hearers would not have registered the lack of a conclusion, since they already knew what it was from the kerygma. But G. Koch deals in even more radical fashion with the set of questions posed by Marxsen when he asks the decisive question about the community's experience before the Parousia:

> In Mark, does Easter come out of the interpretation of the community, which would have transposed onto Jesus a Christology of the Son of Man, or, alternatively, is Easter the response of the community to the revelation of the Kyrios . . .

a revelation which Koch interprets as experience of the 'presence of the Kyrios', itself 'the foundational principle on whose basis Mark has written his gospel'.[182] Here Easter and Parousia would merge indifferently into each other – which in no way corresponds to Mark's apocalyptic tone. The question thus left open is a grievous one, since we are ignorant as to whether we may, or should, make of the missing ending a theologoumenon or not. Hitherto, however, the exegete has proved unable to give the theologian any positive counsel here: that is why the theologian, until he be better informed, must interpret the ending of Mark in the context of the other gospels, and not venture to relativise the other three in favour of some special Marcan theology of the Parousia.

(bb) The problem of *Galilee and Jerusalem* presents us with a choice of quite a different kind. Where the appearances are concerned, the reports point in both directions. Mark, the first evangelist to write, indicates an unmistakable displacement of Jerusalem in favour of Galilee as the country of the appearances. Matthew follows him, though not without inserting an appearance of Jesus 'on the way', made to the women in the area of the tomb. John (if one includes his appendix into the count) on the whole preserves the direction 'from Jerusalem to Galilee' but 'takes over' the '*en route* appearances': that to Mary Magdalen from Matthew, and the appearance to the Twelve in Jerusalem from Luke. Luke is the sole evangelist to place all the appearances in Jerusalem, not without weakening, by an adroit twist in the tail (Luke 24, 6), the angel's reference to Galilee (Mark 16, 7) – which rests in Mark on a prediction by Jesus (14, 28), while Matthew leaves this open (Matthew 28, 7, and in despite of Matthew 26, 32).[183] If we opt for Galilee as the location of the first appearances, neither an angelic message nor a reference by Jesus need necessarily have been the original occasion for a change of venue. One can either think of a flight on the part of the disciples (difficult on the Sabbath day, and rendering impossible the women's announcement on the third day that the tomb was empty: so Grass),[184] or accept a sojourn by the disciples in Jerusalem until the third day, followed by the disturbing message from the women who had been the first to venture to the tomb, and thereupon the departure of the disciples under the leadership of Peter in whom Jesus' promise was fulfilled (Luke 22, 31ff: so H. von Campenhausen). Both hypotheses require a first appearance to Peter in Galilee and then a second to the Eleven, and so strongly are these associated by a Galilaean colouration, that Luke, in all probability, felt himself obliged to strip the appearance to Peter, which he alone mentions, of all its narrative character, whilst perhaps introducing its concrete substance into the account of the call, which is special material of his own (Luke 5, 1–11). The so-called 'third' appearance in John (21, 14) may contain traces of the first and probably also of the second.[185] By no means self-evident is the justice of H. von Campenhausen's reconstruction for which:

> the decisive impulse which set everything off ... was the discovery of the empty tomb[186]

and more precisely, because the announcement made by the women to the disciples is what led them to set out.

In the face of all this, the thesis which would give priority to the appearances at Jerusalem is going to have a hard time. Luke, who is its first thoroughgoing representative, has in that theological preoccupations (E. Lohse),[187] while a Jerusalem origin for the confessing formula of I Corinthians 15, 3–5, a case argued by H. Conzelmann,[188] is barely satisfactory. Admittedly, a 'departure' or 'flight' of the apostles into their own region is nowhere referred to, any more than is a 'return' occurring by Pentecost at the latest. One can, as between the Galilee appearances and those of Jerusalem, point out differences of theological theme,[189] but the rise of the two-fold tradition is not explained by that. It is quite certain that the tomb shows a tendency to draw the appearances into proximity with itself;[190] whether, however, the (Jerusalem) tomb-tradition and the (Galilaean) appearances tradition were, at their origins, historically bound up with each other (as the 'departure' hypothesis would have it) or 'first arose in independence of each other[191] (as in the acceptance of a 'flight' hypothesis) can scarcely be determined.

(cc) The question of the *empty tomb* offers a problematic with a quite different structure. In favour of its historicity is the eloquent fact that it cannot count as a *proof* of Christ's Resurrection,[192] and was not exploited apologetically in such a way in the oldest tradition. It spread, at first, only terror and confusion.[193]

> The discovery of the empty tomb is an ambiguous sign,
> which prepares the way for the Easter appearances and
> is only interpreted through them.[194]

'The empty tomb is not proposed as a proof of the
Resurrection, but as a pointer to it, and a sign': it is the
mouth of the angel which first interprets it.[195] There are
marked differences of opinion as to whether the ancient
Pauline Resurrection formula, which mentions the burial,
implies the emptiness of the grave, and – supposing that it
does – whether this should be credited to the account of the
intellectual perspective of Jewish apocalypticism which could
only conceive of a resurrection of the dead in the material
mode of the resuscitation of a corpse.[196] Whilst the historicity
of the fact that the tomb was found empty can scarcely be
doubted – although, admittedly, without an empty tomb the
Resurrection of Jesus could not have been proclaimed in the
Jewish world (least of all in Jerusalem) – it is, on the other
hand, certain that this fact was subsequently exploited
apologetically – something which could hardly have been
avoided, given that the sign, by virtue of its ambiguity, was
going to receive a polemical interpretation from the opposing
side as well.[197] That this apologetic tendency of the
Matthaean account is 'also at work in John',[198] especially in
the portrayal of Jesus as a gardener – for in the Jewish reply
there figured an alleged 'gardener Judah' who had moved the
body of Jesus without the knowledge of the Christians –
cannot be stated as fact. At most, one may say that John
turns the motifs of apologetic discussion to his own (symbolic
and allegorical) ends.[199] It has been asked whether the Marcan
ending with its queer detail that the order given by the
angel to announce the Resurrection to the disciples goes
unexecuted may not also betray an apologetic tendency. On
this point, one can gladly agree with von Campenhausen that
this incoherence (suppressed by Matthew and Luke)
constitutes 'a secondary, and wilful, modification of the
tradition'. But is the reason for it really the desire to protect
the disciples who, in this way, have nothing to do with the
tomb? The thesis is possible, yet the impression it makes is

one of artifice. If it is true, then Luke 24, 12 must be struck out as an interpolation and in that case, the race scene in John 20, 3–10 (which may be the provenance of the Lucan verse) is non-historical also. Given the state in which the Markan ending finds itself, one will forego the luxury of a decision. The Christophany to the women, inserted by Matthew, (there is a corresponding scene in John) may be judged differently. Above all, the objection can be raised:

> Why the Risen One should appear to the women in Jerusalem, but then send on the disciples to Galilee, is incomprehensible.[200]

It is possible, however, with P. Benoit to find in John 20, 2–10 (in connexion with Luke 24, 12) traces of the most ancient tradition: a visit to the tomb by Peter, without an appearance, and a Christophany to the Magdalen (which Matthew would then have reproduced in summary form).[201] The question of the Christophany to the women is mixed up, moreover, with the question of priority as between the women and the apostles. We shall have more to say about that below (3).

(dd) Also bound up with this question and by and large not less significant is the matter of the *appearances of the angels* at the tomb: in Mark one angel ('young man') who interprets the empty space; in Luke two of them, with the same function; in Matthew one, who, with radiant aspect, descends from heaven, rolls away the stone, and then interprets the emptiness of the tomb which has now become patent; in John, none at first, just the awful emptiness, but then in the second Mary Magdalen episode two, who, however, do nothing by way of interpretation, and so seem to have lost their specific task (but see below under '3').[202] Those who have a priori objections against *angeli interpretes* will regard these appearances as mere interpretations of inner inspiration and certitude. One can perhaps take in this sense the modest correction which the text of Mark undergoes at the hands of Matthew: in Mark the angel refers to the words of Jesus ('There you will see him, as he told you', 16, 7 with reference to 14, 28), whereas in Matthew (and despite 26, 32) he sends the disciples to Galilee on his own responsibility ('Lo, I have told you', 28, 7). And this means, then, that:

> No word of Jesus led the disciples to Galilee but an angelic word: namely, the working of the divine action (P. Seidensticker)[203]

The role of the angel here *can* be excluded, just as in the stories of the annunciation, the Nativity, the Temptation and the Ascension. The question is, however, whether, bearing in mind the tenor of biblical revelation as a whole, one would be justified in so doing.

(ee) The ancient formula of faith contains the assertion: Christ 'was raised *on the third day* according to the Scriptures'. The significance of the expression 'on the third day' is exegetically difficult and controversial. J. Kremer is certainly right when he remarks that 'the simplest and most natural explanation' is that

> the mention of the third day rests on an historical datum, – either the discovery of the empty tomb or the first appearance of the Risen One at that point in time.[204]

In this case, the Resurrection remains – so far as its becoming known is concerned, for in itself it is not dateable – an historically determinable event, just as are the death and the burial. It would also be possible to relate the expression 'according to the Scriptures', at least in the first place, to the Resurrection as such (which is, as we have seen, the culminating point of the saving action of God), and not to the 'third day' – or, at best, to present the two in merely indirect relation.[205] So far as scriptural proof is concerned, the only text worth considering here is Hosea 6, 1ff in its Septuagint form.

After two days he will revive us;
on the third day he will raise us up,
(*anastēsometha*),
that we may live before him.

Rabbinic exegesis drew from this text the conviction that 'the resurrection of the dead will take place on the third day after the world's end'.[206] But against such a reference to this text is the elequent fact that nowhere in the New Testament is it adduced as a scriptural support. If, however, one is not content to consign the matter to a purely historical explanation, it would still be possible to have recourse to a 'dogmatic' explanation, for which there is a plenitude of references but no knock-down proof. The parallels provided by the history of religions are too remote for a Palestinian kerygma[207], and the text itself is too ancient to have cultic foundations (in the celebration of Sunday).[208]

The bringing into relation of the Sign of Jonah, in Matthew 12, 30, with Jonah's sojourn 'three days and three nights in the belly of the sea-monster' is a late formulation, as comparison with Luke 11, 29ff and Matthew 16, 4 would show. But perhaps one should not take the expression 'on the third day' in a rigorously chronological sense, as indeed the already cited formulation of the Sign of Jonah would suggest. Moreover, 'on the third day' is parallel with 'after three days'.[209] The expression might mean just a brief lapse of time in general. Its more probable meaning, however, is that of a return to an initial state after an interruption or counter-movement. J. Jeremias places in close proximity to Jesus' words of prediction that he would 'rise again on the third day' a series of quite different 'three days' sayings. After three days, Jesus says, he will erect the New Temple (Mark 14, 58 and parallels).

Behold, I cast out demons and perform cures today and tomorrow, and the third day I finish my course (Luke 13, 32). Today, tomorrow, and the following day he must go on his way, then to suffer in Jerusalem the fate of a prophet (Luke 13, 32–33). Yet a little while and they will see him no more, and again a little while and they will see him. Today, community with him;

tomorrow, separation; and on the third day, the return (John 16, 16).[210]

Remarkable, too, is the fact that Elijah, after his transport, was for three days sought and not found (II Kings 2, 17). We may be forgiven for not mentioning other attempts at explanation here.[211] All in all, one will have to choose between the historical interpretation (from which in due course Jesus' words of prediction may find themselves excluded as *vaticinia ex eventu*) and a less clear-cut, dogmatic and salvation-historical interpretation, to which many of Jesus' sayings seem to point forward, and for which this or that representative manner of the period might have proved a more concrete background.

(ff) Luke alone mentions (Luke 24, 51; Acts 1, 2) and describes (Acts 1, 9), an *Ascension* of the Lord in the presence of his disciples. In his second work (the Book of the Acts) he dates it as the conclusion of the *forty days* during which Jesus appeared to his disciples.[212] The concept of a round number here creates no difficulties. It is patterned on the stories of Moses[213] and Elijah,[214] and on Jesus' stay in the desert, and, correspondingly, asks to be understood as a sacred number.[215] The difficulty lies in the representation of an Ascension detached from the Resurrection, and in the meaning to be attached to that special time of the appearances sandwiched between the two. Here again there are exegetical options to choose from. One can take the view that the original Easter accounts knew of no appearances, or at best only appearances of a spiritual and transfigured kind (on the model of Paul's Damascus Road vision, or the idealised scene of the appearing exalted Kyrios in Matthew) – and that what are alleged to be the increasingly earthly and realistic scenes (in Luke and in John 20, 19ff) are, by contrast, apologistic coarsenings of perception. Then, in a second moment of reflection, the time occupied by such appearances has to be nicely distinguished from the succeeding time of the Church where the Spirit, and the faith that does not see, are our guides. But the hypothesis of an ever-increasing coarseness may well be over facile. Who could decide a priori in what modalities the ('analogy-less') Risen One can and may manifest himself, and why should the Damascus Road vision (of whose realistic quality we, in any case, know nothing) be made into the measure of all the rest? The representatives of the 'coarsening' hypothesis, as well as those are sympathetic to the thesis of a uniformity of relationship between Christ and the community[216], tread down the barrier Luke set up between the time of the Resurrection (of revelation) and the time of the Church. In this, they find sturdy support in the countless texts which see the event of Resurrection and Ascension as one single happening: the exaltation of the humiliated Son by the Father, his enthronement as Kyrios and his sitting on the Father's right hand.[217] Yet the Acts of the Apostles itself places just such texts into the apostles' mouths (for example, 2, 32ff; 5, 30; 13, 33). And that must mean that Luke himself can have experienced no contradiction between an 'Ascension' identical with the Resurrection, and a manifestation of that Ascension at the end of the time of the appearances. H. Schlier and G. Lohfink have travelled down the road opened up by P. Benoit, and done so to its end – Lohfink in the justified conviction that a *glorificatio in fieri* and *in facto* are scarcely distinguishable for an event which takes place outside the time and space of the old aeon, and also (as Benoit rightly saw) that the One who, in the Resurrection, was exalted by the Father ever disposes of the freedom, in his manifestations to the disciples, to bring out now one, now another aspect, without there being any need to insert here a chronological element (this is at its clearest in two scenes we have yet to speak about: John 20, 11–18: *in fieri*; 20, 19–23: *in facto*). One can quite agree with H. Conzelmann that Luke has removed the apocalyptic factor from the time of salvation,[218] but one must then observe that Luke has established wholly immediate relationships both between Resurrection and Ascension (between which he inserts the earthly time of the forty days) and between Ascension and Parousia (between which he inserts the earthly time of the Holy Spirit and the Church). The first of these has already been mentioned in the foregoing (in the Acts of the Apostles, Luke lets both modes of exaltation stand side by side). The second inter-relation is disclosed by the way in which, at the Ascension, the cloud of the Danielic Son of man functions as an 'eschatological vehicle' and the *angeli interpretes* underline the similarity of departure and return. One can then, as already suggested, frankly admit a certain periodisation of the time of salvation by Luke, without having to call into question the specific character of Jesus' final appearance (as a separation marked by blessing). For:

> the same transcendent event can manifest itself in any number of appearances. The manifestations are historically differentiated events, the manifested event remaining, however, always the same. Moreover, the infinite richness of the transcendent event can never be perfectly shown forth in the finite (Lohfink).[219]

(3) The Imagistic Development of the Theological Aspects

(a) *The necessity of a transposition into images*

The self-disclosure of fundamentally transcendent events *vis-à-vis* witnesses in space and time requires not only that free room for manoeuvre which befits the One who reveals himself, but also free room for interpretation into human words and images, for which the interpreter must take responsibility in his own freedom as well as in the obligation incumbent on him to speak out. G. Koch has described the difference which opens up here as that between 'form' and 'formation'[220]. Words, like (scenic) images remain of necessity 'limit-expressions'[221] for a reality which − since it has absorbed in itself in a transcendent way the entire reality of the old aeon − overflows on all sides the latter's receptive capacities. Depending on just how one interprets the concept, one can call the images which contain the 'holy saga' 'mythical'[222] or one can refuse to use that much abused expression and speak rather of the 'need for a work of translation' into 'figural language' in which

> the decision about the choice of appropriate concepts and expressive media ... was already made by the apostles and evangelists.[223]

It has often been remarked that amplifying the scope of 'saga' or 'legend' need not be at the expense of historicity.[224] And yet − to take up again a metaphor of our own − legitimate refractions of the single inexpressible reality into the multiple colours of the spectrum may set these various shades in contrast one with another. In order to grasp the real meaning of particular affirmations − a *theological* meaning, and therefore a kerygmatic one as well − it is not good policy to wish to reconcile, at any price, particular images at the level of the earthly, phenomenal order. Rather must one consider them first and foremost in their relatively autonomous affirmatory value (as with particular *logia*) of the Gospels), and draw them into harmony by reference to the transcendent common source which they express. This general principle deprives the chronology and topography of the appearances of much of their importance as well. Naturally, this is not a matter of giving unilateral audience to a sheerly 'kerygmatic theology';[225] nevertheless, one should not overlook the 'genuine dialectic' of the accounts. Jesus

> is recognised, and yet unrecognised. He makes himself present in his self-warranty and at the same time in withdrawal. He gives himself to be touched, and refuses such contact. He is there in his boldiness, but in an ungraspable heavenly otherness,

and the gospels leave

> their varying, and, in part contradictory traditions standing next to one another with only the lightest touches of attempted harmonisation.[226]

So H. Schlier, and K. Barth agrees:

> We are not required to translate the Inexpressible which
> they attest ... into the expressible. Every such translation
> can only obscure and obliterate the decisive word here
> given us.[227]

Christ's Resurrection and Ascension are for our temporal
and mortal world something eschatological. They had to be
experienced first as Parousia and even after subsequent
distinguishing therefrom (*quoad nos*) left in the closest relation
with it. Protological and eschatological affirmations – such as
Genesis and Apocalypse venture – remain always limit-
affirmations. Linguistically, they are ordered to a shifting
mid-point which – in the marked sobriety and reticence of the
affirmations of the Resurrection[228] – they respect in an
extraordinary manner, when compared with the products of
the Apocrypha. We have seen that, in many of their forms,
they are *on the way to* a fully formed myth which subsequently
appears in untrammelled form in the Apocrypha, but that
they come to a halt before crossing this frontier – not from
considerations of aesthetic taste, but because the norm of
theological assertion so requires. The objective character of
the achieved encounter can have its objectivity exhibited in
different fashions – as is shown by, for example, the three
subtly divergent accounts of the meeting on the Damascus
Road where the author offers variations, in a manifestly
conscious way – on a foundational theme – whilst not
undergoing a distancing process from the affirmation of a
self-identical Object.[229] That the frontier with myth is not
crossed – in other words, that the so–called mythical world
picture remains irrelevant to the underlying intention of the
account – allows the biblical affirmations to retain their
meaning for us, over and above all changes in the historically
conditioned picture of the world, and absolve us from the
need to make important excisions or alterations (through de-
mythologisation). The 'naked facts' (inasmuch as there are
such things in human history) are so clothed that their
theological import becomes visible, without, however,

rendering the historical aspect unrecognisable because hidden behind the kerygmatic. And here 'historical' means the self-presentation of the Risen One, now become meta-historical, to determinate persons situated in time and space. Nevertheless, certain theological affirmations could possess such a weight that the historical data at our disposal are constrained to adapt themselves to those affirmations in the most complete manner possible (up to the point where an allegorical scene could arise out of this process). The witnesses of the Resurrection, whose whole existence is engaged in their testimony, take responsibility for that as an expression of the truth that has *happened*, and in no way as some kind of poetic truth.

(b) The event of the Resurrection

Rightly enough, it has always been emphasised that there can have been no witnesses to the event of the Son's Resurrection by the Father – any more than there can to the act of the Incarnation. And yet the two actions are foundational events of a salvation which is *for* man, and God does not simply bring about these events without man, any more than he allowed the Passion to happen without human co-operation. Evidently, it is not enough for Mary to take cognisance after the event that she is pregnant, nor for the women to find the empty tomb after the act. Matthew felt that when – moving close to the border of mythology but not over-stepping that boundary – he made the women witnesses not, to be sure, of the Resurrection itself, but of the opening of the tomb by the angel of dazzling brightness (28, 2ff). Luke and John go, each in their own fashion, further still. That Resurrection and Ascension are substantially identical we have already recognised in the case of Luke. On the Mount of Olives, the disciples are witnesses of the disappearance from earth of him who is going to the Father – but only the disappearing remains within view, the cloud ensuring that the 'journey' enters the realm of the invisible. The Lucan disciples, therefore, 'see' the invisible end-point of the event whose point of departure Mary had 'seen' in her conversation with the angel of the Annunciation. They are testimonies to the final 'proof' (Acts 1, 3). In her own manner, Mary Magdalen is also, on Easter morning, when she meets the Lord who has 'not yet ascended to the Father', and who is understood, therefore, as on the way between death and life, Hell and Heaven, in the event of the Resurrection. To this *resurrectio in fieri*, she must give her consent by not holding back the Risen One (John 20, 17), but letting him go free, in the same way that Mary as Mother had to let the Spirit act when it covered her with its shadow, and Mary of Bethany, in her loving gesture of anticipation, accorded with all that the Lord decided, even with his burial, even with his Passion. For the three chief articulations of the redemption *in fieri*, the 'Yes' of the three Marys is required. Beyond all contestation they symbolise here the believing and loving Church (*personam Ecclesiae gerens*). Naturally, one can say of the image used that it is an 'extremely mythological representation'.[230] But if one realises what it seeks theologically to express, then the mythological element disappears completely – all the more so in that what is in question is not a movement of place but an event which cannot be expressed otherwise and in which the believing person must at all costs – *in actu primo!* – obtain a share.

The narrative presents texts that have been woven together. It is surprising that the two angels offer no interpretation, that both the angels and subsequently Jesus put the same question to Mary Magdalen, that the latter says three times that they have taken the Lord from the tomb (v. 2. 13, 15) and that she returns twice (v. 14, 16). Older sources have been, perhaps, touched up, without, however, attaining a definitive unity of a literary kind. And yet Mary is essentially she who, with fixed gaze, searches for the One who has disappeared, leaning over the empty tomb where he should be. The shining angels, 'sitting where the body of Jesus had lain, one at the head and one at the feet', pronounce an eloquent discourse without use of words. They give the measure of the emptiness of the tomb by making visible the glory which indirectly issues from it, and in them the One who has disappeared is present in an inexpressible way. The twofold 'returning' is also theologically correct: the first, a physical return, moves towards the unknown neighbour who is Jesus; the second, spiritual, after Mary's calling by her name, towards the divine Lord. Of the highest theological importance is the replacement of the gesture of clasping (here John may be correcting Matthew who attributes two things to the women, clasping and mission, Matthew 28, 9ff) by the mission of testifying to the brothers, which Mary carries out to the letter[231] (contrary to what one finds in Mark).

In the 'returnings' of Mary, which in the last analysis are a shift of orientation from the Lord in his ascending to the brethren, is reflected the warning given to the women, as to the disciples, by the angels of Easter and the Ascension. In Luke, the women enter the tomb, but do not find the corpse; when they encounter the angels, they are afraid and 'bow their faces to the ground' (24, 5). This lowering of the gaze is remarked on by the angels: 'Why do you seek the living among the dead? He is not here, but has risen'. At the Ascension, the disciples 'were gazing into heaven', seeking the One who had disappeared. And now the warning of the angel interpreter is reversed: 'Why do you stand looking into heaven?'. Until the Lord's return, there is nothing more to see. The disciples are sent back to his words of mission (Acts 1, 7–8) and thereby to making their way throughout the world.

(c) The Condition of the Risen One

That the condition of the Risen One is absolutely unique has already (1) been shown above. That absolute uniqueness is theological in character, since in the greatest possible difference of conditions – deepest abasement and the highest exaltation, God-abandonment and union with God – is expressed not only the supreme identity of the person, but also the identity of his 'dispositions' (Philippians 2, 5) – an identity which John expresses in his unitary vision of the contraries as 'exaltation' and 'glorification', or in the image of the slain Lamb upon the throne. In both phases, what is involved is the sovereignty and, indeed, the divinity of the

Son's obedience as representation of the Trinitarian Love both in itself and for the world.[232] But inasmuch as this unique event signifies the turning of the ages, and the foundation of the new world through the death of the old, one cannot decide a priori how the Risen One will appear to his disciples – whether alike or unlike, near or distant, familiar or strange. There is, therefore, no point in setting up a determinate mode of appearance (for example that to Paul, or that described at the end of his Gospel by Matthew) as norm for the rest.

Through all the Resurrection stories runs the theme of the Lord's spontaneous self-revelation. The 'strange form' under which he appears may seem mythical – H. Gunkel, for this reason, excluded the Emmaus story as legend, since it reminded him of the ancient myths of unrecognised fellow-travelling deities and might have occurred in the Iliad or in Genesis.[233] Is that a decisive reason if in fact precisely this theme brings to expression the distinctively Christian message? What is needful for recognising Jesus is not only his words of address (in Luke and John there is also dialogue without recognition) but also his will to be recognised. That can be understood, and virtually postulated, on the basis of the central Old Testament theology of the Word of God. Again, the conversation can preserve the form of complete concealment (Mary and the 'gardener') or tend to an unveiling ('Did not our hearts burn within us?') or, differently again, signify a breakthrough recognition ('Mary!'). And the situation of explicit recognition can spark off all kinds of reactions; 'shock and fright' (Luke 24, 37); 'doubt'(ibid., 38); 'joy and wonderment' (ibid., 41); 'fear and great joy' (Matthew 28, 8); and finally sheer 'joy' (John 20, 20), and yet, once again, a reluctance to accept the conversation offered, a reticence, perhaps wrong-headed, at that morning meal where Jesus seems to establish a pure familiarity (John 21, 12ff; cf. Mark 9, 32).

What becomes manifest here is not only the freedom of the Risen One to offer himself when and as he wills, but also a leaving free of man (this, too, is an aspect of Easter grace) to react just as *he* wills. Here we find the significance, celebrated by the Church Fathers, of the disciples' doubt (as a confirmation of our faith). It is possible that this theme has been exploited and given extra emphasis for apologetic reasons [234] – but that is no reason for ruling it out of court as a whole. It will not be said that the appearances of the Risen One are insufficiently potent to impose themselves by the force of their own evidence. For he can also reveal himself in a self-evident sovereignty, as the Thomas episode shows. On other occasions, the evidence appears so extraordinarily powerful that it surpasses human measure (Luke 24, 41). Where doubt arises, one must rather say: the Risen One has so mighty a freedom that, for the sake of the encounter, he communicates a part of this freedom to the man whom he meets. In the same sense, he can be the absolute Sovereign (to whom 'all power has been given', Matthew 28, 18), and, at the same time, the One who, first and precisely then, calls his own 'my brothers' (Matthew 28, 10; John 20, 17): he who compels adoration (Matthew 28, 9, 17; Luke 24, 52?) and he who, as in the days of old, 'sits with them at table' (Acts 1, 4; Luke 24, 41ff; John 21, 12ff). This tension is maintained in Paul: insofar as we are 'in Christ', 'one body' with him, is he

> as much separated from us and distant ('above', 'in heaven': II Corinthians 5, 6; Philippians 1, 23; Colossians 3, 1) as also present in our midst and active in us (Colossians 1, 27).[235]

Starting from this principle, one will, yet again, be sceptical about the critique offered of the so-called 'massive realism' of the Resurrection stories. Even the Pauline *sōma pneumatikon*, when considered from the vantage point of the old aeon, is self-contradictory. To say that the transfigured body of Christ can no longer eat and drink (and thus cannot transform into the new aeon the realities of the old) is an undemonstrable assertion. Karl Barth opposed this critical spiritualism with equal 'massiveness',[236] without, however, finding much support. No gospel is free from the so-called 'massive' realism. Ascribing to Mark spiritualising tendencies is to create myths; Matthew 28, 9 is bypassed when arguments are built on Matthew 28, 16–22 alone; no explanation can sidestep the transition from John 20, 1–18 to 20, 19–28: why should John have been compelled to add to his 'spiritual' theology such 'massive' scenes which in any case express his own theology with adequacy and precision? And of course the saying about those who 'do not see and yet believe' is not directed against the validity of eye-witness, but is spoken from out of the perspective, and the pre-occupations, of the second generation.[237] Whoever spiritualises unilaterally the accounts of the Resurrection very frequently shows a tendency also to spiritualise unilaterally the Eucharist of the Church.[238]

Finally, the ultimate tension between God's revelation and his hiddenness is to be maintained in this very closing word of his self-disclosure: *in tanta similitudine 'maior dissimilitudo'* (DS 806). Precisely as the supremely manifest One, God can only manifest himself in his total otherness. This abstract proposition receives its concrete content in the history of salvation, wherein the Son, according to the clear declarations of Scripture, far from 'rising again into history' (G. Koch, followed by J. Moltmann), returns, in his leave-taking, to the Father, sending in his stead the 'other Paraclete', the Spirit who explains and convicts. 'You will seek me and you will not find me' (John 7, 34); 'You will not see me again' (Matthew 23, 39). Moreover, what the Spirit will manifest of the Son for history will always remain a sign of contradiction, and will never be imposed in a direct and non-dialectical manner in the history of the world. That God has manifested the Risen One: 'not to all the people, but to us who were chosen by God as witnesses' (Acts 10, 41), and has given the faith of the nations the precarious foundation of this witness ('Lord, who has believed what he has heard from us?': Isaiah 53, 1, = Romans 10, 16, and yet: 'Faith comes from what is heard' 10, 17) is in itself not only daring, but also 'scandal and folly'. Jesus was able to make known the hidden God, who is faithful to his covenant till the end, only 'because he himself shared and shares in the hiddenness of God'.[239]

(d) The founding of the Church

(aa) The appearances of the Risen One always issue in *mission*.

Insasmuch as Mary does not hold back Jesus but goes with her message to the brethren, she experiences Easter. The accounts outdo one another in insistence and solemnit. Luke is the most detailed, making the great instruction on Scripture and the Kingdom of God finish up by reference to mission on two occasions (Luke 24, 44ff; Acts 1, 3, 8). Matthew shows the Lord sending out the disciples, equipped with word and sacraments, into the whole domain of his power, by virtue of the sovereignty conferred on him over all peoples and periods (cf. Daniel 7, 14). John makes this mission flow forth from the Trinitarian mission of the Son himself: 'As the Father has sent me, even so I send you' (John 20, 21). Although much in the founding of the Church was prepared in the time before Easter – in the disciples' training in discipleship, and their instruction – the real act of founding could not take place until the Risen One had completed his own work, and, in the power of his death and Resurrection, could breathe out his Spirit upon the Church-in-the-founding. That, from the very outset, this Church was *hierarchically constituted* is quite clear from the words of foundation as from the self-understanding of the apostles. The conferment of office on Peter narrated by John (and perhaps ante-dated by Matthew) grounds Peter's primacy. Paul acknowledges him (he always calls him Cephas). The disciples, as eye-witnesses of the Resurrection, know themselves to be at one and the same time both those called and those sent forth. Paul, as a latecomer, closes the series of these foundation-laying sending-out through his vision of the Risen One (I Corinthians 15, 8). Other visions and charisms (including in the life of Paul himself) never enter into competition with these fundamental missions: Over against R. Sohm's idea that the community had at the origins a charismatic constitution, K. Holl has rightly sustained the thesis that, with the conclusion of the list of founders:

the notions of authority and tradition . . . at once come to take precedence over charism[240] . . . Thus, from the start, we find in the Christian community a regular hierarchy, a divinely established order, a divine law for the Church, a Church-institution in which individual persons are received.[241]

It is the Risen One himself who opens up for the disciples, assembled as these are around him, the *total meaning of Scripture*. Delivered from their narrow perspectives (Luke 24, 19ff;) and false orientations, they must learn to look at the whole from the high-point: at the Law ('Moses'), the prophets, and the wisdom books ('psalms': Luke 24, 44ff). The Risen One seals the primordial understanding of Scripture in the *memoria* of the Church. And to the Scripture is joined the sacrament. Crystal clear in John, this means in the first place, along with the inbreathing of the Spirit, the plenary power to forgive sins (also recorded in Matthew 16 as the primary object of the power of the keys). Then in Matthew we find the command to baptise and, by way of the repetition of meal scenes with a eucharistic character, the (at any rate implicit) instruction to do 'this in memory of me' and so proclaim the death of Jesus and God's supreme work of love (I Corinthians 11, 25ff). The Eastertide meals may for Jesus himself already be the eschatological banquet (Mark 14, 25 and parallels; Apocalypse 3, 20); for the disciples, they are the 'first-fruits' of that definitive feasting, annunciatory signs 'until he comes again'. Beyond the awed reticence which marks the turning point between the two ages (John 21, 12), the meals remain an intimate communion, an essential participation in the altar ('in the blood of Christ') and so in the reconciliatory character of every cultic meal,[242] and create therefore, finally, a unity of being among those taking part (I Corinthians 10, 16ff). The fact that Jesus, after Easter, 'shares the meal' of the disciples (*sunalizomenos*, Acts 1, 4) is not at all something slipped in by way of 'massive realism', but is rather a symbolic feature of a theologically indispensable kind.[243]

(bb) The directly masculine and hierarchical aspect of the history of the Church's foundation receives a counter-weight in the strongly emphasised rôle of the women at the Crucifixion, the burial and the discovery of the empty tomb.

The interplay between the feminine and masculine representatives of the Church at Easter, as that appears in the Synoptic accounts, John deepens into an allegory which forms part of the ecclesiology, so subtly and meditatively thought out, of his two closing chapters. The Mother of Jesus is entrusted to the beloved disciple, and the author of the Apolcalypse sees the Church, as woman, give birth to the Messiah. He has a feeling for the femininity of the Church in relation to the Lord. In the last analysis much more is going on here than some 'rivalry' between the women and the apostles as to who enjoys priority in bearing testimony; even the view that, in Jewish law, women could not count as witnesses plays only a subordinate part. What is in question is the delicate equilibrium between the Church as 'bride' of Christ and the Church as hierarchical institution. Paul allows the testimony of the women to fall out of the picture. He knows only appearances before males – first before Peter, and then, before the Twelve. In Mark, the women, to be sure, see the angel, but not the Lord. The disciples and Peter (he is mentioned separately) will see him in Galilee. In Luke, similarly, the women see only the angels, their message goes unreceived; Peter races to the tomb and sees 'with astonishment' the burial clothes, not yet believing (if we assume that 24, 12 is authentically Lucan); the Lord appears to the disciples at Emmaus, and they, when they arrive in Jerusalem and before they can recount their own experience; are greeted by the disciples with the words, 'The Lord has risen indeed, and has appeared to Simon'. Only afterwards can they tell their story. The first appearance remains, therefore, that granted to Peter. Matthew breaks out of this framework because, inbetween the angelophany to the women and the great final appearances in Galilee in the presence of the disciples, he inserts the 'appearance on the road' to Jerusalem before the women. Here Peter's right of priority seems put in question. Matthew knows no particular appearance to Peter, but sums everything up in two images: a first appearance to the women, which points on to the second and so is preliminary (and yet indisputably first), followed by the great official appearance to the disciples. It is

almost as though Matthew could not tolerate the thought
that the women, who alone had persevered at the Cross and
burial, should not have been the first to see the Risen One.
John joins together Luke's intentions with those of Matthew
by deepening the theological understanding both of Peter's
running to the tomb and the appearance to Mary Magdalen.
First we have the woman alone at the tomb (but no vision).
She announces to Peter and the beloved disciple that the
tomb is open. Then the disciples run to the tomb; Peter
registers the fact that the corpse has not been stolen (the
folded napkin).[244] John believes without seeing the Lord
(believing by way of the sign). Thus this faith which at once
sees and does not see receives a priority over the appearance
(of Jesus ascending to the Father) to Mary Magdalen which
now follows. Mary becomes the witness of this *resurrectio in
fieri* and is sent with this vision to the disciples. The disciples
then encounter the Risen One *in facto esse* and receive the
decisive mission. We have already noted how the appearance
to Mary Magdalen develops in phases, each of which remains
significant in its own right. There is a vision of the absent
One in his *doxa*, represented by the angels; next, a veiled
vision of him who is present incognito, and lastly an
uncovered vision of him, granted, however, in withdrawal
and in mission.

(cc) To this problem of the Church as feminine and
masculine there is linked in John a developed allegory on the
relation between the Church of office (Peter) and the Church
of love (John, the 'disciple whom Jesus loved'). Only the
reader who sees the two apostles as real symbols of these two
aspects of the Church of Christ understands the evangelist's
intention.[245] The traditional material incorporated into this
allegory surely derives from a Galilean tradition left over for
the next, complementary, chapter. It contained, in all
probability, a confession of guilt by Peter and a call to him
(cf. the echo of this in Luke 5). Whether Luke 24, 12 should
be considered as the foundation of John 20, 3–10 (a much
contested point), whether an historical kernel can be identified
within this account; whether this story is located between the

announcement of the women and the departure of the disciples for Galilee, in which case they would have still been in Jerusalem – all these questions we must leave unanswered.

A first and permanently valuable observation is that the two disciples run together, *homou*. And this thought is not cancelled out by a second consideration, namely, that love, unencumbered as it is by burdens, 'runs ahead', whilst the hierarchical function, with its many preoccupations, reaches the goal later. Love sees what can be seen (from without), yet allows authority to overtake it. The latter, looking at everything (even what is not visible from without) and seeing the napkin at the head rolled up in an orderly way, comes up with a kind of *nihil obstat* which lets love enter freely, in such a way that (whether through seeing the signs or by participating in what Peter has seen in his discovery) love attains faith. This faith is however, entirely vague since 'they did not yet understand that he was to rise from the dead' (the additional reference to the word of 'Scripture' here should be suppressed). This first episode suggests a Church with two poles: the Church of office and the Church of love, with a harmonious tension between them, the official function working for love, love respectively allowing first place to office.

The additional chapter takes the symbolism further. Peter has the initiative at the first moment of departure of the ship of the Church without its Lord. This initiative remains fruitless: effort and harvesting are never proportionate to each other in the supernatural work of mission. Then there comes the dialogue with the still hidden Lord and the Church's obedience to his counsel, even though she does not recognise him. At the miracle, love recognises the Lord, but at once says so to office which knows what should be done: in the right kind of clothing, and as quickly as possible, rejoin the Lord. There then follow various images: the Lord with Peter on the shore (symbol of eternity, and of *terra firma*, an 'infallible' foundation), the others coming towards Peter and Jesus and bringing the produce from their fishing trip. Next there is Peter who, as the one responsible for the whole gathering, climbs into the boat and fetches for the Lord the net filled to overflowing. Lastly, we have the common meal. On the strength of this, there follows the conferment of the office by way of the question which for Peter, the agent in the denial, can receive no reply, 'Do you love me more than these?' There is no other solution than for Peter to let John lend him the greatest love (in the communism of the 'communion of saints'), so as to give thereby the answer which is absolutely demanded.[246] The primacy of Peter is raised up on John's renunciation of a 'private' love for the Lord. To Peter, with the command to feed the flock, is promised immediately martyrdom for the sheep in the Lord's own footsteps. In this way, the unity of love and office is sealed in Peter's person. The gospel of love thus ends with an apotheosis of office, an apotheosis in which particular love renounces itself. And yet there remains a residue which will not go away (21, 20–25). Peter sees that the beloved disciple (who should have disappeared into him) is still there, and he remembers his mediating rôle between office and the Lord (John 13, 23ff; cf. 18, 15ff; 21, 7). He does not comprehend, but he feels from the fact of his function the duty to comprehend, and consequently he asks, 'Lord, what about this man?'. The question is an understandable one in the mouth of an office-holder, and, indeed, a legitimate one, but the answer given it remains obscure, since it rests entirely on the freedom of the Church's Lord. Peter must fulfil his task as servant, and the rest in no way concerns him – the rest, that is, the question of knowing how on earth the exact limits between the Church of office and the Church of love are drawn. The latter will 'remain' until the Lord returns, but how and where only the Lord knows. Peter *should* love, and should therefore inasmuch as he is able, also be himself the Church of love. It is in this spirit that he is to pastor the Church. No way can he allow himself to think that every religion is equally good – for if someone has simply that love which Christ by his death for all likewise earned for all and offers, as a supernatural reality, at the disposal of all, why should that not suffice for anyone?[247] But no more can Peter harden into the opposite view, for which only those kept within his visible sheepfold have the guarantee of authentic love and so of everlasting salvation. Between these two unacceptable ecclesiologies the gospel of John leaves us and releases us at a hovering mid-point whose fixed place depends uniquely on the Lord. The last word addressed to that servant who is Peter, the last word of the Lord in the gospel, is the warning (for the Church, and for the theology, of all ages), 'What is that to you?'.

(dd) The entire founding of the Church is linked in the closest possible manner to the *sending of the Spirit*. Whether (as in Luke) this described as a future happening – the Lord's withdrawal in an official event, as well as a suitable preparation of the community by prayer, being pre-requisite for the Spirit's descent, or whether (as in John) the sending is portrayed as an already present reality, since the Risen One is already and as such the Man of the Spirit, he who disposes of the Spirit, it remains anyhow the case that the existence of a visible Church of the Lord in the midst of history can only have a remote analogy with profane 'peoples', 'States' or 'communities'. Her visibility (her institutional character) most certainly cannot be severed, in its inner ties, from her pneumatic character. That does not mean that the Spirit, who is freedom and blows where he will, may capriciously turn away from the foundation given by Christ (for he is sent to 'be with you for ever', John 14, 16). It does mean, contrariwise, that the visible frame, in a case where it ceases to house the animating Spirit, ceases to be a reliable support. This becomes very clear in the word of testimony which the Church is given that she may bear it before the nations. In its substance, it is a word of the Spirit who 'dwells with you and will be in you', (14, 17), who 'teaches' you and 'brings to your remembrance' (14, 26), 'guiding you into all the truth' (16, 13). The religion of Christ will be no book-religion.

The . . . new covenant . . . is not in a written code, but in the Spirit, for the written code kills, but the Spirit gives life. (22 Corinthians 3, 6)

Just as Christ is not his own word, but the Father's, so what the Spirit addresses to us in Scripture and preaching is not the literal word of Christ but Christ's word in the language of the Spirit. Only so is it truly a Trinitarian word, only so, too, a word which ever raises from the dead and brings new life. On this basis, we can understand the prohibition, 'Do not hold me!' The freedom of the Resurrection (and of the Church which takes her birth from the Resurrection) tolerates no confining. Doubtless, it admits a 'fingering' in faith, perhaps a naive touching of the 'hem of his garment' (Matthew 9, 20) – but it rules out an 'assurance' based on what is, in a way that can be isolated, visible and tangible. That applies equally well to the 'sacramental magic' of Catholicism, as to the 'Bible magic' of Protestantism. *Nolui per atramentum* . . . (III John 13; cf. II Corinthians 3, 3). This enables us to situate the combined rebuke and promise which meets Thomas' demand for assurance, and with which word John finishes his gospel. 'Not to see and yet to believe': a formula to which John gave exemplary expression in his attitude to the tomb (20, 8). Signs pointing in a certain direction: those suffice John as the means of coming to faith. He looks with the 'eyes of faith', with the 'eyes of (the) heart enlightened' (Ephesians 1, 18). Basically, in Jesus Christ's death, Descent into Hell and Resurrection, only one reality is there to be seen: the love of the triune God for the world, a love which can only be perceived through a co-responsive love.

Existence in the *Mysterium Paschale*

The founding of the Church is not an end in itself. That is shown to us in the dialectic in which the ecclesiology of the final gospel issues. The Church is open to the world in its entirety, and to that world the Almighty sends her out in an unrestricted fashion (Matthew 28). It is not the Church, it is the whole world which is reconciled with God through the Cross and Resurrection of Christ (Colossians 1, 19ff). And yet the achieved reconciliation has need of the Church's ministry in its service – a ministry which constitutes, according to Paul, the meaning of the mission Christ has conferred.

> So we are ambassadors for Christ, God making his appeal through us. We beseech you on behalf of Christ: be reconciled to God (II Corinthians 5, 20).

The ministry of reconciliation of the Christian person is not merely, however, a supplication (of an impotent kind), but a engagement of all existence even to the point of being 'poured as a libation' (Philippians 2, 17; II Timothy 4, 6).

The detailed evocation of this relationship is not the task of this essay. What follows in its original setting, in the series *Mysterium Salutis*, sets out the great lines of the soteriology of the *Mysterium Paschale*: the reconciliation of the whole creation with God; the exaltation of the Mediator above all profane powers, whether cosmic or historical – since he had been installed as 'heir of all things' in the creative work of the Father (Hebrews 1, 2); the fulfilment in him of the Covenant once made with Israel, in such a way that the *dikaiosunē theou* comes to its completion since, as God and man, Christ embodies in its perfection a Covenant which is henceforth new and everlasting, and he who lives in Christ (by the faith which is a gift of existence, Galatians 2, 19–20) shares in this justice of God and in the peace which it establishes between God and the world. All of this is presupposed in this concluding section.

And yet none of it resolves the question of how man, living in the old aeon, can receive the Risen One who addresses him (in the kerygma of the witnesses) and respond to his call. By way of God-abandonment on the Cross and the Descent into Hell, Christ has triumphed over the world (John 16, 33), but I am still in the world (John 17, 11). By his call, by the fact that he takes me actively into his total destiny, I am to die to the world, to be buried and raised again with Christ (Romans 6, 2ff; Ephesians 2, 6). I have to seek 'the things that are above', things which, however, remain 'hidden' to me (Colossians 3, 1ff). That one is already on the way towards that which can only be grasped in believing 'hope' and must therefore be waited for in patience' (Romans 8, 24ff): that stretches out the Christian on the Cross formed by the criss-crossing beams of the old aeon and the new. This is a harder cross than that of the natural man who, as spirit, stands homeless on the frontier between the created world and the absolute God. As we have seen, Gnosis and philosophical dialectic ever again attempt to reduce this hard Cross to the gentler 'cross of light'. But, through the victory of the Jesus of history, and his exaltation as Lord of the world, the Christian remains all the more ineluctably obliged to take up the historical Cross of Christ, torn between the anticipated possession of the heavenly polity (Hebrews 12, 22ff) and the excessive demand to initiate what is realised there above into a world essentially lacking the prior conditions for such a real transformation and resistant, with all its instincts of self-preservation, to the inbreaking of the eschatological Kingdom of God.

The individual thus crucified cannot understand his own position except in terms of that unique point of reference which is his mission. And that itself can never be grasped in static fashion; it is only actual when in absolute motion.

> Not that I have already obtained this or am already perfect; but I press on to make it my own, because Jesus Christ has made me his own ... one thing I do, forgetting what lives behind and straining forward to what lies ahead ... (Philippians 3, 12ff)

Existence is lived as a trajectory. One might term this Utopian, except that, behind the Christian mission, there stands the

> Old Testament background: salvation, *sōtēria*, must also be understood as *shalom* ... It signifies not only the soul's salvation, individual deliverance from an evil world, consolation for a troubled conscience, but also the realisation of an eschatological hope for justice, the humanisation of man, the socialisation of humanity,

> peace for all creation. This 'other face' of the
> reconciliation with God has always been short-changed
> in the history of Christianity, because people ceased to
> understand themselves in the light of eschatology,
> abandoning the earthly anticipation of the eschaton to
> the ultra – pious and to 'enthusiasts'.[248]

Certainly, the 'patience' spoken of in the New Testament is
more than a passive enduring, and contains indeed a fair
share of impatience not only in resisting but also in seizing
opportunities and in transformation, as well as in the general
determination to hold open the self-enclosing horizon of the
world to the Kingdom of God which is coming (because
already present in a hidden way). The New Testament
exhortation to submit oneself to existing authority (Romans
13, 1ff; I Peter 2, 13ff), to work peacefully (II Thessalonians
3, 12), to live quiet and upright lives among the pagans
(I Peter 2, 11 and 15; 3, 6) and, when circumstances require
it, to undergo unjust suffering for the Lord do not exhaust
the reality of Christian ethics. The audacious demands of the
Sermon on the Mount and the Letter of James take further
the postulates of Old Testament social ethics, and allow the
Christian Cross to appear as their respective term, the normal
result, in Christ, of the attempt to put them into practice.
Christ himself was for thirty years a manual worker, and a
spiritual worker for only three years, before the three days of
his Passion, death and Resurrection. The ethics of Matthew
and James should not be counterposed, as something of lesser
worth, to the ethics of Paul. The Constitution *Gaudium et
Spes* undertook the difficult task of their synthesising – of
which we can only say, in the last analysis, that no human
being can dominate its unifying centre, since it lies in Christ
alone. And we are not thinking of the individual Christ only
when we say this, but of Christ as Head of the Church (and,
through her, of all that is) who plunges ever anew into his
own being those whom he sends out as his disciples. Since we
stand under the law of the Risen One, he places us on the
way of the Cross, and we travel our way of the Cross only
in his power, and his hope who, as the Risen One, has

already won the victory. This is why the Church, and Christians, can occupy no determinate place within the *Mysterium Paschale*. Their place is neither in front of the Cross nor behind it, but on both its sides: without ever settling for the one vantage point or the other they look from now one, now the other, as ceaselessly directed. And yet this see-saw by no means lacks a support, because the Unique One is the identity of Cross and Resurrection, and Christian and ecclesial existence is disappropriated into him:

None of us lives to himself, and none of us dies to himself. If we live, we live to the Lord, and if we die we die to the Lord; so then, whether we live or whether we die, we are the Lord's. For to this end Christ died and lived again, that he might be Lord both of the dead and of the living (Romans 14, 7ff).

References

[1] K. Barth, *Kirchliche Dogmatik* IV/1 (Zollikon 1953), p. 371. But it should be noted with what prudence Barth introduces these concepts and employs them.

[2] L. Goppelt, *Das Osterkerygma heute*, cited from B. Klappert, *Diskussion um Kreuz und Auferstehung* (Wuppertal 1967), p. 212.

[3] H. Schlier, *Über die Auferstehung Jesu Christi* (Einsiedeln 1968), p. 15.

[4] W. Marxsen, *Die Auferstehung als historisches und theologisches Problem* (Gütersloh 1965). Cited from *Die Bedeutung der Auferstehungsbotschaft für den Glauben an Jesus Christus* (Gütersloh 1967[4]), pp. 12ff.

[5] W. Künneth, *Theologie der Auferstehung* (Munich 1968[5]), p. 109.

[6] H. Schlier, op. cit., p. 11; W. Künneth, op. cit., p. 107; L. Goppelt, op. cit., p. 213.

[7] H. Grass, *Ostergeschehen und Osterberichte* (Göttingen 1961[2]), p. 263; G. Koch, *Die Auferstehung Christi* (Tübingen 1965[2]), pp. 325ff; F. X. Durrwell, *La résurrection de Jésus, mystère du salut* (Le Puy – Paris 1954[2]), pp. 183ff.

[8] *Der christliche Glaube* II., para. 99, 'The facts of Christ's Resurrection and Ascension cannot be considered as constitutive elements for the doctrine of his Person' (Berlin 1831[2]), p. 92.

[9] Hence the primacy of theology in the treatise on the Resurrection as presented by, for example, K. Barth, W. Künneth, K. H. Rengstorf – *Die Auferstehung Jesu*, (Witten-Ruhr 1952[5]), F. X. Durrwell, A. M. Ramsey, *The Resurrection of Christ* (London 1956[2]), despite the violent protest of E. Käsemann, 'Die Gegenwart der Gekreuzigten', in *Christus unter uns* (Stuttgart 1967[3]).

[10] Especially since U. Wilckens, *Die Missionsreden der Apostelgeschichte* (Neukirchen 1963[2]) has called into question the antiquity of the so-called 'archaic' formulae in the sermons of Peter.

[11] List in K. Kremer, *Das älteste Zeugnis von der Auferstehung Christi* (Stuttgart 1966), p. 25.

[12] J. Jeremias, *Die Abendmahlsworte* Jesu (Zurich 1949), p. 96; E. Fascher, 'Die Auferstehung Jesu und ihr Verhältnis zur urchristlichen Verkündigung', ZNW 26 (1927), pp. 1–26. U. Wilckens' view that the formula might also derive from Antioch or Damascus, and present Hellenistic features, as set forth in his 'Der Ursprung der Überlieferung der Erscheinungen des Auferstandenen', in W. Joest and W. Pannenberg (eds.), *Dogma und Denkstrukturen* (Göttingen 1963), and H. Conzelmann's contestation of the Semitic character of the primitive formula, as made in his 'Zur Analyse der Bekenntnisformel I Korinther 15, 3–5', EvTh 25 (1965), pp. 1–11, were rejected by G. Delling, *Die Bedeutung der Auferstehung Jesu für den Glauben an Jesus Christus. Ein exegetischer Beitrag*, cf. above, n. 4. For the whole question, see also B. Klappert, 'Zur Frage der semitischen oder griechischen Urtextes von I Korinther 15, 3–5', NTS 13 (1967), pp. 168–173, and J. Kremer, op. cit., pp. 82ff. This is why one should not speak simply, in a stereotypical way, of the 'Antiochene formula of faith', as does P. Seidensticker in *Die Auferstehung Jesu in der Botschaft der Evangelien* (Stuttgart 1967), pp. 24ff.

[13] Above all, E. Bammel, 'Herkunft und Funktion der Traditions-elemente in I Korinther 15, 1–11', ThZ 11 (1955), pp. 401–419.

[14] Correctly, then, H. Grass, op, cit., p. 298.

[15] As does P. Seidensticker, op. cit., pp. 27ff in wanting to identify this single appearance with the single Galilaean encounter of Matthew 28, 16ff. Against this opinion, J. Kremer, op. cit., p. 71, no. 30, who thus maintains the plurality of the appearances.

[16] As does G. Koch, op. cit., pp. 200ff.

[17] In affirmations about the Resurrection, the formula 'according to the Scriptures' is related primarily to the Resurrection and not to the circumstance of the 'third day': thus J. Kremer, op. cit., pp. 35; 39. See further on this below.

[18] In the phrase 'dead and buried', K. H. Rengstorf sees 'a fixed formula already frequently used in the Old Testament, employed in the history of Israel for important personalities and probably having its place of origin in royal annals', op. cit., p. 52. He reminds us that, in the parable of Lazarus, it is said of the rich man that he died and was buried, whereas of the poor man only that he died (Luke 16, 22) 'and that must include the fact of his dying without receiving a monument'.

[19] *Kirchliche Dogmatik* IV/1, pp. 335ff. 'A new action of God, independent in relation to the event of the Cross . . . and not just the revelation and explanation of the Cross's positive meaning and importance' (as Bultmann thinks). In the same sense, see also J. Schniewind, *Antwort an R. Bultmann* (text in B. Klappert, op. cit., pp. 76–89), and L. Goppelt (ibid., pp. 207–221). H. Grass (op. cit., pp. 245ff) writes, 'God has acted in Christ before acting in his witnesses, and he acts in them by acting in Christ . . . No anthropology, however attractive it may be in its discovery of the inner roots of our humanity, and contained in this proclamation, can be allowed to justify retrospectively, so to speak, this

proclamation itself. Similarly, H. S. Iwand, *Kreuz und Auferstehung Christi* (in B. Klappert, op. cit., pp. 275–297).

20 'Can talk about Chist's Resurrection be something other than the expression of the meaningfulness of the Cross?': 'Neues Testament und Mythologie', in H. W. Bartsch (ed.), *Kerygma und Mythos* I (1948), pp. 47–48. What is meant is meaningfulness *pro me* as 'presence in the concrete realisation of life in the believer', p. 46.

21 It is on this text that F. X. Durrwell built his entire theology of the Resurrection. Cf. also K. H. Rengstorf, op. cit., pp. 63–64, 'The most astonishing thing . . . is expressed in I Corinthians 15, 17, 'If Christ be not raised, you are still in your sins'. What is said, when considered with precision, tends to make one think that, for Paul, a confrontation with the Crucified does not suffice to let a man come to God . . . and to come, finally, to himself.

22 R. Bultmann, op. cit., p. 45: 'The significance of his (Jesus') history is disengaged by what God wants me to say through it'. In stout opposition to this thesis: H. Grass, op. cit., pp. 268; 275; 323.

23 'Here all analogies are lacking': W. Künneth, op. cit., p. 62, cf. pp. 78ff. 'That is why the death of Jesus necessarily escapes all analogy with the death of other men', ibid., p. 159. 'The Resurrection is an event without analogy, that is, lacking all correspondence with history', B. Klappert, op. cit., p. 17. 'The analogy-less event of Easter', G. Koch, ibid., p. 208. 'We simply lack for that any possibility of comparison, and any corresponding category', J. Kremer, op. cit., p. 61; 'comparisons with other resurrections of deceased individuals are aberrant', ibid., p. 46. 'The understanding of Jesus' Resurrection goes totally beyond, thereby, every analogy', G. Delling, op. cit., p. 86.

24 A point contested, and reasonably so, by W. Künneth (against, especially, P. Althaus), op. cit. pp. 246–281. For the Resurrection as the *finishing* of time: ibid., pp. 191–192.

25 K. Barth, op. cit., p. 368. Barth corrects his more radical affirmations contained in *Die Auferstehung der Toten* (Munich 1924), where history had been devalued in favour of a sheer 'fact of revelation'.

26 W. Pannenberg, *Grundzüge der Christologie* (Gütersloh 1964), p. 95. For a criticism, see B. Klappert, op. cit., p. 22: there is produced in this way 'a flattening out of the eschatological to the level of universal history'.

27 B. Klappert, op. cit., p. 18.

28 H. Grass, op. cit., pp. 12ff.

29 B. Klappert, op. cit., p. 50.

30 W. Marxsen, op. cit., p. 18. In a significant fashion, the apocryphal Gospel of Peter for the first time sought to describe in concrete terms the Resurrection event: Schneemelcher, *Neutestamentliche Apokryphen* op. cit., I. pp. 122ff.

31 K. H. Rengstorf, op. cit., pp. 60–62.

32 F. Mussner, *Zōē. Die Anschauung vom 'Leben' im vierten Evangelium* (Munich 1952), pp. 6ff.

33 G. von Rad, ' "Gerechtigkeit" und "Leben" in den Psalmen', *Festschift A. Bertholet* (Tübingen 1950), pp. 418–437, also found as *Gesammelte Studien zum Alten Testament* (Munich 1965), pp. 244–245.

35   H. W. Bartsch, *Das Auferstehungszeugnis. Sein historisches und thehologisches Problem* (Hamburg 1965), pp. 12–15.

36   P. Seidensticker, op. cit., p. 52; idem.; *Zeitgenössische Texte zur Osterbotschaft der Evangelien* (Stuttgart 1967), pp. 43–51.

37   Op. cit., p. 55; cf. also G. Koch, op. cit., pp. 62–63; against H. W. Bartsch, cf. H. Conzelmann, *Historie und Theologie in den synoptischen Passionsberichten. Zur Bedeutung des Todes Jesu* (Gütersloh 1967²), p. 41. n. 10. See also the criticism by L. Goppelt, op. cit., p. 218.

38   P. Seidensticker, op. cit., p. 56.

39   Criticism in W. Künneth, op. cit., pp. 28ff; B. Klappert, op. cit., pp. 22ff; H. G. Geyer, 'Die Auferstehung Jesu Christi. Ein Überblick über die Diskussion in gegenwartigen Theologie', in *Die Bedeutung der Auferstehungsbotschaft für den Glauben an Jesus Christus* (Gütersloh 1967⁴), pp. 110 ff. Scarcely worth mentioning is the attempt to interpret the New Testament eye-witnesses to the Resurrection by the categories of the late Jewish apocalyptic seers of the hidden mysteries of the world to come. The witnesses to the Resurrection do not meet a Danielic Son of Man strange to them, even less are they 'ravished' in their vision. They meet the Lord who is familiar to them, they recognise him by his wounds, at the breaking of the bread and so forth. They deal with him on this earth, and not in a celestial sphere foreign to the world. So this apocalyptic category is also insufficient where the understanding of the Resurrection is concerned.

40   *Erniedrigung und Erhöhung bei Jesus und seinen Nachfolgern* (Basle 1955).

41   W. Popkes, *Christus traditus* (Zurich 1967), pp. 55, 56; E. Sjöberg, *Der verborgene Menschensohn in den Evangelien* (Lund 1955), pp. 255ff; 262ff; E. Lohse, *Die Geschichte des Leidens und Sterbens Jesu Christi* (Gütersloh 1964), pp. 14ff; cf. E. Schweizer, op. cit., p. 49.

42   G. Koch, op. cit., p. 53.

43   'For the most ancient testimony, the Resurrection and exaltation coincide . . . That very old saying, Acts 2, 36, which has it that God has made Lord and Christ this Jesus whom you have crucified, clearly draws into unity Resurrection and exaltation. Similarly: Acts 5. 30ff: 'The God of our fathers raised Jesus whom you killed by hanging him on a tree. God exalted him at his right hand as Leader and Saviour, to give repentance to Israel and forgiveness of sins' does not want to say, apparently, that the Resurrection took place first, and the exaltation afterwards. Rather do the two formulae express the same thing,' H. Grass, op. cit., pp. 229–230. Cf. J. Kremer, op. cit., pp 90–91. K. H. Rengstorf, op. cit., p. 70, speaks doubtless in the first place of a 'careful distinction' between Resurrection and exaltation, but then grants that in many texts the two things are mentioned in tandem. H. Schlier, op. cit., pp. 26ff, has it that 'From the moment of his Resurrection, Christ appears essentially as the 'Exalted One'. In a certain sense, his Resurrection from among the dead anticipates his 'exaltation'. For his Resurrection is a movement of exaltation to God – exaltation takes place in the power of the Resurrection'. Doubtless, for Schlier, it is possible that originally Resurrection and exaltation were 'autonomous interpretations of the same event. But from the start one could see between them a certain relationship,

which, however, has not acheived formal elucidation in our texts'. cf. G. Koch, op. cit., p. 56; W. Künneth, op. cit., p. 132, note 30.

44 Discussion on this category and the limitation of its importance in W. Künneth, op. cit., pp. 31–39.

45 W. Michaelis, *Die Erscheinungen des Auferstandenen* (Basle 1944), p. 82; G. Delling, 'analémpsis', TWNT IV, pp. 8–9.

46 H. Grass, op. cit., p. 64.

47 Cf. R. Bultmann, *Theologie des Neuen Testaments* (Tubingen 1948), p. 124.

48 'For out of the whole Old Testament, this is the only passage where one finds, "He died for our sins". How this two fold reference to Isaiah 53 has ever been queried will ever remain a mystery to me'. J. Jeremias, *Der Opfertod Jesu Christi* (Stuttgart 1963), p. 21.

49 Decisive criticisms of such analogies have been made by K. Holl, 'Urchristentum und Religionsgeschichte' (originally 1918), in idem., *Gesammelte Aufsätze zur Kirchengeschichte* II (Tübingen 1928), pp. 1–32, and A. Schweitzer, *Geschichte der Leben-Jesu-Forschung* (Tübingen 1921), pp. 536ff. Cf. K. H. Rengstorf, op. cit., pp. 30–31; W. Künneth, op. cit., pp. 43ff who also remarks, however, that the Resurrection is the deepest fulfilment of myth, p. 184; H. Grass, op. cit., p. 237; L. Goppelt, op. cit., p. 221; W. Pannenberg, in B. Klappert, op. cit., p. 239. To Bultmann's renewed attempt to derive Christology from Gnostic myth, there have been replies from E. Stauffer, *Entmythologisierung oder Realtheologie* (Stuttgart 1949), pp. 10ff; and C. Colpe, *Die religionsgeschichtliche Schule. Darstellung und Kritik ihres Bildes von gnostischen Erlösermythus* (Gottingen 1961). Cf. also H. M. Schenke, *Der Gott 'Mensch' in der Gnosis* (Gottingen 1962).

50 G. Delling, *Die Bedeutung der Auferstehung*, op. cit., pp. 86–88.

51 'The meeting with the Risen One opens the understanding of Scripture: it is not that the meeting with the Risen One is born from minute reflection on Scripture', H. Grass, op. cit., p. 236.

52 'In fact, one has to say that none of the attempted psychological or historical explanations of the faith of the disciples in the Resurrection has led until now to any convincing result', H. Grass, p. 234.

53 K H. Rengstorf, op. cit., p. 22.

54 F. X. Durrwell, op, cit., pp. 36ff; W. Künneth, op. cit., pp. 162ff, and his reference to E. Schäder, *Die Bedeutung des lebendigen Christus für die Rechtfertigung* (Gütersloh 1893); H. Grass, op. cit., p. 42.

55 J. Jeremias, op. cit., n. 45.

56 Foerster, 'Kyrios', ThW III, pp. 1085–1095.

57 If we abstract from the debated text of Romans 9, 5.

58 E. Lohmeyer, '*Sun Christōi*', in *Festgabe für Deissmann* (Tübingen 1927);, pp. 218ff; idem., *Grundlagen paulinischer Theologie* (Tübigen 1929), pp. 139ff.

59 W. Künneth, op. cit. p. 217

60 'O vere beate nox, quae sola meruit scire tempus et horam, in qua Christus ab inferis resurrexit', *Exsultet* from Liturgy of the Vigil of Easter.

61 Op cit., pp. 39–43.

62 R. Schnackenburg, *Das Johannesevangelium* I (Freiburg 1965), pp. 207ff; G.

Ziener, 'Wesiheitsbuch und Johannesevangelium', *Biblica* 38 (1957), pp. 396–418; 39 (1958), pp. 37–60.

63 K. H. Rengstorf, op. cit., pp. 34ff, 669ff, 108.

64 H. Schlier, op. cit., p. 21. For the terminology, cf. E. Fascher, 'Anastasis-Resurrectio-Auferstehung', ZNW 40 (1942), pp. 166–229; E. Lichtenstein, 'Die älteste christliche Glaubensformel', ZKG 63 (1950), pp. 1–74; K. H. Rengstorf, op. cit., p. 29; P. Seidensticker, op. cit., p. 11; G. Delling, op. cit., pp. 76–78. 'The Resurrection of Jesus is the divine act of the Resurrection and, as such, the breaking in of the Eschaton ... That is why the wish to uncover diversity of traditon in the words "being raised" and "to rise" should really not be allowed, nor, for example, the ascribing of "being raised" to the Palestinian, "rising" to the Hellenistic tradition', G. Koch, op, cit, p. 55.

65 W. Künneth, op. cit., p. 127.

66 Ibid., pp. 166ff; K. H. Rengstorf, op. cit., pp. 91ff.

67 H. Grass, op. cit., p 225; L. Goppelt, op. cit., p. 216: 'Thus it is not by chance that the Old Testament theophanies constitute the closest analogy, where historic form is concerned, to the appearance narratives'. Cf. K. Koch, op. cit., pp. 27, 65, 178; this author writes, 'The *Doxa* of God has in him (the Risen One) appeared in the world', op. cit., p. 192. Cf. also K. H. Rengstorf, op. cit., pp. 67–68. In II Corinthians 4, 5, where we read, 'For it is the God who said, "Let light shine out of darkness", who has shone in our hearts to give the light of the knowledge of the glory of God in the face of Christ', many exegetes tend to see an allusion by Paul to his experience on the Damascus road.

68 P. Seidensticker, op. cit., pp. 40–41. Reservations are entered by H. v. Campenhausen, op. cit., pp 9 and 48 n. 193.

69 W. Künneth, op. cit., pp. 144–145 who writes. 'Whether the words of the Jesus of history must themselves be considered as simple wisdom teachings or simple prophetic acts of knowledge on the part of the rabbi of Nazerth, or, on the contrary, be thought of as words of an incomparable nature – this question can receive no answer save through the Resurrection. Without reference to the Resurrection, all Jesus' words belong to the level of the history of religions ... (but, through the Resurrection) all of his *logia* are set free from their temporal historicity and raised to absolute universality. The Resurrection enables one to see that there is divine authority behind them. And so, in retroactive fashion, the words of Jesus become "words of the Lord", possessing the quality of the Word of God'.

70 P. Seidensticker, op. cit., pp. 44ff.

71 F. X. Durrwell, op. cit., passim. but especially pp. 80–93 On the representation of the Resurrection as the great high priest's entry, by virtue of his own bloody sacrifice, into the Holy of holies, in the Letter to the Hebrews, see ibid., pp. 88ff. On the sacrificial theory of the French School, see H. Bremond, *Histoire du Sentiment Réligieux en France* III (Paris 1935). See also M. de la Taille, *Mysterium Fidei* (Paris 1931³), and notably *Elucidatio* XII–XV. F. X. Durrwell, op. cit., p. 85.

73 U. Wilckens, 'Die Überlieferungsgschicthe der Auferstehung Jesu', in *Die Bedeutung der Auferstehungs-botschaft für den Glauben an Jesus Christus* (Gütersloh

1967[4]), p. 45. 'Son' may be the special designation of the Exalted One: Romans 1, 3ff; 1 Thessalonians, 1, 10.

74 'Wort und Glaube', *Gesammelte Aufsätze* (Tübingen 1960), p. 317. For a critique: G. Eicholz, 'Die Grenze der existentialen Interpretation. Fragen zu Gerhard Ebelings Glaubensbegriff', *Tradition und Interpretation* (Munich 1965), p. 219

75 On the hidden character of God in the Resurrection of Christ, cf. the explications of K. H. Rengstorf, op, cit., pp. 95–107.

76 L. Goppelt, op. cit., p. 217

77 Ibid., p. 220

78 W. Künneth, op. cit., pp. 125ff

79 'Who God is and what is divine, that we have to learn there where God has revealed himself, and revealed his own nature, the essence of the divine. And if now it is in Jesus Christ that he has thus revealed himself as God, it is not our business to wish to be wiser than he, and to assert that all this is incompatible with the divine nature . . . The common opinion that God can and should only be absolute in contrast to everything relative, only infinite in his exclusion of everything finite, only high in contrast to all that is low, only active over against all suffering, only unmoved in opposition to all that is vulnerable, only transcendent in contrast to all immanence: this opinion shows itself to be untenable, perverse and pagan in the light of what God is and does factually and precisely as such, in Jesus Christ': K. Barth, *Kirchliche Dogmatik* IV/1 p. 203.

80 'Faith in the New Testament sense recognises the person of Jesus behind the word, and calls out to him in prayer . . . The call to faith becomes a legal demand when the living Lord disappears behind the kerygma', L. Goppelt, in B. Klappert, op. cit., p. 33; cf. ibid., p. 218.

81 'Antwort an R. Bultmann', *Kerygma und Mythos* I (Hamburg 1967[5]), p. 92. Bultmann's reply to Schniewind (ibid. p. 127) says clearly, 'I must avow . . . that I also hold as mythological the expression of personal relationship with Christ'

82 E. Güttgemanns, *Der leidende Apostel und sein Herr. Studien zur paulinischen Christologie* (Göttingen 1966); U. Wilckens, 'Weisheit und Torheit', BHTh 26 (1959).

83 E. Lohse, 'Die Bedeutung des Pfingstberichtes im Rahmen des lukanischen Geschichtswerkes', EvTh 13 (1953), pp. 422–436.

84 U. Wilckens, *Die Missionsreden der Apostelgeschichte. Form-und tradition-segeschichtliche Untersuchungen* (Neukirchen 1963[2]), p. 95.

85 P. Seidensticker, op. cit., p. 24.

86 Ibid., pp. 100–101

87 The extended and coherent account of the healing miracle in Jesus' name at the Beautiful Gate, the courageous testifying before the Great Council ('filled with the Holy Spirit', Acts 4, 8), the prayer of the community 'in the spirit' (4, 31), the whipping of the apostles who suffered 'dishonour for the Name' (5, 41) and the stoning of Stephen, successively develop different aspects of the presence of the Spirit.

88 The anticipated dating of the revelation of the Trinity in Luke 1, 28, 31 and 35, indicates a post-paschal composition: A. Resch, *Das Kindheits-evangelium nach*

Lukas und Matthäus (Leipzig 1897); R. Laurentin, *Structure et théologie de Luc I-II* (Paris 1957).

89 D. M. Stanley, *Christ's Resurrection in Pauline Soteriology* (Rome 1961), p. 251.

90 K. H. Rengstorf, op. cit., p. 38.

91 Ibid., p. 108.

92 Thomas Aquinas, *Super Joannem* 16, 7 (Ed. Marietti, Rome 1952, n. 2088); cf. idem., *In Libros Sententiarum* III., d. 22, q. 3, a. 1, ad v.

93 H. Schlier, op. cit., p. 41.

94 *Die Auferstehing Christi* (Tübingen 1965²). On this, see H. Grass, op. cit., p. 324; W. Koepp, ThLZ 84 (1959), pp. 927–933.

95 G. Koch, op. cit., pp. 9–11.

96 Ibid., p.p. 21, 40ff.

97 Ibid., p. 314.

98 Ibid., pp. 71, 237.

99 Ibid., pp. 67ff.

100 Ibid., pp. 268ff.

101 Ibid.

102 Ibid., pp. 6; 153ff; 293ff.

103 Ibid., pp. 26ff: 'Between Resurrection and appearance one can introduce no distinction', p. 179.

104 Ibid., p. 174.

105 Ibid., p. 179.

106 Ibid., p. 54.

107 Ibid., p. 17.

108 'The form of the appearance had to be brought within the adventurous exercise of formation . . . There the language and imagery of myth offered their services', ibid., p. 73. The communication must remain a 'responsive formation', ibid., p. 224; but the appearance itself is 'never without form', ibid., p. 206.

109 'Jesus is the image; he is the form of God, in him God comes to appearance . . . Here is what corresponds to God'. This correspondence is unique, since here 'divine fidelity' and 'human confidence' are one, ibid., p. 257.

110 Ibid., p. 295. Cf. p. 305: 'The signs of the presence of Christ emerge into the visible realm. They are indicative signs, the form of a hidden reality which makes itself present. The signs point back to foundation and essence'.

111 Ibid., pp. 271ff.

112 Ibid., p. 57.

113 Ibid., p. 264.

114 'In this form, the heart of God has turned towards men', ibid., p. 265. 'The co-being of Christ with the world is therefore being in-love', ibid., p. 122.

115 Ibid., pp. 305ff.

116 Ibid., pp. 21; 47, 61, 201ff; 301ff.

117 Ibid., pp. 280–297.

118 Ibid., pp. 308ff.

119 H. Schlier, op. cit., p. 43.

120 K. H. Rengstorf, op cit., p. 56.

121 Rengstorf wishes to see the in use of this word a protest of Christianity against

the vision-hypothesis: ibid., p. 58.

122 *Homilia in Lucam* 3 (ed. Rauer, 9, 20–23). Origen regards it, then, as possible that Jesus could have appeared at the same time before some human beings as glorified, and to others as not glorified; cf. *Commentarium in Matthaeum, Sermo* 35 (ed. Klostermann-Benz, 11, 65); cf. *In Matthaeum* 12, 37–38 (ibid., 10, 152–4).

123 J. Kremer, op. cit., p. 86, especially for the 'Angel of YHWH', Exodus 3, 2; cf. Acts 7, 30 and 35; other examples in Kremer, op. cit., p. 35.

124 W. Künneth, op. cit., p. 84. Reservations are expressed in U. Wilckens, *Überlieferungsgeschichte*, op. cit., p. 56. *Ophthē* is not used exclusively, but alternates with several other expressions: critical analysis in H. Grass, op. cit., pp. 186–189. And yet Grass tends to restrict the content of the expression to that of 'seeing' or 'becoming visible', since he regards the original phenomenon as 'a meeting in visual contemplation', a 'seeing which engendered faith', op. cit., p. 258. The content of *ophthē* is even more reduced by W. Marxsen. What in Grass was correctly called the 'objective vision hypothesis' (op. cit., pp. 233ff) becomes in Marxsen the simple 'happening' of a faith which 'deals with objective visions' and subsequently arrives 'by way of reflective interpretation at the affirmation that Jesus has been raised by God', Similarly, according to Marxsen, the New Testament knows of another possible interpretation: thus *Die Auferstehung Jesu als historisches und theologisches Problem*, op. cit., pp. 115–131; cf. also U. Wilckens, op. cit., G. Delling, op. cit., B. Klappert, op. cit., pp. 45–51.

125 G. Koch, op. cit., p. 58.

126 J. Kremer, op. cit., p. 61, n. 119.

127 Ibid., p. 63.

128 G. Koch, op. cit., pp. 295ff.

129 'For what is decisive in the fact of the appearances, is that the disciples *recognised Jesus* in him who appeared to them', U. Wilckens, op. cit., p. 51.

130 G. Koch, op. cit., pp. 48–49.

131 H. Grass, op. cit., pp. 250–253.

132 G. Koch, op. cit., p. 303.

133 'The shepherd knows his sheep and "calls each one by name", John 10, 3, and when they hear his voice they recognise him', R. Bultmann, *Johannes*, op. cit., p. 532.

134 Ibid., p. 102.

135 Ibid., pp. 46, 63.

136 On John 20, 8, see below

137 Even such attributes as 'Son of God' (John 1, 49), 'the Christ (the Messiah)' (Mark 8, 29) or 'the Christ, the Son of the living God' (Matthew. 16, 16) could be products of post-Easter insight. That does not rule out the fact that elements belonging to an understanding of the divine mission of Jesus could and must have been present in the minds of the disciples: H. Schürmann, *Die vorösterlichen Anfängen der Logientradition* (1960), now in *Traditionsgeschichtliche Untersuchungen zu den synoptischen Evangelien* (Düsseldorff 1968), pp. 39–65, especially at p. 49: 'If there could be a post-Easter confession of Christ, was it not because – despite all the differences – there was already a pre-Easter confession in the circle of the disciples? There had to be, before Easter, a least a messianic "presumption", in

order for the event of Easter to be capable of understanding as a "fulfilment".'

138 Note the sharp contrast with Luke where the pre-Easter faith of the disciples on the Emmaus road goes no further than the image of a 'prophet mighty in deed and word before God and all the people' (24, 19).

139 G. Delling, op. cit., p. 87.

140 H. Grass, op. cit., p. 70.

141 G. Koch, op. cit., pp. 64ff.

142 'The whole New Testament is written in the light of Resurrection faith', F. V. Filson, *Jesus Christ the Risen Lord* (New York 1956), p. 31. 'It is absolutely correct to say that the way in which the Gospels present Jesus is, from start to finish, in the light of the Easter experience', G. Kittel, 'Der historische Jesus', *Mysterium Christi* (1931), pp. 64ff.

143 W. Künneth, op. cit., pp. 152–153.

144 Collection of these scriptural evidences in H. Grass, op. cit., pl 262.

145 J. Kremer, op. cit., pp. 53 ff.

146 P. Seidensticker, op. cit., pp. 124ff.

147 E. Lohse, 'Die alttestamentliche Bezüge zum neutestament lichen Zeugnis vom Tode Jesu Christi', in *Zur Bedeutung des Todes Christi* (Gütersloh 1967), p. 104.

148 H. Schlier, op. cit., p. 57.

149 'Eschatologie und Geschichte im Lichte der Qumrantexte', *Zeit und Geschichte. Dankgabe an R. Bultmann* (Tübingen 1064), p. 14.

150 W. Kunneth, op. cit., p. 92.

151 J. Kremer, op. cit., p. 134.

152 H. Schlier, op. cit., pp. 69–70.

153 'Dogmatischen Thesen zur Lehre von der Offenbarung', in W. Pannenberg (ed.), *Offenbarung als Geschichte* (Göttingen 1961), p. 98.

154 Ibid., pp. 113–114.

155 *Summa Theologiae* IIIa., q. 55, a. 2, ad i.

156 See on this my 'Schau der Gestalt', = *Herrlichkeit* I (Einsiedeln 1968²).

157 Dibelius-Kümmel, *Jesus* (Berlin 1966⁴), pp. 117 ff Cf. also the citation of F. C. Baur in H. Grass, op. cit., p. 233. Baur recognises that 'no psychological analysis can penentrate into the interior psychic process whereby, in the disciples' awareness, their incredulity at the moment of the death of Jesus became faith in his Resurrection'.

158 W. Pannenberg, *Grundzüge der Christologie* (Gütersloh 1964), pp. 79ff.

159 K. Barth, *Kirchliche Dogmatik* IV/1, p. 368.

160 On this see the considerable arguments developed by W. Künneth, op. cit., pp. 185–194, under the title 'Der christologische Zeitsbegriff'. With these Teilhard de Chardin, in his own fashion, might well be agreed.

161 On such differences of importance, see W. Künneth, op. cit., p. 108.

162 J. Kremer, op. cit., p. 84.

163 Who would claim to demonstrate that the appearance to five hundred brethren is identical with that which took place before the eleven disciples in Galilee, recounted by Matthew (Seidensticker), or that it could only have happened in Galilee, in the open air (Lohmeyer, von Campenhausen), or, yet again, that it is identical with the Pentecost event (Dobschütz, Bousset and others), or, once

again still, that it could only have happened after Pentecost, because only then was the community sufficiently numerous (Grass), etc? Kremer's reserve is the only attitude possible. Only the fact is expressed; the rest remains obscure (op. cit., p. 72). The same is true of the appearance granted to James.

[164] On the hypotheses proposed, cf. H. Grass, op. cit., pp. 102–104.

[165] Ibid., p. 38.

[166] Ibid., pp. 176ff.

[167] E. Haenchen, 'Historie und Geschichte in den johanneischen Passionsberichten', in *Zur Bedeutung des Todes Jesu* op. cit., p. 65. On the atempt to cover up the flight of the disciples, see already Wellhausen, *Evangelium Marci* (1903[2]), p. 136.

[168] H. Grass, op. cit., p. 29.

[169] H. Grass: for the location of the scene, ibid., pp. 91ff; 120; for the closing images, p. 114.

[170] This is the central thesis which Grass sustains.

[171] P. Seidensticker, op. cit., pp. 97–98.

[172] Thus H. Grass, op. cit., pp. 34, 54. The opposite is not excluded if the conclusion to John's Gospel is allowed an explicitly symbolic or allegorical character. See below.

[173] P. Benoit, *Passion et résurrection du Seigneur* (Paris 1966), pp. 321–322.

[174] E. Hirsch, *Die Auferstehungsgeschichte und der christliche Glaube* (Tübingen 1940) p. 3. Against his position, W. Michaelis, op. cit., pp. 31–34; against all retrojection of what were originally Easter accounts into the life of Jesus, K. H. Rengstorf, op. cit., excurses 4, pp. 146–154. For the relation of John 21 to Luke 5, cf. M. E. Boismard, 'Le chapitre XXI de Saint Jean. Essai de critique litteraire', RB 54 (1957), pp. 471–501. O. Cullmann maintains that the first appearance was to Peter, which would, once again, have affirmed his authority among the disciples. He seeks therefore to explain how the memory of this first appearance might have faded, *Petrus: Jünger-Apostel-Märtyrer* (Zurich 1952[2]), pp. 64ff.

[175] *Gospel of Peter*, 28–29 (Schneemelcher, op. cit., I., pp. 122ff.

[176] H. Grass, op. cit., p. 16.

[177] Cf ibid., pp. 16–23.

[178] R. Bultmann, *Synoptische Tradition* (Göttingen 1957[3]) p. 309, n. 1; L. Brun, *Die Auferstehung Christi in der urchristlichen Überlieferung* (Lund 1925), pp. 9–11.

[179] Cf. H. Schlier, op. cit., pp. 56–57.

[180] *Der evangelist Markus* (Göttingen 1959[2]). A position worked out earlier by Lohmeyer, *Galiläa und Jerusalem* (Göttingen 1936). For the latter, the appearance narratives are objectifications intended to validate a passage, a 'shifting centre-point', to the Parousia, p. 13.

[181] H. Grass, op. cit., p. 289. On p. 300. he calls it 'fantastic'. For H. von Campenhausen, *Der Ablauf der Ostereignisse und das leere Grab* (Heidelberg 1966[3]), p. 38, 'this linkage of mythological with contemporary theological ideas seems already something rather astonishing' and its exegetical justification 'more than fragile'.

[182] G. Koch, op. cit., pp. 38–40.

[183] Cf. on this P. Seidensticker, op. cit., p. 88.

[184] Op. cit., pp. 113–116.

185 Some of the apocrypha support the Galilee hypothesis, and notably the *Gospel of Peter* 58 (Schneemelcher, op. cit., I. p. 124).

186 Op. cit., p. 50.

187 E. Lohse, 'Die Auferstehung Jesu Christi im Zeugnis des Lukasevangeliums', *Biblische Studien* 21 (1961), pp. 8ff; J. Kremer, op. cit., p. 69.

188 RGG³ I., pp. 699ff. So also W. Michaelis, *Die Erscheinungen des Auferstandenen* (Basle 1944).

189 K. Koch, op. cit., p. 46.

190 H. Grass, op. cit., pp. 120ff.

191 H. Schlier, op. cit., p. 9.

192 K. H. Rengstorf, op. cit., pp. 60–62.

193 W. Nauck, 'Die Bedeutung des leeren Grabs für den Glauben an den Auferstandenen', ZNW 47 (1956), pp. 243–267. For Nauck, the accounts of the empty tomb are most ancient and reliable traditions, but in their oldest form they simply prepare the Easter appearances without constituting an independent testimony to them.

194 L. Goppelt, op. cit., p. 216.

195 H. Schlier, op. cit., pp. 32–33.

196 Kremer thinks that, in Paul, the empty tomb is presupposed 'in the mention of the burial . . . and so attested implicitly', pp. 38ff. He indicates, n. 33, quite a large number of authors who have written in this sense. After Grass's deepened study of what the 'spiritual body' signified for Paul, pp. 146–173, von Campenhausen in the later editions of his already mentioned study is less categorical than in the earlier: 'Probably (first edition: 'undoubtedly') Paul envisages a real transformation and transfiguration of the dead body, and, to this extent, an 'emptying' of the tomb', p. 20. In favour of the hypothesis that Paul would have definitely thought that the tomb had to be empty, W. Künneth, op. cit., pp. 96ff, cites the somewhat dated study by K. Bornhäuser, *Die Gebeine der Toten* (Gütersloh 1921) which, admittedly, locates itself exclusively within the horizon of Jewish thought, which Paul to some degree breaks away from by his theory of the spiritual body. Despite II Corinthians 5,1, what seems decisive in a difficult *crux* is the term and idea of the 'swallowing up' of the mortal by the immortal (v. 4; cf. I Corintians 15, 55). But all of this fails to inform us as to whether Paul was familiar with the historic tradition of the empty tomb, that is to say, whether this tradition existed – abstracting from all discussion of backdrops of thought. Nor are we further advanced thereby in the question of whether such a horizon of thought still keeps its value for us today. On the first of these issues, E. Stauffer responds by an energetic affirmative: 'Only an uncriticised criticism can still today qualify as legendary the story of the empty tomb. All the historic indications and all the critical considerations in the sources tend to make one believe that, on Easter morning, the tomb of Jesus was empty', *Entmythologisierung oder Realtheologie* (Stuttgart 1949), p. 20; cf. idem., 'Der Auferstehungsglabube und das leere Grab', in *Zeitschrift für Religions-und Geistesgeschichte* 6 (1954), pp. 146ff. H. Grass enters however a reservation: none of the arguments in favour of historicity seem to him 'absolutely coercive' (p. 183), though the 'gap in the historical demonstration of the empty tomb (is)

very narrow', p. 184. On the second problem, J. Kremer says rightly (uniting himself in this to W. Künneth, op. cit., p. 85; cf. also P. Althaus, *Die Wahrheit des kirchlichen Osterglaubens* (Gutersloh 1941²), p. 27: 'From the purely theoretical and abstract viewpoint, a resurrection of the dead, a new creation of man in body and spirit, may be conceivable even if the corpse remains in the tomb', p. 143; the empty tomb is thus in reality only a *sign*. But it remains a sign in every case, no matter what horizon of thought one chooses to adopt.

[197] In Matthew, this tendency is clear, and his account of the guard on the tomb, asked for the Pilate (27, 62–66; 28, 4 and 11–15) bristles with internal contradictions (H. von Campenhausen, op. cit., p. 29). The account is half-way towards the exaggerations of the apocrypha, where the sureties with which the tomb is surrounded are 'increased to the level of the fantastic', and a large number of neutral or hostile witnesses invoked, witnesses who, in the Gospel of Peter, and contrary to all the (canonical) Gospels, are present at the Resurrection event.

[198] H. von Campenhausen, op. cit., pp. 31ff.

[199] See below.

[200] H. Grass, op. cit., p. 27.

[201] P. Benoit, 'Marie-Madeline et les disciples au Tombeau selon Jean 20, 1–18', in *Judentum Urchristentum, Kirche. Festschrift für J. Jeremias* (1960), pp. 14ff. So also. C. H. Dodd, 'The Appearances of the Risen Christ', in *Studies in the Gospels for R. H. Lightfoot* (1957), pp. 18ff.

[202] For the whole question, see P. Gaechter, 'Die Engelserscheinungen in den Auferstehungsberichten', ZKTh 89 (1967), pp. 191–202.

[203] Op. cit., p. 88. One cannot argue by using Matthew 28, 6 and 10, because it is there that Jesus repeats the words of the angel at the tomb: the angel's word enjoys priority.

[20] J. Kremer, op. cit., p. 45. H. von Campenhausen supports the discovery of the empty tomb on the third day, op. cit., pp. 11–12; 42; 59. Anyone who wishes to transfer the first appearances into Galilee will have difficulty in using this chronological marker. This objection is raised by Grass, op. cit., p. 129, against F. Hahn, *Christologische Hoheitstitel* (Göttingen 1964²) and others.

[205] J. Kremer, op. cit., pp. 35; 49.

[206] H. Grass, op. cit., p. 137.

[207] Resurrection of Osiris or Attis (Adonis) on the third day: references and bibliography in H. Grass, op. cit., p. 133.

[208] J. Kremer, op. cit., p. 51; H. Grass, op. cit., pp. 131ff.

[209] Texts in J. Kremer, op. cit., p. 47. n. 55.

[210] J. Jeremias, in B. Klappert, op. cit., p. 180; see also P. Seidensticker, 'Das antiochenische Glaubens-bekenntnis I Korinther 15, 3–7 im Lichte seiner Traditionsgeschichte', ThGl 57 (1967), pp. 299–305: the formula proclaims only the coming of salvation and does not constitute a piece of exact dating – which Seidensticker proves by the linguistic usage of the Septuagint.

[211] On this theme: J. Dupont, 'Ressuscité "le troisime jour"', *Biblica* 40 (1959), pp. 742–763. On this, see also E. Lohse, 'Die alttestamentliche Bezüge zum neutestamentlichen Zeugnis vom Tode Jesu Christi', art. cit., p. 108; J. B. Bauer,

'Drei Tage', BB 38 (1958), pp. 354–358; F. Mildenberger, '"Auferstandenen am dritten Tag nach den Schriften"', EvTh (1963) pp. 265–280; F. Nötscher, 'Zur Auferstehung nach den drei Tagen', *Biblica* 35 (1954), pp. 313–319; K. Lehmann, *Auferweckt am Dritten Tag nach der Schrift* (Freiburg 1968: appeared too late for use in the present work).

212 For what follows, see above all, P. Benoit, 'L'Ascension', RB 56 (1949), pp. 161–203; idem., 'Himmelfahrt', BL[2], pp. 738ff; A. M. Ramsey, 'What was the Ascension?' *Studies for the New Testament Society Bulletin* 2 (1951), pp. 43–50; G. Kretschmar, 'Himmelfahrt und Pfingsten', *Zeitschrift für Kirchengeschichte* 66 (1954–55), pp. 209–253; H. Schlier, 'Jesu Himmelfahrt nach den lukanischen Schriften', *Korrespondenzblatt des Collegium Canisianum* 95 (1961), pp. 2–11, articles which can be consulted in, and are here cited from: *Besinnung auf das Neue Testament* (Freiburg 1964), pp. 227–241; G. Lohfink, 'Der historische Ansatz der Himmelfahrt Christi', *Catholica* 17 (1963), pp. 44–84.

213 Exodus 24, 18; 34, 38; Deuteronomy 9, 11, 15 and 18; 10, 10; cf. the forty years of Israel's desert journey.

214 II Kings 19, 8.

215 H. Grass, op. cit., p. 48.

216 So naturally G. Koch, for which Christ, in rising into history, meets the community on each occasion with ever new originality: op. cit., pp. 279–280.

217 Commentary on these texts in P. Benoit, as in G. Lohfink, arts. cit.

218 H. Conzelmann, *Die Mitte der Zeit* (Tübingen 1954).

219 Op. cit., p. 73.

220 G. Koch, op. cit., pp. 17ff; 53; 73, 224ff.

221 W. Künneth, op. cit., p. 89.

222 Thus W. G. Kümmel, who distinguishes between the dispensable mythic traits (dispensable since dependent on their epoch and thus capable of removal) and the 'indispensable mythic traits': indispensable if divine revelation is to be translated into human Representations: *Mythische Rede und Heilsgeschehen im Neuen Testament* (1947), cited from B. Klappert, op. cit., pp. 94–104, and especially p. 99. Cf. J. Schniewind in 'Antwort an R. Bultmann', art, cit., pp. 79–84.

223 W. Künneth, op. cit., pp. 55ff. Cf. H. Schlier, 'Was heisst Auslegung der Heiligen Schrift?', in *Besinnung auf das Neue Testament*, op. cit., pp. 43–44.

224 W. Nigg, *Der Glanz der Legende* (Zurich 1964); H. Grass, op. cit., p. 301.

225 Cf. the energetic protests of H. Grass against this tendency, as the emphasis, too, of W. Pannenberg.

226 H. Schlier, op. cit., pp. 324–325; cf. p. 40.

227 K. Barth, *Kirchliche Dogmatik* IV/1 p. 337.

228 H. Schlier, op. cit., p. 15.

229 G. Lohfink, *Paulus vor Damaskus* (Stuttgart 1965).

230 H. Grass, op. cit., p. 60.

231 For the unity which holds good between the Johannine Ascension and that of Luke, cf. Lohfink, 'Der historische Ansatz', art. cit., pp. 68–75.

232 Cf. K. H. Rengstorf, op. cit., pp. 22ff.

233 *Zum religionsgeschichtlichen Verständnis des Neuen Testaments* (Göttingen 1903), p. 71.

234 H. Grass, op. cit., p. 29. In the final, ideal scene in Matthew, the incident in which 'some doubted' has the effect of a 'signalling cry, breaking the entire atmosphere of the power-filled coming of the Easter Lord', P. Seidensticker, op. cit., p. 91. It gives the impression, above all, of a schematic formula. It must have been taken from other, more concrete, reports, and inserted here as an element contributing to this whole account.

235 J. Kremer, op. cit., p. 94.

236 K. Barth, *Kirchliche Dogmatik* III/2, pp. 530ff.

237 H. Grass, op. cit., pp. 71ff. For the whole problem of seeing and believing in John, which is much more complex than can be indicated here, see O. Cullmann, '*Eiden kai episteusen. Aux sources de la traditon chrétienne*', *Mélanges Goguel* 1950, pp. 52–61; K. Lammers, *Hören, Sehen und Glauben im Neuen Testament* (Stuttgart 1967²); F. Mussner, *Die Johanneische Sehweise und die Frage nach dem historischen Jesus* (Freiburg 1965); H. Schlier, *Glauben, Erkennen, Liete nach dem Johannesevangelium* (1962), all described in *Besinnung auf das Neue Testament* op. cit., pp. 279–293; H. Wenz, 'Sehen und Glauben bei Johannes', ThZ 17 (Basle 1961), pp. 17–25. For other works, see P. Seidensticker, op. cit., p. 108, n. 3.

238 Cf. the entire problematic of John 6 and 7, 38–39. On this, see F. X. Durrwell, op. cit., pp. 109ff.

239 K. H. Rengstorf, op. cit., p. 104.

240 K. Holl, 'Der Kirchenbegriff des Paulus in seinem Verhaltnis zu dem Urgemeinde' (originally 1921), in idem., *Gesammelte Aufsätze zur Kirchengeschichte* II (1927), pp. 50ff.

241 Ibid., p. 54.

242 J. Jeremias, *Die Abendmahlsworte Jesu* (Göttingen 1960³), p. 196.

243 Bibliography for the understanding of this word in W. Bauer, ThW 1552. Even if it is not a matter here to table-fellowship, the meals in Luke and John still suffice as proofs. For the theology involved, see F. X. Durrwelll, op. cit., pp. 83ff; 94, 369ff.

244 This interpretation is found first in Chrysostom, *Homilia in Johannem* 85, 4; cf. H. von Campenhausen, op. cit., p. 35, n. 138.

245 Bultmann's interpretation, in Johannes, op. cit., p. 531, founded as it is on the distinction between a Jewish Christianity (Peter) and a Gentile (John) is also erroneous and non-objective, as is that, analogously, of Gregory the Great, in *Homilia in Evangelium* 22. Of course, it does not suffice either to show the possible rivalries between communities with a Petrine orientation and those with a Johannine. These rivalries were certainly, for John, and long after Peter's death, to which he looks back in John 21, 18ff, the occasion for reflecting again on the relationship which existed between them: but the event goes far beyond this passing occasion and takes on a value for all ages.

246 A. von Speyr, *Johannes* IV (Einsiedeln 1949), pp. 420ff.

247 Augustine, *In Joannem Tractatus* 45, 2 (PL 35,1720)

248 J. Moltmann, *Theologie der Hoffnung* (Munich 1965³), p. 303; on this theme, see also W. Kreck, *Die Zukunft des Gekommenen. Grund probleme der Eschatologie* (Munich 1965²); G. Sauter, *Zukunft und Verheissung. Das Problem der Zukunft in der gegenwärtigen theologischen und philosophischen Diskussion* (Zurich 1965).

Select Bibliography

I. Incarnation and Passion; The Death of God as Wellspring of Salvation, Revelation and Theology; Going to the Cross.

1. Encyclopaedia articles.
DACL III (1914) 3045–3131: 'Croix et Crucifix' (H. Leclercq).
DBS VI (1960) 1419–1492: 'Passion' (X. Léon-Dufour).
DSAM II (1953) 2607–2623: 'Croix, Mystère de la' (M. Olphe-Galliard).
LThK VI (^{1}1934) 242–254: 'Kreuz' (J. Sauer).
LThK VI (^{2}1961) 605–615: 'Kreuz' (J. Hasenfuss – J. Sauer – J. Blinzler – G. Römer – E. Lucchesi-Palli – D. Schaefers).
RGG IV (^{3}1960) 45–49: 'Kreuz' (C.-M. Edsman – E. Dinkler – H.-U. Haedeke).
ThW VII (1966) 572–580: σταυρός (J. Schneider).

2. General
Althaus, P., 'Das Kreuz Christi' = *Theologische Aufsätze* (Gütersloh 1929) 1–50.
Bartsch, H. W., 'Die Passions- und Ostergeschichten bei Matthäus' = *Entmythologisierende Auslegung* (Hamburg 1962) 80–92.
– 'Historische Erwägungen zur Leidensgeschichte', EvTh 22 (1962) 449–459.
– 'Die Bedeutung des Sterbens Jesu nach den Synoptikern', ThZ 20 (1964) 87–102.
Benoit, P., 'La Loi et la Croix d'après S. Paul', RB 47 (1938) 481–509.

– *Passion et résurrection du Seigneur* (Paris 1966).

Bertram G., *Die Leidensgeschichte Jesu und der Christuskult* (Göttingen 1922).

– 'Die Himmelfahrt Jesu vom Kreuz aus und der Glaube an seine Auferstehung', *Festgabe für G. A. Deissmann*, (Tübingen 1927) 187–217.

Bousset W., 'Platons Weltseele und das Kreuz Christi', ZNW 14 (1913) 273ff.

Bouyer L., *Le Mystère Pascal*, Paris [5]1957.

Burkill T. A., 'St. Mark's Philosophy of the Passion', NT 2 (1958) 245–271.

Dahl, N. A., 'Der gekreuzigte Messias' = H. Ristow – K. Matthiae, *Der historische Jesus und der kerygmatische Christus* (Berlin [2]1961) 149–169.

Dillistone F. W., *Jesus Christ and his Cross* (London 1953).

Dinkler E., *Das Apsismosaik von S. Apollinare in Classe*, (Cologne and Opladan 1964).

– *Signum Crucis. Aufsätze zum Neuen Testament und zur Christlichen Archäologie* (Tübingen 1967).

Favre R., 'Credo in Filium Dei ... Mortuum et sepultum', RHE 33 (1937) 687–724.

Gnilka J., 'Mein Gott, mein Gott, warum hast du mich verlassen? Mk 15, 34 par', BZNF 3 (1959) 294–297.

Grelot P., 'Aujourd'hui tu seras avec moi au paradis', RB (1967) 196–214.

Grillmeier A., *Der Logos am Kreuz. Zur christologischen. Symbolik der älteren Kreuzigungsdarstellung* (Münich 1956).

Güttgemanns E., *Der leidende Apostel und sein Herr* (Göttingen 1966).

Hasenzahl W., *Die Gottverlassenheit des Christus nach dem Kreuzeswort bei Mt und Mk, und das christologische Verständnis des griechischen Psalters* (Gütersloh 1937).

Heer J., *Der Durchbohrte* (Rome 1966).

Holzmeister U., *Crux Domini atque Crucifixio* (Rome 1934).

– 'Die Finsternis beim Tode Jesu', *Biblica* 22 (1961) 404–441.

Hülsbusch W., *Elemente einer Kreuzestheologie in den Spätschriften Bonaventuras* (Düsseldorf 1968).

Journet C., *Les sept paroles du Christ en Croix* (Paris 1952).

Kähler W., *Das Kreuz, Grund und Mass der Christologie* (Gütersloh 1911).

Käsemann E. et al., *Zur Bedeutung des Todes Jesu. Exegetische Beiträge* (Gütersloh 1967).

Kruse H., 'Pater noster et Passio Christi', VD 46 (1968) 3–29.

Kühn G. H., 'Jesus in Gethsemane', Ev. Th. 12 (1952–3) 260 bis 285.

Leal J., 'Christo confixus sum Cruci', VD (1939) 76–80, 98–105.

Lebreton J., 'L'agonie de Notre Seigneur' = Rev. Apol. 33 (1922).

Lohse E., *Die Geschichte des Leidens und Sterbens Jesu Christi*, (Gütersloh 1964).

Luther M., 'Sermon von der Betrachtung des heiligen Leidens Christi 1519', *Werke, Weimar Ausgabe 2*, 136f.

Morris L., *The Apostolic Preaching of the Cross* (London 1955).

Ortkemper F. J., *Das Kreuz in der Verkündigung des Apostels Paulus* (Stuttgart 1967).

Pascal B., 'Le Mystère de Jésus', in: *Pensées* (ed. Chevalier Nr. 736).

Pascher J., *Theologie des Kreuzes* (Münster 1948).

Przywara E., *Deus semper maior. Theologie der Exerzitien. 2. Bd. 3. Woche* (Freiburg 1940).

Rahner H., 'Das Mysterium des Kreuzes' in *Griechische Mythen in christlicher Deutung* (Zürich 1945) 73–100.

Riggenbach E., *Das Geheimnis des Kreuzes Christi* (Stuttgart and Basle ³1927).

Schelkle K. H., *Die Passion Jesu in der Verkündigung des Neuen Testamentes* (Heidelberg 1949).

Schlatter A., *Jesu Gottheit und das Kreuz*, (Gütersloh ²1913).

Schmidt W. H., 'Das Kreuz Christi bei Paulus', ZSTh 21 (1950) 145–159.

Schnackenburg R., 'Das Ärgernis des Kreuzes', GuL 30 (1957) 90–95.

Schneider J., *Die Passionsmystik bei Paulus* (Leipzig 1929).

Schweizer E., 'Die »Mystik« des Sterbens und Auferstehens mit Christus bei Paulus', EvTh 26 (1966) 239–257.

Shaw J. M., 'The Problem of the Cross', *Expository Times* 47 (1935/6) 18–21.

Steffen B., *Das Dogma vom Kreuz* (Gütersloh 1920).

Stommel E., 'Σημεῖον ἐπεκτάσεως', RQ 50 (1955) 1ff.

Taylor V., *The Cross of Christ* (London 1956).

Vierig F., *Das Kreuz Christi. Interpretation eines Theologischen Gutachtens* (Gütersloh 1969).

Vosté V., *De Passione et Morte Christi* (Rome 1937).

Wiencke G., *Paulus über Jesu Tod* (Gütersloh 1939).

Zöckler O., *Das Kreuz Christi. Religionsgeschichtliche und kirchlich-archäologische Untersuchungen* (Gütersloh 1875).

II. Going to the Dead

1. Encyclopaedia articles

DACL IV, (1920) 682–696: 'Descente du Christ aux enfers d'après la Liturgie' (F. Cabrol – A. de Meester).

DBS II (1934) 395–431: 'Descente du Christ aux enfers' (J. Chaîne, overwhelmingly biblical).

DThC IV (1920) 565–619: 'Descente de Jésus aux enfers' (H. Quillet, much patristic material).

LThK V (²1960) 450–455: 'Höllenabstieg' (A. Grillmeier – E. Lucchesi-Palli).

RGG III (³1959) 407–411: 'Höllenfahrt' (W. v. Soden – B. Reicke – R. B. Breen).

2. On the history of the problem:

Dietelmayer J. A., *Historia Dogmatis de Descensu Christi ad Inferos Litteraria* (Altdorf ²1762).

König J. L., *Die Lehre von Christi Höllenfahrt* (Frankfurt 1842).

Monnier J., *La Descente aux Enfers* (Paris 1905).

Petavius D., *De Theologicis Dogmatibus* V, lib. 13 c 15ff. (Venice 1757).

3. General:

Bernard J. H., 'The descent into Hades and Christian baptism, a Study of 1 Peter 3, 19ff', *The Expositor* II (1915) 241–274.

Bieder W., *Die Vorstellung von der Höllenfahrt Christi. Beitrag zur Entstehungsgeschichte der Vorstellung des sogenannten Descensus ad inferos* (Zürich 1949).

Biser E., 'Abgestiegen zu der Hölle', MThZ 9 (1958) 205–212, 283 bis 293.

Braun F. M., 'La sépulture de Jésus', RB 45 (1930) 34–52, 168–200, 346–363.

Cabrol F., 'La descente du Christ aux enfers d'après la liturgie mozarabe et les liturgies gallicanes', *Rassegna gregoriana* 8 (1909) 233, 242.

Caird G. B., 'The Descent of Christ', in Cross(ed.), *Studia Evangelica* II, Berlin 1964, 535–545.

Clavier H., 'Le Drame de la mort et de la vie dans le Nouveau Testament', in Cross(ed.), *Studia Evangelica* III, Berlin 1964, 166, 177.

Clemen C., *Niedergefahren zu den Toten* (Giessen 1900).

Dalton J., *Christ's Proclamation to the Spirits, A Study of 1 Peter 3,18–4,6* (Rome 1965).

Delling B., ἡμέρα: ThW II (1935) 945–956.

Dieterich A., *Nekyia. Beiträge zur Erklärung der neuentdeckten Petrusapokalypse* (Leipzig ²1913).

Frings J., 'Zu 1 Petr 3,19 und 4,6', BZ 17 (1926) 75–88.

Galot J., 'La Descente du Christ aux enfers' NRT 93 (1961) 471–491.

Gaschienietz R., 'Katabasis', Pauli-Wissowa X/2 (1919) 2359–2449.

Grillmeier A., 'Der Gottessohn im Totenreich', ZKTh 71 (1949) 1–53, 184–203.

Gschwind, K., *Die Niederfahrt Christi in die Unterwelt* (Münster 1911).

Güder E., *Die Lehre von der Erscheinung Jesu Christi unter den Todten* (Berne 1853).

Jeremias J., 'Zwischen Karfreitag und Ostern. Descensus und Ascensus in der Karfreitagstheologie des NT', ZNW 42 (1949) 124–201.

– *Der Opfertod Jesu Christi* (Stuttgart 1963).

Johnson S. E., 'The Preaching to the Dead', JBL 79 (1960) 48–51.

Kroll, J., *Gott und Hölle* (Leipzig 1932).

Loofs F., 'Christ's descent into Hell', *Transactions of the Third International Congress for the History of Religions* II, Oxford 1908, 280–301.

– 'Descent to Hades', *Hastings* IV (1911) 654–663.

Lundberg P., *La typologie baptismale dans l'ancienne Église* (Uppsala 1942).

MacCulloch J. A., *The Harrowing of Hell. A Comparative Study of an Early Christian Doctrine* (Edinburgh 1930).

Perdelwitz R., *Die Mysterienreligion und das Problem des 1. Petrusbriefs* (Giessen 1911).

Ploig D., 'De Descensu in 1 Petr 3,19', *Theologische Tijdschrift* 47 (1913) 145–160.

Rahner H., *Griechische Mythen in christlicher Deutung* (Zürich 1948).

Rahner K., 'Karsamstag', GuL 30 (1957) 81–84.

Reicke B., *The Disobedient Spirits and Christian Baptism* (Copenhagen 1946).

Riesenfeld H., 'La descente dans la mort. Aux sources de la tradition chrétienne' *Mélanges Goguel* (Neuchâtel 1950) 207–217.

Rousseau O., 'La descente aux Enfers, fondement sotériologique du baptême chrétien', RSR 40 (1952) (*Mélanges Lebreton*) 173–197.

Rushforth G. M., 'The Descent into Hell in Byzantine Art', *Papers of the British School at Rome* (London 1902).

Schmidt C., *Der Descensus in der alten Kirche* = TU 43 (1919) 376–453.

Schulz H. J., 'Die »Höllenfahrt« als «Anastasis«', ZKTh 81 (1959) 1–66.

Selwyn E., *The First Epistle of S. Peter* (London 1947) 302–315.

Spicq C., *Les Epîtres de S. Pierre* 35, (Paris 1966) 133f.

Spitta F., 'Christi Predigt an die Geister (1 Petr 3,19ff)', *Evangelische Kirchenzeitung* 52 (1900) 883ff, 1025ff.

Turmel J., *La descente du Christ aux enfers*, Paris 1905.

Vorgrimler H., 'Fragen zum Höllenabstieg Christi', *Concilium* 2 (1966) 70–76.

Williams C., *Descent into Hell* (Grand Rapids [2]1949).

III. Going to the Father

Althaus, P., *Die Wahrheit des kirchlichen Osterglaubens* (Gütersloh 21941).

Barth, K., *Credo* (Munich 1939).

– *Kirchliche Dogmatik* IV § 59.

– *Die Auferstehung der Toten* (Munich 1926; responded to by R. Bultmann in *Glauben und Verstehen* I (Tübingen [5]1964) 38–64).

Bartsch H. W., 'Das Auferstehungszeugnis und sein historisches und theologisches Problem', *Theologische Furschung* 41 (1965).

Benoit P., *Passion et Résurrection du Seigneur* (Paris 1966).

– 'Ascension', RB 56 (1949) 161–203.

– 'Marie-Madelaine et les Disciples au Tombeau selon Jo. 20,1–18', in *Festschrift J. Jeremias* (Berlin 1960) 141–152.

Bertram G., 'Himmelfahrt Jesu vom Kreuz', in *Festgabe für Deissmann* (Tübingen 1927).

Boismard M. E., 'Le Chapitre XXI de S. Jean. Essai de critique littéraire', RB 54 (1947) 471–501.

Brun L., *Die Auferstehung Christi in der urchristlichen Überlieferung* (Oslo 1925).

Bultmann R., *Das Verhältnis der urchristlichen Christusbotschaft zum historischen Jesus* (Heidelberg 1960).

Campenhausen H. v., Zur Analyse der Bekenntnisformel 1 Kor 15, 3–5', EvTh 25 (1965) 1–11.

– Der Ablauf der Osterereignisse und das leere Grab ([3]Heidelberg 1966).

Conzelmann H., 'Jesus von Nazareth und der Glaube an den Auferstandenen' in H. Ristow – K. Matthiae, *Der historische Jesus und der kerygmatische Christus* (Berlin [2]1961) 188–199.

Delling G., 'Die Bedeutung der Auferstehung Jesu für den Glauben an Jesus Christus. Ein exegetischer Beitrag' in *Die Bedeutung der Auferstehungsbotschaft für den Glauben an Jesus Christus* (Gütersloh [4]1967) 65–90.

Dobschütz E. v., 'Ostern und Pfingsten. Eine Studie zu 1 Kor 15', DLZ 24 (1903) 266f.

Durwell F. X., *La Résurrection de Jésus. Mystère de Salut* (Le Puy-Paris [2]1954).

Ebert H., 'Die Krise des Osterglaubens', *Hochland* 60 (1968) 305, 331.

Fascher E., 'Die Osterberichte und das Problem der biblischen Hermeneutik', H. Ristow – K. Matthiae, Berlin [2]1961, 200–207.

– 'Anastasis-Resurrectio-Auferstehung', ZNW 40 (1941) 166–229.

Gaechter P., 'Die Engelserscheinungen in den Auferstehungsberichten', ZKTh 89 (1967) 191–262.

Geyer H. G., 'Die Auferstehung Jesu Christi. Ein Überblick über die Diskussion in der gegenwärtigen Theologie'. *Die Bedeutung der Osterbotschaft für den Glauben an Jesus Christis*, Gütersloh [4]1967, 93–117.

Goppelt L., 'Das Osterkerygma heute', *Lutherische Monatshefte* 3 (1934) 50–57.

Grass H., *Ostergeschehen und Ostergeschichte* (Göttingen [2]1962).

– 'Zur Begründung des Osterglaubens', ThLZ 89 (1964) 405–414.

Gutwenger E., 'Zur Geschichtlichkeit der Auferstehung Jesu', ZKTh 88 (1966) 257–282.

– 'Auferstehung und Auferstehungsleib Jesu', ZKTh 91 (1969) 32, 58.

Hirsch, E., *Die Auferstehungsgeschichte und der christliche Glaube* (Tübigen 1940).

Klappert B. (ed.), *Diskussion um Kreuz und Auferstehung* (Wuppertal [2]1967).

Koch G., *Die Auferstehung Jesu Christi* (Tübingen 1965).

Kreck W., *Die Zukunft der Gekommenen. Grundprobleme der Eschatologie* (Munich [2]1966).

Kremer J., *Das älteste Zeugnis von der Auferstehung Christi* (Stuttgart 1966).

– *Die Osterbotschaft der vier Evangelien* (Stuttgart 1968).

Kühn M., 'Das Problem der zureichenden Begründung der christlichen Auferstehungshoffnung', KuD 9 (1963) 1–17.

Künneth, W., *Entscheidung heule. Jesu Auferstehung – Brennpunkt der theologischen Diskussion* (Hamburg 1966) *Theologie der Auferstehung* (Munich 51968).

Lehmann K., *Auferweckt am Dritten Tag nach der Schrift* (Freiburg 1968; = *Quaestiones Disputatae* 38).

Lichtenstein E., 'Die älteste christliche Glaubensformel', ZKG 63 (1950–1952) 1–74.

Lohfink G., 'Die Auferstehung Jesu und die historische Kritik', *Bibel und Leben* 9 (1968) 48–51.

Lohbmeyer E., *Galiläa und Jerusalem* (Göttingen 1936).

Lohse E., *Die Auferstehung Jesu Christi im Zeugnis des Lukasevangeliums* (Neukirchen 1961).

Martini C. M., *Il problema storico della risurrezione negli studi recenti* = Anal. Greg. 104, (Rome 1959).

Marxsen W., 'Die Auferstehung Jesu als historisches und als theologisches Problem' in *Die Bedeutung der Auferstehungsbotschaft für den Glauben an Jesus Christus* (Gütersloh ⁴1967) 11–39.

– *Die Auferstehung Jesu von Nazareth* (Gütersloh 1968).

Michaelis W., *Die Erscheinungen des Auferstandenen* (Basle 1944).

Nauck, W., 'Die Bedeutung des leeren Grabes für den Glauben an den Auferstandenen', ZNW 47 (1956) 243–267.

Nicolaipen A., *Der Auferstehungsglaube in der Bibel und ihrer Umwelt* (Helsinki; I 1944, II 1946).

Odenkirchen P. C., 'Praecedam vos in Galilaeam', VD (1968) 193–223 (Lit.).

Oepke A., Arts. ἀνίστημι and ἐγείρω: ThW I, 368–372 und II, 332, 336.

– 'Wie entsteht nach den Schriften des NT der Glauben an die Auferstehung Jesu?', *Wissenschaftliche Zeitfunk der Karl-Marx-Univ. Leipzig* 3 (1953–1954) *Gesellschafts- und sprachwissenschaftliche Reihe* 1, 109–115.

Pannenberg W., 'Die historische problematik der Auferweckung Jesu in *Grundzüge der Christologie* (Gütersloh 1964).

– *Offenbarung und Geschichte* (Göttingen ²1963).

Rahner K., 'Dogmatische Fragen der Osterfrömmigkeit, *Schriften* IV, 157–172.

Ramsey A. M., *The Resurrection of Christ* (London ⁴1956).

Rengstorf K. H., *Die Auferstehung Jesu. Form, Art und Sinn der urchristlichen Osterbotschaft* (Witten ⁴1960, ⁵1967).

Ruckstuhl E. and Pfammatter J., *Die Auferstehung Jesu Christi. Heilsgeschichtliche Tatsache und Brennpunkt des Glaubens*, (Lucerne 1968).

Schäder E., *Die Bedeutung des lebendigen Christus für die Rechtfertigung* (Gütersloh 1893).

Schlier H., *Über die Auferstehung Jesu Christi* (Einsiedeln ²1968; Leipzig ²1971).

Schmitt J., *Jésus ressuscité dans la prédication apostolique* (Paris 1949).

Schubert K., 'Die Entwicklung der Auferstehungslehre von der nachexilischen bis zur frührabbinischen Zeit', BZ NS 6 (1962) 177–214.

Seidensticker P., *Die Auferstehung Jesu in der Botschaft der Evangelien* (Stuttgart 1967).

– *Zeitgenössische Texte zur Osterbotschaft der Evangelien* (Stuttgart 1967).

Sint J., 'Die Auferstehung Jesu in der Verkündigung der Urgemeinde', ZKTh 84 (1962) 129–251.

Stanley D. M., *Christ's Resurrection in Pauline Soteriology* (Rome ²1963).

Strobel A., *Kerygma und Apokalyptik* (Göttingen 1967).

Wilckens U., 'Der Ursprung der Überlieferung der Erscheinungen des Auferstandenen' in *Dogma und Denkstrukturen*, edited by W. Joest, et al. (Göttingen 1963), 56–95.

– 'Die Überlieferungsgeschichte der Auferstehung Jesu', in *Die Bedeutung der Auferstehungsbotschaft für den Glauben an Jesus Christus* (Gütersloh ⁴1967) 43–63.

Index

Adler, N. 145
Alain 63–65, 85
Alain of Lille 167
Albert the Great 94
Albinus 58
Alexander of Hales 86, 103, 163, 166
Altaner-Stuiber 42
Althaus, P. 33, 46, 142, 146, 168, 268, 278, 281, 286
Ambrose 21, 90, 146, 181
Ambrosiaster 165, 166, 187
Anastasius of Sinai 45
Andrew of Crete 165
Angela of Foligno 47, 78, 87
Anselm of Canterbury 38, 89, 120, 140
Anthony of Egypt 38
Apollinarius of Laodicea 25
Arius 25
Arnold, F. X. 48
Athanasius 20, 25, 36, 41, 42, 47, 48, 167
Athenagoras 42
Aubineau, M. 185
Audet, J.-P. 145
Augustine 22, 26, 29, 31, 38, 45, 49, 59, 76, 86, 90, 120, 140, 146, 162, 163, 164, 181, 185, 187, 280

Baader, F. v. 65, 147, 185
Baillie, M. 46
Bammel, E. 268
Bardy, G. 46
Barth, C. 42
Barth, K. 79–82, 124, 141, 142, 143, 193, 205, 215, 217, 253, 266, 268, 275, 280, 286, 287
Bartsch, H.-W. 197, 268, 269, 281, 287
Basil 38

Bauer, J. B. 278
Bauer, M. 186
Bauer, W. 143
Baur, F. C. 275
Bea, A. 47
Bede 38, 163
Bellarmine 94
Benedict 38
Benoit, P. 143, 241, 245, 276, 278, 279, 281, 287
Bensow, O. 44, 46
Benz, E. 85, 274
Bernard, J. H. 284
Bernardakis, P. 42
Bernard of Clairvaux 22–23, 38, 39, 78, 104, 144
Bertholet, A. 268
Bertram, G. 282, 287
Bertrand, F. 46
Bérulle, P. de 34, 141
Bieder, W. 151, 152, 159, 183, 185, 188, 284
Bihlmeyer 87
Biser, E. 284
Blank, J. 122, 143
Blanke, J. 147
Blinzler, J. 142, 183, 281
Boismard, M.-E. 145, 276, 287
Bonaventure 38, 39, 103, 104, 169
Bornhäuser, K. 277
Boros, L. 147, 177
Bossuet, J. B. 94, 144
Botte, B. 144
Bouëssé, H. 144
Bourdaloue, L. 94
Bourgoing, F. 94
Bousset, W. 83, 151, 183, 275, 282

Bouyer, L. 47, 282
Brandt, H. 147
Braun, F. M. 145, 285
Braun, H. 85
Breen, R. B. 284
Bremond, H. 47, 183, 271
Brentz, J. 30–31
Breton, S. 47, 63, 85
Brox, N. 86
Brun, L. 287
Bruno, G. 184
Bückler, F. W. 144
Bulgakov, S. N. 35, 46
Bultmann, R. 96, 143, 193, 203, 215, 217, 268, 270, 274, 276, 280, 287
Burkill, T. A. 282

Cabrol, F. 284, 285
Caesarius 151, 187
Caird, G. B. 285
Callaey, F. 47
Calvin, J. 169–170
Campenhausen, H. v. 238–239, 240, 275, 276, 278
Carra de Vaux Saint Cyr 144
Casel, O. 47
Cassian 188
Castelli, E. 184
Catherine of Siena 78, 94
Cepko 86
Ceppède, J. de la 40
Cerfaux, L. 44
Chaîne, J. 284
Chardin, P. Th. de 61, 275
Chardon, L. 41, 94, 141
Chemnitz, M. 30–31
Chrysostom 21, 30, 89, 140, 187, 280
Claudel, P. 188
Clavier, H. 285
Clemen, C. 285
Clement of Alexandria 187
Clement of Rome 38
Colpe, C. 270
Condren, C. de 206
Congar, Y. 47
Conzelmann, H. 239, 245, 268, 269, 279, 287
Cornelius, G. 186
Coste, J. 42
Courcelle, P. 184
Cullmann, O. 146, 276, 280
Cyril of Alexandria 25, 26, 30, 36, 185, 187

Cyril of Jerusalem 21, 84, 130, 151

Dahl, N. A. 143, 224, 282
Dalton, W. J. 183
Davis, C. T. 47
Dehau, P.-T. 146
Deissmann, G. A. 270, 282
Delling, B. 285
Delling, G. 146, 267, 268, 270, 271, 274, 275, 287
Dermenghen, E. 87
Descartes, R. 64
Diadochus of Photikē 77, 78
Dibelius, M. 143, 228, 275
Diekamp-Jüssen 185
Dietelmayer, J. A. 284
Dietrich, A. 285
Dietrich of Freiberg 76
Dillistone, F. W. 282
Dinkler, E. 84, 281, 282
Dobschütz, F. von 275, 287
Dodd, C. H. 278
Dölger, F. J. 187
Dörries, H. 86
Dorner, J. A. 178
Dostoievskii, F. M. 65
Dubarle, A. M. 145
Duguet, J. J. 40, 183
Dupont, J. 44, 278
Durrwell, F. X. 206, 266, 268, 270, 280, 287

Ebeling, G. 147, 206
Ebert, H. 287
Ebner, M. 47, 78
Edsman, C.-M. 281
Eicholz, G. 272
Eizenhöfer, L. 185
Elizabeth of Thuringia (Elizabeth of Hungary) 39
Ephraem 188
Eriugena 76, 163, 173
Eusebius 188
Eutyches 25
Evagrius 38, 77, 78, 86
Evodius of Uzalis 162

Faber, F. M. 94
Fairbairn, A. M. 46
Fascher, E. 27, 287
Favre, R. 282
Ferré, M.-F. 87

Feuerbach, L. 63
Feuillet, A. 44, 146
Ficino, M. 163, 184
Filson, F. V. 275
Firmicus Maternus 84
Florand, P. F. 41, 141
Foerster 270
Forsyth, P. T. 35–36
Frank, F. H. R. 45
Frank, S. 31–32, 86
Franz, A. 48
Francis of Assisi 39, 174
Francis de Sales 78, 94
Frings, J. 285
Füglister, N. 145
Fulgentius of Ruspe 183, 185

Gaechter, P. 278, 288
Galot, J. 285
Galtier, P. 90, 140
Gaschienietz, R. 285
Gertrude of Helfta 39, 47
Gess, W. F. 46
Gewiess, J. 44
Geyer, B. 141
Geyer, H. G. 269, 288
Giorgi, F. 184
Gnilka, J. 144, 186, 282
Görres, J. J. 87
Goethe, J. W. v. 85
Goppelt, L. 167, 266, 267, 269, 272, 288
Gore, C. 32
Gorodetsky, N. 46
Grandchamp, F. 141
Grass, H. 267, 269, 270, 271, 273, 274,
    275, 276, 277, 278, 280, 288
Greban, A. 47
Green, R. B. 187
Green, T. H. 32
Gregory the Great 167, 175–176, 187,
    280
Gregory of Elvira 46, 146
Gregory of Nazianzus 21, 41, 47, 187
Gregory of Nyssa 20, 33, 77, 84, 167, 181
Grelot, P. 145, 146, 282
Gressmann, H. 183
Gretser, J. 40
Grillmeier, A. 141, 282, 284, 285
Grünhut, L. 86
Gschwind, K. 156, 285
Güder, E. 177, 285
Gügler, A. 174

Guénon, R. 60
Güttgemanns, E. 141, 146, 272, 282
Gunkel, H. 252
Guny, A. 47
Gutwenger, E. 288

Haedeke, H.-U. 281
Haenchen, E. 276
Hahn, F. 278
Hamann, J. H. 65, 85
Hamon, M. 87
Harlé, P. A. 141
Harnack, A. v. 192
Hartmann, C. 44
Hasenfuß, J. 281
Hazenzahl, W. 144, 282
Hausherr, I. 86
Heer, J. 47, 144, 145, 146, 282
Hegel, G. W. F. 31, 32, 35, 52, 62, 177
Hegermann, H. 86
Henry, P. 24, 44, 45, 46
Herder 174, 186
Hermas 151, 187
Herrmann, J. 193
Hilary 21, 26–27, 29, 32, 103, 144,
    181
Hildebrand, D. v. 145
Hillmann, W. 142
Hilton, W. 78, 87
Hippolytus 21, 167
Hirsch, E. 235, 276, 288
Holl, K. 255–256, 270
Holland, H. S. 84
Holzmeister, U. 282
Homer 130
Honorius of Autun 76
Hornschuh, M. 83
Hormisdas 185
Hülsbusch, W. 282
Hugh of St Victor 104
Huidekopper, F. 182
Husserl, E. 216

Ignatius of Antioch 37
Ignatius of Loyola 39, 78, 94
Innitzer, T. 142
Isaac of Niniveh 77
Irenaeus 21, 38, 43, 83, 90, 125, 151, 175,
    184, 187
Isidore of Seville 176
Iwand, H. S. 268

Jacopone da Todi 39
James, M. R. 83
Jansen 144
Jeremias, J. 141, 183, 237, 243, 267, 270, 278, 285
Jerome 66
Joest, W. 268
John Damascene 37
John of the Cross 39, 76, 78
Johnson, S. E. 285
Josephus 127
Jossua, J. P. 44
Jouassard, G. 143
Journet, C. 282
Jungmann, J. A. 184
Justin 151

Kähler, M. 14
Kähler, W. 282
Käsemann, E. 24, 44, 86, 140, 143, 260, 283
Kaftan, J. 61
Kattenbusch, F. 147
Kierkegaard, S. 53, 65
Kittel, G. 275
Klappert, B. 266, 267, 268, 272, 278, 279, 288
Klein, R. 184
Kneller, K. A. 47
Klostermann, E. 274
Koch, G. 215–217, 224, 229, 237, 246, 268, 269, 270, 271, 274, 275, 276, 277, 279, 288
König, J. L. 182, 284
Koepp, W. 273
Krebs, E. 86
Kreck, W. 280, 288
Kremer, J. 146, 181, 242, 267, 268, 269, 274, 276, 278, 280, 288
Kretschmar, G. 279
Krinetzki, L. 44
Kroll, J. 182, 285
Kruse, H. 283
Kühn, M. 288
Kümmel, W. G. 275
Kuhn, G. H. 283
Künneth, W. 220, 266, 268, 270, 271, 272, 275, 277, 279, 288

Laktantius 84, 130
Lammers, K. 280
Landgraf, A. 83, 185

Langmann, A. 81
Latour, J. J. 144
Laurentin, R. 273
Leal, J. 283
Lebreton, J. 283
Leclercq, H. 281
Leese, K. 85
Lehmann, K. 279, 288
Lehmann, W. 87
Leibrecht, W. 85
Leo the Great 21, 25, 26, 44, 140, 146
Leonardi, T. 93
Léon-Dufour, X. 281
Lichtenstein, E. 271, 288
Lieb, F. 85
Liebner, K. T. A. 45
Lightfoot, R. H. 278
Lindeskog, G. 144
Loewenich, W. v. 147
Lohfink, G. 245, 279, 288
Lohmeyer, E. 85, 145, 270, 275, 276, 288
Lohse, E. 141, 142, 145, 269, 272, 278, 283, 289
Loofs, F. 285
Lossky, V. 30
Lot-Borodine, M. 86
Louis of Granada 26, 45
Lubac, H. de 41, 46, 48, 83, 84, 86, 182
Lucchesi-Palli, E. 281, 284
Ludolph of Saxony 186
Lüthi, K. 142
Lundberg, P. 285
Luther, M. 39, 52, 53, 61, 62, 78, 139, 169, 283
Lyonnet, S. 141, 143, 182

MacCulloch, J. A. 286
Magdalena, dei Pazzi 78
Mahieu, L. 144
Malevez, L. 86
Malevez, P. 44
Malmberg, F. 141
Marcellus of Ancyra 181
Marcion 62–63
Marheinecke, P. 178
Marie de l'Incarnation 47
Marie des Vallées 78
Marius Victorinus 46
Martini, C. M. 289
Marxsen, W. 68, 85, 220, 239, 268, 274, 289

Matthiae, K. 143, 282, 287
Maximus Confessor 21, 38, 78
Maximus of Turin 84
Maxsein, A. 145
Mechthild of Magdeburg 47, 78, 87
Meester, A. de 284
Melanchthon, P. 169
Ménard, J. E. 145
Meyer, E. 237
Michaelis, W. 270, 276, 277
Michel, O. 44, 147
Mildenberger, F. 279
Moltmann, J. 280
Monnier, J. 186, 284
Morris, L. 141, 283
Müller, A. 146
Mussner, F. 268, 280

Nacchiante, J. 141
Nauck, W. 277, 289
Nautin, P. 46, 84, 145
Nazari, J.-P. 141
Nelis, J. 86, 183
Nestorius 24, 25, 44
Nicetas of Remesiana 181
Nicholas Cabasilas 22
Nicholas of Cusa 76, 163, 170–171, 172
Nicolaipen, A. 289
Nierenberg, J. E. 88
Nigg, W. 279
Nilus 38
Nötscher, F. 279

Odenkirchen, P. C. 289
Oepke, A. 42, 289
Oetinger, F. 185
Olphe-Galliard, M. 281
Origen 29–30, 36, 38, 77, 144, 179, 185, 187, 208, 218
Ortkemper, F. J. 283

Pablo, Bas. de S. 47
Pannenberg, W. 197, 268, 275, 289
Paris, G. 47
Pascal, B. 65, 283
Pascher, J. 283
Paul, J. 83
Paul of the Cross 47
Paz, A. de 87
Pelletier, A. 144, 145
Pelster, F. 83
Pelzer, A. 83

Perdelwitz, R. 286
Petavius, D. 284
Peter Chrysologus 184, 185
Peterson, E. 85
Peter Lombard 103
Pfammatter, J. 289
Philo Carpasius 186
Philo of Alexandria 127
Philastrius of Brescia 187
Phythian-Adams 131
Plato 58, 163, 173
Ploig, D. 286
Plotinus 38, 163, 173
Pohle-Gierens 184
Polycarp 184
Popkes, W. 85, 86, 142, 269
Prestel, J. 47
Proclus of Constantinople 186
Ps.-Ambrose 187
Ps.-Augustine 182, 186, 187
Ps.-Denys 38
Ps.-Epiphanius 151, 188
Ps.-Gregory of Nyssa 45
Ps.-Hippolytus 58, 145
Przywara, E. 283
Puccini, V. 87
Pulleyn 163
Pullus, R. 102–103, 162

Quillet, H. 284

Rad, G. v. 268
Rahner, H. 47, 84, 145, 146, 283, 286
Rahner, K. 141, 146–147, 177, 286, 289
Ramsey, A. M. 32, 44, 260 279, 289
Ratzinger, J. 141
Raven, C. E. 60
Raynaud, G. 47
Read, D. H. C. 144
Rehm, M. 144
Reicke, B. 183, 284, 286
Rengstorf, K. H. 266, 267, 268, 269, 270, 271, 272, 273, 276, 277, 279, 289
Resch, A. 272
Richard of St. Victor 29, 94, 166
Richtstätter 47
Riesenfeld, H. 286
Rigaldus, O. 103
Riggenbach, E. 147, 283
Ristow, H. 143, 282, 287
Robert, A. 182

Robert of Melun 83
Römer, G. 281
Romanos ho Melōdos 50–51, 83
Rondet, H. 47
Rose of Lima 78
Rosenthal, K. 46
Rothemund, H. 186
Ruckstuhl, E. 289
Rousseau, O. 286
Rousset, J. 47
Rücker, A. 43
Rufinus 149
Rufus, R. 83
Rushforth, G. M. 286
Ruysbroeck, J. 94

Sailer 174
Salaville, S. 43
Sauer, J. 281
Sauter, G. 280
Schäder, E. 270, 289
Schäferdiek, K. 83
Schaefers, D. 281
Scheeben, M. J. 186
Schelkle, K. H. 142, 283
Schelling, F. W. 35
Schenke, H. M. 270
Schille, G. 142
Schille, L. 142
Schlatter, A. 143
Schleiermacher, F. 177, 191
Schlier, H. 59, 84, 142, 143, 183, 203, 220, 227, 245, 266, 269, 271, 273, 276, 277, 279, 280, 289
Schmid, J. 143
Schmidt, C. 152, 286
Schmidt, K. L. 142
Schmidt, W. H. 283
Schmitt, J. 290
Schnackenburg, R. 270, 283
Schneemelcher, W. 84, 182, 187, 268, 276
Schneider, J. 281, 283
Schneider, R. 65
Schniewind, J. 267, 279
Schönwolf, O. 187
Schram, D. 88
Schubert, K. 290
Schürmann, H. 274–275
Schultze, B. 186
Schulz, J. H. 186, 286
Schumacher, H. 44

Schweitzer, A. 197–198, 270
Schweizer, E. 141, 142, 145, 197, 283
Schwendimann, F. 47
Schwind, G. 182
Scotus Eriugena 76, 163, 173
Seeberg, E. 61
Seidensticker, P. 85, 197, 268, 269, 271, 272, 276, 278, 290
Selwyn, E. 286
Shaw, J. M. 283
Siewerth, G. 145
Silesius, A. 86
Sint, J. 290
Sjöberg, E. 269
Soden, W. v. 284
Sohm, R. 255
Socrates 62
Soloviev, V. 46
Speyr, A. v. 83, 185, 280
Spicq, C. 141, 146, 156, 286
Spindeler, A. 41, 43, 44
Spitta, F. 286
Stamm, J. J. 86
Stanley, D. M. 213, 273, 290
Stauffer, E. 52, 54, 270, 277
Steckx, D. S. 84
Steffen, B. 283
Stein, C. 145
Stibbs, A. M. 141
Stommel, E. 145, 284
Strack-Billerbeck 85
Straubinger, J. 47
Strauch, P. 87
Strobel, A. 290
Stuhlmacher, P. 143
Surin, J. 78
Surius 39
Surkau, H.-W. 86
Suso, H. 39, 78
Swedenborg, E. 185
Symeon of Mesopotamia 38

Taille, M. de la 206, 271
Tarejev 46
Tauler, J. 39, 78, 87, 94
Taurisano, P. I. 87
Taylor, V. 284
Temple, W. 36
Tertullian 45, 164
Theresa of Avila 20, 38, 78
Thérèse de Lisieux 78
Thomasius, G. 31, 32, 45, 178

Thomas Aquinas 31, 89, 140, 146, 164, 166, 176, 181, 184, 186, 228, 273
Thomas à Kempis 94
Thüsing, W. 122, 143
Tillich, P. 42
Trilling, W. 143
Tromp, S. 146
Turmel, J. 286

Ubertino di Casale 39
Unger, R. 85

Valentinus 62
Vierig, F. 284
Villette, J. 187
Völter, E. 187
Vogelsang, E. 185
Vogt, J. 43
Volz, P. 183

Vorgrimler, H. 286
Vosté, V. 284

Waldhäuser, M. 44, 185
Weil, S. 65
Weis-Liebersdorf, J. E. 38
Wellhausen, J. 142, 276
Wenz, H. 280
Weston, F. 32
Wichmann, W. 86, 142
Wiencke, G. 284
Wilckens, U. 42, 54, 83, 267, 268, 271, 272, 274, 290
Williams, C. 286
Wolff, H. W. 86

Zeller, H. 145
Zerwick, M. 145
Ziener, G. 145
Zöckler, O. 284